JOHN DEWEY

The Essential Writings

Edited by David Sidorsky

HARPER TORCHBOOKS
Harper & Row, Publishers
New York, Hagerstown, San Francisco, London

The Essential Writings of the Great Philosophers is published under the editorship of Charles M. Sherover.

Designed by Eve Callahan

First edition: HARPER TORCHBOOKS, 1977

LIBRARY OF CONGRESS CATALOG CARD NUMBER: 76–51587

ISBN: 0-06-131926-0

77 78 79 80 81 10 9 8 7 6 5 4 3 2 1

Contents

Introduction

John Dewey was the most influential figure in American philosophical thought in the first half of the twentieth century. His influence was both broad in scope and deep in impact. Dewey's philosophical writings were the focal point of discussion in American universities in such diverse fields as logic, metaphysics, ethics, aesthetics, and epistemology for five decades. During much of this period, his works were also at the center of debate or controversy among professional theorists and practitioners in the areas of education, art criticism, social psychology, and political science. At the same time, Dewey's commentaries on current social and political events often set the framework of public discourse and generated intellectual excitement about the relevant issues of the civic agenda. Alfred North Whitehead, the British mathematician and philosopher who came to the United States to teach at Harvard after his retirement from Cambridge, found the American philosophical atmosphere pervasively Deweyan when he wrote in 1939: "John Dewey is the typical effective American thinker; and he is the chief intellectual force providing that environment with coherent purpose."

The impact of Dewey's ideas upon American philosophical and social thought was so great that it must be considered a major phenomenon of American cultural history of the twentieth century. Almost as striking a phenomenon, however, was the rapidity and completeness with which interest in Dewey's work virtually ended in most American philosophical discussion after World War II. This was accompanied by a severe decline of interest in Dewey's writings and in his proposals on social and educational problems as well.

The shift in the public receptivity to John Dewey's thought reflected, in some manner, the change in public mood and in the public's sense of the political and social agenda after World War II. In the Academy, however, it reflected an abrupt and extreme change in philosophical style and philosophical self-consciousness, that is to say, more specifically, in the understanding by many philosophers of what were the possibilities and the tasks of philosophical inquiry. This change took place between 1930 and 1950.

I also think it is demonstrable that the abandonment of interest in Dewey's writings stemmed to some degree from the fulfillment of some of his programs and aspirations, just as it derived in part from the apparent, decisive refutation of some of his most important theses. Further, the fate accorded to the ideas of John Dewey was similarly bestowed upon the works of most of the other figures of the American pragmatic movement in philosophy that had dominated American philosophy from the turn of the century.

This kind of phenomenon—the rise and fall of a once dominant philosophical movement or figure—affords a parallel in certain ways to that favorite theme of historical study, the passing of a dynasty. It is an event that inevitably generates historical curiosity and seems to demand some sort of rational explanation. In most cases of fluctuation in the fortunes of a scientific or philosophical set of ideas, the historical inquiry has often been of secondary interest. I believe that is so because, independent of the investigation of the origins, influence, or acceptance of a thinker's work, there is also the question of the truth of his premises, the validity of his arguments, or more generally, the adequacy of his intellectual accomplishment.

Accordingly, in the case of John Dewey we are confronted with two important kinds of inquiry. The first is an examination of the context of his philosophical activity, which helps to account for the extraordinary destiny of his philosophical work. The second is an effort to appraise the philosophical adequacy of Dewey's main theses and positions.

In this essay I propose to sketch the major themes of Dewey's philosophy in the context of their development. First, the salient biographical events of Dewey's life as they relate to his philosophical evolution are presented. Second, the American context of the pragmatic movement in philosophy of which Dewey became the major figure is examined. Dewey characteristically formulated his own philosophical views by a dialectical criticism of the representative conflicting theses of other philosophers. Accordingly, in the third part of this essay several important positions on knowledge and scientific method are discussed in terms of Dewey's response to what he took to be the challenge of Darwinism for philosophy. Similarly, in the fourth part of this essay I investigate how Dewey's fundamental theses on the nature of liberalism, empiricism, and ethical judgments constituted a critical reworking of the ruling liberal, empiricist, and moral theories of John Stuart Mill. Fifth, we see how Dewey's philosophical work comprehended the programs for pragmatic philosophy embryonically sketched by Charles Peirce and William James, particularly in epistemology and in metaphysics. And finally, a retrospective assessment of the place of Dewey in the philosophy of the twentieth century is made.

The Life of John Dewey

Many elements in Dewey's life formed an appropriate background for a philosophy that came to be considered an authentic expression of American attitudes and values. Dewey's career cut across numerous areas of American social and intellectual activity over the approximate century from the forging of the unified nation in the Civil War to America's emergence as a major world power after World War II.

Dewey was born in Burlington, Vermont, in 1859. His childhood was brushed by the Civil War. Dewey's father, Archibald, was a Burlington grocer who became the quartermaster of the Vermont cavalry regiment. He was stationed in the South throughout the war. In 1865, his wife moved with the children to Virginia to end the long family separation. John Dewey later was able to remember the devastation of the Virginia countryside.

After the war, the Deweys returned to Burlington, and John was raised in a New England rural village environment that seems to have possessed many of the familiar features of the nineteenth-century American pastoral idyll. These included John Dewey's daily paper route, the fishing and hunting trips in the woods, and the monotonous drill and recitation of the traditional public school.

Dewey attended the University of Vermont and was one of the eighteen graduates of the class of 1879. The courses, all of which were required, included geology, physiology—in which T. H. Huxley's text was used—psychology, and philosophy. In philosophy, Dewey was introduced to the then influential school of Scottish intuitionism, as well as to German idealism by way of Coleridge as presented by the American philosopher, the Reverend James Marsh. Outside the prescribed curriculum, Dewey read the contemporary

English fortnightly reviews. In these he followed the discussion on the significance of the theory of evolution and also became interested in the writings of Auguste Comte.

After graduation, Dewey taught in the high school of South Oil City, Pennsylvania, at the time of the first mining of oil there. He published his first philosophical article, "The Metaphysical Assumptions of Materialism," in 1882, and decided to take up graduate study in philosophy at Johns Hopkins University. Hopkins had been established as the first American university to be based on the German model of emphasis upon graduate study, seminar teaching, and a research orientation. There the young Dewey studied with Charles Peirce, whose work was to become a major influence on his philosophical ideas only many years later. At Hopkins, Dewey adopted the philosophical position of his teacher George S. Morris, which was one of Hegelian idealism modified by Aristotelianism. That combination was to remain a permanent component of Dewey's philosophical development, though it became transformed by his commitment to naturalism—to the naturalistic biology of Darwin and the naturalistic psychology of William James.

Dewey taught philosophy and psychology at the University of Michigan and at the University of Minnesota for the decade between 1884 and 1894. His publications during that period show the wide range of interests that characterized his career. These included his *Psychology*, a study of the philosophy of Leibniz, and articles on the British Hegelian philosopher T. H. Green and on ethical theory. Dewey also asserted his interest in education, and co-authored two books for teachers in training.

In 1894 Dewey moved to the University of Chicago and became head of its new Department of Pedagogy, as well as of the Department of Philosophy, a year later. Under his leadership, the former department sponsored and supervised an elementary school, known officially as "The Laboratory School" and commonly as "The Dewey School." Dewey's involvement in public affairs in Chicago extended beyond education, and brought him into close contact with Jane Addams and the work of Hull House. Hull House was then the pioneer of settlement houses, leading in the effort of social work to solve the urban crises of America's mass immigration at the end of the century. One of the remarkable aspects of Dewey's career was his ability to assimilate into the texture of his obviously rugged New England character an understanding and sympathy for the changing features of American society through the decades of America's rapid transformation.

The period of Dewey's teaching at Michigan and Chicago also

marked his gradual shift from Hegelianism to pragmatism. Dewey himself attributed this shift primarily to the impact of his study of William James's *Principles of Psychology*, the book that motivated Dewey to develop his own instrumentalist theory of mind. In 1903, as part of the decennial celebration of the founding of the University of Chicago, Dewey published a monograph entitled *Studies in Logical Theory* that included essays by him and by graduate students in the Department of Philosophy. William James referred to the authors as the "Chicago School" and found in their philosophical position the coming wave of pragmatic philosophy. After Dewey's move to Columbia University in New York in 1905, he became the recognized leader of the pragmatic movement in philosophy, at a time when pragmatism began to dominate American philosophy.

Dewey's move to New York coincided with that city's emergence as an international cultural center. At the same time, there was a parallel expansion in Dewey's participation in civic, national, and international affairs. An example of this was his leadership of a group of educators at Teachers College, Columbia, who brought about the growth of progressive education throughout the United States and had an important impact upon educational reform in several foreign countries.

Educational leaders in several countries that were undergoing rapid social or cultural change sought in Dewey's philosophy of education a guide in the planning of their schools. Dewey lectured in Japan shortly after World War I and then spent two years at the universities of Peking and Nanking during the period of the modernization of Chinese education in the early years of the Chinese Republic. Dewey also observed the postrevolutionary educational institutions of Turkey, Mexico, and the Soviet Union and analyzed their efforts at reconstruction of their traditional educational systems.

Dewey's interest in education also led him to a concern with academic autonomy and freedom of inquiry. He was a founder of the American Association of University Professors, and a charter member of the first teachers union in New York City.

A major vehicle of Dewey's influence in public affairs was his regular contribution to the liberal journalism that developed in America between the two world wars. From the founding of *The New Republic* in 1914, Dewey wrote regularly both reviews of current works in philosophy and articles on such favored topics as women's suffrage and the peace movement of the 1920's. Dewey's traditional mistrust of American involvement in the international balance of power led him to argue that the United States ought not to join the League of Nations. Yet he undertook leadership in a movement for the "outlawing" of war.

Certainly the most dramatic of Dewey's political activities was his chairing of a Commission of Inquiry into the Charges against Leon Trotsky at the Moscow Trial in 1938. The commission exonerated Trotsky from the particular set of charges that Stalin had directed against him. This episode provided Dewey with an insight into the phenomenon of totalitarianism. Consequently, Deweyan liberalism became antitotalitarian and extremely realistic about the problem of American collective security in confrontation with Nazi Germany or the Soviet Union.

Despite the great disappointment that the rise of totalitarianism and World War II brought to Dewey's liberal optimism, he continued in his writings from the end of the war until his death in 1952 to insist on the possibilities inherent in human intelligence. This intelligence, if applied scientifically to social and political problems, would result in the achievement of freer, more democratic societies throughout the world.

Parallel with his political and civic activity, Dewey influenced several generations of philosophical students. He elaborated his philosophical position in a series of major books, as well as in the innumerable articles and wide correspondence that continued until his death at the age of ninety-four. The relationship between Dewey's life and thought was close so that the landmarks of his philosophical achievement are also major events of his biography.

Dewey and American Pragmatism

Pragmatism has generally been recognized as the first indigenous movement of philosophical thought to develop in the United States. As such, it has exercised a peculiar fascination for historians, interpreters, and critics of American society and culture. This fascination raises an interesting problem of the appropriate focus in which philosophical movements, like pragmatism, should be interpreted.

From the perspective of the philosophical practitioner, the rise of a philosophical movement indicates that a small number of philosophers have arrived at similar or converging responses to some of the questions posed by their predecessors. Thus, between 1880 and 1950, Charles Peirce, William James, John Dewey, George Herbert Mead, Clarence Irving Lewis, and a number of their colleagues and students advanced similar "pragmatic" theses (and some dissimilar ones as well) about certain traditional philosophical issues—most prominently the definition of truth, the nature of morality, and the relationship between what is experienced and what is real.

From the perspective of the cultural historian, the emergence of such a philosophical movement represents the development of the cultural self-consciousness of a society. It exhibits and reflects the spirit of the age, and can be understood by reference to other manifestations of the cultural self-consciousness in literature, art, music, or indeed any other contemporaneous expression of human activity.

From the broad and admittedly speculative perspective of some cultural historians, pragmatism, accordingly, must be viewed as the philosophical expression of the tendency around the turn of the century—a tendency that was only partly intentional or aware of its own direction—to articulate a native American expression in all aspects of culture.

Many items can be entered as evidence of the expression of American self-consciousness at that time, although their uniqueness in comparison with other periods of American history might be disputed. It is true that within a brief period a number of movements arose that were explicitly committed to the development of an American national style in painting, music, architecture, and even science. Walt W. Rostow has suggested that these movements were related to a general American assertiveness and self-confidence, which found expression in American activism in international affairs at the time of the Spanish-American War. Yet the evidence is complex, since most American cultural activity, including philosophy, was characterized by a willingness to accept, absorb, or modify European models and influences.

Consider, for example the eight American painters of the first decade of this century who had set for themselves the aim of realistically portraying the American urban scene. This group, later known as the "Ashcan School," had their first show in New York (in 1907) coincident with William James's presentation of his lectures entitled "Pragmatism" at Columbia. Yet almost without exception, each had studied in Europe and most continued a close connection with European painters.

Another illustration is that of Gertrude Stein, who was a student—and favorite—of William James's in psychology, though not in philosophy. In *Three Lives*, Stein took as her subject matter, probably for the first time in American literature, the life and thought of an American black woman. Stein aggressively asserted her view that America was the first country to have entered the twentieth century, primarily by suffering the "precocious" ordeal of the Civil War. Yet Stein's parents (like James's) had shuffled between Europe and America, and Gertrude Stein herself chose to live and write as an expatriate in Paris.

Examples of the mixing of native and foreign influences, of regional or parochial and cosmopolitan or universal elements in the development of American culture can be constantly multiplied. Perhaps certain aspects of the career of William James, a founding father of American pragmatic philosophy, provide the most pertinent and complex illustration. There is some evidence that James believed it was both possible that the values found in American society and history should ultimately receive a mature expression in American cultural activity. There may be some relevance to James's insistence, during the youthful period when he planned to become a painter, on returning from Europe to study under an American master on native grounds. One of the more interesting sequences in his correspondence with his brother, Henry, is his recurrent chiding of Henry for a tendency to dwell on America's "omissions, silences, vacancies," without indicating the possibilities for their amelioration. Most important, James understood pragmatism as providing a new direction for human faith in progress and meliorism, at least in part in opposition to those dominant European philosophies of the nineteenth century that he believed had come to a dead end.

On the other hand, James's life and thought also faced toward Europe. Even though he had pioneered the development of experimental psychology in the United States, when he resigned from the teaching of psychology he brought over an experimental psychologist from Germany as his replacement. In this connection, though James had virtually founded an empirical approach to psychology in this country, his comment to Freud on the latter's one visit to America was that "the future of psychology belongs to your work." In James's long dialogue with his expatriate brother on European and American values and styles, it was to Europe that William looked for the rectification or filling in of America's "omissions, silences, vacancies."

Further, the source of his earliest philosophical conversion to a "pragmatic" theory of free will against the prevalent European versions of philosophical materialism and idealism had been the French philosopher Renouvier. The contemporary who James believed had demonstrated the foundation for the future of the pragmatic tendency in philosophy was Henri Bergson. It is difficult to see nativist American self-consciousness asserting itself in James's expression: "I thank heaven that I have lived to this date—that I have witnessed the Russo-Japanese war, and seen Bergson's new book appear—the two great modern turning-points of history and of thought."

Despite the ambiguity of interpreting American pragmatism as an expression of the American *Zeitgeist*, this mode of interpretation has been continuous from its inception. Bertrand Russell, who remained a constant critic of John Dewey's philosophy, first examined pragmatic philosophy in a review of James's *Pragmatism* titled ironically "Transatlantic Truth." Russell wrote in 1909:

> The appearance in the world of a genuinely new philosophy is at all times an event of very great importance. More particularly is this the case when the new philosophy embodies the prevailing temper of the age better than any of its older rivals; for in that case it is likely to establish itself in popular favor, to colour the thoughts of the educated and half-educated public and to strengthen those elements in the mental atmosphere to which it owes its success. . . . The philosophy which is called *Pragmatism* . . . is genuinely new and is singularly well adapted to the predominant intellectual temper of our age. . . .

Along somewhat similar lines, George Santayana developed a more complex thesis about the role of American pragmatism in American thought. In his remarkable essay "The Genteel Tradition in American Thought," Santayana argued that American intellectual activity has been bifurcated. On one side, there is an inherited religious approach, which dominates American philosophy and is prevalent throughout the American university. On the other side, there is the American experimental and inventive attitude, which asserts itself in industry and social organization. In Santayana's analogy, this division is stated as follows:

> This division may be found symbolized in American architecture: a neat reproduction of the colonial mansion—with some modern comforts introduced surreptitiously—stands beside the sky-scraper; the American Will inhabits the sky-scraper; the American intellect inhabits the colonial mansion. The one is all aggressive enterprise; the other is all genteel tradition.

Santayana's assertion was that the American pragmatic movement "played havoc with the genteel tradition." Santayana mentioned in some detail the ways in which pragmatism connects the domain of American practicality with philosophical theory. Of special importance is the pragmatic conception of all knowledge, including intellectual speculation, as instrumental. The human mind in knowing is functioning "to prepare us to meet events." Within the genteel tradition, human purposes are derived by the unfolding of transcendental law. For pragmatic philosophy, however, human purposes are the experimental goals of individuals derived from their wants and needs. In Santayana's view, pragmatism was able to reintegrate the division between American philosophical theory and American practice. It could then become a genuine American philosophy, in Santayana's terms, because "it inspires and expresses the life of those who cherish it."

Though Santayana was a critic of pragmatism, his appraisal of its role as a philosophy that aimed at integrating American values significantly resembled Dewey's own formulation. Dewey placed great stress—as we shall see later both in this essay and in the selections from his own works—on his diagnosis of American culture as having a deep split in its fundamental attitudes. He found a significant gap between the willingness to apply scientific methodology to all aspects of the physical environment or the technological culture, on the one hand, and the resistance to any extension of scientific methods to the resolution of economic, social, or political problems on the other.

To a marked degree, pragmatism provided Dewey with a philosophical rationale for the consistent adoption of scientific inquiry as the single methodology to be used in resolving all problematic situations. Much of Dewey's social polemic becomes a call for the application of scientific method to the critical problems of economic depression or international conflict. The application of scientific method to all social and political affairs, as well as to the evaluation of the various moral issues implicit in such affairs, would entail a significant reconstruction of American social institutions and attitudes. In advocating such a reconstruction, Dewey believed that the split in current attitudes would be bridged. Pragmatism could provide America with a coherent philosophical attitude that would close the dangerous gap between the adoption of scientific method in some domains and the rejection of scientific method in ethical and social affairs.

This interpretation of the role to be fulfilled by Deweyan pragmatism is also present in the single most ambitious and systematic formulation of the place of pragmatism in the context of American intellectual history, developed by Morton White in his book *Social Thought in America: The Revolt against Formalism*. White's argument is that the development of American industrial society in the early years of this century helped to precipitate a new and heightened realism among many American social theorists. There was, in consequence, a rejection of the "formalist" frameworks that had previously characterized American social thought in many areas of inquiry. In economics, Thorstein Veblen rejected the framework of classical economic theory in favor of an analysis of the actual functioning of American economic institutions. In legal theory, Oliver Wendell Holmes suggested that the governing conceptions of jurisprudence should be replaced by an account of the law that would realistically demonstrate how courts actually functioned and what were, in fact, the procedures of legal decision making. Similarly, James Harvey Robinson pioneered a new school of historical writing that focused on the realistic description of the events and motives occurring in society, rather than on the ways in which ideal national or political goals were fulfilled.

According to White, Dewey's contribution is central to the revolt against formalism. Dewey had advanced an account of the nature of morality that rejected any transcendental source for moral imperatives. Instead, he interpreted ethical ideals as optimal and pragmatic resolutions of conflicts among human desires or needs within the individual or the group. This naturalistic ethical theory —which I shall discuss at a later point in this essay—certainly supported a realistic account of how ethical decisions are made, rather than a "formalist" analysis of how they ought to be made. In White's view, Dewey was therefore able to exhibit the gap between the ideal aspirations of American society and its actual practice.

In sum, the pragmatic philosophy of Dewey, like the "institutional economics" of Thorstein Veblen, the "legal realism" of Oliver Wendell Holmes, or the "new history" of James Harvey Robinson, advanced a critical and realistic appraisal of American society. In so doing, it lays the foundation for a more effective structure for American social ideals.

This interpretation of pragmatism as a vehicle of social criticism is consistent with the severely critical attitudes that both James and Dewey expressed toward the development of American industrial society in their times. It is in extreme contrast with a familiar interpretation of pragmatism, often asserted by European critics of James or Dewey, in which pragmatism becomes a justification or apology for American industrial capitalism. Georges Sorel, the French radical syndicalist, delivered a series of lectures on pragmatism in which he stated that it was a philosophy that was "calculated to justify all the assumptions of American society." (By way of digression, it is noteworthy that Sorel then advanced the analogy between pragmatism and his own conception of the justification of an ideology through its consequences when applied directly to action —a sort of "ideology of the act." It was this kind of "pragmatism" that later led Mussolini to label himself a pragmatist. Possibly both

Mussolini and Lenin heard Sorel deliver these lectures in Paris in 1908.) In this vein, Santayana wrote of Dewey that he was "the devoted spokesman of the spirit of enterprise, of experiment, of modern industry."

Similarly, Bertrand Russell remarked that he had found "the love of truth obscured in America by commercialism, of which pragmatism is the philosophical expression." This last comment prompted Dewey's reply that it was of an "order of interpretation which would say that English neo-realism is a reflection of the snobbish aristocracy of the English and the tendency of French thought to dualism an expression of the alleged Gallic disposition to keep a mistress in addition to a wife."

The irony of the situation is that to the limited degree to which pragmatic philosophy implied an explicit analysis of American society, that analysis was severely critical. In the Deweyan view, it was legitimate, not utopian, to demand that the methods of scientific inquiry be applied to the conflicts among social, political, and economic groups in a society. Dewey believed that just as the use of scientific method in a particular area of scientific inquiry could achieve a rational consensus among the community of inquirers, so the adoption of scientific method in areas of social inquiry could result in a rational consensus within a democratic society on controversial issues of social policy. It seems obvious that disagreements on questions of interest and value in economics or politics do not lend themselves readily to such a rational resolution by the introduction of a scientific methodology. Accordingly, the Deweyan social philosophy was critical of the methods used by the major institutions of American society in their decision making.

In point of fact, few foreign critics of American society have been as harsh in their assessment or severe in their demands as was John Dewey. Dewey wrote, for example:

> Anthropologically speaking, we are living in a money culture. Its cult and rites dominate. . . . Our law and politics and the incidence of human association depend upon a novel combination of the machine and money, and the result is the pecuniary culture characteristic of our civilization. The spiritual factor of our tradition, equal opportunity and free association and intercommunication, is obscured and crowded out.

Dewey's criticism of American education, the main arena of social activity, was equally blunt when he referred to it as "the art of taking advantage of the helplessness of the young." It is true that these criticisms were a point of departure for Dewey's efforts to

reconstruct or to reassert values like equality of opportunity, freedom of association and expression, or democracy in education that
he believed could flourish in American society. The relevant point
in this context, however, is how remote Dewey's social theory is
from any naïve reading of pragmatism as a justification of American
commercial or industrial civilization.

It is true, of course, that a philosophy critical of the society in
which it has developed will still reflect that society and its values.
However, it is, I believe, still inexplicable just how that process
takes place. It is difficult to understand what aspects of French
society led to impressionism in art, or how the New York environment brought forth the movement of abstract-expressionist painting,
or why Vienna produced twelve-tone music, and so on. To a significant degree, these movements do not seem to connect to aspects
of their immediate milieu as much as they represent the unfolding
or development of an autonomous cultural tradition or technique.

Dewey's own assessment of the American character of pragmatic
philosophy in his essay "The Development of American Pragmatism" placed special emphasis upon the ways in which pragmatists
like Peirce or James had responded critically to arguments advanced
by European philosophers, prominently Kant and Mill. Dewey
wrote that

> for long years our [American] philosophical thought was merely an
> echo of European thought. The pragmatic movement . . . as well as
> neo-realism, behaviorism, the absolute idealism of Royce, the na-
> turalistic idealism of Santayana, are all attempts at re-adaptation. . . .
> They have their roots in British and European thought. Since these
> systems are re-adaptations they take into consideration the distinctive
> environment of Americal life. . . .

Dewey often asserted his opposition to a conception of philosophical activity as a kind of "dialogue in limbo," in which the
contemporary philosopher debated the thesis of his predecessor so
that all philosophy stretched back in one chain of ideas as an extended footnote to the writings of Plato. For Dewey, each philosopher should and must take into consideration, as the phrase above
quoted goes, "the distinctive environment" in which the philosophical issues were formulated and the philosophical themes re-
adapted. Dewey's account of the development of pragmatism, however, does shift the focus from the way in which this philosophical
movement may have reflected the contemporary temper to the ways
in which its spokesmen inherited, criticized, and reformulated the
philosophical and cultural tradition of their predecessors. In the

thought of Dewey, specifically, there was a conscious and explicit effort to come to terms with what Dewey took to be the philosophically usable tradition of his time. The effort included, in a crucial way, an account of the implications of Darwinism for philosophy. It also included a response to the perceived inadequacies of the current reigning formulations of the empiricism and liberalism of John Stuart Mill. And it involved Dewey in a critical extension of the distinctive points of view, already termed "pragmatic philosophy," advanced by Charles Peirce and William James. It is in tracing the record of Dewey's adaptation of these sources of and precursors to his own distinctive pragmatic philosophy that many of the main features of Dewey's thought are exhibited clearly.

There is a symbolically appropriate point of departure in investigating Dewey's philosophy as a response to the intellectual challenge posed by his predecessors. The year of Dewey's birth, 1859, was that *annus mirabilis* in which, among others, were published Charles Darwin's *Origin of Species* and John Stuart Mill's essay *On Liberty*. These works set the philosophical agenda for many later philosophers of naturalist or liberal bent, particularly for Dewey.

Dewey and the Implications of Darwinism

Interpretations of the implications of Darwin's theory for philosophy flourished from the day his works were published. Some theologians claimed that Darwin had demonstrated how animal and human adaptation to the environment could take place without any appeal to the hypothesis of divine design; others saw in Darwin's description of the evolutionary process the sketch of the instrumentalities of that design. Many conservative political philosophers found in Darwin's account of the struggle for survival a rationale for the ineffectiveness of any socially planned intervention in social or economic conflict among groups. Other political philosophers, like Marx, who had hoped to dedicate *Capital* to Darwin, found in that account a model for the possibilities of evolutionary social transformation through conflict among groups.

There were several systematic efforts to show how the major metaphysical systems of the nineteenth century—both materialist and idealist—could readily be accommodated to Darwin's analysis of the biological realm. Materialists, despite Bergson's views on creative evolution, found in Darwinism an illustration of the application of deterministic laws to biological events. In their view, these laws would ultimately be explainable by deterministic chemical or physical theories. Idealists who had interpreted all natural and social processes as the unfolding of the career of the transcendental self were not dismayed by the seeming incompatibility of Darwin's account of evolution. His description more simply documented from the material standpoint the evolutionary process that they depicted from the formal standpoint.

Dewey believed that both materialist and idealist metaphysical systems were incompatible with the true implications of Darwinian biology. This belief did not derive, however, from any incompatibility between their metaphysical picture of the world and Darwin's evolutionary schema. For Dewey, one of the significant consequences of Darwinism was a new interpretation of the nature of knowledge or mind. Thinking through the implications of Darwinism for epistemology would lead to a new conception of knowledge, mind, or intelligence that would be incompatible with the traditional metaphysical accounts, whether materialist or idealist.

Darwinian biology had demonstrated how various species adjusted and adapted to their environment. It had shown intelligence evolving as an instrument of human adaptation and adjustment, capable of bringing about significant changes in the environment. From this account stemmed an interpretation of the process of knowledge as an interaction between the organism and the environment so as to result in an effective adaptation to environment. Dewey generalized that "thought has its origin in biological adaptive behavior and the ultimate function of its cognitive aspect is a prospective control of the conditions of the environment." It was this pragmatic—or in Dewey's preferred term, "instrumental"—function of thought that the theory of knowledge of all current metaphysical systems failed to explain.

For the materialist, the human mind or brain was somehow capable of discovering the structures of reality. Knowledge of an event or entity represented some correspondence or mirroring by the mind of the antecedently given real thing or process. Thus, according to Dewey, in the materialist theory of knowledge, when a human mind knew the world it was not involved in changing the world. It followed that the materialist could not explain how minds intervened to effect changes in the world. Yet unless thought and knowledge could effect such change, their character as instruments of human adaptation and control of the environment was denied. The materialist conclusion was not only at variance with what was taken to be the Darwinian account; it also made the prizing of knowledge for its prospective or guiding function a mystery of human experience.

In a parallel pattern of argument, Dewey contended that in the theory of knowledge of idealist metaphysics, to know an object or event was to be able to place that object or event in its proper place as part of a coherent, rational totality. The human mind is capable of inferring or deducing the structures or patterns of that antecedently coherent reality. Yet, according to this thesis, human intelligence cannot intervene to effect change in the world. Dewey believed that the idealist was also incapable of explaining those functions of knowledge as an instrument of adaptation, prediction, control, and of the adjustment of the organism to the biological environment that have rendered human intelligence a cherished entity throughout human history.

Such considerations, which were explicitly traced back to Darwinism in biology, account for the fact that theory of knowledge became the most critical question at issue between the proponents and the critics of pragmatism. Dewey later outlined a theory of nature or metaphysical position compatible with the belief that mind functions in the world as an instrument of adaptation and control. Most characteristically, however, the pragmatists' theme was the novelty and significance of an interpretation of knowledge, mind, or truth that could make sense of the utilitarian and practical function of cognition. There are many variations on this theme that signify its importance for pragmatism.

At the very outset of pragmatic philosophy, Charles Peirce had argued that all inquiry began with the biological irritation he termed "doubt," and culminated with the appeasement of that irritation he termed "belief." The function of inquiry was to effect the appeasement of irritation satisfactorily. Analogously, James, in his *Principles of Psychology*, had written that "the pursuance of future ends and the choice of means for their attainment are . . . the mark and criterion of the presence of mentality in phenomena" —a passage that Dewey asserted was critical for the development of his own pragmatic point of view. Subsequently, in *Pragmatism*, James sought to define truth in terms of what it is expedient for mankind to believe over the long run. The most comprehensive program to connect the concept of truth with biological adaptation was developed in Dewey's interpretation of logical principles. For Dewey, all the formal canons of logic—the rules of deductive inference and the requirement of consistency, as well as all the rules for inductive inference and experimental methodology—are justified as instruments of inquiry in resolving problematic situations. Pragmatists would disagree over the differing formulations of Peirce, James and Dewey. But the three shared the belief that the related cluster of concepts, including the nature of knowledge or of truth, the concept of mind or of human intelligence, require an explication in terms of the ability of the human species to predict or control features of its environment.

John Dewey advanced a second thesis regarding the ways in which philosophy must come to terms with the achievement of Darwinian biology. And here Darwinism was the key to a revolutionary turn in philosophical method. Dewey developed his argument in an essay entitled "The Influence of Darwinism on Philosophy," written in 1909 on the occasion of the fiftieth anniversary of the publication of *The Origin of Species*.

Dewey's argument was that there is a methodology common to all metaphysical systems of philosophy: metaphysical philosophers have sought to understand the nature of reality by discovering what are the basic or underlying species, classes, or kinds of reality. In a sense, the materialist philosopher derives the world from the ultimate nature or class of matter, just as the Platonist, presumably, would trace all things back to different kinds of forms, or the Aristotelian would subsume the events and processes of the world into classes of actualizations of potencies. There is a measure of credibility to Dewey's view that many philosophers who saw their function to be the discovery of what is *necessarily true* about the nature of things, if the *contingent truths* of everyday experience and scientific observation are to be explained, could legitimately be interpreted as providing a classification of the ultimate kinds or species of things. The underlying methodological assumptions are twofold: first, that there are fixed species of things or events; and second, that explanation consists in classifying things or events in their appropriate species.

In contrast with these methodological assumptions, Darwin had provided a new model for philosophical explanation. First, Darwin had shown that there were no fixed species. Second, explanation consisted in specifying the conditions that generate change in species. The methodological revolution most applicable to what Dewey termed the "metaphysical quest for certainty" was to realize that there was no ultimate categorization of things. Philosophical theories could then turn to the more fruitful task of explaining how categories or theories changed. This task would involve philosophy in the more empirical methodology of identifying the conditions that generated changes in events.

Dewey characteristically used the contrast in methodology as a polemical device for criticizing the achievement of traditional metaphysical philosophy. One significant illustration is his criticism of the Kantian effort to deduce the ultimate categories by which the mind categorized or intuited reality. Dewey's objection was that these categories were themselves the product of evolution, resulting from their function as optimal instruments for the coherence, prediction, or control of experience. They would be revised in the light of the development of new ways of comprehending or grasping experience. For Dewey, even the most seemingly certain kinds of knowledge, such as the axioms of logic or the truths of mathematics, were subject to revision as a consequence of their success or failure in permitting men to predict or control their environment. (It is worth noting that this position, arrived at by Dewey from the general methodological consideration that since all knowledge was instrumental, there could be no ultimate categories or "givens" in experience, was developed for much more specific reasons by the American logician Willard van Quine in what has been termed a "neo-pragmatic" thesis. Quine argued that the analytical statements of logical languages were open to change by the press of empirical experience.)

But the most significant consequence of Dewey's acceptance of the post-Darwin model of explanation was that philosophy must use scientific method as its sole method of inquiry or analysis. There is an obvious problem for the practice of philosophy implicit in this consequence. If Dewey's characterization of the traditional philosophical methodology as antithetical to scientific method is correct, and if Dewey's view that this methodology can be replaced by a scientific inquiry into the conditions that generate specified changes in particular groups of phenomena is accepted, then it would seem that philosophy should come to an end—to be replaced by the empirical or positive sciences. This was precisely the moral of the story of the shift in methodology asserted by positivist philosophers and sociologists. Auguste Comte, the well-known founder of sociology whose writings Dewey had read in his undergraduate years, had argued that the replacement of philosophy by the empirical sciences was an inevitable consequence of the development of science in modern society. And many other positivists, of diverse tendencies within the diverse positivistic movements of the late nineteenth and early twentieth century, had asserted that to accept scientific method as the sole form of legitimate, rational inquiry mandated some kind of termination to most philosophical activity.

Like the positivists, Dewey argued—often in the most sustained polemical manner—for the complete adoption of scientific method by philosophy. Unlike many positivists, Dewey then argued that this adoption would not entail the end of philosophy, but rather would bring about a reconstruction and rebirth of philosophical activity.

There were several reasons for Dewey's belief that a commitment by philosophy to the scientific method of inquiry would result in a renewal of philosophical activity rather than in the displacement of philosophy by science. The fundamental one was Dewey's conception of the function of philosophy. The task of philosophy, he believed, was to provide intellectual coherence and systematic criticism of the values and traditions of society. Ultimately, philosophers have not aimed so much at an overarching metaphysical account or schema of what there is in the world as they have sought to critically examine the general beliefs and methods of inquiry of the society in which they have practiced their discipline. Dewey illustrated this interpretation by indicating how medieval philosophy had sought to reconcile its inherited tradition of Greek rationalism with the cultural heritage of Christian revelation, or how Greek thinkers like Plato or Aristotle could be interpreted as philosophers who had provided critical analyses of the social institutions of their culture in the light of the new methodologies developed by Greek mathematicians, scientists, and Sophists. For Dewey, as we noted, American society—in fact, the whole of modern Western society— is bifurcated by the gap between the general acceptance of scientific method in the areas of technological achievement and the physical sciences, and the continued reliance upon methodologies of convention and tradition, with an accompanying rejection of the scientific method, in the areas of social action or humanistic inquiry.

In accordance with Dewey's conception of philosophy, the primary philosophical challenge of our society would be to critically examine and to provide some kind of intellectual resolution to this bifurcation. For Dewey, the resolution of the conflict necessitated the demonstration that the standards of knowledge exhibited in the great achievements of science and technology are also appropriate for economic, social, and political inquiry. Philosophy must then provide an analysis of the methodology of science and the rationale for its application to all domains of inquiry. Far from suggesting the abandonment of philosophy, such an enterprise requires a philosophical account of the nature of knowledge and a philosophical inquiry into the feasibility and potential of the social sciences. Further, it requires philosophical investigation into the question of whether moral issues can be clarified or decided by a scientific methodology.

It follows that the shift in philosophical methodology does bring about a reordering of philosophical priorities in subject matter. Metaphysical or theological questions that had previously been given primacy in philosophical tradition were now replaced in the Deweyan canon by issues stemming from education, politics, psychology, or the social sciences. Dewey saw this change as one that "introduces responsibility into the intellectual life." And he described the change in the primary subject matter of philosophy in the following way:

> To idealize and rationalize the universe at large is after all a confession of inability to master the courses of things that specifically concern us. As long as mankind suffered from this impotency, it naturally shifted a burden of responsibility that it could not carry over to the more competent shoulders of the transcendent cause. But if insight into the specific conditions of value and into specific consequences of ideas is possible, philosophy must in time become a method of locating and interpreting the more serious of the conflicts that occur in life and a method of projecting ways for dealing with them: a method of moral and political diagnosis and prognosis.

It is true that Dewey did not propose the complete abandonment of metaphysical thought, in spite of the view stated in the passage above. He also believed in the possibility of an empirical metaphysics that would make no appeal to transcendental causes. Dewey's claim was that an empirical metaphysics, consistent with the methodology of scientific inquiry, could describe those general features of the world in which knowledge and action can take place, or formulate a credible account of the relationship between what is experienced and what is real.

The crucial consequence, nonetheless, of the philosopher's adoption of scientific method as his instrument of inquiry is the shift in philosophical subject matter to the domain of the social and political, or for Dewey, the moral, problems of man. Metaphysician and antimetaphysician might converge in the belief that an abandonment of transcendent metaphysical philosophy would deprive philosophy of its central area of concern. Dewey's claim was that philosophy had implicitly always had as its function the resolution of social problems, broadly conceived. With its new commitment to scientific method and its new awareness of its social function, philosophy could more explicitly focus on those areas that Dewey termed the "problems of men."

Dewey did not simply confine his thesis to a continuing polemic for the adoption of scientific method and for philosophical concern with human problems, though such a polemic recurs constantly through many of his writings. He also sought to exhibit in his philosophical work the fruit of such a shift in method and subject matter. Perhaps the single book that best exemplifies this commitment is Dewey's pioneering effort to write a work in what may be considered the newly developing field of social psychology—his *Human Nature and Conduct*, published in 1922.

There are several salient elements in *Human Nature and Conduct* that document Dewey's effort to respond adequately to the implications of Darwinism. The recurrent thesis of the book is that there is no fixed human nature. Even those patterns of human behavior that seem to be instinctive have not been immutable but are the product of preceding successful ways of organizing and channeling human impulses and drives. Man is a creature of plural impulses and needs, with no fixed list of instincts and no essential nature.

Patterns of conduct, or habits, have been instituted to satisfy human needs and integrate human impulses. These patterns are not completely determined by antecedent structures, like the genetic code, nor are they the product of random and spontaneous innovation. Intelligence functions to identify latent conflict among impulses and to innovate modifications of established habits so that they can better integrate impulses or needs. Intelligence is not, in Hume's phrase, "the slave of the passions," although it cannot legislate patterns of conduct or generate new impulses. When established habits no longer resolve the conflicting impulses and needs of the human being adequately, however, intelligence can project the modification or change that will reconstitute an adequate adjustment of habit to impulse.

It is important to note how much of Dewey's liberal social philosophy is embedded in this social-psychological account.

The thesis of the malleability of human nature was continuous with the moral insight that man is perfectible. This malleability meant that there could be no fixed limits for human growth, nor any antecedent pattern for social planning or social change. It provided the basis for Dewey's confidence in the significance of educational reform and for his belief in the beneficial possibilities of change.

The role ascribed to intelligence in organizing individual conduct is paradigmatic for the application of human intelligence in society. Social institutions often do not function optimally. Their malfunction characteristically involves either a misapprehension of the nature of human needs or an unresolved conflict among legitimate human impulses. It may indicate that a previously adequate institutional arrangement has become dysfunctional, or that there is a discrepancy between the formulated end of a particular institution and the means being employed to attain that end. The function of social intelligence, which is the analogue of the application of scientific method to social problems, is to mediate social conflict in an optimal way and to propose new patterns of institutional reconstruction that will allow for a more appropriate, fuller channeling of human expression.

There is an irony in Dewey's use of Darwinian biology as the point of departure for a liberal social philosophy. Darwin's work had been utilized by conservative social theorists to justify the contention that social reform and humanitarian legislation were ineffective or harmful to social progress. For these nineteenth-century moralists, Darwin had demonstrated the quasi-permanent biological residue of human nature, which was impervious to reform or to revolutionary changes in social environment. Conservatives often cited Darwin's data to show that the path of progress or evolution was unavoidably marked by conflict, force, suffering, and not by intelligent, humanitarian social planning.

Dewey was not seeking to derive an alternative, substantively liberal social philosophy from a Darwinian basis. His argument hinged upon a different kind of reading of the record, one that was crucially related to his methodological claim. The achievement of Darwin was, he believed, the most important vindication of the possibility of the study of man by the empirical sciences. Such study does not determine the essence of man and derive the implications of this essential nature; rather, it seeks to understand how changes in human nature and in social institutions take place. Since a scientific study of the human condition is attainable, the commitment of a liberal social philosophy is not contained in any particular substantive program, whether traditionally liberal or conservative, but is instead directed to undertake the scientific study of social conflict and to apply the policies derived from that study.

Partly in consequence of this interpretation of liberalism, Dewey was led to a reexamination of the major doctrines of the nineteenth-century liberal tradition, such as "economic individualism" and "negative liberty." And this reexamination was one of the major factors in Dewey's criticism of that century's dominant philosophical figure in the interpretation of empiricism and liberalism: John Stuart Mill.

Dewey and Mill: Liberty, Experience, and Morals

William James had dedicated *Pragmatism*—his book of public lectures on pragmatic philosophy that first gave the movement and the word itself its great popular recognition—to the "memory of John

Stuart Mill . . . whom my fancy likes to picture as our leader were he alive today." The solid grounds for James's fancy are readily found. Mill had formulated a complete empiricist philosophy in metaphysics and had developed an empirical, inductive interpretation of logic. He had set forth a modified, cogent form of utilitarianism in ethics, and had provided the tradition of British liberalism with a forceful and persuasive examination of fundamental theses on liberty, equality, and democracy.

It is a familiar fact of philosophical and intellectual debate—of which the most famous historical example must be Aristotle's critique of Plato—that progress is sometimes pursued by the sharpest kind of confrontation with intellectual allies rather than by sweeping disagreement with adversaries. The reason would seem to be that such confrontation permits the issues on which there is disagreement within the framework of certain common purposes or intentions to be drawn more rigorously and refined more carefully. In any case, it is instructive to observe how John Dewey developed his own philosophical position by articulating his disagreement with John Stuart Mill in crucial areas of philosophy—even though Dewey's philosophical commitments in broadly stated terms were like those of Mill, both being empiricists in the theory of knowledge, naturalists in ethical theory, and liberals and democrats in political philosophy.

The most dramatic and publicly relevant area of the confrontation between Dewey and Mill was Dewey's effort to reformulate liberalism as defined by Mill. Mill's essay *On Liberty* had achieved canonic status in the latter part of the nineteenth century. Dewey believed that the major assumption of *On Liberty* was mistaken.

Mill asserts that a line can be drawn between the domain of the private individual, in which his acts affect only himself, and the domain of the public, in which the acts of the individual affect others. Mill had asserted this distinction in order to recognize and to demarcate the domain of the sovereign individual, whose decisions regarding his own health, education, welfare, morals, or manners would be immune from the intervention of government or the coercion of the public. The marking out of such a domain is, for Mill, a condition for the definition of liberty, which is seen as the protection of the domain of the individual from the incursion of government or society.

Dewey's interpretation of human nature, and particularly his account of the way the character of the individual is formed by processes of social interaction, provided one basis of his disagreement with Mill on the distinction between the private, or self-regarding, domain and the public, or other-regarding, domain.

Dewey criticized Mill for positing an "atomic individual," isolated from the society in which his individuality was formed and from the environment in which his actions became defined. The sources of Dewey's criticism would seem to be both his social-psychological theory of the development of individuality and his general philosophical view of the inclusiveness of the category of the social.

With the shift in the analysis of the relationship between individual and society, Dewey also advocated an alternative account of the nature of liberty or freedom. The individual is not perceived as a completed entity in potential conflict with an interventionist or coercive society; rather, he is a developing person whose career is continuously conditioned by the social environment. In this view, the context of the growth of liberty becomes the conditions required for the development of self and for the realization of a person's ends or goals. Like the Hegelians, Dewey defined liberty in terms of the ability of a person to realize his aims rather than to limit external interference. The significance of the adoption of this theory, recently phrased as the concept of "positive liberty" in contrast with Mill's concept of "negative liberty," has usually been a preference for a more active role of government in economic affairs. Dewey's doctrine bears some relationship to the general shift in American liberal theory from support of the sovereign individual's freedom of contract in a market economy to support of governmental intervention with that freedom, on the grounds that such intervention can foster personal security, promote greater equality, or make possible greater expression of other freedoms.

Dewey's views could justify such a shift in economic policy. But the major themes of his own writing on the topic of freedom were not connected to economic theory. Dewey's concern was with the social conditions that enhance the possibilities for the development of a free personality. It was this concern that led to his stress on educational reform, social pluralism, and political democracy.

John Dewey was unique among the major philosophers of our time in the priority he ascribed to educational theory and practice.

The schools of a nation are one of the major institutions for determining conditions of cultural freedom and for developing the character of the individual citizen. Dewey believed that America's schools ought to be major agencies for the development of free personalities, while recognizing that in fact they were often institutions that repressed or inhibited personal expression and stunted growth. Dewey helped to initiate a series of reforms—in student participation in the classroom, in the change of curricula, in revision of the processes of decision making in education—that resulted in a virtual remaking of American education. This movement for reform, subsequently termed "progressive education," was to become the most controversial and possibly the most caricatured product of Dewey's philosophical thought.

Dewey wrote on many of the concrete issues of education. He believed that students should participate in the decisions that affect them in the school in a way consistent with both the responsibility of the teacher and the rights of the community. He argued that curricula should respond to the vital needs of students and not to an established tradition or convention, but he did not interpret this to mean that students should learn only what they wished. As the movement for progressive education generated experimental models in American education, Dewey was applauded or condemned for programs that were in fact remote from his philosophical or educational theories.

There was one area of Dewey's practical educational activity that seemed closely connected to his political philosophy. Dewey actively supported the rights of teachers and their autonomy on questions related to academic subject matter or method, which should be safeguarded from intervention by political, economic, or other interest groups. The autonomy of the schools, he felt, was part of a concept of pluralism that was a necessary condition for political democracy. Aside from the value of democratic pluralism, freedom of inquiry was to be valued as an expression of free personality.

Dewey's most characteristic defense of freedom of inquiry resembled that of Mill in the argument that intellectual inquiry, particularly scientific inquiry, has an implicit connection with progress. Consequently, restrictions on freedom of inquiry could result in the adoption of views that have not been verified under open competition. This procedure would have self-defeating consequences in practice, even for those who initially stood to benefit from an authoritarian censorship of ideas.

It is noteworthy that Dewey believed that the schools of a democracy could be a model for democratic society. They could exhibit a form of life in which conflicting views would be mediated by intellectual inquiry, and in which social policy would result from the free participation of all elements of the school community. This kind of freedom and democracy would inevitably be more difficult to achieve in the larger political and economic institutions of the society. But schools could demonstrate the potential direction of a free, democratic society.

The rise of totalitarianism in the 1930's represented a major challenge to the assumptions of Dewey's political philosophy. Totalitarian societies cast doubt on such Deweyan tenets as faith in progress through scientific inquiry and the adoption of positive liberty as a social ideal involving individual self-realization. This was particularly telling when a concept of "positive liberty" was accompanied by confidence in greater participation by the masses in political and social life as an instrument for lessening human oppression. John Stuart Mill, like Benjamin Constant and other nineteenth-century liberals, had envisaged "negative liberty" as a brake to the conformism of mass democracy. With the rise of totalitarian societies that had involved or used mass participation, many social theorists asserted the need for a revised interpretation of democratic liberty—one that would discard Dewey's beliefs entirely.

Friedrich von Hayek, for example, argued anew for the restoration of the free market economy without governmental intervention as a necessary condition for a free market place of ideas and economic limits upon excessive state power. Walter Lippmann advanced the thesis that only an agreed "public philosophy," with an absolute commitment to human rights and to the humane values of the Western spiritual tradition, could save democratic societies from their totalitarian potential. Reinhold Niebuhr, Jacques Maritain (and later Aleksandr Solzhenitsyn), saw totalitarian societies as the consequence of a secular belief in human perfectibility unprotected by a religious awareness of the limits and norms of the human condition. Accordingly, for them, a revision of the assumptions of most forms of liberalism, including that of John Dewey, was in order.

Dewey's response to the phenomenon of totalitarianism, and to the philosophical reaction it engendered, was to reassert the significance of the values of pluralism and of scientific methodology, both in theory and in practice. On theoretical grounds, Dewey noted that totalitarian ideologies asserted monistic conceptions of history. In the ideologies of Marxism, fascism, and Nazism, a historical event is not seen as the product of plural activities of men resulting in an unpredictable future. Rather, it is the realization of an antecedently determined career of race, nation, or class. The protagonists of such monistic theories of history resisted validation or verification of their hypothesis by scientific methods. In the theoretical sphere, only the application of critical intelligence, which Dewey believed to be continuous with the scientific method, could serve as antidote to totalitarian ideology.

Practically, a defense against totalitarianism, in Dewey's view, did not call for the abandonment of the ideal of positive liberty or of governmental intervention; instead, it called for a stronger awareness of the position that plural, secondary associations had in democratic society. Democracy did not comprise, as Mill's model would lead one to believe, a mass public confronting an autonomous individual. There were plural publics or associations, including the schools, trade unions, diverse informational media, corporations, families, and other voluntary or quasi-voluntary groups. Years before the issue of totalitarianism had come to the fore, Dewey had argued that the framework for expression of the individual could no longer be the small village or rural community of an earlier America. Democracy in America would require the articulation of many kinds of voluntary associations in which the citizen might affirm his identity or express his individuality. Such plural associations were also the effective brake to the totalitarian potential of mass society.

Dewey recognized plural groups—not just plural political parties —existing under conditions of freedom as a necessary condition of political democracy. Democracy was to be a method of resolving or mediating conflicts among the interests and beliefs of these plural groups in society. He emphasized the analogy between democratic method and scientific method, since both mediated conflicting opinions by an appeal to the experimental consequences of adopting a particular opinion or hypothesis. In my view, Dewey did not sufficiently confront the important lack of analogy between democracy and scientific method. He saw in democracy the best social method for articulating and resolving all points of view in a continuing process of decision and inquiry. Scientific method also was the optimal method for resolving conflicting opinions. But the analogy breaks down when one examines the specific social functions of voting as contrasted with the procedures of scientific verification.

Dewey understood, of course, the difference between an election and scientific research. I believe that his focus upon the elements of the analogy stemmed from his sense of the urgent need to implement scientific methods in the study and reform of society. As noted, Dewey believed that the crisis of Western civilization was caused by the gap between our readiness as a culture to apply scientific methods in technology, including the arts of war, and our inability and refusal to apply them to social problems. Since every democratic society had to permit freedom of inquiry, the practice of freedom of inquiry in a pluralistic society would require social scientific research on the full agenda of the problems of men. Liberalism in social philosophy for Dewey meant a commitment to freedom of inquiry in social issues and to the implementation of the empirical fruits of that inquiry.

I have suggested that Dewey's criticism of Mill's concept of the "atomic individual" provides one appropriate departure for the development of Dewey's own philosophy of liberalism. Similarly, Dewey's criticism of Mill's concept of experience as a "subjective, atomic sensation" was, in many ways, the appropriate foil for the adumbration of his own empirical naturalism. No other polemic in his criticism is more recurrent than that directed—primarily against Mill, but often against the entire tradition of British empiricism from Locke to Russell—to the interpretation of the concept of experience.

For Dewey, experience denoted an interaction between an organism and the environment. The units of experience, so to speak, may be transactions, happenings, occurrences, episodes, events, involvements, processes, and other characterizations of actions that take place in time. Experience refers to objective occurrences that may involve particular things in a particular place. In his view, it seemed an anomaly bordering on the perverse that the empirical philosophical tradition that locates the source of knowledge in concrete, empirical experience should have locked itself into an account of the world as comprising classes of sense data—the subjective apprehensions of taste, touch, sight, smell, and sound. In fairness, it was in some measure the desire on the part of the empiricists to avoid a hypothetical source of error and to realize certainty of knowledge that motivated their reading of experience as the immediate apprehension of the experientially given datum. For these empiricists, it seemed plausible to believe that while I might be mistaken about my memory or inference about a moment of experience, I could be certain about the here-and-now datum or immediately given experience as described in phenomenal terms, such as "here," "yellow," "now."

The misidentification of experience with a subjective apprehension of the immediately given, alleged data of sense was the root, Dewey argued, of the major inadequacies of the British empirical tradition in philosophy. Once the object or event of experience is transformed into a collection of ideas or a class of subjective sense data, then a series of spurious metaphysical issues are generated.

One example of such a metaphysical conundrum is the problem of the existence of the external object. Since the ordinary cup, saucer, tree, moon, have been transformed into classes of sense data, the problem arises about the existence of the external object beyond the sense data. Another example is the problem of the existence of other minds. Since the episodes of response to environmental probes by another person are classes of ideas, the existence of a mind as a source of these ideas becomes an issue for philosophical inquiry.

Further, Dewey held that it was this misreading of experience in terms of subjective sensation that generated a theory of knowledge in which truth could be understood as a correspondence between the ideas in the mind and the sense data. Such a theory could not explain how the having of knowledge was related to the ability to predict or control the objective environment in which men had to function. Since it identified certainty with the immediate having of an experience, it could not account for the corrigible factor in knowledge that leads to revision even of the most seemingly certain claims for knowledge in the light of future experience.

Stemming from this criticism of Mill's inadequate account of experience, Dewey advanced three related claims in metaphysics and theory of knowledge. First, as noted, he sought to provide a systematic account of the concept of experience as an objective term for the public transactions of organisms with their environment. This enterprise led Dewey to attempt a descriptive metaphysics, most prominently in his book *Experience and Nature*. There he attempted to formulate some of the more pervasive and general characteristics of experience. His effort resembles in some respects a descriptive phenomenology of certain aspects of human experience.

Second, and I believe most fundamentally, Dewey attempted to demonstrate how the correction of the empiricist misidentification of experience with atomic sensationalist data could eliminate the spurious questions mentioned earlier, and others, from the philosophical agenda. This elimination of metaphysical questions was carried out without any general manifesto on the theoretical impossibility of metaphysics, unlike similar enterprises in the decades after Dewey. Yet many of Dewey's writings on metaphysics were clearly antimetaphysical in that their goal was to demonstrate that there was no general problem of the existence of the external world, or of other minds, or of the mind-body question, and so on. Dewey's antimetaphysical claim was that the shift in the characterization of experience replaced this kind of metaphysical question with specific questions. And the specific questions that related to specified occurrences in experience were, unlike the spuriously metaphysical problems, empirically verifiable ones.

Third, the reinterpretation of the concept of experience provided Dewey with an additional justification for his account of the nature of knowledge. Knowledge was not the correspondence of "passive, spectator" mind with the external data, nor was it the grasping of the immediately incorrigible given. Knowledge was an interaction of organism with environment in which the agent actively intervened to predict future experience and to control it. Dewey, in some contexts, ranked metaphysical views in terms of their making plausible this account of human knowledge, which in turn determined an attitude toward experience and the world. On the theory of mind as a passive spectator, the shaping of the future was not within human power. But on the theory of experience that had room in it for human intervention, man could correctly understand himself as an agent with some degree of freedom to reform his environment. It was the account compatible with human freedom that more adequately reflected the truth about human experience and the human condition. In that sense, Dewey's account of experience justified his theory of knowledge; and, reciprocally, that theory of knowledge provided some confirmation for his account of experience.

In one other important area of Dewey's philosophy, ethical theory, Dewey's views represented a critical development of those of John Stuart Mill. It is true that for Dewey's ethics, as for his political philosophy or his metaphysics, there were plural sources for his point of view. Yet it is instructive to note in what respects his views are similar to those of Mill's utilitarian ethical theory—the dominant empirical moral philosophy before him—and how his views diverged from those of Mill.

Dewey shares four fundamental theses with Mill. First, like Mill, he is an ethical naturalist, who rejects any transcendental or supernatural source for moral values or ethical imperatives. Second, Mill and Dewey are in agreement on the thesis of the objective character of value judgments. Both deny that assertions of value are expressions of subjective taste, arbitrary preference, emotive attitude, or conventional manners. Rather, and this is a third point of agreement, judgments of value are empirical appraisals of which policy among several is the best to pursue for the realization of human ends. Moral judgment thus functions in a context of decision making among choices for the resolution of concrete problems. This claim of the relevant context and function of moral judgment differs from the claim of those who would see in moral assertion some absolute vindication of moral principle or some aesthetic effort at cultivation of human excellence. Morality is social; it involves choice among the feasible alternatives in particular social situations. Fourth, both Mill and Dewey locate the source of morality in the desires and wants of human nature. A fundamental key to determining the norms or standards of morality is the correct account of human nature, of its diverse needs and ranked preferences.

Despite these four major areas of agreement, however, Dewey was often a severe critic of utilitarian ethical theory. For notwithstanding their ethical naturalism and their recognition of the place of human nature in ethical theory, the utilitarians provided an interpretation of man as motivated by the desire to maximize the sensations of pleasure and to minimize those of pain. This interpretation is a caricature of the many complex motives that are present in human behavior, according to Dewey. Again, as in the cases of the "atomic individual" or the "atomic sensation," empirical philosophers have reduced the processes by which human beings satisfy their needs and gratify their demands, drives, or desires to a model of atomic sensations of isolable and incrementally measurable units of pleasure or pain. Consequently, Dewey's criticism was directed against the psychological theory of utilitarianism, and not against the empirical and naturalistic character of its ethics.

The most explicit documentation of the connection between Mill and Dewey is Dewey's defense of the connection between the "desired" and the "desirable." Mill had argued that the only ultimate proof that something is visible is that it is seen, or audible that it is heard; consequently, the only ultimate proof that something is desirable is that it is desired. Critics of Mill have countered that there is a logical error in Mill's formulation, for while "audible" means capable of being heard and "visible" means capable of being seen, the term "desirable" carries with it the connotation that something ought to be desired. Mill's error is to miss the distinction between what *is* the case and what *ought to be* the case—a distinction that cannot be blurred or evaded. A familiar criticism of Mill and all ethical naturalists or empiricists is that they fail adequately to recognize the gulf that lies between the factual assertion of human desires, needs, wants, or aims and the moral prescription of values, imperatives, or ideals.

Dewey argued that there is no source of derivation for what ought to be desired or what ought to be done morally except the facts of human desires, needs, and preferences. Accordingly, there is a close connection between the "desirable" and the "desired," as Mill had claimed. The belief that some policy is desirable is an assertion that human beings would desire it under certain conditions. Characteristically, one of those conditions is that human beings understand the nature of their own desires, or that they have correctly assessed the consequences of a policy; another may be that they have made the correct factual judgments about the options available to them or about the means of their realization. For example, if I say that a policy of permitting abortion of the fetus is desirable—that is, ought to be desired—then in Dewey's analysis I am claiming that human beings would approve of this policy if they knew the nature of their own desires, learned its actual consequences, and determined the consequences of the alternatives.

"Desirable" is not the unique or even the preferred term for this kind of linguistic function. Dewey's theory applies for all judgments of value. The claim that any particular policy is the "right" one or the "good" one is, for Dewey, an empirical prediction about how the implementation of that policy will meet genuine human needs. It is to be evaluated like all empirical claims by its consequences in experience.

Dewey advanced a number of specific criticisms of utilitarian ethical theory. His aim was to develop a naturalistic and empirical ethical theory that would more adequately reflect the facts of social psychology and his own sense of the way in which normative moral judgments functioned in society. I believe that Dewey's reformulation of ethical naturalism marks one of his lasting contributions to the philosophy of our times. Ethical naturalism has allegedly been refuted several times in the twentieth century, first, brilliantly by G. E. Moore in his assertion of a "naturalistic fallacy" and, again, seemingly devastatingly by logical positivists in their assertion of the emotive and attitudinal characteristics of ethical judgment. The themes of Dewey's ethical naturalism, however, if not the idiom of his formulation, are continuously restated even after the apparent refutation. The relevance of facts for the determination of moral judgment, the connection between human inclinations or desires and moral values, the significance of a commitment to rational method for resolving moral conflict about the substantive moral worth of the proposed resolution, are three specific Deweyan themes that recur in recent ethical theory. The recurrence suggests that Dewey's naturalistic ethical theory contains some elements that no adequate account of morals can ever completely ignore or reject.

Peirce, James, and Dewey on Meaning, Truth, and Metaphysics

In the two preceding sections of this essay, I have traced the fundamental themes of Dewey's philosophy as they emerged from his critical assessment of the traditions of Darwin's naturalism and Mill's empiricism. I have done so because Dewey characteristically develops his own views by a dialectical criticism of the theses of his predecessors'. It is true, of course, that Dewey provided significant reinterpretations of many other major figures of the Western philosophical tradition. Of special importance, however, is his adoption

and reformulation of salient features of the two American philosophers of pragmatism who preceded him: Charles Peirce and William
James. Dewey's pragmatic epistemology and his naturalistic metaphysics clearly reflect his interpretation and his extension of doctrines or views first asserted by Peirce in epistemology and James in
metaphysics.

Charles Peirce provided the basis for the pragmatic account of
truth in his philosophical papers, which Dewey termed "seminal."
In his short paper "How to Make Our Ideas Clear," Peirce advanced
the thesis that inquiry is a process initiated by a biological irritation
of "doubt" about a practical decision to be made and terminated
by "belief," which appeases the irritation of doubt by instituting a
decision. It follows that "belief," in the Peircean sense of the term,
involves instituting a practical decision, or initiating a habit of
action, or some change in the observable state of affairs, so that the
state after inquiry differs from what it was before.

Peirce's shrewd and original ploy was to raise the question of
whether two beliefs, formulated in differing verbal phrases but resulting in the identical practical decision, habit, or features of the
observable situation, should be counted as the same belief or not.
His reply was that unless there is a difference in the conceivable
practical consequences between the two beliefs that would manifest
itself at some time in the future, they are the same belief. It follows
that any belief, assertion, or hypothesis—whether in common sense,
science, or metaphysics—that does not have conceivably distinctive
consequences in practice cannot be significant. It cannot serve as an
appropriate terminus of inquiry.

Further, Peirce contended that beliefs are evaluated in terms of
their efficacy in resolving doubt. Doubt is resolved only when a
decision is made that will have observable consequences in the
future. As a methodological rule of human practicality, men accept
the belief that more adequately resolves the situation that originally
led to doubt, that is, the belief whose future consequences are verified. Similarly, we reject the belief whose future consequences are
confuted by our ongoing experience. If two beliefs had identical
consequences, there would be no procedure for evaluating their
acceptability. Disputation for or against the adoption of such beliefs—that is, the hypotheses or assertions that had no distinctive
consequences for future experience—would be pointless. It would
constitute a verbal or semantic argument that could admit of no
empirical resolution.

This line of argument led Peirce, James, and Dewey to the conclusion that metaphysical dispute can be significant only if it has issue in empirical or practical consequences. Peirce developed a metaphysical hypothesis that he believed could be verified by human evolutionary experience. James claimed that the adoption of differing metaphysical hypotheses had momentous implications for practice, although critics have often accused him of confusing the psychological consequences that may stem from a person's believing in a particular hypothesis with the set of consequences that are logically derivable from that particular hypothesis. The most familiar illustration of that confusion points out that while a believer's faith in the existence of God may have many consequences for his actions and his attitudes, the hypothesis that God exists does not thereby become, in Peircean terms, a hypothesis with verifiable consequences in the future.

As we have noted, Dewey attempted to develop a naturalistic metaphysics that would describe pervasive characteristics of experience. Since his metaphysics was naturalistic, in ways that I shall subsequently detail, Dewey made no appeal to transcendental entities. Accordingly, he believed that his metaphysical theses were consistent with Peirce's criterion for significant belief; in other words, they were verifiable by future experience.

Peirce had anticipated and adumbrated in some detail a criterion for the significance of hypotheses or assertions that was later to be both celebrated and castigated as the "verifiability theory of meaning." The theory asserted as the criterion for the significance or meaningfulness of any proposition that it should be capable of verification by future sense experience. By using this criterion, many logical positivist philosophers were to deny significance to all metaphysical hypotheses. It was their contention that not only transcendental metaphysical systems, which presumably invoked nonverifiable transcendent entities, but also those metaphysical systems that were naturalistic and empirical—such as those of Peirce, James, or Dewey—would violate the verifiability theory of meaning. This was so because it is impossible even in a naturalistic metaphysical theory to specify a set of empirical consequences that hold if the theory is true and are refuted if the theory is false.

Pierce's argument generated philosophical tension over the legitimacy of metaphysical inquiry. For the logical positivists who elaborated a more rigorous reading of his argument than he had provided, Pierce had suggested a criterion of meaning that would banish metaphysics as meaningless. For the pragmatists, particularly Dewey, Peirce had laid the foundation for a pragmatic criticism of the nonfunctional character of transcendental metaphysics. He had thereby provided the guidelines for a metaphysical inquiry that must be limited to an account of natural processes and empirically experienced events.

Peirce's argument in "How to Make Our Ideas Clear" defines a significant belief in terms of its conceivable practical consequences. Those beliefs whose consequences are confirmed in future experience are accepted. Those beliefs that are confuted by the course of future experience generate anew the irritation of doubt. After a renewed process of inquiry, they are replaced by a new belief that points in turn to other experiential consequences. And the process continues with no final end.

This description of the process of inquiry involved Peirce in three interesting theses, each of which he explicitly recognized and championed. First, every belief is fallible. This conclusion is mandated by the openness of every belief or hypothesis to the test of future experience. No belief is certain, since in pointing to experiential consequences there is always the possibility that future experience will refute the belief and generate a new inquiry aimed at its replacement.

Second, every belief is corrigible. Since beliefs are fallible, they are open to replacement. Since they are replaceable only if the new belief can more adequately predict the course of future experience, every belief is open to correction in the light of new evidence.

Third, it follows that the method of replacement of one belief by another is a progressive method. Since the process of replacing fallible beliefs is one of continuous correction, the newer belief must be an improvement on its predecessor. This progressiveness is procedurally implicit in the criterion of acceptance of a new hypothesis only if the hypothesis is capable both of accounting for all the past predictions its predecessor had made and of predicting future consequences more adequately. In explaining this procedure, Peirce argued that he was explicating the methodology of empirical science.

The significance of this interpretation of the progressive character of scientific method is easily grasped. It explains the belief that the currently accepted scientific theory or hypothesis, even when developed by a team of ordinary scientists, is superior to earlier theories like the biology of Aristotle or the physics of Newton. In other areas of human activity, there is no similar technique of methodological progress. Eighteenth-century drama may well be inferior to Shakespeare; painting after the Renaissance may represent a deterioration in both technique and vision; in many areas of cultural style or fashion, one concept or norm may replace another in cyclical manner with no convergence of attitude by connoisseurs and, certainly, with no claim that the newer is in any way superior to its predecessor. Yet, on the whole, we do not believe that contemporary scientific theories represent a generational fashion, to be replaced by a previously dominant theory or by highly novel speculation as scientific styles change. Peirce had provided a plausible explanation for the progressive character of scientific views that is compatible with the recognition that human societies have periods of advance and deterioration in many areas, that there may be times of efflorescence of scientific genius and other times when only mediocrity flourishes. The progressive character of science is, for Peirce, a consequence of the methodological criteria in scientific inquiry for the acceptance of new hypotheses.

In effect, Peirce had formulated a theory of the nature of truth, the first formulation of the "pragmatic theory of truth." Since every statement is fallible, it is not certainly true, but probable. Its probability is some measure of the degree of its confirmation. Peirce sought to quantify this measure of degree of confirmation according to a frequency theory of probability. The hypothesis that ought to be accepted at any particular time is that hypothesis which can best explain past data and, most crucially, successfully predict future consequences. Absolute truth is unattainable. The true opinion is the one that would be arrived at as the limit or convergence of the process of scientific inquiry—a process that, by definition, could not end. Thus Peirce does provide us with a criterion for absolute truth, even though it is defined asymptotically.

Peirce had sketched these doctrines of the nature of meaning and of truth in a few published papers and many diverse uncompleted manuscripts. Dewey agreed with his approach, and developed a comprehensive, related series of works on logic, the theory of knowledge, the definition of truth, and the place of mind in nature. There was an important shift of emphasis in Dewey's works. Dewey stressed the characteristics of human intelligence or mind that make it an instrument in man's adjustment to his environment and in his ability to predict and control change. Accordingly, the term "pragmatic," which Peirce had introduced to stress the connection of inquiry with practical consequences, was often replaced in Dewey's epistemology by the term "instrumental." Further, Dewey's much greater concern with social issues led him to a concern with the ways in which scientific inquiry could serve as a paradigm for the rational and optimal resolution of social conflict. In many ways, however, the themes just formulated in Peirce's papers were accepted by Dewey and received a complex elaboration in his works.

Dewey's major work in logical theory, *Logic: The Theory of Inquiry*, traced the genesis of all inquiry to its biosocial matrix. Thought always began in an unresolved, problematic situation, a highly elaborate replacement for Peircean "doubt." The termination of inquiry was the provisional resolution of the problematic situation. In describing the process of inquiry, Dewey sought to identify the particular functions provided by the various techniques of deductive inference and inductive method as described in the texts of traditional logic. And in stressing the function of these techniques in problem solving, Dewey usually revised the ways in which earlier logicians had understood or interpreted them.

Since Dewey believed that every resolution of a problematic situation is provisional, he was committed to the view that every conclusion of logical or scientific inquiry is not certain or finally fixed. The illusion of certainty, Dewey argued in one of his major books, *The Quest for Certainty*, has perennially been harmful in philosophical interpretations of knowledge. Whether certainty is alleged to reside in logical first principles or in incorrigibly given sense data, whether it is asserted as self-evident truth or is the product of arduous effort at illumination, it inevitably distorts the continuing nature of inquiry. The quest for certainty has fostered absolutism in morals and politics, whereas a correct appreciation of the process of inquiry would lead to fallibility and an openness to the possibility of change.

It has often been countered that Dewey's commitment to the process of inquiry is itself a tacit absolute. Dewey's response was that he posited no *substantive*, ultimately certain or absolute doctrine in his philosophy. The commitments implicit in scientific inquiry are *methodological*: a belief in freedom of inquiry, for example, or a decision to accept the outcome of inquiry. In rejoinder, it is obviously possible to argue that freedom of inquiry should be abridged. And indeed, in research in certain aspects of genetic control and of cobalt-bomb technology, there have been cogent arguments in favor of blocking the further progress of inquiry. It may sometimes be the path of psychological wisdom or prudence for a person to refuse to acknowledge the outcome of an inquiry, preferring to remain with an inconsistency in his beliefs or to ignore evidence that is inimical to cherished preconceptions. The response of the Deweyan is that the commitment to scientific method does not categorically exclude the decision to adopt these options in any particular case. The relevant point supporting Dewey's methodological principle is that the person who advocates such seemingly non-rational options as abridging an inquiry or rejecting the conclusions of an inquiry must support his advocacy—

on pain of irrationality—with evidence that the decisions he favors will be justified by their consequences in future experience.

The close connection between the methodology of science and the methods of critical social inquiry motivated much of Dewey's analysis of the nature of scientific method. Dewey did not seek to provide a technical analysis of how his concept of the instrumental truth of scientific methodology could be explicated by a probabilistic notion of "degree of confirmation," or how it could be related to the notions in statistical inference of strategies of hypothesis acceptance or rejection. This theme was more general. Dewey sought to demonstrate that an instrumental concept of truth explained how knowledge could effect social change, while other theories of truth held by rationalists or empiricists could only make this a miracle or mystery. Further, he argued that the understanding of scientific method provided a paradigm for the peaceful and rational resolution of social conflict.

For Dewey, scientific method was a method of mediating among conflicting opinions by an appeal to future consequences under conditions of free inquiry. The conclusions of scientific inquiry were true—that is, *warrantedly assertible* in the process of inquiry, while still open to revision in the light of new hypotheses and future evidence. In contrast to this method, decisions among conflicting social opinions often require a resort to force, pressure, manipulation, or other kinds of coercion. Conflicting social opinions are frequently presented as contending absolute ideological claims or other species of moral certainty.

With the successful institutions of science as a model, it should become increasingly possible for men to transpose their social claims from the idiom of ideological or moral certainty into that of hypotheses that they believe can best meet the needs of the situation. As empirical hypotheses, these opinions must indicate the kind of intersubjective evidence that will serve as confirmation or refutation of their claim. The process of social conflict can then begin to approximate the ways in which science mediates conflicting opinion. Further, since science is inherently methodologically progressive, some of the possibility for social progress is transferred to the social process of decision making.

This process had begun to take place as social-scientific inquiry was developed in areas like economics. Dewey argued that issues of economic policy had previously been examined from the vantage point of ideological or moral attitudes or from points of view derived from vested interests. The adoption of the methodology of the social scientist provided a new perspective on these issues.

Accordingly, his demonstration of the continuity of scientific method in both the natural and social sciences was, for Dewey, the intellectual presupposition for the regular use of that method for progressive improvement of the human condition.

In the context of the pragmatic movement, Dewey was the major philosophical figure who transformed insights and programs into coherent formulations of a philosophical point of view. His instrumentalist epistemology—that is, the series of works on knowledge, logic, truth, and mind—shows Dewey systematically articulating and critically developing the earlier pragmatic insights of Charles Peirce. And his formulation of a theory of naturalistic metaphysics carried out a program first sketched by William James in *Pragmatism* in 1907.

In that book, James had deplored the condition of contemporary philosophy, in which all philosophy seemed divided into two camps, materialism and idealism. In contrast to the ideal of rational inquiry, in which open-minded persons collaborate toward a convergent truth, materialist or idealist philosophers were not capable either of perceiving the cogency of each other's arguments or of persuading each other of the grounds for their firm conviction of truth.

James suggested that those persons who were temperamentally "tough minded" chose materialism, with its picture of the universe as an antecedently determined system of matter, governed by mechanical laws. They found in the contemporaneous discoveries of the natural and biological sciences sufficient evidence to support this philosophical point of view. Conversely, those persons who were temperamentally "tender minded" chose idealism, with its picture of the universe as an antecedently determined system of ideas, evolving in accordance with the dialectically logical patterns of reason. The idealists found in the argument that all experienced events are structured by the categories of mind or reason, the logical ground that required the universe of human experience to be interpreted as the product of mind or reason.

James argued that pragmatism should provide the framework for an alternative picture of the world. From his point of view, materialism and idealism commit a similar error of metaphysical method. They choose a method that seeks to explain events by deriving them from a single, logically necessary, causal schema, instead of seeking to explain plural events by an empirical account of their careers and consequences. For persons of James's temperament, which was remarkably open to the novelties of experience and interested in the capacity of individuals to affect the world for better or worse, a conception of the universe as antecedently determined seemed to deny the most pervasive aspects of the world: plurality, accident, change, unpredictability, and the arena of human effort.

Similarly, Dewey's metaphysical viewpoint is set by the need to provide an interpretation of the world that is consistent with his naturalistic theory of knowledge. His theory interprets knowing as the interaction of an organism with an environment in order to adjust to that environment, but also to control or change some of its features. It follows that the Deweyan picture of the world had to be one that made sense of the fact that knowledge could change the world. This would lead to a rejection of any metaphysical account of the world as antecedently determined structure, whether of matter or of mind. Further, Dewey's theory of knowledge is an empirical one. Inquiry begins with a problematic situation and terminates with a new hypothesis that can more adequately respond to the facts of experience and predict the course of future experience. There is no room in this account for the introduction of entities that transcend experience. Accordingly, Dewey's metaphysical theory is naturalistic and empirical.

Within that empirical and naturalistic metaphysics, there are four special themes of great importance. First is the special emphasis Dewey places upon the conception of the world as irreducibly plural. Second is his stress on the reality of so-called secondary and tertiary qualities. Third is the parallel belief that experience may comprehend different kinds of entities; it is not restricted to sensations. Fourth is the view that some of the processes of nature may be legitimately understood as means-ends processes. Each of these themes provides a clarification of some aspect of Dewey's metaphysical naturalism that distinguished it from preceding naturalistic interpretations of the world.

First, Dewey's pluralism leads him to disagree with those interpretations of naturalism, like that of Spinoza, in which all events are to be ultimately explained as parts of a single system of nature, whether conceived as immanent deity or as the axioms of mathematical physics. These interpretations presume that scientific knowledge mirrors some parts of the world, and that ultimate scientific knowledge would be an account of the total system. For Dewey, the scientific investigator categorizes or selects—depending on his interests and subject matter—those aspects of experienced things which he can meaningfully connect in laws or theories that correlate with or predict other experiences. He does not simply mirror some portion of a single block universe. A simple example may clarify the issue.

A seismologist selects specific physical phenomena that allow him to predict or understand, and it is hoped, at some time to prevent, earthquake phenomena. An economist studies specific social phenomena, such as supply and demand of money, that allow him to predict and understand, and it is hoped, at some time to prevent, economic recession. There is no single super-science that comprehends seismology, economics, and all the other data of experience in order to predict all occurrences. The sciences are inevitably *plural* inquiries. A mountain of gold will represent a different characteristic in seismology than it will in economic theory. There is no metaphysical single substance that will acontextually comprehend the only "real" mountain of gold in all its potential experience.

This recognition of the plural aspects of all experienced things is crucial for Dewey's metaphysics. Since experience contains events of irreducible plurality, it is never completely predictable by any rational or scientific account. A plural and unpredictable world is one in which the precariousness of existence is not illusory. But Dewey argued that the abilities of men to organize rationally certain selected aspects of their experience means that men can gain a measure of control over their environment in order to partially overcome the precarious nature of existence.

Second, Dewey argued that experience is not reducible to any particular set of properties selected from experience, like extension in motion. Modern science, particularly physics and chemistry, can abstract certain specified, quantitative properties of things (such as extension, mass, motion), and incorporate these properties as variables in theories that predict the occurrence of other variables. It is tempting to conclude that the explanatory properties are somehow primary or real and the other properties of experienced things secondary or less real. This was the thought grasped in the aphorism of the first materialist atomist, Democritus, who held that bitter and sweet are "by convention," while "nothing is real but atoms and the void."

In Dewey's account of science and of experience, even if physics and chemistry can explain or predict the properties of sweetness in terms of other variables, such as carbon and hydrogen, it is still the case that the experience of sweet things is an objective experience. "Sugar is sweet" is an objective description of a real property of sugar. Further, experienced events may be exciting or boring, paintings may be ugly or beautiful, relationships may be nauseating or cloying, independent of the success or failure of the sciences adequately to explain or predict these events, paintings, and relationships by physical or chemical theories. Materialistic metaphysics is mistaken, according to Dewey, if it believes that the possibility of a scientific understanding of aspects of experience provides us with a primary world of material entities of which the experienced world is an apparent duplication. It is precisely because experienced events are real that the scientific theories may be useful in enhancing the quality of human experience.

Third, Dewey was also opposed to the view, characteristic of Mill and some British empiricists, that experience could be understood as a structure of subjective sensations. For Dewey, there is no preferred entity that constitutes the stuff of experience. A horse running, for example, may be an episode in a race for one person and a biological event for another. It may appear as a surface of color to the artist seeking to paint the event and as a blur of sensations to the photographer focusing on a particular instant. To the horse's trainer, it may represent a heroic effort; while for the geneticist, it is a predictable performance. The characterization of experience depends upon context and purpose. Characterization of experienced objects as things like tables, stars, or salt may be preferred for everyday communication. In some contexts of control, their consideration as physical or chemical entities may be more desirable. In special contexts of epistemological confirmation, it may be appropriate to construe these things as observable occurrences or sense data. Experience admits of diverse characterization, and the empiricist is not committed to afford primacy to the language of sensory happenings or sense data.

Fourth, for Dewey, events are often interpretable or characterizable as means to ends. In terms of human achievement, it is this aspect of experience that is most important. It was this importance that misled Aristotelian naturalists to interpret all natural processes as teleological, although they too were forced to realize the operation of chance, spontaneity, and necessity in the events of the natural world. For Dewey, just as it was a mistake to read purposiveness in all natural processes, so it would be an error to read out of nature the various ways in which men make use of the things that are natural. Dewey argued that many philosophical traditions had interpreted man as an alien spectator in an external and completed world. He in turn sought to restore a frame of reference in which natural processes are part of the human environment and human actions are viewed as part of nature.

There is no doubt that Dewey's primary motives in philosophy were those of the moralist and social philosopher. His ambitious efforts at a metaphysical theory, however, which were aimed at providing an account of "the general features of experienced things," in order "to interpret their significance for a philosophic theory of the universe in which we live," were more than a detour providing the relevant context for morals and social philosophy. They represented Dewey's systematic effort to complete his conception of naturalism as an adequate framework for all realms of human experience.

This developmental survey has demonstrated Dewey's thought in his four major areas of philosophical activity: metaphysics, theory of knowledge, ethics, and social philosophy. It has shown the significance of Dewey's conception of philosophy for his own philosophical work and partially explored the importance for him of the philosophy of education. Yet, as the selections from Dewey's own writings show, these areas do not exhaust the full range of his interests in and contributions to philosophy.

Illustrative of this range is the way in which Dewey explored the consequences of his naturalistic and empirical interpretation of the concept of experience for both religion and aesthetics. In 1934, Dewey published both *A Common Faith* and *Art as Experience*. *A Common Faith* proposed a definition of religious experience that would deny the traditional identification of the religious with the supernatural, or with any transcendent domain marked off from the area of natural human inquiry or activity. For Dewey, "the religious function in experience" is "the unification of the self through allegiance to inclusive ideal ends, which imagination presents to us and to which the human will responds as worthy of controlling our desires and choices." Consequently, a naturalistic account of the function of religion in projecting or formulating "inclusive ideal ends" could provide a basis for criticism of the transcendental metaphysical presuppositions of religion while providing a basis for the support of the moral and aesthetic function of religion in human experience. Analogously, in *Art as Experience* he developed a theory of the experience of art that denied any sharp split between human activity in the practical arts and the fine arts, or in Dewey's terms, between the "instrumental" and the "consummatory." The aesthetic process, however, is a clarification and intensification of experience. Whether in producing or in appreciating a work of art, men are involved in experiences that possess cumulative powers and are marked by a consummation or finality. Accordingly, Dewey's aesthetic theory provides a basis for criticism of any theory of art that would introduce a single explanatory schema for the appreciation or production of a work of art. For Dewey, "Marxist" theory that considers art works as projections of class consciousness, "Freudian" theory that considers art works as sublimations of libidinal energies, and any theory that would explain art as the product of a transcendent spirit equally illustrate a tendency to reduce the aesthetic experience to one of its causal factors or partial components. Dewey seeks to establish a basis for an aesthetic theory that can provide an account of the place of art in human affairs as continuous with the various ways in which human beings naturally seek consummatory experiences. An investigation of the consummating experiences of art can exhibit specifically how different kinds of material are given significant form.

I do not propose to propound here Dewey's philosophy of religion or of art. But I cite both works as evidence of the comprehensiveness with which he sought to work out his interpretation of naturalism. It is this comprehensiveness that motivates the belief that Dewey was one of the last philosophers of the "classic" tradition or in the "grand" manner. Dewey understood this tradition when he defined philosophy for the *Encyclopedia of the Social Sciences* as a "survey of existence from the standpoint of value."

A Retrospective Appraisal

The broad range of Dewey's philosophy reflected a confidence about the possibilities open to philosophical inquiry in our historical period. This confidence was twofold. First, it asserted both explicitly and implicitly the task of the contemporary philosopher to respond to the great chain of philosophical debate from Plato to the present. Since the contemporary philosopher was armed with the instrument of scientific methodology, he could critically confront and intellectually reconstruct crucial aspects of that tradition. Second, since Dewey criticized the interpretation of philosophy as a dialogue between the generations, he affirmed the ability of the philosopher to deal with the social and political problems of contemporary culture. Since the philosopher was particularly equipped to analyze the relevant normative and methodological considerations, he was uniquely capable of providing guidance on fundamental aspects of those problems. Both aspects of this confidence have been virtually abandoned in most contemporary philosophy. Consequently, there has been a major discontinuity in philosophical discussion since Dewey wrote. It is this discontinuity of discussion that complicates any retrospective assessment of Dewey's philosophical achievement and even makes difficult a critical verdict on the intellectual adequacy of many of his philosophical works.

The realization that the empirical sciences, and not philosophy, offered the best method for arriving at truth on any particular question led to Dewey's insistence that philosophy should adopt scientific method in order to analyze the philosophical problems of the Western intellectual tradition and of modern society. For many other philosophers, however, the belief that the empirical sciences offered the best method of inquiry implied that these sciences, and not philosophy, were competent to respond to any factual or "first order" questions that came within their purview. Philosophy restricted its competency to conceptual or methodological questions. Questions about the ways in which habits integrated impulses, for example, referred to in the Deweyan social psychology and social philosophy, were presumably within the domain of an increasingly specialized empirical psychology. Analysis of the criteria for confirming competing hypotheses in psychology, a so-called "second order" question, could be a continuing part of philosophical investigation. Thus most philosophers distinguished themselves from empirical scientists by a limitation of their inquiry to the formal subject matter, rather than to the substantively empirical or experimental research. This included the analysis of the concepts and the methods of inquiry, which in practice meant an analysis of the linguistic framework of the empirical science.

Further, the analysis of these conceptual and methodological questions was significantly changed by technical advances in logic and in the understanding of language. The nature of logic as a symbolic or mathematical language was explored, with revolutionary implications for the clarification of traditional issues in logical theory. For many philosophers, philosophy became a highly rigorous analysis of the formal, logical language in which the concepts of science were expressed. For others, philosophy was the analysis of the linguistic contexts in ordinary language in which philosophical concepts like "truth," "mind," or "cause" were used.

In summary, for those who shared Dewey's vision of the competence of scientific method to resolve the empirical issues relating to experience and the problems of men, the framework of philosophical discussion shifted. The philosophical debate about the nature of the world and the place of mind in nature became transformed into a series of rigorous technical analyses of linguistic concepts. Of course, philosophers could still involve themselves in political and social problems, but in these areas they discussed the issues or justified their positions like any other interested citizens, with no unique disciplinary competence.

The tradition of philosophical discussion about the pervasive character of experienced things, or about the values to be discovered and invented in human transactions, continued primarily among phenomenological and existentialist philosophers. But they had refused to accept Dewey's belief that scientific methods were to be the instrument for human inquiry into empirical problems.

The evolution of this philosophical state of affairs deprived the once active and powerful Deweyan school of philosophers of philosophical continuity in their investigations. It is for this reason that it is difficult to render an adequate critical judgment of Dewey's philosophical achievement, since his works are no longer the locus of an active critical discussion that would support some aspects of his philosophy and develop criticism or refutation of other parts. His philosophical theses have not been refuted; yet they have been abandoned by a shift in philosophical interest and a transposition of philosophical method.

Individual themes or theses from Dewey's work often emerge in the new context of linguistic philosophy, or even existentialist philosophy—but formulated in an idiom that is remote from their function in the Deweyan framework. Examples illustrating the changes in philosophical context abound. Thus an important feature of Dewey's metaphysics was, as noted, the criticism of those empiricists who interpreted things as classes of sensations. One of the more interesting works in contemporary linguistic analysis is John Austin's demonstration of the misuse of language involved in empiricist accounts of things in terms of the language of sense data. Dewey believed that his analysis led to a reconstruction of metaphysics; an Austinian would suggest that a clarification of the way in which we use words about sensory experiences serves as a purgative for metaphysical inquiry. There remain interesting similarities between the views of Austin and Dewey on traditional empiricist sensationalism.

Again, no view is more central to Dewey's theory of knowledge than the idea of knowing as an interaction between organism and environment. This involved Dewey in a polemic against the Cartesian concept of mind as a disembodied rational substance that can know entities by intellectual inference. Gilbert Ryle's *Concept of Mind*—a major analysis of the concepts of mental conduct—involved a similar polemic against the misuse of language in Descartes's interpretation of human rationality. While Dewey saw his work as laying the foundation for a theory of inquiry and for an interpretation of the place of mind in nature that would ultimately further human reconstruction of social institutions, Ryle suggested that he is showing how philosophers distorted the conceptual contours embedded in ordinary discourse about thinking, imagining, remembering, and so on. Again, there remain interesting parallels between the works of Ryle and Dewey on the nature of mind.

Only in ethical theory has there been significant continuity between Dewey's formulation of ethical naturalism and the current discussion of the relevant issues, both pro and con. And even here the prominent advocates of positions analogous to those maintained by Dewey speak for the most part within the framework of a discussion that has transposed the context in which Dewey perceived the issues. Dewey argued for ethical naturalism in order to show how scientific method could be applied to the resolution of normative moral dispute. The current context of the ethical discussion is the demonstration that "good" or other terms of our moral vocabulary do not function only to command imperatives, to express emotive attitudes, or to intuit non-natural moral properties; rather, their prescriptive or commending function is related to their function in asserting descriptive or factual beliefs. Once more, there are significant areas of overlap and interesting analogies between Dewey's ethical naturalism and the ethical naturalism of the analysts of moral language.

The conclusion is that for most areas of philosophical discussion, Dewey's point of view surfaces only within a framework of inquiry that he himself would not have accepted. The reason for Dewey's rejection of that framework was his belief that a philosophy that conceived its task as the clarification of the concepts of either scientific or ordinary language was not carrying out its primary function. In its remoteness from the "problems of men," in Dewey's sense of the phrase, linguistic philosophy also fails to confront the central moral problems of the culture. Yet for Dewey, involvement in the central moral problems of the society is the unique prerequisite for philosophical inquiry.

In addition to the change in philosophical style that accompanied the emergence of linguistic philosophy, another cultural development has had a major impact on Deweyan philosophy: the progress of the social sciences. Dewey played the role of a moral prophet on behalf of social-scientific inquiry, contending that only with the application of scientific method to the social and political problems of the times could there be any possibility of social progress. Twenty-five years after Dewey's death it would seem that his confidence in the capacity of social science to achieve social reconstruction was excessive.

But while the social reality of the recent past seems dissonant with Dewey's prophecy about the progress attendant upon the development of the social sciences, it is not clear in which specific way his projection was disproved by events.

One interpretation of the rise of totalitarianism in advanced industrial societies would suggest that the practice of science is compatible with an increase in barbarism in human relations. Moral sensitivity, moral courage, and even a passion for truth in personal and political affairs do not seem to be significantly correlated with the development of the social sciences. It would follow that the Deweyan view is not only erroneous but harmful in the direction it suggests for social policy.

Another interpretation, however, could find some measure of confirmation of Dewey's view that there is a gap between our society's enormously increased technological capacities and our social knowledge and skills in the use and control of these capacities. To a degree, development of social-scientific knowledge can lessen the gap.

Yet on either view, there is no longer the optimistic assessment that motivated much of Dewey's writing in the period from the turn of the century through the 1930's. The historical context in which Dewey's philosophy could gain adherence by presenting a vision of progress through the application of scientific method to social issues has passed. That vision may continue to motivate men; but it does so a generation later by involving them in the established social-scientific disciplines, not in the philosophical elaboration of the promise of those disciplines. Dewey's projection is caught in a destructive dilemma. If the promise of the social sciences for progress is illusory, then he was in error. Yet if that promise is being partially fulfilled, then there is little point to the prophetic advocacy of a method that is being tested routinely in practice. At a time when specific evaluations of the success or failure of the social sciences— the performance of the economists on inflation or of the sociologists on school integration—are so mixed and controversial, Dewey's confident elaboration of the long-term implications of a social-scientific approach that would replace social generalities with empirical hypotheses has become remote.

The appraisal of Dewey's thought takes place, accordingly, in an intellectual environment in which there have been modifications of philosophical technique and purpose and a significant shift in cultural attitudes about science. In light of those changes, it is possible to interpret the philosophy of John Dewey as a great, isolated American monument—a monument to that period in American culture which made possible a confident, optimistic vision of the potential application of the methods of the sciences to the dominant traditions of philosophy and the major institutions of society. In developing that vision with boldness and comprehensiveness, Dewey presented an interpretation of the human condition in full experiential context at one stage of history. It is still an instructive vision.

There is evidence that Dewey would reject any assessment of his work as a didactic relic or monument of the American philosophical past. He lived long enough to have observed the change in philosophical interest away from his own work; yet he believed that the need for normative evaluation of social policies and intellectual methodologies exists in every society. That need would bring with it a discussion of the themes of Dewey's thought. And his thought would then survive, not as a monument to be respected or cherished but as a hypothesis that demands correction by better ones in the continuous, open frontier of inquiry.

I

The Function of Philosophy

A fundamental feature of John Dewey's thought was his conception of the nature and function of philosophy. Dewey viewed philosophy as a phenomenon of human culture. Every philosophy is intrinsically connected with the history, the institutions, and the other intellectual achievements of the society in which it has developed. Philosophy, for Dewey, is an effort to bring to critical self-consciousness the values and interests—in his phrase, the "meaning"—of the culture.

This view of philosophy had been advanced earlier by Hegel. It was probably part of that permanent residue left by his youthful Hegelianism, which Dewey acknowledged when he prepared his intellectual autobiography for the volume *The Philosophy of John Dewey*.* Dewey seems to be following Hegel in asserting that "there is no specifiable difference between philosophy and its role in the history of civilization." Accordingly, it is important to note the distinctive ways in which Dewey understood the function of philosophy in its effort to make coherent the meaning of the civilization of which it is a part.

In the essay "Philosophy and Civilization," in which he explicitly formulated his account of the relationship between a philosophy and its culture, Dewey asserted that philosophy had been "chiefly conservative" in the relationship, "justificatory of selected elements

---

* This volume was the first in the series entitled "The Library of Living Philosophy," in which the philosopher being examined opened the volume with an autobiography and closed with a reply to his critics. In Dewey's case, the biography was written by his daughters "from material which he furnished."

of tradition and received institutions." In contrast, what marks Dewey's own philosophy is the stress on the liberal or radical potential of any effort at cultural coherence: "Thus philosophy marks a change of culture. In forming patterns to be conformed to in future thought and action, it is additive and transforming in its role in the history of civilization."

A second distinctive way in which Dewey develops the Hegelian view that philosophy is the critical self-consciousness of a culture is his stress on pluralism. Most versions of a Hegelian concept of philosophy or culture assume that there is a single cultural self-consciousness for every historical epoch. Dewey, on the other hand, recognizes the diversity of philosophical positions and attitudes in any society.

Further, Dewey asserts the unique relevance of scientific method for philosophy. To the degree to which the "meaning" of an event or occasion in the culture necessarily implies or presupposes some facts about the nature of things, it is open to investigation by the methods of science. Many interpreters of Dewey would see in this acceptance of the epistemic priority of the methods of science the source of his ultimate rejection of a Hegelian approach. Although Dewey retained the conception of philosophy as cultural coherence, he did not view science as only one facet of culture to be synthesized with others, but as providing the criterion for the truth of any theses asserted in the society.

One of the interesting consequences of this view would be that American civilization should develop its unique philosophy expressive of its distinctive cultural values and interests. In point of fact, many students of American philosophy—particularly outside observers such as Santayana, Whitehead, and Russell—had suggested that American pragmatism was indeed an articulation of America's self-consciousness. Dewey's own conclusion in "Philosophy and Civilization" is that American society has not yet developed an "imaginative formulation of itself," and so a distinctive American philosophy has yet to be created.

American society has not yet produced an American philosophy, Dewey goes on, because it has not yet forced a successful confrontation between its inherited cultural traditions and the dynamism of its own intellectual energy, particularly in the sciences. Philosophy perennially has tried to "effect a junction . . . of the new and the old, of deep-sunk customs and unconscious dispositions, that are brought to the light of attention by some conflict with newly emerging directions of activity." In our time, Dewey believed that the most significant such conflict and emergent direction was provided by the impact of Darwinism. Accordingly, the essay "The Influence of Darwinism on Philosophy" is paradigmatic for Dewey's conception of philosophy as an effort to formulate a coherent self-consciousness out of the tensions between various dominant, valued intellectual traditions arising when they are challenged by the results of intellectual or scientific inquiry.

In that essay, Dewey argued that the crucial implication of Darwin's scientific achievement for philosophy would be the transformation of philosophical method. Philosophy before Darwin could aim at an explanation or justification of kinds of natural events by reference to their essences or ends. Philosophy since Darwin must become an investigation into specified conditions of value and into specific consequences of ideas. Accordingly, philosophy abandons the conception of itself as an activity that can "rationalize the universe at large," and becomes instead a "method of moral and political diagnosis and prognosis." Dewey wrote the essay in 1909, in commemoration of the fiftieth anniversary of Darwin's *Origin of Species.* The conception of philosophy outlined there was one he would maintain in most of his philosophical work for nearly the next half century.

1

Philosophy and Civilization

Volumes have been written about each term of our theme. What *is* civilization? philosophy? Yet time passes, and ambiguities and complexities cannot be eliminated by definition; we can only circumvent them by begging questions. But as to one of the terms at least, namely, philosophy, we shall frankly make what is begged explicit. A statement of the relations of philosophy to civilization will, after all, only expound, in some indirect manner, the view of philosophy to which one is already committed. Unless this fact is faced, we shall not only beg the issue, but we shall deceive ourselves into thinking that we are setting forth the conclusions of an original inquiry, undertaken and executed independently of our own philosophical conceptions.

As for myself, then, the discussion is approached with the antecedent idea that philosophy, like politics, literature and the plastic arts, is itself a phenomenon of human culture. Its connection with social history, with civilization, is intrinsic. There is current among those who philosophize the conviction that, while past thinkers have reflected in their systems the conditions and perplexities of their own day, present-day philosophy in general, and one's own philosophy in particular, is emancipated from the influence of that complex of institutions which forms culture. Bacon, Descartes, Kant each thought with fervor that he was founding philosophy anew because he was placing it securely upon an exclusive intellec-

Source: Reprinted by permission of G. P. Putnam's Sons and the Center for Dewey Studies from *Philosophy and Civilization* by John Dewey. Copyright 1931 by John Dewey; renewed 1958 by Roberta L. Dewey.

tual basis, exclusive, that is, of everything but intellect. The movement of time has revealed the illusion; it exhibits as the work of
philosophy the old and ever new undertaking of adjusting that
body of traditions which constitute the actual mind of man to
scientific tendencies and political aspirations which are novel and
incompatible with received authorities. Philosophers are parts of
history, caught in its movement; creators perhaps in some measure
of its future, but also assuredly creatures of its past.

Those who assert in the abstract definition of philosophy that it
deals with eternal truth or reality, untouched by local time and
place, are forced to admit that philosophy as a concrete existence is
historical, having temporal passage and a diversity of local habita-
tions. Open your histories of philosophy, and you find written
throughout them the same periods of time and the same geograph-
ical distributions which provide the intellectual scheme of histories
of politics, industry or the fine arts. I cannot imagine a history of
philosophy which did not partition its material between the oc-
cident and the orient; which did not find the former falling into
ancient, medieval and modern epochs; which, in setting forth Greek
thought, did not specify Asiatic and Italian colonies and Athens.
On the other hand, those who express contempt for the enterprise
of philosophy as a sterile and monotonous preoccupation with un-
solvable or unreal problems, cannot, without convicting themselves
of Philistinism, deny that, however it may stand with philosophy
as a revelation of eternal truths, it is tremendously significant
as a revelation of the predicaments, protests and aspirations of
humanity.

The two views of the history of thought are usually proffered as
irreconcilable opposites. According to one, it is the record of the
most profound dealings of the reason with ultimate being; according to the other, it is a scene of pretentious claims and ridiculous
failures. Nevertheless, there is a point of view from which there is
something common to the two notions, and this common denomina-
tor is more significant than the oppositions. Meaning is wider in
scope as well as more precious in value than is truth, and philosophy
is occupied with meaning rather than with truth. Making such a
statement is dangerous; it is easily misconceived to signify that
truth is of no great importance under any circumstances; while the
fact is that truth is so infinitely important when it is important at
all, namely, in records of events and descriptions of existences, that
we extend its claims to regions where it has no jurisdiction. But
even as respects truths, meaning is the wider category; truths are but
one class of meanings, namely, those in which a claim to verifia-

bility by their consequences is an intrinsic part of their meaning. Beyond this island of meanings which in their own nature are true or false lies the ocean of meanings to which truth and falsity are irrelevant. We do not inquire whether Greek civilization was true or false, but we are immensely concerned to penetrate its meaning. We may indeed ask for the truth of Shakespeare's *Hamlet* or Shelley's *Skylark,* but by truth we now signify something quite different from that of scientific statement and historical record.

In philosophy we are dealing with something comparable to the meaning of Athenian civilization or of a drama or a lyric. Significant history is lived in the imagination of man, and philosophy is a further excursion of the imagination into its own prior achievements. All that is distinctive of man, marking him off from the clay he walks upon or the potatoes he eats, occurs in his thought and emotions, in what we have agreed to call consciousness. Knowledge of the structure of sticks and stones, an enterprise in which, of course, truth is essential, apart from whatever added control it may yield, marks in the end but an enrichment of consciousness, of the area of meanings. Thus scientific thought itself is finally but a function of the imagination in enriching life with the significance of things; it is of its peculiar essence that it must also submit to certain tests of application and control. Were significance identical with existence, were values the same as events, idealism would be the only possible philosophy.

It is commonplace that physically and existentially man can but make a superficial and transient scratch upon the outermost rind of the world. It has become a cheap intellectual pastime to contrast the infinitesimal pettiness of man with the vastnesses of the stellar universes. Yet all such comparisons are illicit. We cannot compare existence and meaning; they are disparate. The characteristic life of man is itself the meaning of vast stretches of existences, and without it the latter have no value or significance. There is no common measure of physical existence and conscious experience because the latter is the only measure there is for the former. The significance of being, though not its existence, is the emotion it stirs, the thought it sustains.

It follows that there is no specifiable difference between philosophy and its role in the history of civilization. Discover and define the right characteristic and unique function in civilization, and you have defined philosophy itself. To try to define philosophy in any other way is to search for a will-of-the-wisp; the conceptions which result are of purely private interpretation, for they only exemplify the particular philosophies of their authorship and interpretation.

Take the history of philosophy from whatever angle and in whatever cross-section you please, Indian, Chinese, Athenian, the Europe of the twelfth or the twentieth century, and you find a load of traditions proceeding from an immemorial past. You find certain preoccupying interests that appear hypnotic in their rigid hold upon imagination and you also find certain resistances, certain dawning rebellions, struggles to escape and to express some fresh value of life. The preoccupations may be political and artistic as in Athens; they may be economic and scientific as today. But in any case, there is a certain intellectual work to be done; the dominant interest working throughout the minds of masses of men has to be clarified, a result which can be accomplished only by selection, elimination, reduction and formulation; the interest has to be intellectually forced, exaggerated in order to be focused. Otherwise it is not intellectually in consciousness, since all clear consciousness by its very nature marks a wrenching of something from its subordinate place to confer upon it a centrality which is existentially absurd. Where there is sufficient depth and range of meanings for consciousness to arise at all, there is a function of adjustment, of reconciliation of the ruling interest of the period with preoccupations which had a different origin and an irrelevant meaning. Consider, for example, the uneasy, restless effort of Plato to adapt his new mathematical insights and his political aspirations to the traditional habits of Athens; the almost humorously complacent union of Christian supernaturalism in the middle ages with the naturalism of pagan Greece; the still fermenting effort of the recent age to unite the new science of nature with inherited classic and medieval institutions. The life of all thought is to effect a junction at some point of the new and the old, of deep-sunk customs and unconscious dispositions that are brought to the light of attention by some conflict with newly emerging directions of activity. Philosophies which emerge at distinctive periods define the larger patterns of continuity which are woven in effecting the enduring junctions of a stubborn past and an insistent future.

Philosophy thus sustains the closest connection with the history of culture, with the succession of changes in civilization. It is fed by the streams of tradition, traced at critical moments to their sources in order that the current may receive a new direction; it is fertilized by the ferment of new inventions in industry, new explorations of the globe, new discoveries in science. But philosophy is not just a passive reflex of civilization that persists through changes, and that changes while persisting. It is itself a change; the patterns formed in this junction of the new and the old are prophecies rather than records; they are policies, attempts to fore-stall subsequent developments. The intellectual registrations which constitute a philosophy are generative just because they are selec-tive and eliminative exaggerations. While purporting to say that such and such is and always *has* been the purport of the record of nature, in effect they proclaim that such and such *should* be the significant value to which mankind should loyally attach itself. Without evidence adduced in its behalf such a statement may seem groundless. But I invite you to examine for yourselves any philo-sophical idea which has had for any long period a significant career, and find therein your own evidence. Take, for example, the Platonic patterns of cosmic design and harmony; the Aristotelian perpetually recurrent ends and grooved potentialities; the Kantian fixed forms of intellectual synthesis; the conception of nature itself as it figured in seventeenth and eighteenth century thought. Discuss them as revelations of eternal truth, and something almost childlike or something beyond possibility of decision enters in; discuss them as selections from existing culture by means of which to articulate forces which the author believed should and would dominate the future, and they become preciously significant aspects of human history.

Thus philosophy marks a change of culture. In forming patterns to be conformed to in future thought and action, it is additive and transforming in its role in the history of civilization. Man states anything at his peril; once stated, it occupies a place in a new per-spective; it attains a permanence which does not belong to its existence; it enters provokingly into wont and use; it points in a troubling way to need of new endeavors. I do not mean that the creative element in the role of philosophy is necessarily the dom-inant one; obviously its formulations have been often chiefly con-servative, justificatory of selected elements of traditions and received institutions. But even these preservative systems have had a trans-forming if not exactly a creative effect; they have lent the factors which were selected a power over later human imagination and sentiment which they would otherwise have lacked. And there are other periods, such as those of the seventeenth and eighteenth centuries in Europe, when philosophy is overtly revolutionary in attitude. To their authors, the turn was just from complete error to complete truth; to later generations looking back, the alteration in strictly factual content does not compare with that in desire and direction of effort.

Of the many objections which may be brought against the con-ception that philosophy not only *has* a role, but that it *is* a specifiable role in the development of human culture, there are two misconceptions which I wish to touch upon. What has been said, taken without qualifying additions, might suggest a picture of a dominant system of philosophy at each historic period. In fact there are diverse currents and aspirations in almost every historic epoch; the divergence of philosophic systems instead of being a reproach (as of course it is from the standpoint of philosophy as a revelation of truth) is evidence of sincerity and vitality. If the ruling and the oppressed elements in a population, if those who wish to maintain the *status quo* and those concerned to make changes, had, when they became articulate, the same philosophy, one might well be skeptical of its intellectual integrity. The other point is much more important. In making a distinction between meaning and truth and asserting that the latter is but one type of meaning, important under definite conditions, I have expressed the idea as if there might be in the processes of human life meanings which are wholly cut off from the actual course of events. Such is not the intent; meanings are generated and in some degree sustained by existence. Hence they cannot be wholly irrelevant to the world of existence; they all have some revelatory office which should be apprehended as correctly as possible. This is true of politics, religion and art as well as of philosophy. They all tell something of the realm of existence. But in all of them there is an exuberance and fertility of meanings and values in comparison with which correctness of telling is a secondary affair, while in the function termed science accuracy of telling is the chief matter.

In the historic role of philosophy, the scientific factor, the element of correctness, of verifiable applicability, has a place but it is a negative one. The meanings delivered by confirmed observation, experimentation and calculation, scientific facts and principles, serve as tests of the values which tradition transmits and of those which emotion suggests. Whatever is not compatible with them must be eliminated in any sincere philosophizing. This fact confers upon scientific knowledge an incalculably important office in philosophy. But the criterion is negative; the exclusion of the inconsistent is far from being identical with a positive test which demands that only what has been scientifically verifiable shall provide the entire content of philosophy. It is the difference between an imagination that acknowledges its responsibility to meet the logical demands of ascertained facts, and a complete abdication of all imagination in behalf of a prosy literalism.

Finally, it results from what has been said that the presence and absence of native born philosophies is a severe test of the depth of unconscious tradition and rooted institutions among any people, and of the productive force of their culture. For sake of brevity, I may be allowed to take our own case, the case of civilization in the United States. Philosophy, we have been saying, is a conversion of such culture as exists into consciousness, into an imagination which is logically coherent and is not incompatible with what is factually known. But this conversion is itself a further movement of civilization; it is not something performed upon the body of habits and tendencies from without, that is, miraculously. If American civilization does not eventuate in an imaginative formulation of itself, if it merely rearranges the figures already named and placed—in playing an inherited European game—that fact is itself the measure of the culture which we have achieved. A deliberate striving for an American Philosophy as such would be only another evidence of the same emptiness and impotency. There is energy and activity, among us, enough and to spare. Not an inconsiderable part of the vigor that once went into industrial accomplishment now finds its way into science; our scientific "plant" is coming in its way to rival our industrial plants. Especially in psychology and the social sciences an amount of effort is putting forth which is hardly equaled in any one other part of the world. He would be a shameless braggart who claimed that the result is as yet adequate to the activity. What is the matter? It lies, I think, with our lack of imagination in generating leading ideas. Because we are afraid of speculative ideas, we do, and do over and over again, an immense amount of dead, specialized work in the region of "facts." We forget that such facts are only data; that is, are only fragmentary, uncompleted meanings, and unless they are rounded out into complete ideas—a work which can only be done by hypotheses, by a free imagination of intellectual possibilities—they are as helpless as are all maimed things and as repellent as are needlessly thwarted ones.

Please do not imagine that this is a plea in disguise for any particular type of philosophizing. On the contrary, any philosophy which is a sincere outgrowth and expression of our own civilization is better than none, provided it speaks the authentic idiom of an enduring and dominating corporate experience. If we are really, for instance, a materialistic people, we are at least materialistic in a new fashion and on a new scale. I should welcome then a consistent materialistic philosophy, if only it were sufficiently bold. For in the degree in which, despite attendant esthetic repulsiveness, it marked the coming to consciousness of a group of ideas, it would formulate a coming to self-consciousness of our civilization. Thereby it would furnish ideas, supply an intellectual polity, direct further observations and experiments, and organize their results on a grand scale. As long as we worship science and are afraid of philosophy we shall have no great science; we shall have a lagging and halting continuation of what is thought and said elsewhere. As far as any plea is implicit in what has been said, it is, then, a plea for the casting off of that intellectual timidity which hampers the wings of imagination, a plea for speculative audacity, for more faith in ideas, sloughing off a cowardly reliance upon those partial ideas to which we are wont to give the name of facts. I have given to philosophy a more humble function than that which is often assigned it. But modesty as to its final place is not incompatible with boldness in the maintenance of that function, humble as it may be. A combination of such modesty and courage affords the only way I know of in which the philosopher can look his fellowman in the face with frankness and with humanity.

2

The Influence of Darwinism on Philosophy

I

That the publication of the *Origin of Species* marked an epoch in the development of the natural sciences is well known to the layman. That the combination of the very words origin and species embodied an intellectual revolt and introduced a new intellectual temper is easily overlooked by the expert. The conceptions that had reigned in the philosophy of nature and knowledge for two thousand years, the conceptions that had become the familiar furniture of the mind, rested on the assumption of the superiority of the fixed and final; they rested upon treating change and origin as signs of defect and unreality. In laying hands upon the sacred ark of absolute permanency, in treating the forms that had been regarded as types of fixity and perfection as originating and passing away, the *Origin of Species* introduced a mode of thinking that in the end was bound to transform the logic of knowledge, and hence the treatment of morals, politics, and religion.

No wonder, then, that the publication of Darwin's book, a half century ago, precipitated a crisis. The true nature of the controversy is easily concealed from us, however, by the theological clamor that attended it. The vivid and popular features of the anti-

SOURCE: A lecture in a course of public lectures on "Charles Darwin and His Influence on Science," given at Columbia University in the winter and spring of 1909. Reprinted from the *Popular Science Monthly* for July, 1909. [Footnotes have been omitted.]

Darwinian row tended to leave the impression that the issue was between science on one side and theology on the other. Such was not the case—the issue lay primarily within science itself, as Darwin himself early recognized. The theological outcry he discounted from the start, hardly noticing it save as it bore upon the "feelings of his female relatives." But for two decades before final publication he contemplated the possibility of being put down by his scientific peers as a fool or as crazy; and he set, as the measure of his success, the degree in which he should affect three men of science: Lyell in geology, Hooker in botany, and Huxley in zoology.

Religious considerations lent fervor to the controversy, but they did not provoke it. Intellectually, religious emotions are not creative but conservative. They attach themselves readily to the current view of the world and consecrate it. They steep and dye intellectual fabrics in the seething vat of emotions; they do not form their warp and woof. There is not, I think, an instance of any large idea about the world being independently generated by religion. Although the ideas that rose up like armed men against Darwinism owed their intensity to religious associations, their origin and meaning are to be sought in science and philosophy, not in religion.

II

Few words in our language foreshorten intellectual history as much as does the word species. The Greeks, in initiating the intellectual life of Europe, were impressed by characteristic traits of the life of plants and animals; so impressed indeed that they made these traits the key to defining nature and to explaining mind and society. And truly, life is so wonderful that a seemingly successful reading of its mystery might well lead men to believe that the key to the secrets of heaven and earth was in their hands. The Greek rendering of this mystery, the Greek formulation of the aim and standard of knowledge, was in the course of time embodied in the word species, and it controlled philosophy for two thousand years. To understand the intellectual face-about expressed in the phrase "Origin of Species," we must, then, understand the long dominant idea against which it is a protest.

Consider how men were impressed by the facts of life. Their eyes fell upon certain things slight in bulk, and frail in structure. To every appearance, these perceived things were inert and passive. Suddenly, under certain circumstances, these things—henceforth known as seeds or eggs or germs—begin to change, to change rapidly in size, form, and qualities. Rapid and extensive changes occur, however, in many things—as when wood is touched by fire. But the changes in the living thing are orderly; they are cumulative; they tend constantly in one direction; they do not, like other changes, destroy or consume, or pass fruitless into wandering flux; they realize and fulfill. Each successive stage, no matter how unlike its predecessor, preserves its net effect and also prepares the way for a fuller activity on the part of its successor. In living beings, changes do not happen as they seem to happen elsewhere, any which way; the earlier changes are regulated in view of later results. This progressive organization does not cease till there is achieved a true final term, a τελὸς, a completed, perfected end. This final form exercises in turn a plenitude of functions, not the least noteworthy of which is production of germs like those from which it took its own origin, germs capable of the same cycle of self-fulfilling activity.

But the whole miraculous tale is not yet told. The same drama is enacted to the same destiny in countless myriads of individuals so sundered in time, so severed in space, that they have no opportunity for mutual consultation and no means of interaction. As an old writer quaintly said, "things of the same kind go through the same formalities"—celebrate, as it were, the same ceremonial rites.

This formal activity which operates throughout a series of changes and holds them to a single course; which subordinates their aimless flux to its own perfect manifestation; which, leaping the boundaries of space and time, keeps individuals distant in space and remote in time to a uniform type of structure and function: this principle seemed to give insight into the very nature of reality itself. To it Aristotle gave the name, εἶδος. This term the scholastics translated as *species*.

The force of this term was deepened by its application to everything in the universe that observes order in flux and manifests constancy through change. From the casual drift of daily weather, through the uneven recurrence of seasons and unequal return of seed time and harvest, up to the majestic sweep of the heavens— the image of eternity in time—and from this to the unchanging pure and contemplative intelligence beyond nature lies one unbroken fulfilment of ends. Nature as a whole is a progressive realization of purpose strictly comparable to the realization of purpose in any single plant or animal.

The conception of εἶδος, species, a fixed form and final cause, was the central principle of knowledge as well as of nature. Upon it rested the logic of science. Change as change is mere flux and lapse; it insults intelligence. Genuinely to know is to grasp a permanent

end that realizes itself through changes, holding them thereby
within the metes and bounds of fixed truth. Completely to know
is to relate all special forms to their one single end and good: pure
contemplative intelligence. Since, however, the scene of nature
which directly confronts us is in change, nature as directly and
practically experienced does not satisfy the conditions of knowledge.
Human experience is in flux, and hence the instrumentalities of
sense-perception and of inference based upon observation are
condemned in advance. Science is compelled to aim at realities lying
behind and beyond the processes of nature, and to carry on its
search for these realities by means of rational forms transcending
ordinary modes of perception and inference.

There are, indeed, but two alternative courses. We must either
find the appropriate objects and organs of knowledge in the mutual
interactions of changing things; or else, to escape the infection of
change, we *must* seek them in some transcendent and supernal
region. The human mind, deliberately as it were, exhausted the
logic of the changeless, the final, and the transcendent, before it
essayed adventure on the pathless wastes of generation and transformation. We dispose all too easily of the efforts of the schoolmen
to interpret nature and mind in terms of real essences, hidden
forms, and occult faculties, forgetful of the seriousness and dignity
of the ideas that lay behind. We dispose of them by laughing at the
famous gentleman who accounted for the fact that opium put people
to sleep on the ground it had a dormitive faculty. But the doctrine,
held in our own day, that knowledge of the plant that yields the
poppy consists in referring the peculiarities of an individual to a
type, to a universal form, a doctrine so firmly established that any
other method of knowing was conceived to be unphilosophical and
unscientific, is a survival of precisely the same logic. This identity
of conception in the scholastic and anti-Darwinian theory may well
suggest greater sympathy for what has become unfamiliar as well as
greater humility regarding the further unfamiliarities that history
has in store.

Darwin was not, of course, the first to question the classic philosophy of nature and of knowledge. The beginnings of the revolution
are in the physical science of the sixteenth and seventeenth centuries. When Galileo said: "It is my opinion that the earth is very
noble and admirable by reason of so many and so different altera-
tions and generations which are incessantly made therein," he
expressed the changed temper that was coming over the world; the
transfer of interest from the permanent to the changing. When
Descartes said: "The nature of physical things is much more easily

conceived when they are beheld coming gradually into existence, than when they are only considered as produced at once in a finished and perfect state," the modern world became self-conscious of the logic that was henceforth to control it, the logic of which Darwin's *Origin of Species* is the latest scientific achievement. Without the methods of Copernicus, Kepler, Galileo, and their successors in astronomy, physics, and chemistry, Darwin would have been helpless in the organic sciences. But prior to Darwin the impact of the new scientific method upon life, mind, and politics, had been arrested, because between these ideal or moral interests and the inorganic world intervened the kingdom of plants and animals. The gates of the garden of life were barred to the new ideas; and only through this garden was there access to mind and politics. The influence of Darwin upon philosophy resides in his having conquered the phenomena of life for the principle of transition, and thereby freed the new logic for application to mind and morals and life. When he said of species what Galileo had said of the earth, *e pur se muove*, he emancipated, once for all, genetic and experimental ideas as an organon of asking questions and looking for explanations.

III

The exact bearings upon philosophy of the new logical outlook are, of course, as yet, uncertain and inchoate. We live in the twilight of intellectual transition. One must add the rashness of the prophet to the stubbornness of the partizan to venture a systematic exposition of the influence upon philosophy of the Darwinian method. At best, we can but inquire as to its general bearing—the effect upon mental temper and complexion, upon that body of half-conscious, half-instinctive intellectual aversions and preferences which determine, after all, our more deliberate intellectual enterprises. In this vague inquiry there happens to exist as a kind of touchstone a problem of long historic currency that has also been much discussed in Darwinian literature. I refer to the old problem of design *versus* chance, mind *versus* matter, as the causal explanation, first or final, of things.

As we have already seen, the classic notion of species carried with it the idea of purpose. In all living forms, a specific type is present directing the earlier stages of growth to the realization of its own perfection. Since this purposive regulative principle is not visible to the senses, it follows that it must be an ideal or rational force. Since, however, the perfect form is gradually approximated through the sensible changes, it also follows that in and through a sensible realm a rational ideal force is working out its own ultimate manifestation. These inferences were extended to nature: (*a*) She does nothing in vain; but all for an ulterior purpose. (*b*) Within natural sensible events there is therefore contained a spiritual causal force, which as spiritual escapes perception, but is apprehended by an enlightened reason. (*c*) The manifestation of this principle brings about a subordination of matter and sense to its own realization, and this ultimate fulfillment is the goal of nature and of man. The design argument thus operated in two directions. Purposefulness accounted for the intelligibility of nature and the possibility of science, while the absolute or cosmic character of this purposefulness gave sanction and worth to the moral and religious endeavors of man. Science was underpinned and morals authorized by one and the same principle, and their mutual agreement was eternally guaranteed.

This philosophy remained, in spite of sceptical and polemic outbursts, the official and the regnant philosophy of Europe for over two thousand years. The expulsion of fixed first and final causes from astronomy, physics, and chemistry had indeed given the doctrine something of a shock. But, on the other hand, increased acquaintance with the details of plant and animal life operated as a counterbalance and perhaps even strengthened the argument from design. The marvelous adaptations of organisms to their environment, of organs to the organism, of unlike parts of a complex organ—like the eye—to the organ itself; the foreshadowing by lower forms of the higher; the preparation in earlier stages of growth for organs that only later had their functioning—these things were increasingly recognized with the progress of botany, zoology, paleontology, and embryology. Together, they added such prestige to the design argument that by the late eighteenth century it was, as approved by the sciences of organic life, the central point of theistic and idealistic philosophy.

The Darwinian principle of natural selection cut straight under this philosophy. If all organic adaptations are due simply to constant variation and the elimination of those variations which are harmful in the struggle for existence that is brought about by excessive reproduction, there is no call for a prior intelligent causal force to plan and preordain them. Hostile critics charged Darwin with materialism and with making chance the cause of the universe. Some naturalists, like Asa Gray, favored the Darwinian principle and attempted to reconcile it with design. Gray held to what may be called design on the installment plan. It we conceive the "stream of variations" to be itself intended, we may suppose that each successive variation was designed from the first to be selected. In that case, variation, struggle, and selection simple define the mechanism of "secondary causes" through which the "first cause" acts; and the doctrine of design is none the worse off because we know more of its *modus operandi*.

Darwin could not accept this mediating proposal. He admits or rather he asserts that it is "impossible to conceive this immense and wonderful universe including man with his capacity of looking far backwards and far into futurity as the result of blind chance or necessity." But nevertheless he holds that since variations are in useless as well as useful directions, and since the latter are sifted out simply by the stress of the conditions of struggle for existence, the design argument as applied to living beings is unjustifiable; and its lack of support there deprives it of scientific value as applied to nature in general. If the variations of the pigeon, which under artificial selection give the pouter pigeon, are not pre-ordained for the sake of the breeder, by what logic do we argue that variations resulting in natural species are pre-designed?

IV

So much for some of the more obvious facts of the discussion of design *versus* chance, as causal principles of nature and of life as a whole. We brought up this discussion, you recall, as a crucial instance. What does our touchstone indicate as to the bearing of Darwinian ideas upon philosophy? In the first place, the new logic outlaws, flanks, dismisses—what you will—one type of problem and substitutes for it another type. Philosophy forswears inquiry after absolute origins and absolute finalities in order to explore specific values and the specific conditions that generate them.

Darwin concluded that the impossibility of assigning the world to chance as a whole and to design in its parts indicated the insolubility of the question. Two radically different reasons, however, may be given as to why a problem is insoluble. One reason is that the problem is too high for intelligence; the other is that the question in its very asking makes assumptions that render the question meaningless. The latter alternative is unerringly pointed to in the celebrated case of design *versus* chance. Once admit that the sole verifiable or fruitful object of knowledge is the particular set of changes that generate the object of study together with the consequences that then flow from it, and no intelligible question can be asked about what, by assumption, lies outside. To assert—as is often asserted—that specific values of particular truth, social bonds and forms of beauty, if they can be shown to be generated by concretely knowable conditions, are meaningless and in vain; to assert that they are justified only when they and their particular causes and effects have all at once been gathered up into some inclusive first cause and some exhaustive final goal, is intellectual atavism. Such argumentation is reversion to the logic that explained the extinction of fire by water through the formal essence of aqueousness and the quenching of thirst by water through the final cause of aqueousness. Whether used in the case of the special event or that of life as a whole, such logic only abstracts some aspects of the existing course of events in order to reduplicate it as a petrified eternal principle by which to explain the very changes of which it is the formalization.

When Henry Sidgwick casually remarked in a letter that as he grew older his interest in what or who made the world was altered into interest in what kind of a world it is anyway, his voicing of a common experience of our own day illustrates also the nature of that intellectual transformation effected by the Darwinian logic. Interest shifts from the wholesale essence back of special changes to the question of how special changes serve and defeat concrete purposes; shifts from an intelligence that shaped things once for all to the particular intelligences which things are even now shaping; shifts from an ultimate goal of good to the direct increments of justice and happiness that intelligent administration of existent conditions may beget and that present carelessness or stupidity will destroy or forego.

In the second place, the classic type of logic inevitably set philosophy upon proving that life *must* have certain qualities and values —no matter how experience presents the matter—because of some remote cause and eventual goal. The duty of wholesale justification inevitably accompanies all thinking that makes the meaning of special occurrences depend upon something that once and for all lies behind them. The habit of derogating from present meanings and uses prevents our looking the facts of experience in the face; it prevents serious acknowledgment of the evils they present and serious concern with the goods they promise but do not as yet fulfill. It turns thought to the business of finding a wholesale transcendent remedy for the one and guarantee for the other. One is reminded of the way many moralists and theologians greeted Herbert Spencer's recognition of an unknowable energy from which welled up the phenomenal physical processes without and the conscious operations within. Merely because Spencer labeled his un-knowable energy "God," this faded piece of metaphysical goods was greeted as an important and grateful concession to the reality of the spiritual realm. Were it not for the deep hold of the habit of seek-ing justification for ideal values in the remote and transcendent, surely this reference of them to an unknowable absolute would be despised in comparison with the demonstrations of experience that knowable energies are daily generating about us precious values.

The displacing of this wholesale type of philosophy will doubt-less not arrive by sheer logical disproof, but rather by growing recognition of its futility. Were it a thousand times true that opium produces sleep because of its dormitive energy, yet the inducing of sleep in the tired, and the recovery to waking life of the poisoned, would not be thereby one least step forwarded. And were it a thousand times dialectically demonstrated that life as a whole is regulated by a transcendent principle to a final inclusive goal, none the less truth and error, health and disease, good and evil, hope and fear in the concrete, would remain just what and where they now are. To improve our education, to ameliorate our manners, to advance our politics, we must have recourse to specific condi-tions of generation.

Finally, the new logic introduces responsibility into the intel-lectual life. To idealize and rationalize the universe at large is after all a confession of inability to master the courses of things that specifically concern us. As long as mankind suffered from this impotency, it naturally shifted a burden of responsibility that it could not carry over to the more competent shoulders of the trans-cendent cause. But if insight into specific conditions of value and into specific consequences of ideas is possible, philosophy must in time become a method of locating and interpreting the more serious of the conflicts that occur in life, and a method of projecting ways for dealing with them: a method of moral and political diagnosis and prognosis.

The claim to formulate *a priori* the legislative constitution of the universe is by its nature a claim that may lead to elaborate dialectic developments. But it is also one that removes these very conclusions from subjection to experimental test, for, by definition, these re-sults make no differences in the detailed course of events. But a philosophy that humbles its pretensions to the work of projecting hypotheses for the education and conduct of mind, individual and social, is thereby subjected to test by the way in which the ideas it propounds work out in practice. In having modesty forced upon it, philosophy also acquires responsibility.

Doubtless I seem to have violated the implied promise of my earlier remarks and to have turned both prophet and partizan. But in anticipating the direction of the transformations in philosophy to be wrought by the Darwinian genetic and experimental logic, I do not profess to speak for any save those who yield themselves consciously or unconsciously to this logic. No one can fairly deny that at present there are two effects of the Darwinian mode of thinking. On the one hand, there are making many sincere and vital efforts to revise our traditional philosophic conceptions in accordance with its demands. On the other hand, there is as definitely a recrudescence of absolutistic philosophies; an assertion of a type of philosophic knowing distinct from that of the sciences, one which opens to us another kind of reality from that to which the sciences give access; an appeal through experience to something that essentially goes beyond experience. This reaction affects popular creeds and religious movements as well as technical philosophies. The very conquest of the biological sciences by the new ideas has led many to proclaim an explicit and rigid separation of philosophy from science.

Old ideas give way slowly; for they are more than abstract logical forms and categories. They are habits, predispositions, deeply engrained attitudes of aversion and preference. Moreover, the conviction persists—though history shows it to be a hallucination—that all the questions that the human mind has asked are questions that can be answered in terms of the alternatives that the questions themselves present. But in fact intellectual progress usually occurs through sheer abandonment of questions together with both of the alternatives they assume—an abandonment that results from their decreasing vitality and a change of urgent interest. We do not solve them: we get over them. Old questions are solved by disappearing, evaporating, while new questions corresponding to the changed attitude of endeavor and preference take their place. Doubtless the greatest dissolvent in contemporary thought of old questions, the greatest precipitant of new methods, new intentions, new problems, is the one effected by the scientific revolution that found its climax in the *Origin of Species*.

II

Logical Theory and Methodology

Logic was one of the major areas of Dewey's philosophical concern throughout his career. His first book in this area was *Studies in Logical Theory,* a volume of essays he edited in 1903 and to which he contributed four articles. It was this book that William James hailed as marking the birth of a "Chicago School" whose views represented an alternative version of pragmatic philosophy. It was followed by *Essays in Experimental Logic* in 1916.

Dewey finally formulated a major statement of his developed views in *Logic: The Theory of Inquiry,* published in 1938. In the preface, he pointed out that his *Logic* was a development of the ideas presented in the earlier works.

For the student of logical theory in the twentieth century, Dewey's interest in logic presents an intriguing, seeming paradox. Despite his continuous interest and publication in this area, he did not anywhere discuss the major accomplishments in logic that occurred during his lifetime. There is no reference in Dewey's logical theory to the great works in both the technique and the theory of logic of such logicians as Frege, Whitehead, Russell, Hilbert, Carnap, Tarski, or Gödel.

The reasons for this puzzling fact are twofold. The first one, in my opinion, is that Dewey remained faithful to a more traditional conception of the relationship between logical theory and philosophy. In that conception, a philosopher's theory of logic was his most general formulation of the norms of thought and inquiry that governed successful intellectual activity, including his own philosophical activity. Thus Aristotle's or Hegel's logic is understood as formulating the rules of thought that had been exhibited in their philosophical work and that presumably could be found in nature or in history. Similarly, Mill's logic aimed at the discovery of the canons of empirical inquiry as a formal codification of the empirical methods Mill and others used in moral, social, or even metaphysical philosophy. Dewey believed that he had participated in the development of an experimental and naturalistic philosophy. Accordingly, his logic would develop the pattern of experimental methods of inquiry in its most general form.

The second reason for Dewey's lack of interest in the actual achievements in the field of logic in the twentieth century is that these were set within a framework of mathematical logic or formal analysis of systems of logic. Dewey's concern was the relationship of methods of inquiry, whether formal or experimental, to their biological, social, or psychological context. For the practitioners of logic, then, Dewey could be described as a social psychologist of the theory of logic. For Dewey, in turn, the logicians were the technicians of a mathematical or linguistic symbolism, who were not sufficiently concerned with the context, conditions, or consequences of their methods and symbolic apparatus.

However Dewey's logical theory is judged in the context of the development of logic in the twentieth century, he formulated an interpretation of logic that is an extraordinary polemic in behalf of an experimentalist methodology. Dewey asserts that the formal aspects of logic represent the canonization and codification of the processes of successful experimental inquiry. The interpretation of logic as the methodology of inquiry can, in turn, help to direct human rationality into an experimental approach to all social institutions and practices. These characteristics of Dewey's logical theory are illustrated in the three selections of this section.

In *Reconstruction in Philosophy* (published in 1920), Dewey presented his philosophical position programmatically, as part of an effort directed toward the reform or reconstruction of prevalent institutions as well as current doctrines. In "The Significance of Logical Reconstruction" he argued that the understanding and adoption of the methods of the experimental sciences in all areas of human inquiry would have an ameliorative effect on human life. Dewey believed that among the obstacles to such an understanding and adoption of scientific methodology were theories of logic derived from an aprioristic philosophic tradition, as, for example, in Hegel's logical theory, or from an atomistic empiricistic philosophy, as in Mill's logical theory. In this selection, Dewey sketches the practical significance he placed upon an experimental interpretation of logical theory.

In a famous section of his *Logic*, Dewey formulated the most general account he would offer of the method of scientific inquiry. In it he traced a method that began with an indeterminate situation and ended with its resolution into a "unified whole." In several ways, Dewey aimed to develop the original pragmatic thesis of Charles Peirce, who traced the process of inquiry from "doubt" to the "fixation of belief." Peirce had sought to identify pragmatism with an interpretation of scientific methodology that arrived at fallible, corrigible hypotheses progressively corrected by the result of experiment. Dewey, in this section, "The Pattern and Structure of Inquiry," develops his account of the procedures and practices any scientific method uses in any branch of empirical inquiry.

Dewey was sensitive to the criticism that his logical theory neglected the formal aspects of logical systems. His response was to try to show how formal canons in logic were bound up with normative practices of methodological inquiry. One striking illustration of this response is his interpretation of the traditional "laws" of logic. In much traditional logical theory, special stress was placed on such principles as the "Law of the Excluded Middle," the "Law of Contradiction," or the "Law of Identity." These laws were often interpreted as representing general or invariant traits of reality. In many contemporary logical systems, they are formulated as axioms of the system. In the section on formal canons, also taken from the *Logic*, Dewey advances the view that these principles can be understood as setting ideal or regulative limits to the processes of inquiry.

3

The Significance of Logical
Reconstruction

Logic—like philosophy itself—suffers from a curious oscillation. It is elevated into the supreme and legislative science only to fall into the trivial estate of keeper of such statements as A is A and the scholastic verses for the syllogistic rules. It claims power to state the laws of the ultimate structure of the universe, on the ground that it deals with the laws of thought which are the laws according to which Reason has formed the world. Then it limits its pretensions to laws of correct reasoning which is correct even though it leads to no matter of fact, or even to material falsity. It is regarded by the modern objective idealist as the adequate substitute for ancient ontological metaphysics; but others treat it as that branch of rhetoric which teaches proficiency in argumentation. For a time a superficial compromise equilibrium was maintained wherein the logic of formal demonstration which the Middle Ages extracted from Aristotle was supplemented by an inductive logic of discovery of truth that Mill extracted from the practice of scientific men. But students of German philosophy, of mathematics, and of psychology, no matter how much they attacked one another, have made common cause in attack upon the orthodox logics both of deductive proof and inductive discovery.

Logical theory presents a scent of chaos. There is little agreement as to its subject-matter, scope or purpose. This disagreement

SOURCE: From *Reconstruction in Philosophy* (1920). Reprinted with the permission of The Center for Dewey Studies, Southern Illinois University at Carbondale.

is not formal or nominal but affects the treatment of every topic. Take such a rudimentary matter as the nature of judgment. Reputable authority can be quoted in behalf of every possible permutation of doctrine. Judgment is the central thing in logic; and judgment is not logical at all, but personal and psychological. If logical, it is the primary function to which both conception and inference are subordinate; and it is an after-product from them. The distinction of subject and predicate is necessary, and it is totally irrelevant; or again, though it is found in some cases, it is not of great importance. Among those who hold that the subject-predicate relationship is essential, some hold that judgment is an analysis of something prior into them, and others assert that it is a synthesis of them into something else. Some hold that reality is always the subject of judgment, and others that "reality" is logically irrelevant. Among those who deny that judgment is the attribution of predicate to subject, who regard it as a relation of elements, some hold that the relation is "internal," some that it is "external," and others that it is sometimes one and sometimes the other.

Unless logic is a matter of some practical account, these contrarieties are so numerous, so extensive, and so irreconcilable that they are ludicrous. If logic is an affair of practical moment, then these inconsistencies are serious. They testify to some deep-lying cause of intellectual disagreement and incoherency. In fact, contemporary logical theory is the ground upon which all philosophical differences and disputes are gathered together and focussed. How does the modification in the traditional conception of the relation of experience and reason, the real and ideal affect logic?

It affects, in the first place, the nature of logic itself. If thought or intelligence is the means of intentional reconstruction of experience, then logic, as an account of the procedure of thought, is not purely formal. It is not confined to laws of formally correct reasoning apart from truth of subject-matter. Neither, on the contrary, is it concerned with the inherent thought structures of the universe, as Hegel's logic would have it; nor with the successive approaches of human thought to this objective thought structure as the logic of Lotze, Bosanquet, and other epistemological logicians would have it. If thinking is the way in which deliberate reorganization of experience is secured, then logic is such a clarified and systematized formulation of the procedures of thinking as will enable the desired reconstruction to go on more economically and efficiently. In language familiar to students, logic is both a science and an art; a science so far as it gives an organized and tested descriptive account of the way in which thought actually goes on; an art, so far as on the basis of this description it projects methods by which future thinking shall take advantage of the operations that lead to success and avoid those which result in failure.

Thus is answered the dispute whether logic is empirical or normative, psychological or regulative. It is both. Logic is based on a definite and executive supply of empirical material. Men have been thinking for ages. They have observed, inferred, and reasoned in all sorts of ways and to all kinds of results. Anthropology, the study of the origin of myth, legend and cult; linguistics and grammar; rhetoric and former logical compositions all tell us how men have thought and what have been the purposes and consequences of different kinds of thinking. Psychology, experimental and pathological, makes important contributions to our knowledge of how thinking goes on and to what effect. Especially does the record of the growth of the various sciences afford instruction in those concrete ways of inquiry and testing which have led men astray and which have proved efficacious. Each science from mathematics to history exhibits typical fallacious methods and typical efficacious methods in special subject-matters. Logical theory has thus a large, almost inexhaustible field of empirical study.

The conventional statement that experience only tells us how men have thought or *do* think, while logic is concerned with norms, with how men *should* think, is ludicrously inept. Some sorts of thinking are shown *by* experience to have got nowhere, or worse than nowhere—into systematized delusion and mistake. Others have proved in manifest experience that they lead to fruitful and enduring discoveries. It is precisely in experience that the different consequences of different methods of investigation and ratiocination are convincingly shown. The parrot-like repetition of the distinction between an empirical description of what is and a normative account of what should be merely neglects the most striking fact about thinking as it empirically is—namely, its flagrant exhibition of cases of failure and success—that is, of good thinking and bad thinking. Any one who considers this empirical manifestation will not complain of lack of material from which to construct a *regulative* art. The more study that is given to empirical records of actual thought, the more apparent becomes the connection between the specific features of thinking which have produced failure and success. Out of this relationship of cause and effect as it is empirically ascertained grow the norms and regulations of an art of thinking.

Mathematics is often cited as an example of purely normative thinking dependent upon *a priori* canons and supra-empirical material. But it is hard to see how the student who approaches the matter historically can avoid the conclusion that the status of mathematics is as empirical as that of metallurgy. Men began with counting and measuring things just as they began with pounding and burning them. One thing, as common speech profoundly has it, led to another. Certain ways were successful—not merely in the immediately practical sense, but in the sense of being interesting, of arousing attention, of exciting attempts at improvement. The present-day mathematical logician may present the structure of mathematics as if it had sprung all at once from the brain of a Zeus whose anatomy is that of pure logic. But, nevertheless, this very structure is a product of long historic growth, in which all kinds of experiments have been tried, in which some men have struck out in this direction and some in that, and in which some exercises and operations have resulted in confusion and others in triumphant clarifications and fruitful growths; a history in which matter and methods have been constantly selected and worked over on the basis of empirical success and failure.

The structure of alleged normative *a priori* mathematics is in truth the crowned result of ages of toilsome experience. The metallurgist who should write on the most highly developed method of dealing with ores would not, in truth, proceed any differently. He too selects, refines, and organizes the methods which in the past have been found to yield the maximum of achievement. Logic is a matter of profound human importance precisely because it is empirically founded and experimentally applied. So considered, the problem of logical theory is none other than the problem of the possibility of the development and employment of intelligent method in inquiries concerned with deliberate reconstruction of experience. And it is only saying again in more specific form what has been said in general form to add that while such a logic has been developed in respect to mathematics and physical science, intelligent method, logic, is still far to seek in moral and political affairs.

4

The Pattern and Structure of Inquiry

We may now ask: What is the *definition* of Inquiry? That is, what is the most highly generalized conception of inquiry which can be justifiably formulated? The definition is as follows: *Inquiry is the controlled or directed transformation of an indeterminate situation into one that is so determinate in its constituent distinctions and relations as to convert the elements of the original situation into a unified whole.*

The original indeterminate situation is not only "open" to inquiry, but it is open in the sense that its constituents do not hang together. The determinate situation on the other hand, *qua* outcome of inquiry, is a closed and, as it were, finished situation or "universe of experience." "Controlled or directed" in the above formula refers to the fact that inquiry is competent in any given case in the degree in which the operations involved in it actually do terminate in the establishment of an objectively unified existential situation. In the intermediate course of transition and transformation of the indeterminate situation, *dis*course through use of symbols is employed as means. In received logical terminology, propositions, or terms and the relations between them, are intrinsically involved.

SOURCE: From *Logic: The Theory of Inquiry* by John Dewey. Reprinted with the permission of The Center for Dewey Studies, Southern Illinois University at Carbondale. Footnotes containing cross-references have been omitted and the remaining ones renumbered.

I. *The Antecedent Condition of Inquiry: The Indeterminate Situation*

Inquiry and questioning, up to a certain point, are synonymous terms. We inquire when we question; and we inquire when we seek for whatever will provide an answer to a question asked. Thus it is of the very nature of the indeterminate situation which evokes inquiry to be *questionable*; or, in terms of actuality instead of potentiality, to be uncertain, unsettled, disturbed. The peculiar quality of what pervades the given materials, constituting them a situation, is not just uncertainty at large; it is a unique doubtfulness which makes that situation to be just and only the situation it is. It is this unique quality that not only evokes the particular inquiry engaged in but that exercises control over its special procedures. Otherwise, one procedure in inquiry would be as likely to occur and to be effective as any other. Unless a situation is uniquely qualified in its very indeterminateness, there is a condition of complete panic; response to it takes the form of blind and wild overt activities. Stating the matter from the personal side, we have "lost our heads." A variety of names serves to characterize indeterminate situations. They are disturbed, troubled, ambiguous, confused, full of conflicting tendencies, obscure, etc.

It is the *situation* that has these traits. *We* are doubtful because the situation is inherently doubtful. Personal states of doubt that are not evoked by and are not relative to some existential situation are pathological; when they are extreme they constitute the mania of doubting. Consequently, situations that are disturbed and troubled, confused or obscure, cannot be straightened out, cleared up and put in order, by manipulation of our personal states of mind. The attempt to settle them by such manipulations involves what psychiatrists call "withdrawal from reality." Such an attempt is pathological as far as it goes, and when it goes far it is the source of some form of actual insanity. The habit of disposing of the doubtful as if it belonged only to *us* rather than to the existential situation in which we are caught and implicated is an inheritance from subjectivistic psychology. The biological antecedent conditions of an unsettled situation are involved in that state of imbalance in organic-environmental interactions which has already been described. Restoration of integration can be effected, in one case as in the other, only by operations which actually modify existing conditions, not by merely "mental" processes.

It is, accordingly, a mistake to suppose that a situation is doubtful only in a "subjective" sense. The notion that in actual existence everything is completely determinate has been rendered questionable by the progress of physical science itself. Even if it had not been, complete determination would not hold of existences as an *environment*. For Nature is an environment only as it is involved in interaction with an organism, or self, or whatever name be used.[1]

Every such interaction is a temporal process, not a momentary cross-sectional occurrence. The situation in which it occurs is indeterminate, therefore, with respect to its *issue*. If we call it *confused*, then it is meant that its outcome cannot be anticipated. It is called *obscure* when its course of movement permits of final consequences that cannot be clearly made out. It is called *conflicting* when it tends to evoke discordant responses. Even were existential conditions unqualifiedly determinate in and of themselves, they are indeterminate in *significance*: that is, in what they import and portend in their interaction with the organism. The organic responses that enter into the production of the state of affairs that is temporally later and sequential are just as existential as are environing conditions.

The immediate *locus* of the problem concerns, then, what kind of responses the organism shall make. It concerns the interaction of organic responses and environing conditions in their movement toward an existential issue. It is a commonplace that in any troubled state of affairs *things* will come out differently according to what is done. The farmer won't get grain unless he plants and tills; the general will win or lose the battle according to the way he conducts it, and so on. Neither the grain nor the tilling, neither the outcome of the battle nor the conduct of it, are "mental" events. Organic interaction becomes inquiry when existential consequences are anticipated; when environing conditions are examined with reference to their potentialities; and when responsive activities are selected and ordered with reference to actualization of some of the potentialities, rather than others, in a final existential situation. Resolution of the indeterminate situation is active and operational. If the inquiry is adequately directed, the final issue is the unified situation that has been mentioned.

---

1. Except of course a purely mentalistic name, like *consciousness*. The alleged problem of "interactionism" versus automatism, parallelism, etc., is a problem (and an insoluble one) because of the assumption involved in its statement—the assumption, namely, that the interaction in question is with something mental instead of with biological-cultural human beings.

II. *Institution of a Problem*

The unsettled or indeterminate situation might have been called a *problematic* situation. This name would have been, however, proleptic and anticipatory. The indeterminate situation becomes problematic in the very process of being subjected to inquiry. The indeterminate situation comes into existence from existential causes, just as does, say, the organic imbalance of hunger. There is nothing intellectual or cognitive in the existence of such situations, although they are the necessary condition of cognitive operations or inquiry. In themselves they are precognitive. The first result of evocation of inquiry is that the situation is taken, adjudged, to be problematic. To see that a situation requires inquiry is the initial step in inquiry.[2]

Qualification of a situation as problematic does not, however, carry inquiry far. It is but an initial step in institution of a problem. A problem is not a task to be performed which a person puts upon himself or that is placed upon him by others—like a so-called arithmetical "problem" in school work. *A* problem represents the partial transformation by inquiry of a problematic situation into a determinate situation. It is a familiar and significant saying that a problem well put is half-solved. To find out *what* the problem and problems are which a problematic situation presents to be inquired into, is to be well along in inquiry. To mistake the problem involved is to cause subsequent inquiry to be irrelevant or to go astray. Without a problem, there is blind groping in the dark. The way in which the problem is conceived decides what specific suggestions are entertained and which are dismissed; what data are selected and which rejected; it is the criterion for relevancy and irrelevancy of hypotheses and conceptual structures. On the other hand, to set up a problem that does not grow out of an actual situation is to start on a course of dead work, nonetheless dead because the work is "busy work." Problems that are self-set are mere excuses for seeming to do something intellectual, something that has the semblance but not the substance of scientific activity.

III. *The Determination of a Problem-Solution*

Statement of a problematic situation in terms of a problem has no meaning save as the problem instituted has, in the very terms

---

2. If by "two-valued logic" is meant a logic that regards "true and false" as the sole logical values, then such a logic is necessarily so truncated that clearness and consistency in logical doctrine are impossible. Being the matter of a problem is a primary logical property.

of its statement, reference to a possible solution. Just because a problem well stated is on its way to solution, the determining of a genuine problem is a *progressive* inquiry; the cases in which a problem and its probable solution flash upon an inquirer are cases where much prior ingestion and digestion have occurred. If we assume prematurely that the problem involved is definite and clear, subsequent inquiry proceeds on the wrong tract. Hence the question arises: How is the formation of a genuine problem so controlled that further inquiries will move toward a solution?

The first step in answering this question is to recognize that no situation which is *completely* indeterminate can possibly be converted into a problem having definite constituents. The first step then is to search out the *constituents* of a given situation which, as constituents, are settled. When an alarm of fire is sounded in a crowded assembly hall, there is much that is indeterminate as regards the activities that may produce a favorable issue. One may get out safely or one may be trampled and burned. The fire is characterized, however, by some settled traits. It is, for example, located *somewhere*. Then the aisles and exits are at fixed places. Since they are settled or determinate in *existence,* the first step in institution of a problem is to settle them in *observation*. There are other factors which, while they are not as temporally and spatially fixed, are yet observable constituents; for example, the behavior and movements of other members of the audience. All of these observed conditions taken together constitute "the facts of the case." They constitute the terms of the problem, because they are conditions that must be reckoned with or taken account of in any relevant solution that is proposed.

A *possible* relevant solution is then suggested by the determination of factual conditions which are secured by observation. The possible solution presents itself, therefore, as an *idea,* just as the terms of the problem (which are facts) are instituted by observation. Ideas are anticipated consequences (forecasts) of what will happen when certain operations are executed under and with respect to observed conditions.[3] Observation of facts and suggested meanings or ideas arise and develop in correspondence with each

3. The theory of *ideas* that has been held in psychology and epistemology since the time of Locke's successors is completely irrelevant and obstructive in logical theory. For in treating them as copies of perceptions or "impressions," it ignores the prospective and anticipatory character that defines *being* an idea. Failure to define ideas functionally, in the reference they have to a solution of a problem, is one reason they have been treated as merely "mental." The notion, on the other hand, that ideas are fantasies is a derivative. Fantasies arise when the function an idea performs is ruled out when it is entertained and developed.

other. The more the facts of the case come to light in consequence of being subjected to observation, the clearer and more pertinent become the conceptions of the way the problem constituted by these facts is to be dealt with. On the other side, the clearer the idea, the more definite, as a truism, become the operations of observation and of execution that must be performed in order to resolve the situation.

An idea is first of all an anticipation of something that may happen; it marks a *possibility*. When it is said, as it sometimes is, that science is *prediction,* the anticipation that constitutes every idea an idea is grounded in a set of controlled observations and of regulated conceptual ways of interpreting them. Because inquiry is a progressive determination of a problem and its possible solution, ideas differ in grade according to the stage of inquiry reached. At first, save in highly familiar matters, they are vague. They occur at first simply as suggestions; suggestions just spring up, flash upon us, occur to us. They may then become stimuli to direct an overt activity but they have as yet no logical status. Every idea originates as a suggestion, but not every suggestion is an idea. The suggestion becomes an idea when it is examined with reference to its functional fitness; its capacity as a means of resolving the given situation.

This examination takes the form of reasoning, as a result of which we are able to appraise better than we were at the outset the pertinency and weight of the meaning now entertained with respect to its functional capacity. But the final test of its possession of these properties is determined when it actually functions—that is, when it is put into operation so as to institute by means of observations facts not previously observed, and is then used to organize them with other facts into a coherent whole.

Because suggestions and ideas are of that which is not present in given existence, the meanings which they involve must be embodied in some symbol. Without some kind of symbol no idea; a meaning that is completely disembodied can not be entertained or used. Since an existence (which *is* an existence) is the support and vehicle of a meaning and is a symbol instead of a merely physical existence only in this respect, embodied meanings or ideas are capable of objective survey and development. To "look at an idea" is not a mere literary figure of speech.

"Suggestions" have received scant courtesy in logical theory. It is true that when they just "pop into our heads," because of the workings of the psycho-physical organism, they are not logical. But they are both the conditions and the primary stuff of logical ideas. The traditional empiristic theory reduced them, as has already been pointed out, to mental copies of physical things and assumed that they were *per se* identical with ideas. Consequently it ignored the function of ideas in directing observation and in ascertaining relevant facts. The rationalistic school, on the other hand, saw clearly that "facts" apart from ideas are trivial, that they acquire import and significance only in relation to ideas. But at the same time it failed to attend to the operative and functional nature of the latter. Hence, it treated ideas as equivalent to the ultimate structure of "Reality." The Kantian formula that apart from each other "perceptions are blind and conceptions empty" marks a profound logical insight. The insight, however, was radically distorted because perceptual and conceptual contents were supposed to originate from different sources and thus required a third activity, that of synthetic understanding, to bring them together. In logical fact, perceptual and conceptual materials are instituted in functional correlativity with each other, in such a manner that the former locates and describes the problem while the latter represents a possible method of solution. Both are determinations in and by inquiry of the original problematic situation whose pervasive quality controls their institution and their contents. Both are finally checked by their capacity to work together to introduce a resolved unified situation. As distinctions they represent logical divisions of labor.

IV. *Reasoning*

The necessity of developing the meaning-contents of ideas in their relations to one another has been incidentally noted. This process, operating with symbols (constituting propositions) is reasoning in the sense of ratiocination or rational discourse.[4] When a suggested meaning is immediately accepted, inquiry is cut short. Hence the conclusion reached is not grounded, even if it happens to be correct. The check upon immediate acceptance is the examination of the meaning as a meaning. This examination consists in noting what the meaning in question implies in relation to other meanings in the system of which it is a member, the formulated relation constituting a proposition. If such and such a relation of meanings is accepted, then we are committed to such and such other relations of meanings because of their membership in the same system.

4. "Reasoning" is sometimes used to designate *inference* as well as ratiocination. When so used in logic the tendency is to identify inference and implication and thereby seriously to confuse logical theory.

Through a series of intermediate meanings, a meaning is finally reached which is more clearly *relevant* to the problem in hand than the originally suggested idea. It indicates operations which can be performed to test its applicability, whereas the original idea is usually too vague to determine crucial operations. In other words, the idea or meaning when developed in discourse directs the activities which, when executed, provide needed evidential material.

The point made can be most readily appreciated in connection with scientific reasoning. An hypothesis, once suggested and entertained, is developed in relation to other conceptual structures until it receives a form in which it can instigate and direct an experiment that will disclose precisely those conditions which have the maximum possible force in determining whether the hypothesis should be accepted or rejected. Or it may be that the experiment will indicate what modifications are required in the hypothesis so that it may be applicable, i.e., suited to interpret and organize the facts of the case. In many familiar situations, the meaning that is most relevant has been settled because of the eventuations of experiments in prior cases so that it is applicable almost immediately upon its occurrence. But, indirectly, if not directly, an idea or suggestion that is not developed in terms of the constellation of meanings to which it belongs can lead only to overt response. Since the latter terminates inquiry, there is then no adequate inquiry into the meaning that is used to settle the given situation, and the conclusion is in so far logically ungrounded.

V. *The Operational Character of Facts-Meanings*

It was stated that the observed facts of the case and the ideational contents expressed in ideas are related to each other, as, respectively, a clarification of the problem involved and the proposal of some possible solution; that they are, accordingly, functional divisions in the work on inquiry. Observed facts in their office of locating and describing the problem are existential; ideational subject-matter is non-existential. How, then, do they cooperate with each other in the resolution of an existential situation? The problem is insoluble save as it is recognized that both observed facts and entertained ideas are operational. Ideas are operational in that they instigate and direct further operations of observation; they are proposals and plans for acting upon existing conditions to bring new facts to light and to organize all the selected facts into a coherent whole.

What is meant by calling facts operational? Upon the negative side what is meant is that they are not self-sufficient and complete in themselves. They are selected and described, as we have seen, for a purpose, namely statement of the problem involved in such a way that its material both indicates a meaning relevant to resolution of the difficulty and serves to test its worth and validity. In regulated inquiry facts are selected and arranged with the express intent of fulfilling this office. They are not merely *results* of operations of observation which are executed with the aid of bodily organs and auxiliary instruments of art, but they are the particular facts and kinds of facts that will link up with one another in the definite ways that are required to produce a definite end. Those not found to connect with others in furtherance of this end are dropped and others are sought for. Being functional, they are necessarily operational. Their function is to serve as evidence and their evidential quality is judged on the basis of their capacity to form an ordered whole in response to operations prescribed by the ideas they occasion and support. If "the facts of the case" were final and complete in themselves, if they did not have a special operative force in resolution of the problematic situation, they could not serve as evidence.

The operative force of facts is apparent when we consider that no fact in isolation has evidential potency. Facts are evidential and are tests of an idea in so far as they are capable of being organized with one another. The organization can be achieved only as they *interact* with one another. When the problematic situation is such as to require extensive inquiries to effect its resolution, a series of interactions intervenes. Some observed facts point to an idea that stands for a possible solution. This idea evokes more observations. Some of the newly observed facts link up with those previously observed and are such as to rule out other observed things with respect to their evidential function. The new order of facts suggests a modified idea (or hypothesis) which occasions new observations whose result again determines a new order of facts, and so on until the existing order is both unified and complete. In the course of this serial process, the ideas that represent possible solutions are tested or "proved."

Meantime, the orders of fact, which present themselves in consequence of the experimental observations the ideas call out and direct, are *trial* facts. They are provisional. They are "facts" if they are observed by sound organs and techniques. But they are not on that account the *facts of the case*. They are tested or "proved" with respect to their evidential function just as much as ideas (hypotheses) are tested with reference to their power to exercise the function of resolution. The operative force of both ideas and facts is thus practically recognized in the degree in which they are connected with *experiment*. Naming them "operational" is but a theoretical recognition of what is involved when inquiry satisfies the conditions imposed by the necessity for experiment.

I recur, in this connection, to what has been said about the necessity for symbols in inquiry. It is obvious, on the face of matters, that a possible mode of solution must be carried in symbolic form since it is a possibility, not an assured present existence. Observed facts, on the other hand, are existentially present. It might seem therefore, that symbols are not required for referring to them. But if they are not carried and treated by means of symbols, they lose their provisional character, and in losing this character they are categorically asserted and inquiry comes to an end. The carrying on of inquiry requires that the facts be taken as *re*presentative and not just as *pre*-sented. This demand is met by formulating them in propositions—that is, by means of symbols. Unless they are so represented they relapse into the total qualitative situation.

VI. *Common Sense and Scientific Inquiry*

The discussion up to this point has proceeded in general terms which recognize no distinction between common sense and scientific inquiry. We have now reached a point where the community of pattern in these two distinctive modes of inquiry should receive explicit attention. It was said in earlier chapters that the difference between them resides in their respective subject-matters, not in their basic logical forms and relations; that the difference in subject-matters is due to the difference in the problems respectively involved; and, finally, that this difference sets up a difference in the ends or objective consequences they are concerned to achieve. Because common sense problems and inquiries have to do with the interactions into which living creatures enter in connection with environing conditions in order to establish objects of use and enjoyment, the symbols employed are those which have been determined in the habitual culture of a group. They form a system but the system is practical rather than intellectual. It is constituted by the traditions, occupations, techniques, interests, and established institutions of the group. The meanings that compose it are carried in the common everyday language of communication between members of the group. The meanings involved in this common language system determine what individuals of the group may and may not do in relation to physical objects and in relations to one another. They regulate *what* can be used and enjoyed and *how* use and enjoyment shall occur.

Because the symbol-meaning systems involved are connected directly with cultural life-activities and are related to each other in virtue of this connection, the specific meanings which are present have reference to the specific and limited environing conditions under which the group lives. Only those things of the environment that are taken, according to custom and tradition, as having connection with and bearing upon this life, enter into the meaning system. There is no such thing as disinterested intellectual concern with either physical or social matters. For, until the rise of science, there were no problems of common sense that called for such inquiry. Disinterestedness existed practically in the demand that group interests and concerns be put above private needs and interests. But there was no intellectual disinterestedness beyond the activities, interests and concerns of the group. In other words, there was no science as such, although, as was earlier pointed out, there did exist information and techniques which were available for the purposes of scientific inquiry and out of which the latter subsequently grew.

In scientific inquiry, then, meanings are related to one another on the ground of their character *as* meanings, freed from direct reference to the concerns of a limited group. Their intellectual abstractness is a product of this liberation, just as the "concrete" is practically identified by directness of connection with environmental interactions. Consequently a new language, a new system of symbols related together on a new basis, comes into existence, and in this new language semantic coherence, as such, is the controlling consideration. To repeat what has already been said, connection with problems of use and enjoyment is the source of the dominant role of qualities, sensible and moral, and of ends in common sense.

In science, since meanings are determined on the ground of their relation as meanings to one another, *relations* become the objects of inquiry and qualities are relegated to a secondary status, playing a part only as far as they assist in institution of relations. They are subordinate because they have an instrumental office, instead of being themselves, as in prescientific common sense, the matters of final importance. The enduring hold of common sense is testified to historically by the long time it took before it was seen that scientific objects are strictly relational. First tertiary qualities were eliminated; it was recognized that moral qualities are not agencies in determining the structure of nature. Then secondary qualities, the wet-dry, hot-cold, light-heavy, which were the explanatory principles of physical phenomena in Greek science, were ejected. But so-called primary qualities took their place, as with Newton and the Lockeian formulation of Newtonian existential postulates. It was not until the threshold of our time was reached that scientific inquiries perceived that their own problems and methods required an interpretation of "primary qualities" in terms of relations, such as position, motion and temporal span. In the structure of distinctively scientific objects these relations are indifferent to qualities.

The foregoing is intended to indicate that the different objectives of common sense and of scientific inquiry demand different subject-matters and that this difference in subject-matters is not incompatible with the existence of a common pattern in both types. There are, of course, secondary logical forms which reflect the distinction of properties involved in the change from qualitative and teleological subject-matter to non-qualitative and non-teleological relations. But they occur and operate within the described community of pattern. They are explicable, and explicable only, on the ground of the distinctive problems generated by scientific subject-matter. The independence of scientific objects from limited and fairly direct reference to the environment as a factor in activities of use and enjoyment, is equivalent, as has already been intimated, to their *abstract* character. It is also equivalent to their *general* character in the sense in which the generalizations of science are different from the generalizations with which common sense is familiar. The generality of *all* scientific subject-matter as such means that it is freed from restriction to conditions which present themselves at particular times and places. Their reference is to *any* set of time and place conditions—a statement which is not to be confused with the doctrine that they have no reference to actual existential occasions. Reference to time-place of existence is necessarily involved, but it is reference to whatever set of existences fulfills the general relations laid down in and by the constitution of the scientific object.[5]

5. The consequences that follow are directly related to the statement that the elimination of qualities and ends is intermediate; that, in fact, the construction of purely relational objects has enormously liberated and expanded common sense uses and enjoyments by conferring control over production of qualities, by enabling new ends to be realistically instituted, and by providing competent means for achieving them.

Summary

Since a number of points have been discussed, it will be well to round up conclusions reached about them in a summary statement of the structure of the common pattern of inquiry. Inquiry is the directed or controlled transformation of an indeterminate situation into a determinately unified one. The transition is achieved by means of operations of two kinds which are in functional correspondence with each other. One kind of operations deals with ideational or conceptual subject-matter. This subject-matter stands for possible ways and ends of resolution. It anticipates a solution, and is marked off from fancy because, or, in so far as, it becomes operative in instigation and direction of new observations yielding new factual material. The other kind of operations is made up of activities involving the techniques and organs of observation. Since these operations are existential they modify the prior existential situation, bring into high relief conditions previously obscure, and relegate to the background other aspects that were at the outset conspicuous. The ground and criterion of the execution of this work of emphasis, selection and arrangement is to delimit the problem in such a way that existential material may be provided with which to test the ideas that represent possible modes of solution. Symbols, defining terms and propositions, are necessarily required in order to retain and carry forward both ideational and existential subject-matters in order that they may serve their proper functions in the control of inquiry. Otherwise the problem is taken to be closed and inquiry ceases.

One fundamentally important phase of the transformation of the situation which constitutes inquiry is central in the treatment of judgment and its functions. The transformation is existential and hence temporal. The pre-cognitive unsettled situation can be settled only by modification of its constituents. Experimental operations change existing conditions. Reasoning, as such, can provide means for effecting the change of conditions but by itself cannot effect it. Only execution of existential operations directed by an idea in which ratiocination terminates can bring about the re-ordering of environing conditions required to produce a settled and unified situation. Since this principle also applies to the meanings that are elaborated in science, the experimental production and re-arrangement of physical conditions involved in natural science is further evidence of the unity of the pattern of inquiry. The temporal quality of inquiry means, then, something quite other than that the process of inquiry takes time. It means that the objective subject-matter of inquiry undergoes temporal modification.

5

Formal Canons of Relations and Propositions

The functions of additive and multiplicative conjunction-disjunction go back, as we have seen, to the conjugate relation of affirmation-negation, inclusion-exclusion. Hence they may be further generalized. When so generalized, the fundamental functions involved take the form of logical principles to which the name *Canons* is traditionally applied. These cannons are *Identity, Contradiction* and *Excluded Middle*. On the ground of the position taken, it follows truistically that they express certain ultimate conditions to be satisfied, instead of being properties of propositions as such. Upon the basis of the cosmological-ontological assumptions of the classic logic, it was a sound logical doctrine that treated identity, etc., as necessary *structural properties*. Species, which alone were capable of definition, classification, and scientific demonstration, were immutable. Hence they were inherently self-identical. Any species is always and necessarily just what it is. The canon of identity expressed symbolically in the form *A* is *A* was, accordingly, the proper form in which any proposition having scientific status should be stated. Species were also ontologically exclusive of one another. No transitions or derivations were possible among them

Source: From *Logic: The Theory of Inquiry* by John Dewey. Reprinted with the permission of The Center for Dewey Studies, Southern Illinois University at Carbondale. The footnotes have been renumbered, and one, containing a cross-reference, has been omitted.

because of their necessary ontological exclusion of one another. Hence, *tertium non datur*.[1]

1. Identity. From the standpoint of the position that it is necessary for propositions to satisfy conditions set by membership in a set or a series of propositions, *identity* means the logical requirement that meanings be stable in the inquiry-continuum. The direct and obvious meaning of this statement is that a meaning remain constant throughout a *given* inquiry, since any change in its content changes the force of the proposition of which it is a constituent, thus rendering it uncertain upon what meanings and relation of meanings the conclusion reached actually depends. Fulfilment of this condition does not mean, however, that a given symbol shall have the same meaning in *all* inquiries. If it did have this meaning, progress in knowledge would be impossible. But the judgment which is the final issue of inquiry modifies to some extent, sometimes crucially, the evidential import of some observed fact and the meaning previously possessed by some conception. Unless *identity* has functional force in relation to the subject-matter undergoing inquiry, the canon of identity is violated in every scientific advance.

The deeper and underlying import of the principle of identity is, accordingly, constituted in the very continuum of judgment. In scientific inquiry, every conclusion reached, whether of fact or conception, is held subject to determination by its fate in further inquiries. Stability or "identity," of meanings is a limiting ideal, as a condition to be progressively satisfied. The conditional status of scientific conclusions (conditional in the sense of subjection to revision in further inquiry) is sometimes used by critics to disparage scientific "truths" in comparison with those which are alleged to be eternal and immutable. In fact, it is a necessary condition of continuous advance in apprehension and in understanding.[2]

1. That Aristotle's formulation of the principle of contradiction is somewhat equivocal is frequently noticed by modern exponents of his logical doctrine. It would seem to be a combination of two considerations; one, that any contradiction violates the principle of the necessary identity of a species; the other, that *contrary* propositions not only exist in the case of changes, as signs of lack of complete Being, but are inevitable, since in his cosmology it is the hot which becomes cold, the moist which alters into the dry, etc. Plato, without formulating the principle of contradiction, had argued against the *complete* reality of change on the ground that if it had a full measure of Being contradictory propositions were inevitable, since it then followed that something both was and was not. On the whole, contradiction seems to have been employed as evidence for the principle of identity rather than as an independent principle.

2. The best definition of *truth* from the logical standpoint which is known to

2. Contradiction. The logical condition to be satisfied for the canon of contradiction is independent of that of identity, although necessarily conjunctive with it. Violation of the principle of identity *may* lead to contradiction. But the logically important instances are those in which *observance* of the principle of identity results in a contradiction. For establishment of propositions one of which must be valid if the other is invalid is an indispensable step in arriving at a grounded conclusion. Contradiction is not then just an unfortunate accident which sometimes happens to come about. Complete exclusion, resulting in grounded disjunction, is not effected until propositions are determined as pairs such that if one is valid the other is invalid, and if one is invalid the other is valid. The principle of contradiction thus represents a condition to be satisfied. Direct inspection of two propositions does not determine whether or not they are related as contradictories, as would be the case if contradiction were an inherent relational property. The contrary doctrine is often affirmed, as when it is said that the two propositions *A is M* and *A is not M* directly contradict each other. But unless *A* has already been determined conjunctively-disjunctively, by prior inquiry, some part of *A,* or *A* in some relation, may be *M,* and some other part of *A,* or *A* in some other relation, may be *not M*. The relation of *A* to *M* and *not M* can be determined only by operations of exclusion which reach their logical limit in the relation of contradiction.

3. Excluded Middle. It was stated earlier that complete satisfaction of the conditions of conjunctive-disjunctive functions, additive and multiplicative, is formally represented in the form *either-one-or-other-but-not-both*. The principle of excluded middle presents the completely generalized formulation of conjunctive-disjunctive functions in their conjugate relation. The notion that propositions are or can be, in and of themselves, such that the principle of excluded middle directly applies is probably the source of more fallacious reasoning in philosophical discourse and in moral and social inquiries than any other one sort of fallacy. That fact that dis-

---

me is that of Peirce: "The opinion which is fated to be ultimately agreed to by all who investigate is what we mean by the truth, and the object represented by this opinion is the real." A more complete (and more suggestive) statement is the following: "Truth is that concordance of an abstract statement with the ideal limit towards which endless investigation would tend to bring scientific belief, which concordance the abstract statement may possess by virtue of the confession of its inaccuracy and one-sidedness, and this confession is an essential ingredient of truth."

junctions which were at one time taken to be both exhaustive and necessary have later been found to be incomplete (and sometimes even totally irrelevant) should long ago have been a warning that the principle of excluded middle sets forth a logical condition *to be* satisfied in the course of continuity of inquiry. It formulates the ultimate *goal* of inquiry in complete satisfaction of logical conditions. To determine subject-matters so that no alternative is possible is the most difficult task of inquiry.

It is frequently argued today that the three principles in question have become completely outmoded with the abandonment of their foundations in the Aristotelian logic. The Aristotelian interpretation of them as ontological, and any interpretation which regards them as inherent relational properties of given propositions, must certainly be abandoned. But as formulations of formal conditions (conjunctive-disjunctive) to be satisfied, they are valid as directive principles, as regulative limiting ideals of inquiry. An example sometimes put forward to show the meaninglessness of the principle of excluded middle is its inapplicability to existences in process of transition. Since all existences are in process of change it is concluded that the principle is totally inapplicable. For example, of water that is freezing and of ice that is melting, it cannot be said that water is either solid or liquid. To avoid this difficulty by saying that it is either solid, liquid or in a transitional state, is to beg the question at issue: namely, determination of the transitional intermediate state. The objection is wholly sound on any other ground than that the canon expresses a condition *to be* satisfied. But taken in the latter sense, it shows the scientific inadequacy of the common sense conceptions of *solid* and *liquid*. As scientific existential inquiry has become occupied with changes and correlations of change, the popular qualitative ideas of solid, liquid, gaseous states have been expelled. They are now replaced by correlations of units of mass, velocity and distance-direction formulated in terms of numerical measurements. The necessity of instituting exclusive disjunctions, satisfying the condition of excluded intermediates, has been a factor in bringing about this scientific change.

III

The Theory of Knowledge

One of the most repeated themes in Dewey's philosophy is that theory cannot be separated from practice. As significant expressions of that leitmotif, Dewey asserts that the theory of logic could not be clarified if it were separated from the study of how men think, or that a theory of ethics requires some connection with how men decide policies or justify decisions, or that a theory of knowledge must help explain how men gain reliable knowledge. Such an account of how men know, for example, would overcome the dualism of a philosophical tradition in which knowledge was alleged to derive exclusively from reason uncontaminated by sensation or exclusively from sense experience unstructured by mind. The truths of logic and mathematics, and sometimes metaphysics, were the paradigmatic instances of rationality, while the truths of such immediately certain paradigms as "Here, yellow patch, now" or, perhaps, "Here what seems to me to be yellow now" provided the truths of sense experience uncorrupted by inference.

The study of how men know things in their everyday experience, and how they put their knowledge to practical use, would reveal—in contrast to the theoretical dualisms—how rational ideas successfully organized, unified, or predicted particular events in experience in an effort to change and to control experience and reality. It would also show—again in contrast to any philosophical dualistic account—how experience provides cues for the genesis of rational hypotheses and serves to verify or to refute those hypotheses. This account of the operations of mind as a pragmatic instrumentality in man's effort to understand and control the environment in which he lives is the main story of Dewey's theory of knowledge.

In developing that account, Dewey utilized a number of approaches. One derived from the psychology of William James in conjunction with his own functional psychology, and involved a psychological theory of the role of knowledge in human adaptation to the environment. In one of his earliest essays, "The Significance of the Problem of Knowledge" (1897), Dewey argued for a different approach in overcoming the untenable dualism between rationalists and empiricists, which he believed blocked the road of progress for any theory of knowledge. Dewey sought to examine the practical motives that may have led to the precipitation of the conflict between rationalists and empiricists. He found them in the difference between those who sought—both as an expression of their temperament and as a result of a preference of policy—to solve human and social problems by an appeal to a structure of authority and those who sought to solve these problems by an appeal to individual change and progress. Dewey concluded that if the antinomy between reason and sensation could not be resolved by argument between the two schools, it might be reconciled or resolved by an appeal to the consequences in experience, including social practice, of adopting those hypotheses that affirm the need for the structure of authority, in contrast to those that affirm the need for change and progress. Dewey claimed that the philosophically insoluble dilemma of reason versus sensation had been legitimately transposed to an experientially soluble problem of the place of rational authority and the place of individualist change in social philosophy. On the basis of this transposition, Dewey offers in this essay an interpretation of the significance of the problem of knowledge for social philosophy. In doing so, however, he had to meet the criticism, frequently applied at that time to James and other pragmatic philosophers, that this shift of concern away from the resolution of the problem of knowledge in traditional terms to its consequences in other domains of human experience is an illegitimate transition.

The most familiar strategy Dewey employed in his perennial effort to overcome the traditional philosophical dualism of reason versus sensation, however, was the interpretation of the concept of experience. Experience, he believed, had been distorted in the empiricist tradition to connote subjectivity, privacy, mental events, or sense data. But when the concept of experience was examined, both in its usage in the language and in its role in human living and knowing, it belied these connotations, having instead a public and objective role. The detailed argument for such an interpretation of experience, and the significance for philosophy of that interpretation, constitute the second selection presented here: an abridged version of Dewey's 1917 paper, "The Need for a Recovery of Philosophy."

In that paper, Dewey showed how an appropriate interpretation of the concept of experience could be connected with his own pragmatic stress on the nature of knowledge. Dewey, like the other pragmatists, insisted on an account of knowledge in which the practical function of "knowing" as related to prediction or control would be recognized. Such an account had significant implications for the future of philosophy. It would mandate an end to various aspects of traditional metaphysics and theory of knowledge; and it could mark a new beginning for a philosophical method that was consonant with empiricism.

6

The Significance of the Problem of Knowledge

It is now something over a century since Kant called upon philosophers to cease their discussion regarding the nature of the world and the principles of existence until they had arrived at some conclusion regarding the nature of the knowing process. But students of philosophy know that Kant formulated the question "how knowledge is possible" rather than created it. As matter of fact, reflective thought for two centuries before Kant had been principally interested in just this problem, although it had not generalized its own interest. Kant brought to consciousness the controlling motive. The discussion, both in Kant himself and in his successors, often seems scholastic, lost in useless subtlety, scholastic argument, and technical distinctions. Within the last decade in particular there have been signs of a growing weariness as to epistemology, and a tendency to turn away to more fertile fields. The interest shows signs of exhaustion.

Students of philosophy will recognize what I mean when I say that this growing conviction of futility and consequent distaste are associated with the outcome of the famous dictum of Kant, that perception without conception is blind, while conception without perception is empty. The whole course of reflection since Kant's time has tended to justify this remark. The sensationalist and the

Source: Delivered before the Philosophical Club of the University of Michigan, in the winter of 1897, and reprinted with slight change from a monograph in the "University of Chicago Contributions to Philosophy," 1897.

rationalist have worked themselves out. Pretty much all students are convinced that we can reduce knowledge neither to a set of associated sensations, nor yet to a purely rational system of relations of thought. Knowledge is judgment, and judgment requires both a material of sense perception and an ordering, regulating principle, reason; so much seems certain, but we do not get any further. Sensation and thought themselves seem to stand out more rigidly opposed to each other in their own natures than ever. Why both are necessary, and how two such opposed factors cooperate in bringing about the unified result of science, becomes more and more of a mystery. It is the continual running up against this situation which accounts for the flagging of interest and the desire to direct energy where it will have more outcome.

This situation creates a condition favorable to taking stock of the question as it stands; to inquiring what this interest, prolonged for over three centuries, in the possibility and nature of knowledge, stands for; what the conviction as to the necessity of the union of sensation and thought, together with the inability to reach conclusions regarding the nature of the union, signifies.

I propose then to raise this evening precisely this question: What is the meaning of the problem of knowledge? What is its meaning, not simply for reflective philosophy or in terms of epistemology itself, but what is its meaning in the historical movement of humanity and as a part of a larger and more comprehensive experience? My thesis is perhaps sufficiently indicated in the mere taking of this point of view. It implies that the abstractness of the discussion of knowledge, its remoteness from everyday experience, is one of form, rather than of substance. It implies that the problem of knowledge is not a problem that has its origin, its value, or its destiny within itself. The problem is one which social life, the organized practice of mankind, has had to face. The seemingly technical and abstruse discussion of the philosophers results from the formulation and statement of the question.

I suggest that the problem of the possibility of knowledge is but an aspect of the question of the relation of knowing to acting, of theory to practice. The distinctions which the philosophers raise, the oppositions which they erect, the weary treadmill which they pursue between sensation and thought, subject and object, mind and matter, are not invented *ad hoc,* but are simply the concise reports and condensed formula of points of view and practical conflicts having their source in the very nature of modern life, conflicts which must be met and solved if modern life is to go on its way untroubled, with clear consciousness of what it is about. As the philosopher has received his problem from the world of action, so he must return his account there for auditing and liquidation.

More especially, I suggest that the tendency of all the points at issue to precipitate in the opposition of sensationalism and rationalism is due to the fact that sensation and reason stand for the two forces contending for mastery in social life: the radical and the conservative. The reason that the contest does not end, the reason for the necessity of the combination of the two in the resultant statement, is that both factors are necessary in action; one stands for stimulus, for initiative; the other for control, for direction.

I cannot hope, in the time at my command this evening, to justify these wide and sweeping assertions regarding either the origin, the work, or the final destiny of philosophic reflection. I simply hope, by reference to some of the chief periods of the development of philosophy, to illustrate to you something of what I mean.

At the outset we take a long scope in our survey and present to ourselves the epoch when philosophy was still consciously, and not simply by implication, human, when reflective thought had not developed its own technique of method, and was in no danger of being caught in its own machinery—the time of Socrates. What does the assertion of Socrates that an unexamined life is not one fit to be led by man; what does his injunction "Know thyself" mean? It means that the corporate motives and guarantees of conduct are breaking down. We have got away from the time when the individual could both regulate and justify his course of life by reference to the ideals incarnate in the habits of the community of which he is a member. The time of direct and therefore unconscious union with corporate life, finding therein stimuli, codes, and values, has departed. The development of industry and commerce, of war and politics, has brought face to face communities with different aims and diverse habits; the development of myth and animism into crude but genuine scientific observation and imagination has transformed the physical widening of the horizon, brought about by commerce and intercourse, into an intellectual and moral expansion. The old supports fail precisely at the time when they are most needed—before a widening and more complex scene of action. Where, then, shall the agent of action turn? The "Know thyself" of Socrates is the reply to the practical problem which confronted Athens in his day. Investigation into the true ends and worths of human life, sifting and testing of all competing ends, the discovery of a method which should validate the genuine and dismiss the spurious, had henceforth to do for man what consolidated and incorporate custom had hitherto presented as a free and precious gift.

With Socrates the question is as direct and practical as the question of making one's living or of governing the state; it is indeed the same question put in its general form. It is a question that the flute player, the cobbler, and the politician must face no more and no less than the reflective philosopher. The question is addressed by Socrates to every individual and to every group with which he comes in contact. Because the question is practical it is individual and direct. It is a question which every one must face and answer for himself, just as in the Protestant scheme every individual must face and solve for himself the question of his final destiny.

Yet the very attitude of Socrates carried with it the elements of its own destruction. Socrates could only raise the question, or rather demand of every individual that he raise it for himself. Of the answer he declared himself to be as ignorant as was any one. The result could be only a shifting of the center of interest. If the question is so all-important, and yet the wisest of all men must confess that he only knows his own ignorance as to its answer, the inevitable point of further consideration is the discovery of a method which shall enable the question to be answered. This is the significance of Plato. The problem is the absolutely inevitable outgrowth of the Socratic position; and yet it carried with it just as inevitably the separation of philosopher from shoemaker and statesman, and the relegation of theory to a position remote for the time being from conduct.

If the Socratic command, "Know thyself," runs against the dead wall of inability to conduct this knowledge, some one must take upon himself the discovery of how the requisite knowledge may be obtained. A new profession is born, that of the thinker. At this time the means, the discovery of how the aims and worths of the self may be known and measured, becomes, for this class, an end in itself. Theory is ultimately to be applied to practice; but in the meantime the theory must be worked out as theory or else no application. This represents the peculiar equilibrium and the peculiar point of contradiction in the Platonic system. All philosophy is simply for the sake of the organization and regulation of social life; and yet the philosophers must be a class by themselves, working out their peculiar problems with their own particular tools.

With Aristotle the attempted balance failed. Social life is disintegrating beyond the point of hope of a successful reorganization, and thinking is becoming a fascinating pursuit for its own sake. The world of practice is now the world of compromise and of adjustment. It is relative to partial aims and finite agents. The sphere of absolute and enduring truth and value can be reached only in and through thought. The one who acts compromises himself with the animal desire that inspires his action and with the alien material that forms its stuff. In two short generations the divorce of philosophy from life, the isolation of reflective theory from practical conduct, has completed itself. So great is the irony of history that this sudden and effective outcome was the result of the attempt to make thought the instrument of action, and action the manifestation of truth reached by thinking.

But this statement must not be taken too literally. It is impossible that men should really separate their ideas from their acts. If we look ahead a few centuries we find that the philosophy of Plato and Aristotle has accomplished, in an indirect and unconscious way, what perhaps it could never have effected by the more immediate and practical method of Socrates. Philosophy became an organ of vision, an instrument of interpretation; it furnished the medium through which the world was seen and the course of life estimated. Philosophy died as philosophy, to rise as the set and bent of the human mind. Through a thousand devious and roundabout channels, the thoughts of the philosophers filtered through the strata of human consciousness and conduct. Through the teachings of grammarians, rhetoricans, and a variety of educational schools, they were spread in diluted form through the whole Roman Empire and were again precipitated in the common forms of speech. Through the earnestness of the moral propaganda of the Stoics they became the working rules of life for the more strenuous and earnest spirits. Through the speculations of the Sceptics and Epicureans they became the chief reliance and consolation of a large number of highly cultured individuals amid social turmoil and political disintegration. All these influences and many more finally summed themselves up in the two great media through which Greek philosophy finally fixed the intellectual horizon of man, determined the values of its perspective, and meted out the boundaries and divisions of the scene of human action.

These two influences were the development of Christian theology and moral theory, and the organization of the system of Roman jurisprudence. There is perhaps no more fascinating chapter in the history of humanity than the slow and tortuous processes by which the ideas set in motion by that Athenian citizen who faced death as serenely as he conversed with a friend, finally became the intellectually organizing centers of the two great movements that bridge the span between ancient civilization and modern. As the personal and immediate force and enthusiasm of the movement initiated by Jesus began to grow fainter and the commanding influence of his own personality commenced to dim, the ideas of the world and of life, of God and of man elaborated in Greek philosophy served to transform moral enthusiasm and personal devotion to the redemption of humanity into a splendid and coherent view of the universe; a view that resisted all disintegrating influences and gathered into itself the permanent ideas and progressive ideals thus far developed in the history of man.

We have only a faint idea of how this was accomplished, or of the thoroughness of the work done. We have perhaps even more inadequate conceptions of the great organizing and centralizing work done by Greek thought in the political sphere. When the military and administrative genius of Rome brought the whole world in subjection to itself, the most pressing of practical problems was to give unity of practical aim and harmony of working machinery to the vast and confused mass of local custom and tradition, religious, social, economic, and intellectual, as well as political. In this juncture the great administrators and lawyers of Rome seized with avidity upon the results of the intellectual analysis of social and political relations elaborated in Greek philosophy. Caring naught for these results in their reflective and theoretical character, they saw in them the possible instrument of introducing order into chaos and of transforming the confused and conflicting medley of practice and opinion into a harmonious social structure. Roman law, that formed the vertebral column of civilization for a thousand years, and which articulated the outer order of life as distinctly as Christianity controlled the inner, was the outcome.

Thought was once more in unity with action, philosophy had become the instrument of conduct. Mr. Bosanquet makes the pregnant remark "that the weakness of medieval science and philosophy are connected rather with excess of practice than with excess of theory. The subordination of philosophy to theology is a subordination of science to a formulated conception of human welfare. Its essence is present, not wherever there is metaphysics but wherever the spirit of truth is subordinated to any preconceived practical intent." (*History of Esthetics,* p. 146.)

Once more the irony of history displays itself. Thought has become practical, it has become the regulator of individual conduct and social organization, but at the expense of its own freedom and power. The defining characteristic of medievalism in state and in church, in political and spiritual life, is that truth presents itself to the individual only through the medium of organized authority.

There was a historical necessity on the external as well as the internal side. We have not the remotest way of imagining what the outcome would finally have been if, at the time when the intellectual structure of the Christian church and the legal structure of the Roman Empire had got themselves thoroughly organized, the barbarians had not made their inroads and seized upon all this accumulated and consolidated wealth as their own legitimate prey. But this was what did happen. As a result, truths originally developed by the freest possible criticism and investigation became external, and imposed themselves upon the mass of individuals by the mere weight of authoritative law. The external, transcendental, and supernatural character of spiritual truth and of social control during the Middle Ages is naught but the mirror, in consciousness, of the relation existing between the eager, greedy, undisciplined horde of barbarians on one side, and the concentrated achievements of ancient civilization on the other. There was no way out save that the keen barbarian whet his appetite upon the rich banquet spread before him. But there was equally no way out so far as the continuity of civilization was concerned save that the very fullness and richness of this banquet set limits to the appetite, and finally, when assimilated and digested, it be transformed into the flesh and blood, the muscles and sinew of him who sat at the feast. Thus the barbarian ceased to be a barbarian and a new civilization arose.

But the time came when the work of absorption was fairly complete. The northern barbarians had eaten the food and drunk the wine of Graeco-Roman civilization. The authoritative truth embodied in medieval state and church succeeded, in principle, in disciplining the untrained masses. Its very success issued its own death warrant. To say that it had succeeded means that the new people had finally eaten their way into the heart of the ideas offered them, had got from them what they wanted, and were henceforth prepared to go their own way and make their own living. Here a new rhythm of the movement of thought and action begins to show itself.

The beginning of this change in the swing of thought and action forms the transition from the Middle Ages to the modern times. It is the epoch of the Renaissance. The individual comes to a new birth and asserts his own individuality and demands his own rights in the way of feeding, doing, and knowing for himself. Science, art, religion, political life must all be made over on the basis of recognizing the claims of the individual.

Pardon me these commonplaces, but they are necessary to the course of the argument. By historic fallacy we often suppose, or imagine that we suppose, that the individual had been present as a possible center of action all through the Middle Ages, but through some external and arbitrary interference had been weighted down by political and intellectual despotism. All this inverts the true order of the case. The very possibility of the individual making such unlimited demands for himself, claiming to be the legitimate center of all action and standard for all organizations, was dependent, as I have already indicated, upon the intervening medievalism. Save as having passed through this period of tremendous discipline, and having gradually worked over into his own habits and purposes the truths embodied in the church and state that controlled his conduct, the individual could be only a source of disorder and a disturber of civilization. The very maintenance of the spiritual welfare of mankind was bound up in the extent to which the claim of truth and reality to be universal and objective, far above all individual feeling and thought, could make itself valid. The logical realism and universalism of scholastic philosophy simply reflect the actual subjection of the individual to that associated and corporate life which, in conserving the past, provided the principle of control.

But the eager, hungry barbarian was there, implicated in this universalism. He must be active in receiving and in absorbing the truth authoritatively doled out to him. Even the most rigid forms of medieval Christianity could not avoid postulating the individual will as having a certain initiative with reference to its own salvation. The impulses, the appetite, the instinct of the individual were all assumed in medieval morals, religion, and politics. The imagined medieval tyranny took them for granted as completely as does the modern herald of liberty and equality. But the medieval civilization knew that the time had not come when these appetites and impulses could be trusted to work themselves out. They must be controlled by the incorporate truths inherited from Athens and Rome.

The very logic of the relationship, however, required that the time come when the individual makes his own the objective and universal truths. He is now the incorporation of truth. He now has the control as well as the stimulus of action within himself. He is the standard and the end, as well as the initiator and the effective force of execution. Just because the authoritative truth of medievalism has succeeded, has fulfilled its function, the individual can begin to assert himself.

Contrast this critical period, finding its expression equally in the art of the Renaissance, the revival of learning, the Protestant Reformation, and political democracy, with Athens in the time of Socrates. Then individuals felt their own social life disintegrated, dissolving under their very feet. The problem was how the value of that social life was to be maintained against the external and internal forces that were threatening it. The problem was on the side neither of the individual nor of progress; save as the individual was seen to be an intervening instrument in the reconstruction of the social unity. But with the individual of the fourteenth century, it was not his own intimate community life which was slipping away from him. It was an alien and remote life which had finally become his own; which had passed over into his own inner being. The problem was not how a unity of social life should be conserved, but what the individual should do with the wealth of resources of which he found himself the rightful heir and administrator. The problem looked out upon the future, not back to the past. It was how to create a new order, both of modes of individual conduct and forms of social life that should be the appropriate manifestations of the vigorous and richly endowed individual.

Hence the conception of progress as a ruling idea, the conception of the individual as the source and standard of rights, and the problem of knowledge were all born together. Given the freed individual, who feels called upon to create a new heaven and a new earth, and who feels himself gifted with the power to perform the task to which he is called—and the demand for science, for a method of discovering and verifying truth, becomes imperious. The individual is henceforth to supply control, law, and not simply stimulation and initiation. What does this mean but that instead of any longer receiving or assimilating truth, he is now to search for and create it? Having no longer the truth imposed by authority to rely upon, there is no resource save to secure the authority of truth. The possibility of getting at and utilizing this truth becomes therefore the underlying and conditioning problem of modern life. Strange as it may sound, the question which was formulated by Kant as that of the possibility of knowledge is the fundamental political problem of modern life.

Science and metaphysics or philosophy, though seeming often to be at war, with their respective adherents often throwing jibes and slurs at each other, are really the most intimate allies. The philosophic movement is simply the coming to consciousness of this claim of the individual to be able to discover not only to direct his own conduct, but to become an influential and decisive factor in the organization of life itself. Modern philosophy is the formulation of this creed, both in general and in its more specific implications. We often forget that the technical problem "*how* knowledge is possible," also means "how *knowledge* is possible"; how, that is, shall the individual be able to back himself up by truth which has no authority save that of its own intrinsic truthfulness. Science, on the other hand, is simply this general faith or creed asserting itself in detail; it is the practical faith at work engaged in subjugating the foreign territory of ignorance and falsehood step by step. If the ultimate outcome depends upon this detailed and concrete work, we must not forget that the earnestness and courage, as well as the intelligence and clearness, with which the task has been undertaken have depended largely upon the wider, even if vaguer, operation of philosophy.

But the student of philosophy knows more than that the problem of knowledge has been with increasing urgency and definiteness the persistent and comprehensive problem. So conscious is he of the two opposed theories regarding the nature of science, that he often forgets the underlying bond of unity of which we have been speaking. These two opposing schools are those which we know as the sensationalist and the intellectualist, the empiricist and the rationalist. Admitting that the dominance of the question of the possibility and nature of knowledge is at bottom a fundamental question of practice and of social direction, is *this* distinction anything more than the clash of scholastic opinions, a rivalry of ideas meaningless for conduct?

I think it is. Having made so many sweeping assertions I must venture one more. Fanciful and forced as it may seem, I would say that the sensational and empirical schools represent in conscious and reflective form the continuation of the principle of the northern and barbarian side of medieval life; while the intellectualist and the rationalist stand for the conscious elaboration of the principle involved in the Graeco-Roman tradition.

Once more, as I cannot hope to prove, let me expand and illustrate. The sensationalist has staked himself upon the possibility of explaining and justifying knowledge by conceiving it as the grouping and combination of the qualities directly given us in sensation. The special reasons advanced in support of this position are sufficiently technical and remote. But the motive which has kept the sensationalist at work, which animated Hobbes and Locke, Hume and John Stuart Mill, Voltaire and Diderot, was a human not a scholastic one. It was the belief that only in sensation do we get any personal contact with reality, and hence, any genuine guarantee of vital truth. Thought is pale, and remote from the concrete stuff of knowledge and experience. It only formulates and duplicates; it only divides and recombines that fullness of vivid reality got directly and at first hand in sense experience. Reason, compared with sense, is indirect, emasculate, and faded.

Moreover, reason and thought in their very generality seem to lie beyond and outside the individual. In this remoteness, when they claim any final value, they violate the very first principle of the modern consciousness. What is the distinguishing characteristic of modern life, unless it be precisely that the individual shall not simply get, and reason about, truth in the abstract, but shall make it his own in the most intimate and personal way? He has not only to know the truth in the sense of knowing about it, but he must feel it. What is sensation but the answer to this demand for the most individual and intimate contact with reality? Show me a sensation-alist and I will show you not only one who believes that he is on the side of concreteness and definiteness, as against washed-out abstractions and misty general notions: but also one who believes that he is identified with the cause of the individual as distinct from that of external authority. We have only to go to our Locke and our Mill to see that opposition to the innate and the *a priori* felt to be opposition to the deification of hereditary prejudice and to the reception of ideas without examination or criticism. Personal contact with reality through sensation seemed to be the only safeguard from opinions which, while masquerading in the guise of absolute and eternal truth, were in reality but the prejudices of the past become so ingrained as to insist upon being standards of truth and action.

Positively as well as negatively, the sensationalists have felt themselves to represent the side of progress. In its supposed eternal character, a general notion stands ready made, fixed forever, without reference to time, without the possibility of change or diversity. As distinct from this, the sensation represents the never-failing eruption of the new. It is the novel, the unexpected, that which cannot be reasoned out in eternal formula, but must be hit upon in the ever-changing flow of our experience. It thus represents stimulation, excitation, momentum onwards. It gives a constant protest against the assumption of any theory or belief to possess finality; and it supplies the ever-renewed presentation of material out of which to build up new objects and new laws.

The sensationalist appears to have a good case. He stands for vividness and definiteness against abstraction; for the engagement of the individual in experience as against the remote and general thought about experience; and for progress and for variety against the eternal fixed monotony of the concept. But what says the rationalist? What value has experience, he inquires, if it is simply a chaos of disintegrated and floating débris? What is the worth of personality and individuality when they are reduced to crudity of brute feeling and sheer intensity of impulsive reaction? What is there left in progress that we should desire it, when it has become a mere unregulated flux of transitory sensations, coming and going without reasonable motivation or rational purpose?

Thus the intellectualist has endeavored to frame the structure of knowledge as a well-ordered economy, where reason is sovereign, where the permanent is the standard of reference for the changing, and where the individual may always escape from his own mere individuality and find support and reinforcement in a system of relations that lies outside of and yet gives validity to his own passing states of consciousness. Thus the rationalists hold that we must find in a universal intelligence a source of truth and guarantee of value that is sought in vain in the confused and flowing mass of sensations.

The rationalist, in making the concept or general idea the all-important thing in knowledge, believes himself to be asserting the interests of order as against destructive caprice and the license of momentary whim. He finds that his cause is bound up with that of the discovery of truth as the necessary instrument and method for action. Only by reference to the general and the rational can the individual find perspective, secure direction for his appetites and impulses, and escape from the uncontrolled and ruinous reactions of his own immediate tendency.

The concept, once more, in its very generality, in its elevation above the intensities and conflicts of momentary passions and interests, is the conserver of the experience of the past. It is the wisdom of the past put into capitalized and funded form to enable the individual to get away from the stress and competition of the needs of the passing moment. It marks the difference between barbarism and civilization, between continuity and disintegration, between the sequence of tradition that is the necessity of intelligent thought and action, and the random and confused excitation of the hour.

When we thus consider not the details of the positions of the sensationalist and rationalist, but the motives that have induced them to assume these positions, we discover what is meant in saying that the question is still a practical, a social one, and that the two schools stand for certain one-sided factors of social life. If we have on one side the demand for freedom, for personal initiation into experience, for variety and progress, we have on the other side the demand for general order, for continuous and organized unity, for the conservation of the dearly bought resources of the past. This is what I mean by saying that the sensationalist abstracts in conscious form the position and tendency of the Germanic element in modern civilization, the factor of appetite and impulse, of keen enjoyment and satisfaction, of stimulus and initiative. Just so the rationalist erects into conscious abstraction the principle of the Graeco-Roman world, that of control, of system, of order and authority.

That the principles of freedom and order, of past and future, or conservation and progress, of incitement to action and control of that incitation, are correlative, I shall not stop to argue. It may be worth while, however, to point out that exactly the same correlative and mutually implicating connection exists between sensationalism and rationalism, considered as philosophical accounts of the origin and nature of knowledge.

The strength of each school lies in the weakness of its opponent. The more the sensationalist appears to succeed in reducing knowledge to the associations of sensation, the more he creates a demand for thought to introduce background and relationship. The more consistent the sensationalist, the more openly he reveals the sensation in its own nakedness crying aloud for a clothing of value and meaning which must be borrowed from reflective and rational interpretation. On the other hand, the more reason and the system of relations that make up the functioning of reason are magnified, the more is felt the need of sensation to bring reason into some fruitful contact with the materials of experience. Reason must have the stimulus of this contact in order to be incited to its work and to get materials to operate with. The cause, then, why neither school can come to rest in itself is precisely that each abstracts one essential factor of conduct.

This suggests, finally, that the next move in philosophy is precisely to transfer attention from the details of the position assumed, and the arguments used in these two schools, to the practical motives that have unconsciously controlled the discussion. The positions have been sufficiently elaborated. Within the past one hundred years, within especially the last generation, each has succeeded in fully stating its case. The result, if we remain at this point, is practically a deadlock. Each can make out its case against the other. To stop at such a point is a patent absurdity. If we are to get out of the cul-de-sac it must be by bringing into consciousness the tacit reference to action that all the time has been the controlling factor.

In a word, another great rhythmic movement is seen to be approaching its end. The demand for science and philosophy was the demand for truth and a sure standard of truth which the new-born individual might employ in his efforts to build up a new world to afford free scope to the powers stirring within him. The urgency and acuteness of this demand caused, for the time being, the transfer of attention from the nature of practice to that of knowledge. The highly theoretical and abstract character of modern epistemology, combined with the fact that this highly abstract and theoretic problem has continuously engaged the attention of thought for more than three centuries, is, to my mind, proof positive that the question of knowledge was for the time being the point in which the question of practice centered, and through which it must find outlet and solution.

We return, then, to our opening problem: the meaning of the question of the possibility of knowledge raised by Kant a century ago, and of his assertion that sensation without thought is blind, thought without sensation empty. Once more I recall to the student of philosophy how this assertion of Kant has haunted and determined the course of philosophy in the intervening years—how his solution at once seems inevitable and unsatisfactory. It is inevitable in that no one can fairly deny that both sense and reason are implicated in every fruitful and significant statement of the world; unconvincing because we are after all left with these two opposed things still at war with each other, plus the miracle of their final combination.

When I say that the only way out is to place the whole modern industry of epistemology in relation to the conditions that gave it birth and the function it has to fulfill, I mean that the unsatisfactory character of the entire neo-Kantian movement lies in its assumption that knowledge gives birth to itself and is capable of affording its own justification. The solution that is always sought and never found so long as we deal with knowledge as a self-sufficing purveyor of reality, reveals itself when we conceive of knowledge as a statement of action, that statement being necessary, moreover, to the successful ongoing of action.

The entire problem of medieval philosophy is that of absorption, of assimilation. The result was the creation of the individual. Hence the problem of modern life is that of reconstruction, reform, reorganization. The entire content of experience needs to be passed through the alembic of individual agency and realization. The individual is to be the bearer of civilization; but this involves a remaking of the civilization that he bears. Thus we have the dual question: How can the individual become the organ of corporate action? How can he make over the truth authoritatively embodied in institutions of church and state into frank, healthy, and direct expressions of the simple act of free living? On the other hand, how can civilization preserve its own integral value and import when subordinated to the agency of the individual instead of exercising supreme sway over him?

The question of knowledge, of the discovery and statement of truth, gives the answer to this question; and it alone gives the answer. Admitting that the practical problem of modern life is the maintenance of the moral values of civilization through the medium of the insight and decision of the individual, the problem is fore-doomed to futile failure save as the individual in performing his task can work with a definite and controllable tool. This tool is science. But this very fact, constituting the dignity of science and measuring the importance of the philosophic theory of knowledge, conferring upon them the religious value once attaching to dogma and the disciplinary significance once belonging to political rules, also sets their limit. The servant is not above his master.

When a theory of knowledge forgets that its value rests in solving the problem out of which it has arisen, viz., that of securing a method of action; when it forgets that it has to work out the conditions under which the individual may freely direct himself without loss to the historic values of civilization—when it forgets these things it begins to cumber the ground. It is a luxury, and hence a social nuisance and disturber. Of course, in the very nature of things, every means or instrument will for a while absorb attention so that it becomes the end. Indeed it is the end when it is an indispensable condition of onward movement. But when once the means have been worked out they must operate as such. When the nature and method of knowledge are fairly understood, then interest must transfer itself from the possibility of knowledge to the possibility of its application to life.

The sensationalist has played his part in bringing to effective recognition the demand in valid knowledge for individuality of experience, for personal participation in materials of knowledge. The rationalist has served his time in making it clear once for all that valid knowledge requires organization, and the operation of a relatively permanent and general factor. The Kantian epistemologist has formulated the claims of both schools in defining judgment as the relation of perception and conception. But when it goes on to state that this relation is itself knowledge, or can be found in knowledge, it stultifies itself. Knowledge can define the percept and elaborate the concept, but their union can be found only in action. The experimental method of modern science, its erection into the ultimate mode of verification, is simply this fact obtaining recognition. Only action can reconcile the old, the general, and the permanent with the changing, the individual, and the new. It is action as progress, as development, making over the wealth of the past into capital with which to do an enlarging and freer business, that alone can find its way out of the cul-de-sac of the theory of knowledge. Each of the older movements passed away because of its own success, failed because it did its work, died in accomplishing its purpose. So also with the modern philosophy of knowledge; there must come a time when we have so much knowledge in detail, and understand so well its method in general, that it ceases to be a problem. It becomes a tool. If the problem of knowledge is not intrinsically meaningless and absurd it must in course of time be solved. Then the dominating interest becomes the *use* of knowledge; the conditions under which and ways in which it may be most organically and effectively employed to direct conduct.

Thus the Socratic period recurs; but recurs with the deepened meaning of the intervening weary years of struggle, confusion, and conflict in the growth of the recognition of the need of patient and specific methods of interrogation. So, too, the authoritative and institutional truth of scholasticism recurs, but recurs borne up upon the vigorous and conscious shoulders of the freed individual who is aware of his own intrinsic relations to truth, and who glories in his ability to carry civilization—not merely to carry it, but to carry it on. Thus another swing in the rhythm of theory and practice begins.

How does this concern us as philosophers? For the world it means that philosophy is henceforth a method and not an original fountain head of truth, nor an ultimate standard of reference. But what is involved for philosophy itself in this change? I make no claims to being a prophet, but I venture one more and final unproved statement, believing, with all my heart, that it is justified both by the moving logic of the situation, and by the signs of the times. I refer to the growing transfer of interest from metaphysics and the theory of knowledge to psychology and social ethics—including in the latter term all the related concrete social sciences, so far as they may give guidance to conduct.

There are those who see in psychology only a particular science which they are pleased to term purely empirical (unless it happen to restate in changed phraseology the metaphysics with which they are familiar). They see in it only a more or less incoherent mass of facts, interesting because relating to human nature, but below the natural sciences in point of certainty and definiteness, as also far below pure philosophy as to comprehensiveness and ability to deal with fundamental issues. But if I may be permitted to dramatize a little the position of the psychologist, he can well afford to continue patiently at work, unmindful of the occasional supercilious sneers of the epistemologist. The cause of modern civilization stands and falls with the ability of the individual to serve as its agent and bearer. And psychology is naught but the account of the way in which individual life is thus progressively maintained and reorganized. Psychology is the attempt to state in detail the machinery of the individual considered as the instrument and organ through which social action operates. It is the answer to Kant's demand for the formal phase of experience—how experience as such is constituted. Just because the whole burden and stress, both of conserving and advancing experience is more and more thrown upon the individual, everything which sheds light upon how the individual may weather the stress and assume the burden is precious and imperious.

Social ethics in inclusive sense is the correlative science. Dealing not with the form or mode or machinery of action, it attempts rather to make out its filling and make up the values that are necessary to constitute an experience which is worth while. The sociologist, like the psychologist, often presents himself as a camp follower of genuine science and philosophy, picking up scraps here and there and piecing them together in somewhat of an aimless fashion—fortunate indeed, if not vague and over-ambitious. Yet social ethics represents the attempt to translate philosophy from a general and therefore abstract method into a working and specific method; it is the change from inquiring into the nature of value in general to inquiring as to the *particular* values that ought to be realized in the life of every one, and as to the conditions which render possible this realization.

There are those who will see in this conception of the outcome of a four-hundred-year discussion concerning the nature and possiblity of knowledge a derogation from the high estate of philosophy. There are others who will see in it a sign that philosophy, after wandering aimlessly hither and yon in a wilderness without purpose or outcome, has finally come to its senses—has given up metaphysical absurdities and unverifiable speculations, and become a purely positive science of phenomena. But there are yet others who will see in this movement the fulfillment of its vocation, the clear consciousness of a function that it has always striven to perform; and who will welcome it as a justification of the long centuries when it appeared to sit apart, far from the common concerns of man, busied with discourse of essence and cause, absorbed in argument concerning subject and object, reason and sensation. To such this outcome will appear the inevitable sequel of the saying of Socrates that "an unexamined life is not one fit to be led by man"; and a better response to his injunction "Know thyself."

7

The Need for a Recovery of Philosophy

I

A criticism of current philosophizing from the standpoint of the traditional quality of its problems must begin somewhere, and the choice of a beginning is arbitrary. It has appeared to me that the notion of experience implied in the questions most actively discussed gives a natural point of departure. For, if I mistake not, it is just the inherited view of experience common to the empirical school and its opponents which keeps alive many discussions even of matters that on their face are quite remote from it, while it is also this view which is most untenable in the light of existing science and social practice. Accordingly I set out with a brief statement of some of the chief contrasts between the orthodox description of experience and that congenial to present conditions.

(i) In the orthodox view, experience is regarded primarily as a knowledge-affair. But to eyes not looking through ancient spectacles, it assuredly appears as an affair of the intercourse of a living being with its physical and social environment. (ii) According to tradition experience is (at least primarily) a psychical thing, infected throughout by "subjectivity." What experience suggests about itself is a genuinely objective world which enters into the actions and sufferings of men and undergoes modifications through their responses. (iii) So far as anything beyond a bare present is recognized by the established doctrine, the past exclusively counts. Registration

SOURCE: From *Creative Intelligence: Essays in the Pragmatic Attitude* (1917). Reprinted with the permission of The Center for Dewey Studies, Southern Illinois University at Carbondale.

of what has taken place, reference to precedent, is believed to be the essence of experience. Empiricism is conceived of as tied up to what has been, or is, "given." But experience in its vital form is experimental, an effort to change the given; it is characterized by projection, by reaching forward into the unknown; connection with a future is its salient trait. (iv) The empirical tradition is committed to particularism. Connections and continuities are supposed to be foreign to experience, to be by-products of dubious validity. An experience that is an undergoing of an environment and a striving for its control in new directions is pregnant with connections. (v) In the traditional notion experience and thought are antithetical terms. Inference, so far as it is other than a revival of what has been given in the past, goes beyond experience; hence it is either invalid, or else a measure of desperation by which, using experience as a springboard, we jump out to a world of stable things and other selves. But experience, taken free of the restrictions imposed by the older concept, is full of inference. There is, apparently, no conscious experience without inference; reflection is native and constant.

These contrasts, with a consideration of the effect of substituting the account of experience relevant to modern life for the inherited account, afford the subject matter of the following discussion.

Suppose we take seriously the contribution made to our idea of experience by biology—not that recent biological science discovered the facts, but that it has so emphasized them that there is no longer an excuse for ignoring them or treating them as negligible. Any account of experience must now fit into the consideration that experiencing means living; and that living goes on in and because of an environing medium, not in a vacuum. Where there is experience, there is a living being. Where there is life, there is a double connection maintained with the environment. In part, environmental energies constitute organic functions; they enter into them. Life is not possible without such direct support by the environment. But while all organic changes depend upon the natural energies of the environment for their origination and occurrence, the natural energies sometimes carry the organic functions prosperously forward, and sometimes act counter to their continuance. Growth and decay, health and disease, are alike continuous with activities of the natural surroundings. The difference lies in the bearing of what happens upon future life activity. From the standpoint of this future reference environmental incidents fall into groups: those favorable-to-life activities, and those hostile.

The successful activities of the organism, those within which environmental assistance is incorporated, react upon the environment to bring about modifications favorable to their own future. The human being has upon his hands the problem of responding to what is going on around him so that these changes will take one turn rather than another, namely, that required by his own further functioning. While backed in part by the environment, its life is anything but a peaceful exhalation of environment. It is obliged to struggle—that is to say, to employ the direct support given by the environment in order indirectly to effect changes that would not otherwise occur. In this sense, life goes on by means of controlling the environment. Its activities must change the changes going on around it; they must neutralize hostile occurrences; they must transform neutral events into co-operative factors or into an efflorescence of new features.

Dialectic developments of the notion of self-preservation, of the *conatus essendi,* often ignore all the important facts of the actual process. They argue as if self-control, self-development, went on directly as a sort of unrolling push from within. But life endures only in virtue of the support of the environment. And since the environment is only incompletely enlisted in our behalf, self-preservation—or self-realization or whatever—is always indirect—always an affair of the way in which our present activities affect the direction taken by independent changes in the surroundings. Hindrances must be turned into means.

We are also given to playing loose with the conception of adjustment, as if that meant something fixed—a kind of accommodation once for all (ideally at least) of the organism *to* an environment. But as life requires the fitness of the environment to the organic functions, adjustment to the environment means not passive acceptance of the latter, but acting so that the environing changes take a certain turn. The "higher" the type of life, the more adjustment takes the form of an adjusting of the factors of the environment to one another in the interest of life; the less the significance of living, the more it becomes an adjustment to a given environment till at the lower end of the scale the differences between living and the nonliving disappear.

These statements are of an external kind. They are about the conditions of experience, rather than about experiencing itself. But assuredly experience as it concretely takes place bears out the statements. Experience is primarily a process of undergoing: a process of standing something; of suffering and passion, of affection, in the literal sense of these words. The organism has to endure, to undergo, the consequences of its own actions. Experience is no slipping along in a path fixed by inner consciousness. Private consciousness is an incidental outcome of experience of a vital objective sort; it is not its source. Undergoing, however, is never mere passivity. The most patient patient is more than a receptor. He is also an agent—a re-actor, one trying experiments, one concerned with undergoing in a way which may influence what is still to happen. Sheer endurance, side-stepping evasions, are, after all, ways of treating the environment with a view to what such treatment will accomplish. Even if we shut ourselves up in the most clam-like fashion, we are doing something; our passivity is an acute attitude, not an extinction of response. Just as there is no assertive action, no aggressive attack upon things as they are, which is all action, so there is no undergoing which is not on our part also a going on and a going through.

Experience, in other words, is a matter of *simultaneous* doings and sufferings. Our undergoings are experiments in varying the course of events; our active tryings are trials and tests of ourselves. This duplicity of experience shows itself in our happiness and misery, our successes and failures. Triumphs are dangerous when dwelt upon or lived off from; successes use themselves up. Any achieved equilibrium of adjustment with the environment is pre-carious because we cannot evenly keep pace with changes in the environment. These are so opposed in direction that we must choose. We must take the risk of casting in our lot with one movement or the other. Nothing can eliminate all risk, all adventure; the one thing doomed to failure is to try to keep even with the whole en-vironment at once—that is to say, to maintain the happy moment when all things go our way.

The obstacles which confront us are stimuli to variation, to novel response, and hence are occasions of progress. If a favor done us by the environment conceals a threat, so its disfavor is a potential means of hitherto unexperienced modes of success. To treat misery as anything but misery, as for example a blessing in disguise or a necessary factor in good, is disingenuous apologetics. But to say that the progress of the race has been stimulated by ills undergone, and that men have been moved by what they suffer to search out new and better courses of action is to speak veraciously.

The preoccupation of experience with things which are coming (are now coming, not just to come) is obvious to any one whose interest in experience is empirical. Since we live forward; since we live in a world where changes are going on whose issue means our weal or woe; since every act of ours modifies these changes and hence is fraught with promise, or charged with hostile energies—what should experience be but a future implicated in a present! Adjust-ment is no timeless state; it is a continuing process. To say that a change takes time may be to say something about the event which is external and uninstructive. But adjustment of organism to environment takes time in the pregnant sense; every step in the process is conditioned by reference to further changes which it effects. What is going on in the environment is the concern of the organism; not what is already "there" in accomplished and finished form. In so far as the issue of what is going on may be affected by intervention of the organism, the moving event is a challenge which stretches the agent-patient to meet what is coming. Experiencing exhibits things in their unterminated aspect moving toward determinate conclusions. The finished and done with is of import as affecting the future, not on its own account: in short, because it is not, really, done with.

Anticipation is therefore more primary than recollection; projection than summoning of the past; the prospective than the retrospective. Given a world like that in which we live, a world in which environing changes are partly favorable and partly callously indifferent, and experience is bound to be prospective in import; for any control attainable by the living creature depends upon what is done to alter the state of things. Success and failure are the primary "categories" of life; achieving of good and averting of ill are its supreme interests; hope and anxiety (which are not self-enclosed states of feeling, but active attitudes of welcome and wariness) are dominant qualities of experience. Imaginative forecast of the future is this forerunning quality of behavior rendered available for guidance in the present. Day-dreaming and castle-building and esthetic realization of what is not practically achieved are offshoots of this practical trait, or else practical intelligence is a chastened fantasy. It makes little difference. Imaginative recovery of the bygone is indispensable to successful invasion of the future, but its status is that of an instrument. To ignore its import is the sign of an undisciplined agent; but to isolate the past, dwelling upon it for its own sake and giving it the eulogistic name of knowledge, is to substitute the reminiscence of old age for effective intelligence. The movement of the agent-patient to meet the future is partial and passionate; yet detached and impartial study of the past is the only alternative to luck in assuring success to passion.

II

This description of experience would be but a rhapsodic celebration of the commonplace were it not in marked contrast to orthodox philosophical accounts. The contrast indicates that traditional accounts have not been empirical, but have been deductions, from unnamed premises, of what experience *must* be. Historic empiricism has been empirical in a technical and controversial sense. It has said, Lord, Lord, Experience, Experience; but in practice it has served ideas *forced into* experience, not *gathered from* it.

The confusion and artificiality thereby introduced into philosophical thought is nowhere more evident than in the empirical treatment of relations or dynamic continuities. The experience of a living being struggling to hold its own and make its way in an environment, physical and social, partly facilitating and partly obstructing its actions, is of necessity a matter of ties and connections, of bearings and uses. The very point of experience, so to say, is that it doesn't occur in a vacuum; its agent-patient instead of being insulated and disconnected is bound up with the movement of things by most intimate and pervasive bonds. Only because the organism is in and of the world, and its activities correlated with those of other things in multiple ways, is it susceptible to undergoing things and capable of trying to reduce objects to means of securing its good fortune. That these connections are of diverse kinds is irresistibly proved by the fluctuations which occur in its career. Help and hindrance, stimulation and inhibition, success and failure mean specifically different modes of correlation. Although the actions of things in the world are taking place in one continuous stretch of existence, there are all kinds of specific affinities, repulsions, and relative indifferences.

Dynamic connections are qualitatively diverse, just as are the centers of action. *In this sense,* pluralism, not monism, is an established empirical fact. The attempt to establish monism from consideration of the very nature of a relation is a mere piece of dialectics. Equally dialectical is the effort to establish by a consideration of the nature of relations an ontological Pluralism of Ultimates: *simple and independent beings.* To attempt to get results from a consideration of the "external" nature of relations is of a piece with the attempt to deduce results from their "internal" character. Some things are relatively insulated from the influence of other things; some things are easily invaded by others; some things are fiercely attracted to conjoin their activities with those of others. Experience exhibits every kind of connection[1] from the most intimate to mere external juxtaposition.

1. The word relation suffers from ambiguity. I am speaking here of *connection*, dynamic and functional interaction. "Relation" is a term used also to express logical reference. I suspect that much of the controversy about internal and external relations is due to this ambiguity. One passes at will from existential connections of things to logical relationship of terms. Such an identification of existences with *terms* is congenial to idealism, but is paradoxical in a professed realism.

Empirically, then, active bonds of continuities of all kinds, together with static discontinuities, characterize existence. To deny this qualitative heterogeneity is to reduce the struggles and difficulties of life, its comedies and tragedies, to illusion: to the nonbeing of the Greeks or to its modern counterpart, the "subjective." Experience is an affair of facilitations and checks, of being sustained and disrupted, being let alone, being helped and troubled, of good fortune and defeat in all the countless qualitative modes which these words pallidly suggest. The existence of genuine connections of all manner of heterogeneity cannot be doubted. Such words as conjoining, disjoining, resisting, modifying, saltatory, and ambulatory (to use James's picturesque term) only hint at their actual heterogeneity.

Among the revisions and surrenders of historic problems demanded by this feature of empirical situations, those centering in the rationalistic-empirical controversy may be selected for attention. The implications of this controversy are twofold: First, that connections are as homogeneous in fact as in name; and, secondly, if genuine, are all due to thought, or, if empirical, are arbitrary by-products of past particulars. The stubborn particularism of orthodox empiricism is its outstanding trait; consequently the opposed rationalism found no justification of bearings, continuities, and ties save to refer them in gross to the work of a hyper-empirical Reason.

Of course, not all empiricism prior to Hume and Kant was sensationalistic, pulverizing "experience" into isolated sensory qualities or simple ideas. It did not all follow Locke's lead in regarding the entire content of generalization as the "workmanship of the understanding." On the Continent, prior to Kant, philosophers were content to draw a line between empirical generalization regarding matters of fact and necessary universals applying to truths of reason. But logical atomism was implicit even in this theory. Statements referring to empirical fact were mere quantitative summaries of particular instances. In the sensationalism which sprang from Hume (and which was left unquestioned by Kant as far as any strictly empirical element was concerned) the implicit particularism was made explicit. But the doctrine that sensations and ideas are so many separate existences was not derived from observation nor from experiment. It was a logical deduction from a prior unexamined concept of the nature of experience. From the same concept it followed that the appearance of stable objects and of general principles of connection was but an appearance.[2]

2. There is some gain in substituting a doctrine of flux and interpenetration of psychical states, *à la* Bergson, for that of rigid discontinuity. But the substitution leaves untouched the fundamental misstatement of experience, the conception of experience as directly and primarily "inner" and psychical.

Kantianism, then, naturally invoked universal bonds to restore objectivity. But, in so doing, it accepted the particularism of experience and proceeded to supplement it from nonempirical sources. A sensory manifold being all which is really empirical in experience, a reason which transcends experience must provide synthesis. The net outcome might have suggested a correct account of experience. For we have only to forget the apparatus by which the net outcome is arrived at, to have before us the experience of the plain man—a diversity of ceaseless changes connected in all kinds of ways, static and dynamic. This conclusion would deal a deathblow to both empiricism and rationalism. For, making clear the nonempirical character of the alleged manifold of unconnected particulars, it would render unnecessary the appeal to functions of the understanding in order to connect them. With the downfall of the traditional notion of experience, the appeal to reason to supplement its defects becomes superfluous.

The tradition was, however, too strongly entrenched; especially as it furnished the subject matter of an alleged science of states of mind which were directly known in their very presence. The historic outcome was a new crop of artificial puzzles about relations; it fastened upon philosophy for a long time the quarrel about the *a priori* and the *a posteriori* as its chief issue. The controversy is today quiescent. Yet it is not at all uncommon to find thinkers modern in tone and intent who regard any philosophy of experience committed to denial of the existence of genuinely general propositions, and who take empiricism to be inherently averse to the recognition of the importance of an organizing and constructive intelligence.

The quiescence alluded to is in part due, I think, to sheer weariness. But it is also due to a change of standpoint introduced by biological conceptions; and particularly the discovery of biological continuity from the lower organisms to man. For a short period, Spencerians might connect the doctrine of evolution with the old problem, and use the long temporal accumulation of "experiences" to generate something which, for human experience, is *a priori*. But the tendency of the biological way of thinking is neither to confirm or negate the Spencerian doctrine, but to shift the issue. In the orthodox position *a posteriori* and *a priori* were affairs of knowledge. But it soon becomes obvious that while there is assuredly something *a priori*—that is to say, native, unlearned, original—in human experience, that something is *not* knowledge, but is activities made possible by means of established connections of neurones. This empirical fact does not solve the orthodox problem; it dissolves it. It shows that the problem was misconceived, and solution sought by both parties in the wrong direction.

Organic instincts and organic retention, or habit-forming, are undeniable factors in actual experience. They are factors which effect organization and secure continuity. They are among the specific facts which a description of experience cognizant of the correlation of organic action with the action of other natural objects will include. But while fortunately the contribution of biological science to a truly empirical description of experiencing has outlawed the discussion of the *a priori* and *a posteriori*, the transforming effect of the same contributions upon other issues has gone unnoticed, save as pragmatism has made an effort to bring them to recognition.

III

The point seriously at issue in the notion of experience common to both sides in the older controversy thus turns out to be the place of thought or intelligence in experience. Does reason have a distinctive office? Is there a characteristic order of relations contributed by it?

Experience, to return to our positive conception, is primarily what is undergone in connection with activities whose import lies in their objective consequences—their bearing upon future experiences. Organic functions deal with things as things in course, in operation, in a state of affairs not yet given or completed. What is done with, what is just "there," is of concern only in the potentialities which it may indicate. As ended, as wholly given, it is of no account. But as a sign of what may come, it becomes an indispensable factor in behavior dealing with changes, the outcome of which is not yet determined.

The only power the organism possesses to control its own future depends upon the way its present responses modify changes which are taking place in its medium. A living being may be comparatively impotent, or comparatively free. It is all a matter of the way in which its present reactions to things influence the future reactions of things upon it. Without regard to its wish or intent every act it performs makes some difference in the environment. The change may be trivial as respects its own career and fortune. But it may also be of incalculable importance; it may import harm, destruction, or it may procure well-being.

Is it possible for a living being to increase its control of welfare and success? Can it manage, in any degree, to assure its future? Or does the amount of security depend wholly upon the accidents of the situation? Can it learn? Can it gain ability to assure its future in the present? These questions center attention upon the significance of reflective intelligence in the process of experience. The extent of an agent's capacity for inference, its power to use a given fact as a sign of something not yet given, measures the extent of its ability systematically to enlarge its control of the future.

A being which can use given and finished facts as signs of things to come; which can take given things as evidences of absent things, can, in that degree, forecast the future; it can form reasonable expectations. It is capable of achieving ideas; it is possessed of intelligence. For use of the given or finished to anticipate the consequence of processes going on is precisely what is meant by "ideas," by "intelligence."

As we have already noted, the environment is rarely all of a kind in its bearing upon organic welfare; its most wholehearted support of life activities is precarious and temporary. Some environmental changes are auspicious; others are menacing. The secret of success— that is, of the greatest attainable success—is for the organic response to cast in its lot with present auspicious changes to strengthen them and thus to avert the consequences flowing from occurrences of ill-omen. Any reaction is a venture; it involves risk. We always build better or worse than we can foretell. But the organism's fateful intervention in the course of events is blind, its choice is random, except as it can employ what happens to it as a basis of inferring what is likely to happen later. In the degree in which it can read future results in present on-goings, its responsive choice, its partiality to this condition or that, become intelligent. Its bias grows reasonable. It can deliberately, intentionally, participate in the direction of the course of affairs. Its foresight of different futures which result according as this or that present factor predominates in the shaping of affairs permits it to partake intelligently instead of blindly and fatally in the consequences its reactions give rise to. Participate it must, and to its own weal or woe. Inference, the use of what happens, to anticipate what will—or at least may—happen, makes the difference between directed and undirected participation. And this capacity for inferring is precisely the same as that use of natural occurrences for the discovery and determination of consequences— the formation of new dynamic connections—which constitutes knowledge.

The fact that thought is an intrinsic feature of experience is fatal to the traditional empiricism which makes it an artificial by-product. But for that same reason it is fatal to the historic rationalisms whose justification was the secondary and retrospective position assigned to thought by empirical philosophy. According to the particularism of the latter, thought was inevitably only a bunching together of hard-and-fast separate items; thinking was but the gathering together and tying of items already completely given, or

else an equally artificial untying—a mechanical adding and sub-
tracting of the given. It was but a cumulative registration, a consolidated merger; generality was a matter of bulk, not of quality.
Thinking was therefore treated as lacking constructive power; even
its organizing capacity was but simulated, being in truth but arbitrary pigeon-holing. Genuine projection of the novel, deliberate
variation and invention, are idle fictions in such a version of experience. If there ever was creation, it all took place at a remote period.
Since then the world has only recited lessons.

The value of inventive construction is too precious to be disposed
of in this cavalier way. Its unceremonius denial afforded an opportunity to assert that in addition to experience the subject has a
ready-made faculty of thought or reason which transcends experience. Rationalism thus accepted the account of experience given by
traditional empiricism, and introduced reason as extra-empirical.
There are still thinkers who regard any empiricism as necessarily
commited to a belief in a cut-and-dried reliance upon disconnected
precedents, and who hold that all systematic organization of past
experiences for new and constructive purposes is alien to strict
empiricism.

Rationalism never explained, however, how a reason extraneous
to experience could enter into helpful relation with concrete experiences. By definition, reason and experience were antithetical, so that
the concern of reason was not the fruitful expansion and guidance
of the course of experience, but a realm of considerations too sub-
lime to touch, or be touched by, experience. Discreet rationalists
confined themselves to theology and allied branches of abstruse
science, and to mathematics. Rationalism would have been a doctrine reserved for academic specialists and abstract formalists had it
not assumed the task of providing an apologetics for traditional
morals and theology, thereby getting into touch with actual human
beliefs and concerns. It is notorious that historic empiricism was
strong in criticism and in demolition of outworn beliefs, but weak
for purposes of constructive social direction. But we frequently overlook the fact that whenever rationalism cut free from conservative
apologetics, it was also simply an instrumentality for pointing out
inconsistencies and absurdities in existing beliefs—a sphere in which
it was immensely useful, as the Enlightment shows. Leibniz and
Voltaire were contemporary rationalists in more senses than one.[3]

3. Mathematical science in its formal aspects, or as a branch of formal logic,
has been the empirical stronghold of rationalism. But an empirical empiricism,
in contrast with orthodox deductive empiricism, has no difficulty in establishing
its jurisdiction as to deductive functions.

The recognition that reflection is a genuine factor within experience and an indispensable factor in that control of the world which secures a prosperous and significant expansion of experience undermines historic rationalism as assuredly as it abolishes the foundations of historic empiricism. The bearing of a correct idea of the place and office of reflecting upon modern idealisms is less obvious, but no less certain.

One of the curiosities of orthodox empiricism is that its outstanding speculative problem is the existence of an "external world." For in accordance with the notion that experience is attached to a private subject as its exclusive possession, a world like the one in which we appear to live must be "external" to experience instead of being its subject matter. I call it a curiosity, for if anything seems adequately grounded empirically it is the existence of a world which resists the characteristic functions of the subject of experience; which goes its way, in some respects, independently of these functions, and which frustrates our hopes and intentions. Ignorance, which is fatal, disappointment, the need of adjusting means and ends to the course of nature would seem to be facts sufficiently characterizing empirical situations as to render the existence of an external world indubitable.

That the description of experience was arrived at by forcing actual empirical facts into conformity with dialectic developments from a concept of a knower outside of the real world of nature is testified to by the historic alliance of empiricism and idealism.[4] According to the most logically consistent editions of orthodox empiricism, all that can be experienced is the fleeting, the momentary, mental state. That alone is absolutely and indubitably present; therefore, it alone is cognitively certain. It alone is *knowledge*. The existence of the past (and of the future), of a decently stable world and of other selves—indeed, of one's own self—falls outside this datum of experience. These can be arrived at only by inference which is "ejective"— a name given to an alleged type of inference that jumps from experience as from a springboard, to something beyond experience. . . .

IV

Why has the description of experience been so remote from the facts of empirical situations? To answer this question throws light

---

4. It is a shame to devote the word idealism, with its latent moral, practical connotations, to a doctrine whose tenets are the denial of the existence of a physical world, and the psychical character of all objects—at least as far as they are knowable. But I am following usage, not attempting to make it.

upon the submergence of recent philosophizing in epistemology—
that is, in discussion of the nature, possibility, and limits of knowledge in general, and in the attempt to reach conclusions regarding
the ultimate nature of reality from the answers given to such
questions.

The reply to the query regarding the currency of a nonempirical
doctrine of experience (even among professed empiricists) is that
the traditional account is derived from a conception once universally entertained regarding the subject or bearer or center of
experience. The description of experience has been forced into
conformity with this prior conception; it has been primarily a deduction from it, actual empirical facts being poured into the moulds
of the deductions. The characteristic feature of this prior notion
is the assumption that experience centers in, or gathers about, or
proceeds from a center or subject which is outside the course of
natural existence, and set over against it—it being of no importance,
for present purposes, whether this antithetical subject is termed
soul, or spirit, or mind, or ego, or consciousness, or just knower or
knowing subject.

There are plausible grounds for thinking that the currency of
the idea in question lies in the form which men's religious preoccupations took for many centuries. These were deliberately and
systematically other-worldly. They centered about a Fall which was
not an event in nature, but an aboriginal catastrophe that corrupted
Nature; about a redemption made possible by supernatural means;
about a life in another world—essentially, not merely spatially,
Other. The supreme drama of destiny took place in a soul or spirit
which, under the circumstances, could not be conceived other than
as nonnatural—extranatural, if not, strictly speaking, supernatural.
When Descartes and others broke away from medieval interests,
they retained as commonplaces its intellectual apparatus: Such as,
knowledge is exercised by a power that is extranatural and set over
against the world to be known. Even if they had wished to make a
complete break, they had nothing to put as knower in the place of
the soul. It may be doubted whether there was any available
empirical substitute until science worked out the fact that physical
changes are functional correlations of energies, and that man is
continuous with other forms of life, and until social life had developed an intellectually free and responsible individual as its
agent.

But my main point is not dependent upon any particular theory
as to the historic origin of the notion about the bearer of experience. The point is there on its own account. The essential thing

is that the bearer was conceived as outside of the world; so that experience consisted in the bearer's being affected through a type of operations not found anywhere in the world, while knowledge consists in surveying the world, looking at it, getting the view of a spectator.

The theological problem of attaining knowledge of God as ultimate reality was transformed in effect into the philosophical problem of the possibility of attaining knowledge of reality. For how is one to get beyond the limits of the subject and subjective occurrences? Familiarity breeds credulity oftener than contempt. How can a problem be artificial when men have been busy discussing it almost for three hundred years? But if the assumption that experience is something set over against the world is contrary to fact, then the problem of how self or mind or subjective experience or consciousness can reach knowledge of an external world is assuredly a meaningless problem. Whatever questions there may be about knowledge, they will not be the kind of problems which have formed epistemology.

The problem of knowledge as conceived in the industry of epistemology is the problem of knowledge *in general*—of the possibility, extent, and validity of knowledge in general. What does this "in general" mean? In ordinary life there are problems a-plenty of knowledge in particular; every conclusion we try to reach, theoretical or practical, affords such a problem. But there is no problem of knowledge in general. I do not mean, of course, that general statements cannot be made about knowledge, or that the problem of attaining these general statements is not a genuine one. On the contrary, specific instances of success and failure in inquiry exist, and are of such a character that one can discover the conditions conducing to success and failure. Statement of these conditions constitutes logic, and is capable of being an important aid in proper guidance of further attempts at knowing. But this logical problem of knowledge is at the opposite pole from the epistemological. Specific problems are about right conclusions to be reached—which means, in effect, right ways of going about the business of inquiry. They imply a difference between knowledge and error consequent upon right and wrong methods of inquiry and testing; not a difference between experience and the world. The problem of knowledge *überhaupt* exists because it is assumed that there is a knower in general, who is outside of the world to be known, and who is defined in terms antithetical to the traits of the world. With analogous assumptions, we could invent and discuss a problem of digestion in general. All that would be required would be to conceive the stomach and food material as inhabiting different worlds. Such an assumption would leave on our hands the question of the possibility, extent, nature, and genuineness of any transaction between stomach and food.

But because the stomach and food inhabit a continuous stretch of existence, because digestion is but a correlation of diverse activities in one world, the problems of digestion are specific and plural: What are the particular correlations which constitute it? How does it proceed in different situations? What is favorable and what unfavorable to its best performance?—and so on. Can one deny that if we were to take our clue from the present empirical situation, including the scientific notion of evolution (biological continuity) and the existing arts of control of nature, subject and object would be treated as occupying the same natural world as unhesitatingly as we assume the natural conjunction of an animal and its food? Would it not follow that knowledge is one way in which natural energies co-operate? Would there be any problem save discovery of the peculiar structure of this co-operation, the conditions under which it occurs to best effect, and the consequences which issue from its occurrence?

It is a commonplace that the chief divisions of modern philosophy, idealism in its different kinds, realisms of various brands, so-called common-sense dualism, agnosticism, relativism, phenomenalism, have grown up around the epistemological problem of the general relation of subject and object. Problems not openly epistemological, such as whether the relation of changes in consciousness to physical changes is one of interaction, parallelism, or automatism have the same origin. What becomes of philosophy, consisting largely as it does of different answers to these questions, in case the assumptions which generate the questions have no empirical standing? Is it not time that philosophers turned from the attempt to determine the comparative merits of various replies to the questions to a consideration of the claims of the questions?

When dominating religious ideas were built up about the idea that the self is a stranger and pilgrim in this world; when morals, falling in line, found true good only in inner states of a self inaccessible to anything but its own private introspection; when political theory assumed the finality of disconnected and mutually exclusive personalities, the notion that the bearer of experience is antithetical to the world instead of being in and of it was congenial. It at least had the warrant of other beliefs and aspirations. But the doctrine of biological continuity or organic evolution has destroyed the scientific basis of the conception. Morally, men are now concerned with the amelioration of the conditions of the common lot in this world. Social sciences recognize that associated life is not a matter of physical juxtaposition, but of genuine intercourse—of community of experience in a non-metaphorical sense of community. Why should we longer try to patch up and refine and stretch the old solutions till they seem to cover the change of thought and practice? Why not recognize that the trouble is with the problem?

A belief in organic evolution which does not extend unreservedly to the way in which the subject of experience is thought of, and which does not strive to bring the entire theory of experience and knowing into line with biological and social facts, is hardly more than Pickwickian. There are many, for example, who hold that dreams, hallucinations, and errors cannot be accounted for at all except on the theory that a self (or "consciousness") exercises a modifying influence upon the "real object." The logical assumption is that consciousness is outside of the real object; that it is something different in kind, and therefore has the power of changing "reality" into appearance, of introducing "relativities" into things as they are in themselves—in short, of infecting real things with subjectivity. Such writers seem unaware of the fact that this assumption makes consciousness supernatural in the literal sense of the word; and that, to say the least, the conception can be accepted by one who accepts the doctrine of biological continuity only after every other way of dealing with the facts has been exhausted.

Realists, of course (at least some of the Neorealists), deny any such miraculous intervention of consciousness. But they[5] admit the reality of the problem; denying only this particular solution, they try to find some other way out that will still preserve intact the notion of knowledge as a relationship of a general sort between subject and object.

Now dreams and hallucinations, errors, pleasures, and pains, possibly "secondary" qualities, do not occur save where there are organic centers of experience. They cluster about a subject. But to treat them as things which inhere exclusively in the subject; or as posing the problem of a distortion of *the* real object by a knower set over against the world, or as presenting facts to be explained primarily as cases of contemplative knowledge is to testify that one has still to learn the lesson of evolution in its application to the affairs in hand.

5. The "they" means the "some" of the prior sentence—those whose realism is epistemological, instead of being a plea for taking the facts of experience as we find them without refraction through epistemological apparatus.

If biological development be accepted, the subject of experience is at least an animal, continuous with other organic forms in a process of more complex organization. An animal in turn is at least continuous with chemico-physical processes which, in living things, are so organized as really to constitute the activities of life with all their defining traits. And experience is not identical with brain action; it is the entire organic agent-patient in all its interaction with the environment, natural and social. The brain is primarily an organ of a certain kind of behavior, not of knowing the world. And to repeat what has already been said, experiencing *is* just certain modes of interaction, of correlation, of natural objects among which the organism happens, so to say, to be one. It follows with equal force that experience means primarily not knowledge, but ways of doing and suffering. Knowing must be described by discovering what particular mode—qualitatively unique—of doing and suffering it is. As it is, we find experience assimilated to a nonempirical concept of knowledge, derived from an antecedent notion of a spectator outside of the world.[6]

V

What are the bearings of our discussion upon the conception of the present scope and office of philosophy? What do our conclusions indicate and demand with reference to philosophy itself? For the philosophy which reaches such conclusions regarding knowledge and mind must apply them, sincerely and wholeheartedly, to its idea of its own nature. For philosophy claims to be one form or mode of knowing. If, then, the conclusion is reached that knowing is a way of employing empirical occurrences with respect to increasing power to direct the consequences which flow from things, the application of the conclusion must be made to philosophy itself. It, too, becomes not a contemplative survey of existence nor

6. It is interesting to note that some of the realists who have assimilated the cognitive relation to other existential relations in the world (instead of treating it as an unique or epistemological relation) have been forced in support of their conception of knowledge as a "presentative" or spectatorial affair to extend the defining features of the latter to all relations among things, and hence to make all the "real" things in the world pure "simples," wholly independent of one another. So conceived the doctrine of external relations appears to be rather the doctrine of complete externality of *things*. Aside from this point, the doctrine is interesting for its dialectical ingenuity and for the elegant development of assumed premises, rather than convincing on account of empirical evidence supporting it.

an analysis of what is past and done with, but an outlook upon future possibilities with reference to attaining the better and averting the worse. Philosophy must take, with good grace, its own medicine.

It is easier to state the negative results of the changed idea of philosophy than the positive ones. The point that occurs to mind most readily is that philosophy will have to surrender all pretension to be peculiarly concerned with ultimate reality, or with reality as a complete (i.e., completed) whole: with *the* real object. The surrender is not easy of achievement. The philosophic tradition that comes to us from classic Greek thought and that was reinforced by Christian philosophy in the Middle Ages discriminates philosophical knowing from other modes of knowing by means of an alleged peculiarly intimate concern with supreme, ultimate, true reality. To deny this trait to philosophy seems to many to be the suicide of philosophy; to be a systematic adoption of skepticism or agnostic positivism.

The pervasiveness of the tradition is shown in the fact that so vitally a contemporary thinker as Bergson, who finds a philosophic revolution involved in abandonment of the traditional identification of the truly real with the fixed (an identification inherited from Greek thought), does not find it in his heart to abandon the counterpart identification of philosophy with search for the truly Real; and hence he finds it necessary to substitute an ultimate and absolute flux for an ultimate and absolute permanence. Thus his great empirical services in calling attention to the fundamental importance of considerations of time for problems of life and mind get compromised with a mystic, nonempirical "Intuition"; and we find him preoccupied with solving, by means of his new idea of ultimate reality, the traditional problems of realities-in-themselves and phenomena, matter and mind, free will and determinism, God and the world. Is not that another evidence of the influence of the classic idea about philosophy?

Even the new realists are not content to take their realism as a plea for approaching subject matter directly instead of through the intervention of epistemological apparatus; they find it necessary first to determine the status of *the* real object. Thus they too become entangled in the problem of the possibility of error, dreams, hallucinations, etc., in short, the problem of evil. For I take it that an uncorrupted realism would accept such things as real events, and find in them no other problems than those attending the consideration of any real occurrence—namely, problems of structure, origin, and operation.

It is often said that pragmatism, unless it is content to be a contribution to mere methodology, must develop a theory of Reality. But the chief characteristic trait of the pragmatic notion of reality is precisely that no theory of Reality in general, *überhaupt,* is possible or needed. It occupies the position of an emancipated empiricism or a thoroughgoing naïve realism. It finds that "reality" is a *denotative* term, a word used to designate indifferently everything that happens. Lies, dreams, insanities, deceptions, myths, theories are all of them just the events which they specifically are. Pragmatism is content to take its stand with science; for science finds all such events to be subject matter of description and inquiry —just like stars and fossils, mosquitoes and malaria, circulation and vision. It also takes its stand with daily life, which finds that such things really have to be reckoned with as they occur interwoven in the texture of events.

The only way in which the term reality can ever become more than a blanket denotative term is through recourse to specific events in all their diversity and thatness. Speaking summarily, I find that the retention by philosophy of the notion of a Reality feudally superior to the events of everyday occurrence is the chief source of the increasing isolation of philosophy from common sense and science. For the latter do not operate in any such region. As with them of old, philosophy in dealing with real difficulties finds itself still hampered by reference to realities more real, more ultimate, than those which directly happen.

I have said that identifying the cause of philosophy with the notion of superior reality is the cause of an *increasing* isolation from science and practical life. The phrase reminds us that there was a time when the enterprise of science and the moral interests of men both moved in a universe invidiously distinguished from that of ordinary occurrence. While all that happens is equally real—since it really happens—happenings are not of equal worth. Their respective consequences, their import, varies tremendously. Counterfeit money, although real (or rather *because* real) is really different from a valid circulatory medium, just as disease is really different from health; different in specific structure and so different in consequences. In occidental thought, the Greeks were the first to draw the distinction between the genuine and the spurious in a generalized fashion and to formulate and enforce its tremendous significance for the conduct of life. But since they had at command no technique of experimental analysis and no adequate technique of mathematical analysis, they were compelled to treat the difference of the true and the false, the dependable and the deceptive, as signifying two kinds of existence, the truly real and the apparently real.

Two points can hardly be asserted with too much emphasis. The Greeks were wholly right in the feeling that questions of good and ill, as far as they fall within human control, are bound up with discrimination of the genuine from the spurious, of "being" from what only pretends to be. But because they lacked adequate instrumentalities for coping with this difference in specific situations, they were forced to treat the difference as a wholesale and rigid one. Science was concerned with vision of ultimate and true reality; opinion was concerned with getting along with apparent realities. Each had its appropriate region permanently marked off. Matters of opinion could never become matters of science; their intrinsic nature forbade. When the practice of science went on under such conditions, science and philosophy were one and the same thing. Both had to do with ultimate reality in its rigid and insuperable difference from ordinary occurrences.

We have only to refer to the way in which medieval life wrought the philosophy of an ultimate and supreme reality into the context of practical life to realize that for centuries political and moral interests were bound up with the distinction between the absolutely real and the relatively real. The difference was no matter of a remote technical philosophy, but one which controlled life from the cradle to the grave, from the grave to the endless life after death. By means of a vast institution, which in effect was state as well as church, the claims of ultimate reality were enforced; means of access to it were provided. Acknowledgment of The Reality brought security in this world and salvation in the next. It is not necessary to report the story of the change which has since taken place. It is enough for our purposes to note that none of the modern philosophies of a superior reality, or *the* real object, idealistic or realistic, holds that its insight makes a difference like that between sin and holiness, eternal condemnation and eternal bliss. While in its own context the philosophy of ultimate reality entered into the vital concerns of men, it now tends to be an ingenious dialectic exercise in professiorial corners by a few who have retained ancient premises while rejecting their application to the conduct of life.

The increased isolation from science of any philosophy identified with the problem of *the* real is equally marked. For the growth of science has consisted precisely in the invention of an equipment, a technique of appliances and procedures, which, accepting all occurrences as homogeneously real, proceeds to distinguish the authenticated from the spurious, the true from the false, by specific modes of treatment in specific situations. The procedures of the trained engineer, of the competent physician, of the laboratory expert, have turned out to be the only ways of discriminating the counterfeit from the valid. And they have revealed that the difference is not one of antecedent fixity of existence, but one of mode of treatment and of the consequences thereon attendant. After mankind has learned to put its trust in specific procedures in order to make its discriminations between the false and the true, philosophy arrogates to itself the enforcement of the distinction at its own cost.

More than once, this essay has intimated that the counterpart of the idea of invidiously real reality is the spectator notion of knowledge. If the knower, however defined, is set over against the world to be known, knowing consists in possessing a transcript, more or less accurate but otiose, of real things. Whether this transcript is presentative in character (as realists say) or whether it is by means of states of consciousness which represent things (as subjectivists say), is a matter of great importance in its own context. But, in another regard, this difference is negligible in comparison with the point in which both agree. Knowing is viewing from outside. But if it be true that the self or subject of experience is part and parcel of the course of events, it follows that the self *becomes* a knower. It becomes a mind in virtue of a distinctive way of partaking in the course of events. The significant distinction is no longer between the knower *and* the world; it is between different ways of being in and of the movement of things; between a brute physical way and a purposive, intelligent way.

There is no call to repeat in detail the statements which have been advanced. Their net purport is that the directive presence of future possibilities in dealing with existent conditions is what is meant by knowing; that the self becomes a knower or mind when anticipation of future consequences operates as its stimulus. What we are now concerned with is the effect of this conception upon the nature of philosophic knowing.

As far as I can judge, popular response to pragmatic philosophy was moved by two quite different considerations. By some it was thought to provide a new species of sanctions, a new mode of apologetics, for certain religious ideas whose standing had been threatened. By others, it was welcomed because it was taken as a sign that philosophy was about to surrender its otiose and speculative remoteness; that philosophers were beginning to recognize that philosophy is of account only if, like everyday knowing and like science, it affords guidance to action and thereby makes a difference in the event. It was welcomed as a sign that philosophers were willing to have the worth of their philosophizing measured by responsible tests.

I have not seen this point of view emphasized, or hardly recognized, by professional critics. The difference of attitude can probably be easily explained. The epistemological universe of discourse is so highly technical that only those who have been trained in the history of thought think in terms of it. It did not occur accordingly, to nontechnical readers to interpret the doctrine that the meaning and validity of thought are fixed by differences made in consequences and in satisfactoriness, to mean consequences in personal feelings. Those who were professionally trained, however, took the statement to mean that consciousness or mind in the mere act of looking at things modifies them. It understood the doctrine of test of validity by consequences to mean that apprehensions and conceptions are true if the modifications affected by them were of an emotionally desirable tone.

Prior discussion should have made it reasonably clear that the source of this misunderstanding lies in the neglect of temporal considerations. The change made in things by the self in knowing is not immediate and, so to say, cross-sectional. It is longitudinal—in the redirection given to changes already going on. Its analogue is found in the changes which take place in the development of, say, iron ore into a watch spring, not in those of the miracle of transubstantiation. For the static, cross-sectional, nontemporal relation of subject and object, the pragmatic hypothesis substitutes apprehension of a thing in terms of the results in other things which it is tending to effect. For the unique epistemological relation, it substitutes a practical relation of a familiar type—responsive behavior which changes in time the subject matter to which it applies. The unique thing about the responsible behavior which constitutes knowing is the specific difference which marks it off from other modes of response, namely, the part played in it by anticipation and prediction. Knowing is the act, stimulated by this foresight, of securing and averting consequences. The success of the achievement measures the standing of the foresight by which response is directed. The popular impression that pragmatic philosophy means that philosophy shall develop ideas relevant to the actual cries of life, ideas influential in dealing with them and tested by the assistance they afford, is correct.

Reference to practical response suggests, however, another misapprehension. Many critics have jumped at the obvious association of the word pragmatic with practical. They have assumed that the intent is to limit all knowledge, philosophic included, to promoting "action," understanding by action either just any bodily movement, or those bodily movements which conduce to the preservation and grosser well-being of the body. James's statement that general conceptions must "cash in" has been taken (especially by European critics) to mean that the end and measure of intelligence lies in the narrow and coarse utilities which it produces. Even an acute American thinker, after first criticizing pragmatism as a kind of idealistic epistemology, goes on to treat it as a doctrine which regards intelligence as a lubricating oil facilitating the workings of the body.

One source of the misunderstanding is suggested by the fact that "cashing in" to James meant that a general idea must always be capable of verification in specific existential cases. The notion of "cashing in" says nothing about the breadth or depth of the specific consequences. As an empirical doctrine, it could not say anything about them in general; the specific cases must speak for themselves. If one conception is verified in terms of eating beefsteak, and another in terms of a favorable credit balance in the bank, that is not because of anything in the theory, but because of the specific nature of the conceptions in question, and because there exist particular events like hunger and trade. If there are also existences in which the most liberal esthetic ideas and the most generous moral conceptions can be verified by specific embodiment, assuredly so much the better. The fact that a strictly empirical philosophy was taken by so many critics to imply an *a priori* dogma about the kind of consequences capable of existence is evidence, I think, of the inability of many philosophers to think in concretely empirical terms. Since the critics were themselves accustomed to get results by manipulating the concepts of "consequences" and of "practice," they assumed that even a would-be empiricist must be doing the same sort of thing. It will, I suppose, remain for a long time incredible to some that a philosopher should really intend to go to specific experiences to determine of what scope and depth practice admits, and what sort of consequences the world permits to come into being. Concepts are so clear; it takes so little time to develop their implications; experiences are so confused, and it requires so much time and energy to lay hold of them. And yet these same critics charge pragmatism with adopting subjective and emotional standards!

As a matter of fact, the pragmatic theory of intelligence means that the function of mind is to project new and more complex ends—to free experience from routine and from caprice. Not the use of thought to accomplish purposes already given either in the mechanism of the body or in that of the existent state of society, but the use of intelligence to liberate and liberalize action, is the pragmatic lesson. Action restricted to given and fixed ends may attain great technical efficiency; but efficiency is the only quality to which it can lay claim. Such action is mechanical (or becomes so), no matter what the scope of the preformed end, be it the Will of God or *Kultur*. But the doctrine that intelligence develops within the sphere of action for the sake of possibilities not yet given is the opposite of a doctrine of mechanical efficiency. Intelligence *as* intelligence is inherently forward-looking; only by ignoring its primary function does it become a mere means for an end already given. The latter *is* servile, even when the end is labeled moral, religious, or esthetic. But action directed to ends to which the agent has not previously been attached inevitably carries with it a quickened and enlarged spirit. A pragmatic intelligence is a creative intelligence, not a routine mechanic.

All this may read like a defense of pragmatism by one concerned to make out for it the best case possible. Such is not, however, the intention. The purpose is to indicate the extent to which intelligence frees action from a mechanically instrumental character. Intelligence is, indeed, instrumental *through* action to the determination of the qualities of future experience. But the very fact that the concern of intelligence is with the future, with the as-yet-unrealized (and with the given and the established only as conditions of the realization of possibilities), makes the action in which it takes effect generous and liberal; free of spirit. Just that action which extends and approves intelligence has an intrinsic value of its own in being instrumental—the intrinsic value of being informed with intelligence in behalf of the enrichment of life. By the same stroke, intelligence becomes truly liberal: knowing is a human undertaking, not an esthetic appreciation carried on by a refined class or a capitalistic possession of a few learned specialists, whether men of science or of philosophy.

More emphasis has been put upon what philosophy is not than upon what it may become. But it is not necessary, it is not even desirable, to set forth philosophy as a scheduled program. There are human difficulties of an urgent, deep-seated kind which may be clarified by trained reflection, and whose solution may be forwarded by the careful development of hypotheses. When it is understood that philosophic thinking is caught up in the actual course of events, having the office of guiding them toward a prosperous issue, problems will abundantly present themselves. Philosophy will not solve these problems; philosophy is vision, imagination, reflection—

and these functions, apart from action, modify nothing and hence resolve nothing. But in a complicated and perverse world, action which is not informed with vision, imagination, and reflection, is more likely to increase confusion and conflict than to straighten things out. It is not easy for generous and sustained reflection to become a guiding and illuminating method in action. Until it frees itself from identification with problems which are supposed to depend upon Reality as such, or its distinction from a world of Appearance, or its relation to a Knower as such, the hands of philosophy are tied. Having no chance to link its fortunes with a responsible career by suggesting things to be tried, it cannot identify itself with questions which actually arise in the vicissitudes of life. Philosophy recovers itself when it ceases to be a device for dealing with the problems of philosophers and becomes a method, cultivated by philosophers, for dealing with the problems of men.

Emphasis must vary with the stress and special impact of the troubles which perplex men. Each age knows its own ills, and seeks its own remedies. One does not have to forecast a particular program to note that the central need of any program at the present day is an adequate conception of the nature of intelligence and its place in action. Philosophy cannot disavow responsibility for many misconceptions of the nature of intelligence which now hamper its efficacious operation. It has at least a negative task imposed upon it. It must take away the burdens which it has laid upon the intelligence of the common man in struggling with his difficulties. It must deny and eject that intelligence which is naught but a distant eye, registering in a remote and alien medium the spectacle of nature and life. To enforce the fact that the emergence of imagination and thought is relative to the connection of the sufferings of men with their doings is of itself to illuminate those sufferings and to instruct those doings. To catch mind in its connection with the entrance of the novel into the course of the world is to be on the road to see that intelligence is itself the most promising of all novelties, the revelation of the meaning of that transformation of past into future which is the reality of every present. To reveal intelligence as the organ for the guidance of this transformation, the sole director of its quality, is to make a declaration of present untold significance for action. To elaborate these convictions of the connection of intelligence with what men undergo because of their doings and with the emergence and direction of the creative, the novel, in the world is of itself a program which will keep philosophers busy until something more worth while is forced upon them. For the elaboration has to be made through application to all the disciplines which have an intimate connection with human conduct: to logic, ethics, esthetics, economics, and the procedure of the sciences formal and natural.

I also believe that there is a genuine sense in which the enforcement of the pivotal position of intelligence in the world and thereby in control of human fortunes (so far as they are manageable) is the peculiar problem in the problems of life which comes home most closely to ourselves—to ourselves living not merely in the early twentieth century but in the United States. It is easy to be foolish about the connection of thought with national life. But I do not see how any one can question the distinctively national color of English, or French, or German philosophies. And if of late the history of thought has come under the domination of the German dogma of an inner evolution of ideas, it requires but a little inquiry to convince oneself that that dogma itself testifies to a particularly nationalistic need and origin. I believe that philosophy in America will be lost between chewing a historic cud long since reduced to woody fiber, or an apologetics for lost causes (lost to natural science), or a scholastic, schematic formalism, unless it can somehow bring to consciousness America's own needs and its own implicit principle of successful action.

This need and principle, I am convinced, is the necessity of a deliberate control of policies by the method of intelligence, an intelligence which is not the faculty of intellect honored in textbooks and neglected elsewhere, but which is the sum-total of impulses, habits, emotions, records, and discoveries which forecast what is desirable and undesirable in future possibilities, and which contrive ingeniously in behalf of imagined good. . . .

IV

Empirical Metaphysics

From its beginnings, pragmatic philosophy in the United States was associated with an effort to resolve the conflicts in metaphysical belief that dominated philosophy in the late nineteenth and early twentieth century. For the pragmatists, particularly Dewey's predecessors, William James and Charles Peirce, both of the metaphysical alternatives contending for philosophical dominance—materialism and idealism—represented the intellectual dead ends of their respective traditions. If metaphysical claims were possible, and the pragmatists shared the view that they could be justified in some sense, then a new method and a new option that departed from materialism and idealism were required.

In *Pragmatism*, William James had argued that the pragmatic philosophical method would mediate the seemingly insoluble conflict between materialists and idealists. In so doing, it would generate a temper of mind that was neither excessively tough-minded and limited to the determined brute facts of experience, nor naïvely tender-minded and committed to the coherently ordered ideal of a rational universe. For James, the new, pragmatic metaphysics, unlike the old, would explain how human knowledge and human effort could affect and change the open future.

There were similar tendencies in the philosophy of Charles Peirce. Some of Peirce's comments on the nature of metaphysical dispute show that conflicting metaphysical claims represent differing verbal formulations of the same empirical set of facts. These comments are an important source of the contemporaneous view that metaphysical dispute is irresolvable and metaphysical claims incapable of being proved. Yet Peirce did sketch an ambitious metaphysical theory, which can be described as evolutionary naturalism or evolutionary idealism, in which he sought to show how both change and determinism, chance and freedom, are ontological attributes of experienced things.

The philosophy of John Dewey is in the mainstream of this metaphysical tradition within pragmatic philosophy. Three aspects of the tradition are stressed in Dewey's writings on metaphysics, and they are illustrated in the selections presented here.

First is the rejection of metaphysics as a transcendental inquiry. In the essay "The Subject Matter of Metaphysical Inquiry," (1915), Dewey asserts his view that questions about "ultimate origin of the entire present state of things" are meaningless. This rejection of one kind of metaphysical quest had been formulated in "The Need for a Recovery of Philosophy" thus: "It is often said that pragmatism, unless it is content to be a contribution to mere methodology, must develop a theory of Reality. But the chief characteristic trait of the pragmatic notion of reality is precisely that no theory of Reality in general, *überhaupt,* is possible or needed." Yet Dewey argues that it is compatible with the elimination of metaphysics as a search for ultimate origins or causes to develop metaphysical inquiry as an account of "the generic traits of existence."

Second, like James and Peirce, Dewey developed many aspects of his metaphysical inquiry by polemicizing against the inadequacies of reductive or deterministic materialism on the one hand, and of rationalistic and antecedently unified idealism on the other. In this inquiry, a fidelity to the actual connection between natural events and ideal outcomes discoverable in experience by the use of scientific methods was celebrated. The viewpoint Dewey advanced on such questions as the relationship of body to mind, or more generally on the relationship of the realm of spirit to that of matter, can be characterized as an empirical naturalism.

Finally, Dewey was active in the reinterpretation of metaphysical inquiry. Like other philosophers of the early twentieth century who had become convinced of the fruitlessness of traditional metaphysics—Bergson, Husserl, even Heidegger—Dewey represented an effort to reinterpret metaphysics as a description of characteristics and conditions of human experience. Henri Bergson has sought to bypass the dispute between rationalist and empiricist by introducing a new goal for metaphysical science: intuition of direct experience. Edmund Husserl had asserted his intention to "bracket," or suspend judgment on, traditional metaphysical questions in order to turn to the immediate phenomenological field. Dewey did not share these methods or their conclusions. Yet his own descriptive metaphysics does examine experience in terms of a series of concerns, intentions, careers, ends-in-view, accomplishments and failures, rather than as a palimpsest of impressions and ideas. The categories of existence that Dewey discusses in the second chapter of *Experience and Nature* (1925), entitled "Existence as Precarious and as Stable," are preeminently those of the precarious and the stable in experience.

It is characteristic of this kind of interpretive or descriptive metaphysics that its goal is not the scientific and nontemporal correlation among abstract properties of reality, but the effort to interpret the flux of temporal existence. For that reason there is special interest in Dewey's account of the reality of time. In the essay "Time and Individuality" (1940), Dewey relates the indeterminacy of historical events and the creativeness of art to his account of the temporal.

8

The Subject Matter of Metaphysical Inquiry

A number of biologists holding to the adequacy of the mechanistic conception in biology have of late expressed views not unlike those clearly and succinctly set forth in the following quotation: "If we consider the organism simply as a system forming a part of external nature, we find no evidence that it possesses properties that may not eventually be satisfactorily analyzed by the methods of physico-chemical science; but we admit also that those peculiarities of ulti-mate constitution which have in the course of evolution led to the appearance of living beings in nature are such that we can not well deny the possibility or even legitimacy of applying a vitalistic or biocentric conception to the cosmic process [considered] as a whole."[1]

The problems connected with the organism as a part of external nature are referred to in the context of the quotation as scientific problems; those connected with the peculiarities of ultimate con-stitution as metaphysical. The context also shows that ultimate constitution is conceived in a temporal sense. Metaphysical ques-tions are said to be those having to do with "ultimate origins." Such questions lie quite beyond the application of scientific method.

SOURCE: From the *Journal of Philosophy*, vol. XII, No. 13 (June 1915), pp. 337–345. Reprinted by permission of the *Journal of Philosophy*. Several footnotes have been omitted and the remaining ones renumbered.

1. Professor Ralph S. Lillie, *Science*, XL (1914), 846. See also the references given in the article, which is entitled "The Philosophy of Biology—Vitalism *vs.* Mechanism."

"Why it [nature] exhibits certain apparently innate potentialities and modes of action which have caused it to evolve in a certain way is a question which really lies beyond the sphere of natural science." These "apparently innate potentialities and modes of action" which have caused nature as a whole to evolve in the direction of living beings are identified with "ultimate peculiarities"; and it is with reference to them that the biocentric idea has a possible legitimate application. The argument implies that when we insist upon the adequacy of the physico-chemical explanation of living organisms, we are led, in view of the continuity of evolution of organisms from nonliving things, to recognize that the world out of which life developed "held latent or potential within itself the possibility of life." In considering such a world and the nature of the potentiality which caused it to evolve living beings, we are forced, however, beyond the limits of scientific inquiry. We pass the boundary which separates it from metaphysics.

Thus is raised the question as to the nature of metaphysical inquiry. I wish to suggest that while one may accept as a preliminary demarcation of metaphysics from science the more "ultimate traits" with which the former deals, it is not necessary to identify these ultimate traits with temporally original traits—that, in fact, there are good reasons why we should not do so. We may also mark off the metaphysical subject matter by reference to certain irreducible traits found in any and every subject of scientific inquiry. With reference to the theme of evolution of living beings, the distinctive trait of metaphysical reflection would not then be its attempt to discover some temporally original feature which caused the development, but the irreducible traits of a world in which at least some changes take on an evolutionary form. A world where some changes proceed in the direction of the appearance of living and thinking creatures is a striking sort of a world. While science would trace the conditions of their occurrence in detail, connecting them in their variety with their antecedents, metaphysics would raise the question of the sort of world which *has* such an evolution, not the question of the sort of world which causes it. For the latter type of question appears either to bring us to an *impasse* or else to break up into just the questions which constitute scientific inquiry.

Any intelligible question as to causation seems to be a wholly scientific question. Starting from any given existence, be it a big thing like a solar system or a small thing like a rise of temperature, we may ask how it came about. We account for the change by linking up the thing in question with other specific existences acting in determinate ways—ways which collectively are termed physico-chemical. When we have traced back a present existence to the earlier existences with which it is connected, we may ask a like question about the occurrence of the earlier things, viewed as changes from something still earlier. And so on indefinitely; although, of course, we meet practical limits in our ability to push such questions beyond a certain indefinite point. Hence it may be said that a question about ultimate origin or ultimate causation is either a meaningless question, or else the words are used in a relative sense to designate the point in the past at which a particular inquiry breaks off. Thus we might inquire as to the "ultimate" origin of the French language. This would take us back to certain definite antecedent existences, such as persons speaking the Latin tongue, others speaking barbarian tongues; the contact of these peoples in war, commerce, political administration, education, etc. But the term "ultimate" has meaning only in relation to the particular existence in question: French speech. We are landed in another historic set of existences, having their own specific antecedents. The case is not otherwise if we ask for the ultimate origin of human speech in general. The inquiry takes us back to animal cries, gestures, etc., certain conditions of intercourse, etc. The question is, how one set of specific existences gradually passed into another. No one would think of referring to latent qualities of the Latin speech as the cause of the evolution of French; one tries to discover actual and overt features which, *interacting* with other equally specific existences, brought about this particular change. If we are likely to fall into a different mode of speech with reference to human language in general, it is because we are more ignorant of the specific circumstances under which the transition from animal cries to articulate speech with a meaning took place. Upon analysis, reference to some immanent law or cause which forced the evolution will be found to be a lazy cloak for our ignorance of the specific facts needed in order to deal successfully with the question.

Suppose we generalize the situation still more. We may ask for the ultimate origin of the entire present state of things. Taken *en masse,* such a question is meaningless. Taken in detail, it means that we may apply the same procedure distributively to each and any of the things which now exist. In each case we may trace its history to an earlier state of things. But in each case, *its* history is what we trace, and the history always lands us at some state of things in the past, regarding which the same question might be asked. That scientific inquiry does not itself deal with any question of ultimate origins, except in the purely relative sense already indicated, is, of course, recognized. But it also seems to follow from what has been said that scientific inquiry does not generate, or leave over, such a question for some other discipline, such as metaphysics, to deal with. The contrary conception with respect to the doctrine of evolution is to be explained, I think, by the fact that theology used to have the idea of ultimate origin in connection with creation, and that at a certain juncture it was natural to regard the theory of evolution as a substitute or rival of the theological idea of creation.

If all questions of causation and origin are specific scientific questions, is there any place left for metaphysical inquiry at all? If its theme can not be ultimate origin and causation, is metaphysics anything but a kind of pseudo-science whose illusory character is now to be recognized? This question takes us to the matter of whether there are ultimate, that is, irreducible, traits of the very existences with which scientific reflection is concerned. In all such investigations as those referred to above we find at least such traits as the following: specifically diverse existences, interaction, change. Such traits are found in any material which is the subject matter of inquiry in the natural science. They are found equally and indifferently whether a subject matter in question be dated 1915 or ten million years B.C. Accordingly, they would seem to deserve the name of ultimate, or irreducible, traits. As such they may be made the object of a kind of inquiry differing from that which deals with the genesis of a particular group of existences, a kind of inquiry to which the name metaphysical may be given.[2]

It may well seem as if the fact that the subject matter of science is always a plurality of diverse interacting and changing existences were too obvious and commonplace to invite or reward investiga-

2. The name at least has the sanction of the historical designation given to Aristotle's consideration of existence as existence. But it should be noted that we also find in Aristotle the seeds (which, moreover, have at places developed into flourishing growths in his own philosophy) of the conception of metaphysics rejected above. For he expressly gives the more general traits of existence the eulogistic title "divine" and identifies his first philosophy with theology, and so makes this kind of inquiry "superior" to all others, because it deals with the "highest of existing things." While he did not himself seek for this higher or supreme real in time, but rather located it, in its fullness of reality, just beyond space, this identification of existence as such with the divine led to such an identification the moment theology became supremely interested in "creation." But unless one approaches the study of the most general traits of the matter of scientific inquiry with theological presuppositions, there is, of course, no ground for the application to them of eulogistic predicates. There is no ground for thinking that they are any better or any worse, any higher or any lower, than other traits, or that any peculiar dignity attaches to a study of them.

tion. Into this point I shall not go, beyond pointing out, in connection with the present theme, that certain negative advantages in the economizing of intellectual effort would at least accrue from the study. Bare recognition of the fact just stated would wean men from the futility of concern with ultimate origins and laws of causation with which the "universe" is supposed to have been endowed at the outset. For it would reveal that, whatever the date of the subject matter which may be successfully reflected upon, we have the same situation that we have at present: diversity, specificality, change. These traits have to be begged or taken in any case. If we face this fact without squeamishness we shall be saved from the recurrent attempts to reduce heterogeneity to homogeneity, diversity to sheer uniformity, quality to quantity, and so on. That considerations of quantity and mathematical order are indispensable to the successful prosecution of researches into particular occurrences is a precious fact. It exhibits certain irreducible traits *of* the irreducible traits we have mentioned, but it does not replace them. When it tries to do so it cuts the ground out from under its own feet.

Let me emphasize this point by comment on a further quotation. "If we assume constancy of the elementary natural processes, and constancy in the modes of connection between them—as exact observation forces us to do—there seems no avoiding the conclusion that—given an undifferentiated universe at the start—only one course of evolution can ever have been possible. Laplace long ago perceived this consequence of the mechanistic view of nature, and the inevitability of [his] conclusion has never been seriously disputed by scientific men. Nevertheless, this is a very strange result, and to many has seemed a *reductio ad absurdum* of the scientific view as applied to the whole of nature."[3]

Note that the inevitable conclusion as to the predetermined course of evolution and the apparent incredibility of the conclusion both depend upon the premise "given an undifferentiated universe at the start." Now this is precisely a premise which a scientific view can not admit, for science deals with any particular existence only by tracing its occurrence to a plurality of prior changing interacting things. Any Laplacean formula would, in any case, be a formula for the structure of *some* existence *in* the world, not for the world as a "whole." The scientific grounds which made it impossible to take the world *en masse* at the present time and to give a comprehensive formula for it in its entirety apply even more strongly, if

3. Lillie, op. cit.

possible, to some earlier state of affairs. For such a formula can be reached only by tracing back a specific present phenomenon to its specific antecedents.

A curious illusion exists as to formulae for the ancient states of nature. It is frequently assumed that they denote not merely some absolute original (which is impossible), but also one from which later events unroll in a mathematically predetermined fashion. We seem to be passing in a one-sided way from the earlier to the later. The illusion vanishes when we ask where the formula came from. How was it obtained? Evidently, by beginning with some present existence and tracing its earlier course, till at some time (relevant to the object of the inquiry) we stop and condense the main features of the course into a formula for the structure of the state of things at the date where we stop. Instead of really deducing or deriving the course of subsequent events from an original state, we are simply taking out of a formula the traits which we have put into it on the basis of knowledge of subsequent events. Let the present state be anything you please, as different as may be from what is actually found, and it will still be true that we could (theoretically) construct a comprehensive formula for its earlier estate. In short, as a matter of fact, a Laplacean formula merely summarizes what the actual course of events has been with respect to some selected features. How then can it be said to describe an original state of nature in virtue of which just such and such things have necessarily happened? A statement that the world is thus and so can not be tortured into a statement of how and why it must be as it is. The account of how a thing came to be as it is always starts and comes back to the fact that it *is* thus and so. How then can this fact be derived according to some law of predestination from the consideration of its own prior history? For, I repeat, this history is *its history*.[4]

This discussion, however, oversimplifies matters. It overlooks the extent to which inference as to a prior state of affairs is dependent upon the diversity and complexity of what is now observed. We should be in a hard case in trying to fix upon the structure of the Latin language if our sole datum were, say, the French language. As a matter of fact, in considering the growth of the French tongue we have other Romance languages to fall back upon. Above all, we have independent evidence as to the characteristics of Latin speech. If we had not, we should be reasoning in a circle. Science is rightly suspicious of accounts of things in terms of a hypothesis for whose

4. Compare Woodbridge, "Evolution," *Philosophical Review*, XXI (1912), 137.

existence nothing can be alleged save that if it existed it would or might account for something which is actually found. Independent evidence of the existence of such an object is required. This consideration has an interesting application to the question in hand. It brings out clearly the absurdity involved in supposing that any formula, of the Laplacean type, about some earlier state of existence, however comprehensive, is comprehensive enough to cover the whole scope of existence of that earlier time.

Let us suppose the formula to be descriptive of a primitive state of the solar system. Not only must it start from and be framed in terms of what *now* exists, but the present datum must be larger than the existing solar system if we are to escape reasoning in a circle. In such cosmological constructions, astronomers and geologists rely upon observation of what is going on outside of the solar system. Without such data, the inquiry would be hopelessly crippled. The stellar field now presents, presumably, systems in all stages of formation. Is there any reason for supposing that a like state of affairs did not present itself at any and every prior time? Whatever formula is arrived at for the beginning of our present solar system describes, therefore, only one structure existing amid a vaster complex. A state of things adequately and inclusively described by the formula would be, by conception, a state of things in which nothing could happen. To get change we have to assume other structures which interact with it, existences not covered by the formula.

As a matter of fact, the conception of a solar system seems to have exercised an hypnotic influence upon Newton's successors. The gathering together of sun, planets, and their satellites, etc., into a system which might be treated as an individual having its own history was a wonderful achievement, and it impressed men's imaginations. It served for the time as a kind of symbol of the "universe." But as compared with the entire stellar field, the solar system is, after all, only a "right little, tight little island." Yet unless its complex context be ignored the idea of "an undifferentiated universe" which, by some immanent potential force, determined everything which has happened since, could hardly arise.[5] That the French language did not evolve out of Latin because of some immanent causality in the latter we have already noted. It is equally true that the contact and interaction of those speaking Latin with those speaking barbaric tongues were not due to the fact that they

5. One who turns to Spencer's chapter on the "Instability of the Homogeneous" (*First Principles*, Part II, Ch. 19) will perceive that his proof of its instability consists in showing that it was really already heterogeneous.

spoke Latin, but to independent variables. Internal diversity is as much a necessity as something externally heterogeneous.[6]

The consideration throws light, I think, upon the meaning of potentiality with reference to any state of things. We never apply the term except where there *is* change or a process of becoming. But we have an unfortunate tendency to conceive a fixed state of affairs and then appeal to a latent or potential something or other to effect change. But in reality the term refers to a characteristic of change. Anything changing might be said to exhibit potentiality with respect to two facts: first, that the change exhibits (in connection with interaction with new elements in its surroundings) qualities it did not show till it was exposed to them and, secondly, that the changes in which these qualities are shown run a certain course. To say that an apple has the potentiality of decay does not mean that it has latent or implicit within it a causal principle which will some time inevitably display itself in producing decay, but that its existing changes (in interaction with its surroundings) will take the form of decay, *if* they are exposed or subjected to certain conditions not now operating upon them. Potentiality thus signifies a certain limitation of present powers, due to the limited number of conditions with which they are in interaction plus the fact of the manifestation of new powers under different conditions. To generalize the idea, we have to add the fact that the very changes now going on have a tendency to expose the thing in question to these different conditions which will call out new modes of behavior, in other words, further changes of a different kind. Potentiality thus implies not merely diversity, but a progressively increasing diversification of a specific thing in a particular direction. So far is it from denoting a causal force immanent within a homogeneous something and leading it to change.

We may say then that an earlier condition of our earth was potential with life and mind. But this means that it was changing in a certain way and direction. Starting where we must start, with the present, the fact or organization shows that the world is of a certain kind. In spots, it *has* organization. Reference to the evolution of this organization out of an earlier world in which *such* organization was not found, means something about that earlier

6. Some contemporary metaphysical theories attempt to start from pure "simple" entities and then refer change exclusively to "complexes." This overlooks the fact that without internal diversification in the alleged simple entity, a complex entity would no more exhibit change than a simple one. The history of the doctrine of atoms is instructive. Such a metaphysics transgresses the conditions of intelligent inquiry in exactly the same way as the metaphysics of ultimate origins.

condition—it means that it was characterized by a change having direction—that is, in the direction of vital and intelligent organization. I do not see that this justifies the conclusion that that earlier world was biocentric or vitalistic or psychic. Yet two conclusions seem to follow. One is negative. The fact that it is possible and desirable to state the processes of an organized being in chemico-physical terms does not eliminate, but rather takes for granted whatever peculiar features living beings have. It does not imply that the distinguishing features of living and thinking beings are to be explained away by resolution into the features found in non-living things. It is the *occurrence* of these peculiar features which it stated in physico-chemical terms. And, as we have already seen, the attempt to give an account of any occurrence involves the genuine and irreducible existence of the thing dealt with. A statement of the mechanism of vital and thinking creatures is a statement of *their* mechanism; an account of their production is an account of *their* production. To give such an account does not prove whether the existence in question is a good thing or a bad thing, but it proves nothing at all if it puts in doubt the specific existence of the subject matter investigated.

The positive point is that the evolution of living and thinking beings out of a state of things in which life and thought were not found is a fact which must be recognized in any metaphysical inquiry into the irreducible traits of the world. For evolution appears to be just one of the irreducible traits. In other words, it is a fact to be reckoned with in considering the traits of diversity, interaction, and change which have been enumerated as among the traits taken for granted in all scientific subject matter. If everything which is, is a changing thing, the evolution of life and mind indicates the nature of the changes of physico-chemical things and therefore something about those things. It indicates that as purely physical, they are still limited in their interactions; and that as they are brought into more and complex interactions they exhibit capacities not to be found in an exclusively mechanical world. To say, accordingly, that the existence of vital, intellectual, and social organization makes impossible a purely mechanistic metaphysics is to say something which the situation calls for. But it does not signify that the world "as a whole" is vital or sentient or intelligent. It is a remark of the same order as the statement that one is not adequately acquainted with water or iron until he has found it operating under a variety of different conditions, and hence a scientific doctrine which regards iron as essentially hard or water as essentially liquid is inadequate. Without a doctrine of evolution we might be able to say, not that matter *caused* life, but that matter under certain conditions of highly complicated and intensified interaction is living. With the doctrine of evolution, we can add to this statement that the interactions and changes of matter are themselves of a kind to bring about that complex and intensified interaction which is life. The doctrine of evolution implies that this holds good of any matter, irrespective of its date, for it is not the matter of 1915, as caused by matter that has now ceased to be, which lives. The matter which was active ten million years ago now lives: this is a feature of the matter of ten million years ago.

I am, however, getting beyond my main point. I am not concerned to develop a metaphysics; but simply to indicate one way of conceiving the problem of metaphysical inquiry as distinct from that of the special sciences, a way which settles upon the more ultimate traits of the world as defining its subject matter, but which frees these traits from confusion with ultimate origins and ultimate ends—that is, from questions of creation and eschatology. The chief significance of evolution with reference to such an inquiry seems to be to indicate the while metaphysics takes the world irrespective of any particular time, yet time itself, or genuine change in a specific direction, is itself one of the ultimate traits of the world irrespective of date.

9

Existence as Precarious and as Stable

A feature of existence which is emphasized by cultural phenomena is the precarious and perilous. Sumner refers to Grimm as authority for the statement that the Germanic tribes had over a thousand distinct sayings, proverbs and apothegms concerning luck. Time is brief, and this statement must stand instead of the discourse which the subject deserves. Man finds himself living in an aleatory world; his existence involves, to put it baldly, a gamble. The world is a scene of risk; it is uncertain, unstable, uncannily unstable. Its dangers are irregular, inconstant, not to be counted upon as to their times and seasons. Although persistent, they are sporadic, episodic. It is darkest just before dawn; pride goes before a fall; the moment of greatest prosperity is the moment most charged with ill-omen, most opportune for the evil eye. Plague, famine, failure of crops, disease, death, defeat in battle are always just around the corner, and so are abundance, strength, victory, festival and song. Luck is proverbially both good and bad in its distributions. The sacred and the accursed are potentialities of the same situation; and there is no category of things which has not embodied the sacred and accursed: persons, words, places, times, directions in space, stones, winds, animals, stars.

Anthropologists have shown incontrovertibly the part played by the precarious aspect of the world in generating religion with its ceremonies, rites, cults, myths, magic; and it has shown the pervasive penetration of these affairs into morals, law, art, and industry.

SOURCE: Acknowledgment is hereby made to Open Court Publishing Company for permission to quote from *Experience and Nature* by John Dewey.

Beliefs and dispositions connected with them are the background out of which philosophy and secular morals slowly developed, as well as more slowly those late inventions, art for art's sake, and business is business. Interesting and instructive as is this fact, it is not the ramifications which here concern us. We must not be diverted to consider the consequences for philosophy, even for doctrines reigning today, of facts concerning the origin of philosophies. We confine ourselves to one outstanding fact: the evidence that the world of empirical things includes the uncertain, unpredictable, uncontrollable, and hazardous.

It is an old saying that the gods were born of fear. The saying is only too likely to strengthen a misconception bred by confirmed subjective habits. We first endow man in isolation with an instinct of fear and then we imagine him irrationally ejecting that fear into the environment, scattering broadcast as it were, the fruits of his own purely personal limitations, and thereby creating superstition. But fear, whether an instinct or an acquisition, is a function of the environment. Man fears because he exists in a fearful, an awful world. The *world* is precarious and perilous. It is as easily accessible and striking evidence of this fact that primitive experience is cited. The voice is that of early man; but the hand is that of nature, the nature in which we still live. It was not fear of gods that created the gods.

For if the life of early man is filled with expiations and propitiations, if in his feasts and festivals what is enjoyed is gratefully shared with his gods, it is not because a belief in supernatural powers created a need for expiatory, propitiatory and communal offerings. Everything that man achieves and possesses is got by actions that may involve him in other and obnoxious consequences in addition to those wanted and enjoyed. His acts are trespasses upon the domain of the unknown; and hence atonement, if offered in season, may ward off direful consequences that haunt even the moment of prosperity—or that most haunt that moment. While unknown consequences flowing from the past dog the present, the future is even more unknown and perilous; the present by that fact is ominous. If unknown forces that decide future destiny can be placated, the man who will not study the methods of securing their favor is incredibly flippant. In enjoyment of present food and companionship, nature, tradition and social organization have coöperated, thereby supplementing our own endeavors so petty and so feeble without this extraneous reinforcement. Goods are by grace not of ourselves. He is a dangerous churl who will not gratefully acknowledge by means of free-will offerings the help that sustains him.

These things are as true today as they were in the days of early culture. It is not the facts which have changed, but the methods of insurance, regulation and acknowledgment. Herbert Spencer sometimes colored his devotion to symbolic experiences with a fact of dire experience. When he says that every fact has two opposite sides, "the one its near or visible side and the other its remote or invisible side," he expresses a persistent trait of every object in experience. The visible is set in the invisible; and in the end what is unseen decides what happens in the seen; the tangible rests precariously upon the untouched and ungrasped. The contrast and the potential maladjustment of the immediate, the conspicuous and focal phase of things, with those indirect and hidden factors which determine the origin and career of what is present, are indestructible features of any and every experience. We may term the way in which our ancestors dealt with the contrast superstitious, but the contrast is no superstition. It is a primary datum in any experience.

We have substituted sophistication for superstition, at least measurably so. But the sophistication is often as irrational and as much at the mercy of words as the superstition it replaces. Our magical safeguard against the uncertain character of the world is to deny the existence of chance, to mumble universal and necessary law, the ubiquity of cause and effect, the uniformity of nature, universal progress, and the inherent rationality of the universe. These magic formulae borrow their potency from conditions that are not magical. Through science we have secured a degree of power of prediction and of control; through tools, machinery and an accompanying technique we have made the world more conformable to our needs, a more secure abode. We have heaped up riches and means of comfort between ourselves and the risks of the world. We have professionalized amusement as an agency of escape and forgetfulness. But when all is said and done, the fundamentally hazardous character of the world is not seriously modified, much less eliminated. Such an incident as the last war and preparations for a future war remind us that it is easy to overlook the extent which, after all, our attainments are only devices for blurring the disagreeable recognition of a fact, instead of means of altering the fact itself.

What has been said sounds pessimistic. But the concern is not with morals but with metaphysics, with, that is to say, the nature of the existential world in which we live. It would have been as easy and more comfortable to emphasize good luck, grace, unexpected and unwon joys, those unsought for happenings which we so significantly call happiness. We might have appealed to good fortune as evidence of this important trait of hazard in nature. Comedy is as genuine as tragedy. But it is traditional that comedy strikes a more superficial note than tragedy. And there is an even better reason for appealing to misfortunes and mistakes as evidence of the precarious nature of the world. The problem of evil is a well-recognized problem, while we rarely or never hear of a problem of good. Goods we take for granted; they are as they should be; they are natural and proper. The good is a recognition of our deserts. When we pull out a plum we treat it as evidence of the *real* order of cause and effect in the world. For this reason it is difficult for the goods of existence to furnish as convincing evidence of the uncertain character of nature as do evils. It is the latter we term accidents, not the former, even when their adventitious character is as certain.

What of it all? it may be asked. In the sense in which an assertion is true that uncontrolled distribution of good and evil is evidence of the precarious, uncertain nature of existence, it is a truism, and no problem is forwarded by its reiteration. But it is submitted that just this predicament of the inextricable mixture of stability and uncertainty gives rise to philosophy, and that it is reflected in all its recurrent problems and issues. If classic philosophy says so much about unity and so little about unreconciled diversity, so much about the eternal and permanent, and so little about change (save as something to be resolved into combinations of the permanent), so much about necessity and so little about contingency, so much about the comprehending universal and so little about the recalcitrant particular, it may well be because the ambiguousness and ambivalence of reality are actually so pervasive. Since these things form the problem, solution is more apparent (although not more actual), in the degree in which whatever of stability and assurance the world presents is fastened upon and asserted.

Upon their surface, the reports of the world which form our different philosophies are various to the point of stark contrariness. They range from spiritualism to materialism, from absolutism to relativistic phenomenalism, from transcendentalism to positivism, from rationalism to sensationalism, from idealism to realism, from subjectivism to bald objectivism, from Platonic realism to nominalism. The array of contradictions is so imposing as to suggest to sceptics that the mind of man has tackled an impossible job, or that philosophers have abandoned themselves to vagary. These radical oppositions in philosophers suggest however another consideration. They suggest that all their different philosophies have a common premise, and that their diversity is due to acceptance of a common premise. Variant philosophies may be looked at as different ways of supplying recipes for denying to the universe the character of contingency which it possesses so integrally that its denial leaves the reflecting mind without a clew, and puts subsequent philosophising at the mercy of temperament, interest and local surroundings.

Quarrels among conflicting types of philosophy are thus family quarrels. They go on within the limits of a too domestic circle, and can be settled only by venturing further afield, and out of doors. Concerned with imputing complete, finished and sure character to the world of real existence, even if things have to be broken into two disconnected pieces in order to accomplish the result, the character desiderated can plausibly be found in reason or in mechanism; in rational conceptions like those of mathematics, or brute things like sensory data; in atoms or in essences; in consciousness or in a physical externality which forces and overrides consciousness.

As against this common identification of reality with what is sure, regular and finished, experience in unsophisticated forms gives evidence of a different world and points to a different metaphysics. We live in a world which is an impressive and irresistible mixture of sufficiencies, tight completenesses, order, recurrences which make possible prediction and control, and singularities, ambiguities, uncertain possibilities, processes going on to consequences as yet indeterminate. They are mixed not mechanically but vitally like the wheat and tares of the parable. We may recognize them separately but we cannot divide them, for unlike wheat and tares they grow from the same root. Qualities have defects as necessary conditions of their excellencies; the instrumentalities of truth are the causes of error; change gives meaning to permanence and recurrence makes novelty possible. A world that was wholly risky would be a world in which adventure is impossible, and only a living world can include death. Such facts have been celebrated by thinkers like Heracleitus and Laotze; they have been greeted by theologians as furnishing occasions for exercise of divine grace; they have been elaborately formulated by various schools under a principle of relativity, so defined as to become itself final and absolute. They have rarely been frankly recognized as fundamentally significant for the formation of a naturalistic metaphysics.

Aristotle perhaps came the nearest to a start in that direction. But his thought did not go far on the road, though it may be used to suggest the road which he failed to take. Aristotle acknowledges contingency, but he never surrenders his bias in favor of the fixed, certain and finished. His whole theory of forms and ends is a theory of the superiority in Being of rounded-out fixities. His physics is a fixation of ranks or grades of necessity and contingency so sorted that necessity measures dignity and equals degree of reality, while contingency and change measure degrees of deficiency of Being. The empirical impact and sting of the mixture of universality and singularity and chance is evaded by parcelling out the regions of space so that they have their natural abode in different portions of nature. His logic is one of definition and classification, so that its task is completed when changing and contingent things are distinguished from the necessary, universal and fixed, by attribution to inferior species of things. Chance appears in thought not as a calculus of probabilities in predicting the observable occurrence of any and every event, but as marking an inferior type of syllogism. Things that move are intrinsically different from things that exhibit eternal regularity. Change is honestly recognized as a genuine feature of *some* things, but the point of the recognition is avoided by imputing alteration to inherent deficiency of Being over against complete Being which never changes. Changing things belong to a purgatorial realm, where they wander aimlessly until redeemed by love of finality of form, the acquisition of which lifts them to a paradise of self-sufficient Being. With slight exaggeration, it may be said that the thoroughgoing way in which Aristotle defined, distinguished and classified rest and movement, the finished and the incomplete, the actual and potential, did more to fix tradition, *the* genteel tradition one is tempted to add, which identifies the fixed and regular with reality of Being and the changing and hazardous with deficiency of Being, than ever was accomplished by those who took the shorter path of asserting that change is illusory.

His philosophy was closer to empirical facts than most modern philosophies, in that it was neither monistic nor dualistic but openly pluralistic. His plurals fall however, within a grammatical system, to each portion of which a corresponding cosmic status is alloted. Thus his pluralism solved the problem of how to have your cake and eat it too, for a classified and hierarchically ordered set of pluralities, of variants, has none of the sting of the miscellaneous and uncoordinated plurals of our actual world. In this classificatory scheme of separation he has been followed, though perhaps unwittingly, by many philosophers of different import. Thus Kant assigns all that is manifold and chaotic to one realm, that of sense, and all that is uniform and regular to that of reason. A single and all embracing dialectic problem of the combination of sense and thought is thereby substituted for the concrete problems that arise through the mixed and varied union in existence of the variable and the constant, the necessary and that which proceeds uncertainly.

The device is characteristic of a conversion such as has already been commented upon of a moral insight to be made good in action into an antecedent metaphysics of existence or a general theory of knowledge. The striving to make stability of meaning prevail over the instability of events is the main task of intelligent human effort. But when the function is dropped from the province of art and treated as a property of given things, whether cosmological or logical, effort is rendered useless, and a premium is put upon the accidental good-fortune of a class that happens to be furnished by the toil of another class with products that give to life its dignity and leisurely stability.

The argument is not forgetful that there are, from Heracleitus to Bergson, philosophies, metaphysics, of change. One is grateful to them for keeping alive a sense of what classic, orthodox philosophies have whisked out of sight. But the philosophies of flux also indicate the intensity of the craving for the sure and fixed. They have deified change by making it universal, regular, sure. To say this is not, I hope, verbal by-play. Consider the wholly eulogistic fashion in which Hegel and Bergson, and the professedly evolutionary philosophers of becoming, have taken change. With Hegel becoming is a rational process which defines logic, although a new and strange logic, and an absolute, although new and strange, God. With Spencer, evolution is but the transitional process of attaining a fixed and universal equilibrium of harmonious adjustment. With Bergson, change is the creative operation of God, or *is* God—one is not quite sure which. The change of change is not only cosmic pyrotechnics, but is a process of divine, spiritual, energy. We are here in the presence of prescription, not description. Romanticism is an evangel in the garb of metaphysics. It sidesteps the painful, toilsome labor of understanding and of control which change sets us, by glorifying it for its own sake. Flux is made something to revere, something profoundly akin to what is best within ourselves, will and creative energy. It is not, as it is in experience, a call to effort, a challenge to investigation, a potential doom of disaster and death.

If we follow classical terminology, philosophy is love of wisdom, while metaphysics is cognizance of the generic traits of existence. In this sense of metaphysics, incompleteness and precariousness is a trait that must be given footing of the same rank as the finished and fixed. Love of wisdom is concerned with finding its implications for the conduct of life, in devotion to what is good. On the cognitive side, the issue is largely that of measure, of the ratio one bears to others in the situations of life. On the practical side, it is a question of the use to be made of each, of turning each to best account. Man is naturally philosophic, rather than metaphysical or coldly scientific, noting and describing. Concerned with prudence if not with what is honorifically called wisdom, man naturally prizes knowledge only for the sake of its bearing upon success and failure in attaining goods and avoiding evils. This is a fact of our structure and nothing is gained by recommending it as an ideal truth, and equally nothing is gained by attributing to intellect an intrinsic relationship to pure truth for its own sake or bare fact on its own account. The first method encourages dogma, and the second expresses a myth. The love of knowledge for its own sake is an ideal of morals; it is an integral condition of the wisdom that rightly conceives and effectually pursues the good. For wisdom as to ends depends upon acquaintance with conditions and means, and unless the acquaintance is adequate and fair, wisdom becomes a sublimated folly of self-deception.

Denial of an inherent relation of mind to truth or fact for its own sake, apart from insight into what the fact or truth exacts of us in behavior and imposes upon us in joy and suffering, and simultaneous affirmation that devotion to fact, to truth, is a necessary moral demand involve no inconsistency. Denial relates to natural events as independent of choice and endeavor; affirmation relates to choice and action. But choice and the reflective effort involved in it are themselves such contingent events and so bound up with the precarious uncertainty of other events, that philosophers have too readily assumed that metaphysics, and science of fact and truth, are themselves wisdom, thinking thus to avoid the necessity of either exercising or recognizing choice. The consequence is that conversion of unavowed morals or wisdom into cosmology, and into a metaphysics of nature, which was termed . . . *the* philosophic fallacy. It supplies the formula of the technique by which thinkers have relegated the uncertain and unfinished to an invidious state of unreal being, while they have systematically exalted the assured and complete to the rank of true Being.

Upon the side of wisdom, as human beings interested in good and bad things in their connection with human conduct, thinkers are concerned to mitigate the instability of life, to introduce moderation, temper and economy, and when worst comes to worst to suggest consolations and compensations. They are concerned with rendering more stable good things, and more unstable bad things; they are interested in how changes may be turned to account in the consequences to which they contribute. The facts of the ongoing, unfinished and ambiguously potential world give point and poignancy to the search for absolutes and finalities. Then when philosophers have hit in reflection upon a thing which is stably good in quality and hence worthy of persistent and continued choice, they hesitate, and withdraw from the effort and struggle that choice demands:—namely, from the effort to give it some such stability in observed existence as it possesses in quality when thought of. Thus it becomes a refuge, an asylum for contemplation, or a theme for dialectical elaboration, instead of an ideal to inspire and guide conduct.

Since thinkers claim to be concerned with knowledge of existence, rather than with imagination, they have to make good the pretention to knowledge. Hence they transmute the imaginative perception of the stably good object into a definition and description of true reality in contrast with lower and specious existence, which, being precarious and incomplete, alone involves us in the necessity of choice and active struggle. Thus they remove from actual existence the very traits which generate philosophic reflection and which give point and bearing to its conclusions. In briefest formula, "reality" becomes what we wish existence to be, after we have analyzed its defects and decided upon what would remove them; "reality" is what existence would be if our reasonably justified preferences were so completely established in nature as to exhaust and define its entire being and thereby render search and struggle unnecessary. What is left over (and since trouble, struggle, conflict, and error still empirically exist, something *is* left over), being excluded by definition from full reality is assigned to a grade or order of being which is asserted to be metaphysically inferior; an order variously called appearance, illusion, mortal mind, or the merely empirical, against what really and truly is. Then the problem of metaphysics alters: instead of being a detection and description of the generic traits of existence, it becomes an endeavor to adjust or reconcile to each other two separate realms of being. Empirically we have just what we started with: the mixture of the precarious and problematic with the assured and complete. But a classificatory device, based on desire and elaborated in reflective imagination, has been introduced by which the two traits are torn apart, one of them being labelled reality and the other appearance. The genuinely moral problem of mitigating and regulating the troublesome factor by active employment of the stable factor then drops out of sight. The dialectic problem of logical reconciliation of two notions has taken its place.

The most widespread of these classificatory devices, the one of greatest popular appeal, is that which divides existence into the supernatural and the natural. Men may fear the gods but it is axiomatic that the gods have nothing to fear. They lead a life of untroubled serenity, the life that pleases them. There is a long story between the primitive forms of this division of objects of experience and the dialectical imputation to the divine of omnipotence, omniscience, eternity and infinity, in contrast with the attribution to man and experienced nature of finitude, weakness, limitation, struggle and change. But in the make-up of human psychology the later history is implicit in the early crude division. One realm is the home of assured appropriation and possession; the other of striving, transiency and frustration. How many persons are there today who conceive that they have disposed of ignorance, struggle and disappointment by pointing to man's "finite" nature—as if finitude signifies anything else but an abstract classificatory naming of certain concrete and discriminable traits of nature itself—traits of nature which generate ignorance, arbitrary appearance and disappearance, failure and striving. It pleases man to substitute the dialectic exercise of showing how the "finite" can exist with or within the "infinite" for the problem of dealing with the contingent, thinking to solve the problem by distinguishing and naming its factors. Failure of the exercise is certain, but the failure can be flourished as one more proof of the finitude of man's intellect, and the needlessness because impotency of endeavor of "finite" creatures to attack ignorance and oppressive fatalities. Wisdom then consists in administration of the temporal, finite and human in its relation to the eternal and infinite, by means of dogma and cult, rather than in regulation of the events of life by understanding of actual conditions.

It does not demand great ingenuity to detect the inversion here. The starting point is precisely the existing mixture of the regular and dependable and the unsettled and uncertain. There are a multitude of recipes for obtaining a vicarious possession of the stable and final without getting involved in the labor and pain of intellectual effort attending regulation of the conditions upon which these fruits depend.

This situation is worthy of remark as an exemplification of how easy it is to arrive at a description of existence via a theory of wisdom, of reflective insight into goods. It has a direct bearing upon a metaphysical doctrine which is not popular, like the division into the supernatural and natural, but which is learned and technical. The philosopher may have little esteem for the crude forms assumed by the popular metaphysics of earth and heaven, of God, nature, and man. But the philosopher has often proceeded in a manner analogous to that which resulted in this popular metaphysics; some of the most cherished metaphysical distinctions seem to be but learned counterparts, dependent upon an elaborate intellectual technique, for these rough, crude notions of supernatural and natural, divine and human, in popular belief. I refer to such things as the Platonic division into ideal archetypes and physical events; the Aristotelian division into form which is actuality and matter which is potential, when that is understood as a distinction of ranks of reality; the noumenal things, things-in-themselves of Kant in contrast with natural objects as phenomenal; the distinction, current among contemporary absolute idealists, of reality and appearance.

The division however is not confined to philosophers with leanings toward spiritualistic philosophies. There is some evidence that Plato got the term Idea, as a name for essential form, from Democritus. Whether this be the case or no, the Idea of Democritus, though having a radically diverse structure from the Platonic Idea, had the same function of designating a finished, complete, stable, wholly unprecarious reality. Both philosophers craved solidity and both found it; corresponding to the Platonic phenomenal flux are the Democritean things as they are in custom or ordinary experience: corresponding to the ideal archetypes are substantial indivisible atoms. Corresponding, again to the Platonic theory is the modern theory of mathematical structures which are alone independently real, while the empirical impressions and suggestions to which they give rise is the counterpart of his realm of phenomena.

Apart from the materialistic and spiritualistic schools, there is the Spinozistic division into attributes and modes; the old division of essence and existence, and its modern counterpart, subsistence and existence. It is impossible to force Mr. Bertrand Russell into any one of the pigeonholes of the cabinet of conventional philosophic schools. But moral, or philosophical, motivation is obvious in his metaphysics when he says that mathematics takes us "into the region of absolute necessity, to which not only the actual world but every possible world must conform." Indeed with his usual lucidity, he says, mathematics "finds a habitation eternally standing, where our ideals are fully satisfied and our best hopes are not thwarted." When he adds that contemplation of such objects is the "chief means of overcoming the terrible sense of impotence, of weakness, of exile amid hostile power, which is too apt to result from acknowledging the all but omnipotence of alien forces," the presence of moral origin is explicit.

No modern thinker has pointed out so persuasively as Santayana that "every phase of the ideal world emanates from the natural," that "sense, art, religion, society express nature exuberantly." And yet unless one reads him wrong, he then confounds his would-be disciples and confuses his critics by holding that nature is *truly* presented only in an esthetic contemplation of essences reached by physical science, an envisagement reached through a dialectic which "is a transubstantiation of matter, a passage from existence to eternity." This passage moreover is so utter that there is no road back. The stable ideal meanings which are the fruit of nature are forbidden, in the degree in which they are its highest and truest fruits, from dropping seeds in nature to its further fructification.

The perception of genetic continuity between the dynamic flux of nature and an eternity of static ideal forms thus terminate in a sharp division, in reiteration of the old tradition. Perhaps it is a caricature to say that the ultimate of reason is held to be ability to behold nature as a complete mechanism which generates and sustains the beholding of the mechanism, but the caricature is not wilful. If the separation of contingency and necessity is abandoned, what is there to exclude a belief that science, while it is grasp of the regular and stable mechanism of nature, is also an organ of regulating and enriching, through its own expansion, the more exuberant and irregular expressions of nature in human intercourse, the arts, religion, industry, and politics?

To follow out the latter suggestion would take us to a theme reserved for later consideration. We are here concerned with the fact that it is the intricate mixture of the stable and the precarious, the fixed and the unpredictably novel, the assured and the uncertain, in existence which sets mankind upon that love of wisdom which forms philosophy. Yet too commonly, although in a great variety of technical modes, the result of the search is converted into a metaphysics which denies or conceals from acknowledgment the very characters of existence which initiated it, and which give significance to its conclusions. The form assumed by the denial is, most frequently, that striking division into a superior true realm of being and lower illusory, insignificant or phenomenal realm which characterizes metaphysical systems as unlike as those of Plato and Democritus, St. Thomas and Spinoza, Aristotle and Kant, Descartes and Comte, Haeckel and Mrs. Eddy.

The same jumble of acknowledgment and denial attends the conception of Absolute Experience: as if any experience could be more absolutely experience than that which marks the life of humanity. This conception constitutes the most recent device for first admitting and then denying the combinedly stable and unstable nature of the world. Its plaintive recognition of our experience as finite and temporal, as full of error, conflict and contradiction, is an acknowledgment of the precarious uncertainty of the objects and connections that constitute nature as it emerges in history. Human experience however has also the pathetic longing for truth, beauty and order. There is more than the longing: there are moments of achievement. Experience exhibits ability to possess harmonious objects. It evinces an ability, within limits, to safeguard the excellent objects and to deflect and reduce the obnoxious ones. The concept of an absolute experience which is only and always perfect and good, first explicates these desirable implications of things of actual experience, and then asserts that they alone are real. The experienced occurrences which give poignancy and pertinency to the longing for a better world, the experimental endeavors and plans which make possible actual betterments within the objects of actual experience, are thus swept out of real Being into a limbo of appearances.

The notion of Absolute Experience thus serves as a symbol of two facts. One is the ineradicable union in nature of the relatively stable and the relatively contingent. The division of the movement and leadings of things which are experienced into two parts, such that one set constitutes and defines absolute and eternal experience, while the other set constitutes and defines finite experience, tells us nothing about absolute experience. It tells us a good deal about experience as it exists: namely, that it is such as to involve permanent and general objects of reference as well as temporally changing events; the possibility of truth as well as error; conclusive objects and goods as well as things whose purport and nature is determinable only in indeterminate future. Nothing is gained—except the delights of a dialectic problem—in labelling one assortment absolute experience and the other finite experience. Since the appeal of the adherents of the philosophy of absolute and phenomenal experience is to a logical criterion, namely, to the implication in every judgment, however erroneous, of a standard of consistency which excludes any possibility of contradictoriness, the inherent logical contradictions in the doctrine itself are worth noting.

In the first place, the contents as well as the form of ultimate Absolute Experience are derived from and based upon the features of actual experience, the very experience which is then relegated to unreality by the supreme reality derived from its unreality. It is "real" just long enough to afford a spring-board into ultimate reality and to afford a hint of the essential contents of the latter and then it obligingly dissolves into mere appearance. If we start from the standpoint of the Absolute Experience thus reached, the contradiction is repeated from its side. Although absolute, eternal, all-comprehensive, and pervasively integrated into a whole so logically perfect that no separate patterns, to say nothing of seams and holes, can exist in it, it proceeds to play a tragic joke upon itself—for there is nothing else to be fooled—by appearing in a queer combination of rags and glittering gew-gaws, in the garb of the temporal, partial and conflicting things, mental as well as physical, of ordinary experience. I do not cite these dialectic contradictions as having an inherent importance. But the fact that a doctrine which avowedly takes logical consistence for its method and criterion, whose adherents are noteworthy for dialectic acumen in specific issues, should terminate in such thoroughgoing contradictions may be cited as evidence that after all the doctrine is merely engaged in an arbitrary sorting out of characters of things which in nature are always present in conjunction and interpenetration.

The union of the hazardous and the stable, of the incomplete and the recurrent, is the condition of all experienced satisfaction as truly as of our predicaments and problems. While it is the source of ignorance, error and failure of expectation, it is the source of the delight which fulfillments bring. For if there were nothing in the way, if there were no deviations and resistances, fulfillment would be at once, and in so being would fulfill nothing, but merely be. It would not be in connection with desire or satisfaction. Moreover when a fulfillment comes and is pronounced good, it is *judged* good, distinguished and asserted, simply because it is in jeopardy, because it occurs and amid indifferent and divergent things. Because of this mixture of the regular and that which cuts across stability, a good object once experienced acquires ideal quality and attracts demand and effort to itself. A particular ideal may be an illusion, but having ideals is no illusion. It embodies features of existence. Although imagination is often fantastic it is also an organ of nature; for it is the appropriate phase of indeterminate events moving toward eventualities that are now but possibilities. A purely stable world permits of no illusions, but neither is it clothed with ideals. It just exists. To be good is to be better than; and there can be no better except where there is shock and discord combined with enough assured order to make attainment of harmony possible. Better objects when brought into existence are existent not ideal; they retain ideal quality only retrospectively as commemorative of issue from prior conflict and prospectively, in contrast with forces which make for their destruction. Water that slakes thirst, or a conclusion that solves a problem have ideal character as long as thirst or problem persists in a way which qualifies the result. But water that is not a satisfaction of need has no more ideal quality than water running through pipes into a reservoir; a solution ceases to be a solution and becomes a bare incident of existence when its antecedent generating conditions of doubt, ambiguity and search are lost from its context. While the precarious nature of existence is indeed the source of all trouble, it is also an indispensable condition of ideality, becoming a sufficient condition when conjoined with the regular and assured.

We long, amid a troubled world, for perfect being. We forget that what gives meaning to the notion of perfection is the events that create longing, and that, apart from them, a "perfect" world would mean just an unchanging brute existential thing. The ideal significance of esthetic objects is no exception to this principle. Their satisfying quality, their power to compose while they arouse, is not dependent upon definite prior desire and effort as is the case with the ideally satisfying quality of practical and scientific objects. It is part of their peculiar satisfying quality to be gratuitous, not purchased by endeavor. The contrast to other things of this detachment from toil and labor in a world where most realizations have to be bought, as well as the contrast to trouble and uncertainty, give esthetic objects their peculiar traits. If all things came to us in the way our esthetic objects do, none of them would be a source of esthetic delight.

Some phases of recent philosophy have made much of need, desire and satisfaction. Critics have frequently held that the outcome is only recurrence to an older subjective empiricism, though with substitution of affections and volitional states for cognitive sensory states. But need and desire are exponents of natural being. They are, if we use Aristotelian phraseology, actualizations of its contingencies and incompletenesses; as such nature itself is wistful and pathetic, turbulent and passionate. Were it not, the existence of wants would be a miracle. In a world where everything is complete, nothing requires anything else for its completion. A world in which events can be carried to a finish only through the coinciding assistance of other transitory events, is already necessitous, a world of begging as well as of beggarly elements. If human experience is to express and reflect this world, it must be marked by needs; in becoming aware of the needful and needed quality of things it must project satisfactions or completions. For irrespective of whether a satisfaction is conscious, a satisfaction or non-satisfaction is an objective thing with objective conditions. It means fulfillment of the demands of objective factors. Happiness may *mark* an awareness of such satisfaction, and it may *be* its culminating form. But satisfaction is not subjective, private or personal: it is conditioned by objective partialities and defections and made real by objective situations and completions.

By the same logic, necessity implies the precarious and contingent. A world that was all necessity would not be a world of necessity; it would just be. For in its being, nothing would be necessary for anything else. But where some things are indigent, other things are necessary if demands are to be met. The common failure to note the fact that a world of complete being would be a world in which necessity is meaningless is due to a rapid shift from one universe of discourse to another. First we postulate a whole of Being; then we shift to a part; now since a "part" is logically dependent as such in its existence and its properties, it is necessitated by other parts. But we have unwittingly introduced contingency in the very fact of marking off something as just a part. If the logical implications of the original notion are held to firmly, a part is already a part-of-a-whole. Its being what it is is not necessitated by the whole or by other parts: its being what it is is just a name for the whole being what it is. Whole and parts alike are but names for existence there as just what it is. But wherever we can say if so-and-so, then some-thing else, there is necessity, because partialities are implied which are not just parts-of-a-whole. A world of "ifs" is alone a world of "musts"—the "ifs" express real differences; the "musts" real con-nections. The stable and recurrent is needed for the fulfillment of the possible; the doubtful can be settled only through its adaptation to stable objects. The necessary is always necessary for, not necessary in and of itself; it is conditioned by the contingent, although itself a condition of the full determination of the latter.

One of the most striking phases of the history of philosophic thought is the recurrent grouping together of unity, permanence (or "the eternal"), completeness and rational thought, while upon another side full multiplicity, change and the temporal, the partial, defective, sense and desire. This division is obviously but another case of violent separation of the precarious and unsettled from the regular and determinate. One aspect of it, however, is worthy of particular attention: the connection of thought and unity. Empiri-cally, all reflection sets out from the problematic and confused. Its aim is to clarify and ascertain. When thinking is successful, its career closes in transforming the disordered into the orderly, the mixed-up into the distinguished or placed, the unclear and ambigu-ous into the defined and unequivocal, the disconnected into the systematized. It is empirically assured that the goal of thinking does not remain a mere ideal, but is attained often enough so as to render reasonable additional efforts to achieve it.

In these facts we have, I think, the empirical basis of the philo-sophic doctrines which assert that reality is really and truly a rational system, a coherent whole of relations that cannot be con-ceived otherwise than in terms of intellect. Reflective inquiry moves in each particular case from differences toward unity; from indeterminate and ambiguous position to clear determination, from confusion and disorder to system. When thought in a given case has reached its goal of organized totality, of definite relations of distinctly placed elements, its object is the accepted starting point, the defined subject matter, of further experiences; antecedent and outgrown conditions of darkness and of unreconciled differences are dismissed as a transitory state of ignorance and inadequate apprehensions. Retain connection of the goal with the thinking by which it is reached, and then identify it with true reality in contrast with the merely phenomenal, and the outline of the logic of rational and "objective" idealisms is before us. Thought like Being, has two forms, one real; the other phenomenal. It is compelled to take on *reflective* form, it involves doubt, inquiry and hypothesis, because it sets out from a subject-matter conditioned by sense, a fact which proves that thought, intellect, is not pure in man, but restricted by an animal organism that is but one part linked with other parts, of nature. But the conclusion of reflection affords us a pattern and guarantee of thought which is *constitutive;* one with the system of objective reality. Such in outline is the procedure of all ontological logics.

A philosophy which accepts the denotative or empirical method accepts at full value the fact that reflective thinking transforms confusion, ambiguity and discrepancy into illumination, definiteness and consistency. But it also points to the contextual situation in which thinking occurs. It notes that the starting point is the actually *problematic,* and that the problematic phase resides in some actual and specifiable situation.

It notes that the means of converting the dubious into the assured, and the incomplete into the determinate, is use of assured and established things, which are just as empirical and as indicative of the nature of experienced things as is the uncertain. It thus notes that thinking is no different in kind from the use of natural materials and energies, say fire and tools, to refine, re-order, and shape other natural materials, say ore. In both cases, there are matters which as they stand are unsatisfactory and there are also adequate agencies for dealing with them and connecting them. At no point or place is there any jump outside empirical, natural objects and their relations. Thought and reason are not specific powers. They consist of the procedures intentionally employed in the application to each other of the unsatisfactorily confused and indeterminate on one side and the regular and stable on the other. Generalizing from such observations, empirical philosophy perceives that thinking is a continuous process of temporal re-organization within one and the same world of experienced things, not a jump from the latter world into one of objects constituted once for all by thought. It discovers thereby the empirical basis of rational idealism, and the point at which it empirically goes astray. Idealism fails to take into account the specified or concrete character of the uncertain situation in which thought occurs; it fails to note the empirically concrete nature of the subject-matter, acts, and tools by which determination and consistency are reached; it fails to note that the conclusive eventual objects having the latter properties are themselves as many as the situations dealt with. The conversion of the logic of reflection into an ontology of rational being is thus due to arbitrary conversion of an eventual natural function of unification into a causal antecedent reality; this in turn is due to the tendency of the imagination working under the influence of emotion to carry unification from an actual, objective and experimental enterprise, limited to particular situations where it is needed, into an unrestricted, wholesale movement which ends in an all-absorbing dream.

The occurrence of reflection is crucial for dualistic metaphysics as well as for idealistic ontologies. Reflection occurs only in situations qualified by uncertainty, alternatives, questioning, search, hypotheses, tentative trials or experiments which test the worth of thinking. A naturalistic metaphysics is bound to consider reflection as itself a natural event occurring *within* nature because of traits of the latter. It is bound to inference from the empirical traits of thinking in precisely the same way as the sciences make inferences from the happening of suns, radio-activity, thunder-storms or any other natural event. Traits of reflection are as truly indicative or evidential of the traits of *other* things as are the traits of these events. A theory of the nature of the occurrence and career of a sun reached by denial of the obvious traits of the sun, or by denial that these traits are so connected with the traits of other natural events that they can be used as evidence concerning the nature of these other things, would hardly possess scientific standing. Yet philosophers, and strangely enough philosophers who call themselves realists, have constantly held that the traits which are characteristic of thinking, namely, uncertainty, ambiguity, alternatives, inquiring, search, selection, experimental reshaping of external conditions, do not possess the same existential character as do the objects of valid knowledge. They have denied that these traits are evidential of the character of the world within which thinking occurs. They have not, as realists, asserted that these traits are mere appearances; but they have often asserted and implied that such things are only personal or psychological in contrast with a world of objective nature. But the interests of empirical and denotative method and of naturalistic metaphysics wholly coincide. The world must actually be such as to generate ignorance and inquiry; doubt and hypothesis, trial and temporal conclusions; the latter being such that they develop out of existences which while wholly "real" are not as satisfactory, as good, or as significant, as those into which they are eventually re-organized. The ultimate evidence of genuine hazard, contingency, irregularity and indeterminateness in nature is thus found in the occurrence of thinking. The traits of natural existence which generate the fears and adorations of superstitious barbarians generate the scientific procedures of disciplined civilization. The superiority of the latter does not consist in the fact that they are based on "real" existence, while the former depend wholly upon a human nature different from nature in general. It consists in the fact that scientific inquiries reach *objects* which are better, because reached by method which controls them and which adds greater control to life itself, method which mitigates accident, turns contingency to account, and releases thought and other forms of endeavor.

The conjunction of problematic and determinate characters in nature renders every existence, as well as every idea and human act, an experiment in fact, even though not in design. To be intelligently experimental is but to be conscious of this intersection of natural conditions so as to profit by it instead of being at its mercy. The Christian idea of this world and this life as a probation is a kind of distorted recognition of the situation; distorted because it applied wholesale to one stretch of existence in contrast with another, re-garded as original and final. But in truth anything which can exist at any place and at any time occurs subject to tests imposed upon it by surroundings, which are only in part compatible and reinforcing. These surroundings test its strength and measure its endurance. As we can discourse of change only in terms of velocity and acceleration which involve relations to other things, so assertion of the permanent and enduring is comparative. The stablest thing we can speak of is not free from conditions set to it by other things. That even the solid earth mountains, the emblems of constancy, appear and dis-appear like the clouds is an old theme of moralists and poets. The fixed and unchanged being of the Democritean atom is now reported by inquiries to possess some of the traits of his non-being, and to embody a temporary equilibrium in the economy of nature's com-promises and adjustments. A thing may endure *secula seculorum* and yet not be everlasting; it will crumble before the gnawing tooth of time, as it exceeds a certain measure. Every existence is an event.

This fact is nothing at which to repine and nothing to gloat over.

It is something to be noted and used. If it is discomfiting when applied to good things, to our friends, possessions and precious selves, it is consoling also to know that no evil endures forever; that the longest lane turns sometime, and that the memory of loss of nearest and dearest grows dim in time. The eventful character of all existences is no reason for consigning them to the realm of mere appearance any more than it is a reason for idealizing flux into a diety. The important thing is measure, relation, ratio, knowledge of the comparative tempos of change. In mathematics some variables are constants in some problems; so it is in nature and life. The rate of change of some things is so slow, or is so rhythmic, that these changes have all the advantages of stability in dealing with more transitory and irregular happenings—if we know enough. Indeed, if any one thing that concerns us is subject to change, it is fortunate that all other things change. A thing "absolutely" stable and unchangeable would be out of the range of the principle of action and reaction, of resistance and leverage as well as of friction. Here it would have no applicability, no potentiality of use as measure and control of other events. To designate the slower and the regular rhythmic events structure, and more rapid and irregular ones process, is sound practical sense. It expresses the function of one in respect to the other.

But spiritualistic idealism and materialism alike treat this relational and functional distinction as something fixed and absolute. One doctrine finds structure in a framework of ideal forms, the other finds it in matter. They agree in supposing that structure has some superlative reality. This supposition is another form taken by preference for the stable over the precarious and uncompleted. The fact is that all structure is structure *of* something; anything defined as structure is a character of *events,* not something intrinsic and *per se*. A set of traits is called structure, because of its limiting function in relation to other traits of events. A house has a structure; in comparison with the disintegration and collapse that would occur without its presence, this structure is fixed. Yet it is not something external to which the changes involved in building and using the house have to submit. It is rather an arrangement of changing events such that properties which change slowly, limit and direct a series of quick changes and give them an order which they do not otherwise possess. Structure is constancy of means, of things used for consequences, not of things taken by themselves or absolutely. Structure is what makes construction possible and cannot be discovered or defined except in some realized construction, construction being, of course, an evident order of changes. The isolation of structure from the changes whose stable ordering it is, renders it mysterious—something that is metaphysical in the popular sense of the word, a kind of ghostly queerness.

The "matter" of materialists and the "spirit" of idealists is a creature similar to the constitution of the United States in the minds of unimaginative persons. Obviously the real constitution is certain basic relationships among the activities of the citizens of the country; it is a property or phase of these possessions, so connected with them as to influence their rate and direction of change. But by literalists it is often conceived of as something external to them; in itself fixed, a rigid framework to which *all* changes must accomodate themselves. Similarly what we call matter is that character of natural events which is so tied up with changes that are sufficiently rapid to be perceptible as to give the latter a characteristic rhythmic order, the causal sequence. It is no cause or source of events or processes; no absolute monarch; no principle of explanation; no substance behind or underlying changes—save in that sense of substance in which a man well fortified with this world's goods, and hence able to maintain himself through vicissitudes of surroundings, is a man of substance. The name designates a character in operation, not on entity.

That structure, whether of the kind called material or of the kind summed up in the word mental, is stable or permanent relationally and in its office, may be shown in another way. There is no action without reaction; there is no exclusively one-way exercise of conditioning power, no mode of regulation that operates wholly from above to below or from within outwards or from without inwards. Whatever influences the changes of other things is itself changed. The idea of an activity proceeding only in one direction, of an unmoved mover, is a survival of Greek physics. It has been banished from science, but remains to haunt philosophy. The vague and mysterious properties assigned to mind and matter, the very conceptions of mind and matter in traditional thought, are ghosts walking underground. The notion of matter actually found in the practice of science has nothing in common with the matter of materialists—and almost everybody is still a materialist as to matter, to which he merely adds a second rigid structure which he calls mind. The matter of science is a character of natural events and changes as they change; their character of regular and stable order.

Natural events are so complex and varied that there is nothing surprising in their possession of different characterizations, characters so different that they can be easily treated as opposites.

Nothing but unfamiliarity stands in the way of thinking of both mind and matter as different characters of natural events, in which matter expresses their sequential order, and mind the order of their meanings in their logical connections and dependencies. Processes may be eventful for functions which taken in abstract separation are at opposite poles, just as physiological processes eventuate in both anabolic and katabolic functions. The idea that matter and mind are two sides or "aspects" of the same things, like the convex and the concave in a curve, is literally unthinkable.

A curve is an intelligible object and concave and convex are defined in terms of this object; they are indeed but names for properties involved in its meaning. We do not start with convexity and concavity as two independent things and then set up an unknown *tertium quid* to unite two disparate things. In spite of the literal absurdity of the comparison, it may be understood however in a way which conveys an inkling of the truth. That to which both mind and matter belong is the complex of events that constitute nature. This becomes a mysterious *tertium quid,* incapable of designation, only when mind and matter are taken to be static structures instead of functional characters. It is a plausible prediction that if there were an interdict placed for a generation upon the use of mind, matter, consciousness as nouns, and we were obliged to employ adjectives and adverbs, conscious and consciously, mental and mentally, material and physically, we should find many of our problems much simplified.

We have selected only a few of the variety of the illustrations that might be used in support of the idea that the significant problems and issues of life and philosophy concern the rate and mode of the conjunction of the precarious and the assured, the incomplete and the finished, the repetitious and the varying, the safe and sane and the hazardous. If we trust to the evidence of experienced things, these traits, and the modes and tempos of their interaction with each other, are fundamental features of natural existence. The experience of their various consequences, according as they are relatively isolated, unhappily or happily combined, is evidence that wisdom, and hence that love of wisdom which is philosophy, is concerned with choice and administration of their proportioned union. Structure and process, substance and accident, matter and energy, permanence and flux, one and many, continuity and discreteness, order and progress, law and liberty, uniformity and growth, tradition and innovation, rational will and impelling desires, proof and discovery, the actual and the possible, are names given to various phases of their conjunction, and the issue of living depends upon the art with which these things are adjusted to each other.

While metaphysics may stop short with noting and registering these traits, man is not contemplatively detached from them. They involve him in his perplexities and troubles, and are the source of his joys and achievements. The situation is not indifferent to man, because it forms man as a desiring, striving, thinking, feeling creature. It is not egotism that leads man from contemplative registration of these traits to interest in managing them, to intelligence and purposive art. Interest, thinking, planning, striving, consummation and frustration are a drama enacted by these forces and conditions. A particular choice may be arbitrary; this is only to say that it does not approve itself to reflection. But choice is not arbitrary, not in a universe like this one, a world which is not finished and which has not consistently made up its mind where it is going and what it is going to do. Or, if we call it arbitrary, the arbitrariness is not ours but that of existence itself. And to call existence arbitrary or by any moral name, whether disparaging or honorific, is to patronize nature. To assume an attitude of condescension toward existence is perhaps a natural human compensation for the straits of life. But it is an ultimate source of the covert, uncandid and cheap in philosophy. This compensatory disposition it is which forgets that reflection exists to guide choice and effort. Hence its love of wisdom is but an unlaborious transformation of existence by dialectic, instead of an opening and enlarging of the ways of nature in man. A true wisdom, devoted to the latter task, discovers in thoughtful observation and experiment the method of administering the unfinished processes of existence so that frail goods shall be substantiated, secure goods be extended, and the precarious promises of good that haunt experienced things be more liberally fulfilled.

10

Time and Individuality

The Greeks had a saying, "Count no man happy till after his death." The adage was a way of calling attention to the uncertainties of life. No one knows what a year or even a day may bring forth. The healthy become ill; the rich, poor; the mighty are cast down; fame changes to obloquy. Men live at the mercy of forces they cannot control. Belief in fortune and luck, good or evil, is one of the most widespread and persistent of human beliefs. Chance has been deified by many peoples. Fate has been set up as an overlord to whom even the Gods must bow. Belief in a Goddess of Luck is in ill repute among pious folks but their belief in providence is a tribute to the fact no individual controls his own destiny.

The uncertainty of life and one's final lot has always been associated with mutability, while unforeseen and uncontrollable change has been linked with time. Time is the tooth that gnaws; it is the destroyer; we are born only to die and every day brings us one day nearer death. This attitude is not confined to the ignorant and vulgar. It is the root of what is sometimes called the instinctive belief in immortality. Everything perishes in time but men are unable to believe that perishing is the last word. For centuries poets made the uncertainty which time brings with it the theme of their discourse—read Shakespeare's sonnets. Nothing stays; life is fleeting and all earthly things are transitory.

It was not then for metaphysical reasons that classic philosophy maintained that change, and consequently time, are marks of inferior reality, holding that true and ultimate reality is immutable

Source: Reprinted by permission of New York University Press from *Time and Its Mysteries*, series II, copyright 1940 by New York University Press.

and eternal. Human reasons, all too human, have given birth to the
idea that over and beyond the lower realm of things that shift like
the sands on the seashore there is the kingdom of the unchanging,
of the complete, the perfect. The grounds for the belief are couched
in the technical language of philosophy, but the cause for the
grounds is the heart's desire for surcease from change, struggle, and
uncertainty. The eternal and immutable is the consummation of
mortal man's quest for certainty.

It is not strange then that philosophies which have been at odds
on every other point have been one in the conviction that the ultimately real is fixed and unchanging, even though they have been as
far apart as the poles in their ideas of its constitution. The idealist
has found it in a realm of rational ideas; the materialist in the laws
of matter. The mechanist pins his faith to eternal atoms and to unmoved and unmoving space. The teleologist finds that all change is
subservient to fixed ends and final goals, which are the one steadfast
thing in the universe, conferring upon changing things whatever
meaning and value they possess. The typical realist attributes to unchanging essences a greater degree of reality than belongs to existences; the modern mathematical realist finds the stability his heart
desires in the immunity of the realm of possibilities from vicissitude.
Although classic rationalism looked askance at experience and empirical things because of their continual subjection to alteration, yet
strangely enough traditional sensational empiricism relegated time
to a secondary role. Sensations appeared and disappeared but in
their own nature they were as fixed as were Newtonian atoms—of
which indeed they were mental copies. Ideas were but weakened
copies of sensory impressions and had no inherent forward power
and application. The passage of time dimmed their vividness and
caused their decay. Because of their subjection to the tooth of time,
they were denied productive force.

In the late eighteenth and the greater part of the nineteenth
centuries appeared the first marked cultural shift in the attitude
taken toward change. Under the names of indefinite perfectability,
progress, and evolution, the movement of things in the universe
itself and of the universe as a whole began to take on a beneficient
instead of a hateful aspect. Not every change was regarded as a sign
of advance but the general trend of change, cosmic and social, was
thought to be toward the better. Aside from the Christian idea of a
millennium of good and bliss to be finally wrought by supernatural
means, the Golden Age for the first time in history was placed in the
future instead of at the beginning, and change and time were
assigned a benevolent role.

Even if the new optimism was not adequately grounded, there

were sufficient causes for its occurrence as there are for all great changes in intellectual climate. The rise of new science in the seventeenth century laid hold upon general culture in the next century. Its popular effect was not great, but its influence upon the intellectual elite, even upon those who were not themselves engaged in scientific inquiry, was prodigious. The enlightenment, the *éclaircissement,* the *Aufklärung*—names which in the three most advanced countries of Europe testified to the widespread belief that at last light had dawned, that dissipation of the darkness of ignorance, superstition, and bigotry was at hand, and the triumph of reason was assured—for reason was the counterpart in man of the laws of nature which science was disclosing. The reign of law in the natural world was to be followed by the reign of law in human affairs. A vista of the indefinite perfectibility of man was opened. It played a large part in that optimistic theory of automatic evolution which later found its classic formulation in the philosophy of Herbert Spencer. The faith may have been pathetic but it has its own nobility.

At last, time was thought to be working on the side of the good instead of as a destructive agent. Things were moving to an event which was divine, even if far off.

This new philosophy, however, was far from giving the temporal an inherent position and function in the constitution of things. Change was working on the side of man but only because of *fixed* laws which governed the changes that take place. There was hope in change just because the laws that govern it do not change. The locus of the immutable was shifted to scientific natural law, but the faith and hope of philosophers and intellectuals were still tied to the unchanging. The belief that "evolution" is identical with progress was based upon trust in laws which, being fixed, worked automatically toward the final end of freedom, justice, and brotherhood, the natural consequences of the reign of reason.

Not till the late nineteenth century was the doctrine of the subordination of time and change seriously challenged. Bergson and William James, animated by different motives and proceeding by different methods, then installed change at the very heart of things. Bergson took his stand on the primacy of life and consciousness, which are notoriously in a state of flux. He assimilated that which is completely real in the natural world to them, conceiving the static as that which life leaves behind as a deposit as it moves on. From this point of view he criticized mechanistic and teleological theories on the ground that both are guilty of the same error, although from opposite points. Fixed laws which govern change and fixed ends toward which changes tend are both the products of a backward look, one that ignores the forward movement of life. They apply only to that which life has produced and has then left behind in its ongoing vital creative course, a course whose behavior and outcome are unpredictable both mechanically and from the standpoint of ends. The intellect is at home in that which is fixed only because it is done and over with, for intellect is itself just as much a deposit of *past* life as is the matter to which it is congenial. Intuition alone articulates in the forward thrust of life and alone lays hold of reality.

The animating purpose of James was, on the other hand, primarily moral and artistic. It is expressed, in his phrase, "block universe," employed as a term of adverse criticism. Mechanism and idealism were abhorrent to him because they both hold to a closed universe in which there is no room for novelty and adventure. Both sacrifice individuality and all the values, moral and aesthetic, which hang upon individuality, for according to absolute idealism, as to mechanistic materialism, the individual is simply a part determined by the whole of which he is a part. Only a philosophy of pluralism, of genuine indetermination, and of change which is real and intrinsic gives significance to individuality. It alone justifies struggle in creative activity and gives opportunity for the emergence of the genuinely new.

It was reserved, however, for the present century to give birth to the out-and-out assertion in systematic form that reality *is* process, and that laws as well as things develop in the processes of unceasing change. The modern Heraclitean is Alfred North Whitehead, but he is Heraclitus with a change. The doctrine of the latter, while it held that all things flow like a river and that change is so continuous that a man cannot step into the same river even once (since it changes as he steps), nevertheless also held that there is a fixed order which controls the ebb and flow of the universal tide.

My theme, however, is not historical, nor is it to argue in behalf of any one of the various doctrines regarding time that have been advanced. The purpose of the history just roughly sketched is to indicate that the nature of time and change has now become in its own right a philosophical problem of the first importance. It is of time as a *problem* that I wish to speak. The aspect of the problem that will be considered is the connection of time with individuality, as the latter is exemplified in the living organism and especially in human beings.

Take the account of the life of any person, whether the account is a biography or an autobiography. The story begins with birth, a temporal incident; it extends to include the temporal existence of parents and ancestry. It does not end with death, for it takes in the influence upon subsequent events of the words and deeds of the one whose life is told. Everything recorded is an historical event; it is something temporal. The individual whose life history is told, be it Socrates or Nero, St. Francis or Abraham Lincoln, is an extensive event; or, if you prefer, it is a course of events each of which takes up into itself something of what went before and leads on to that which comes after. The skill, the art, of the biographer is displayed in his ability to discover and portray the subtle ways, hidden often from the individual himself, in which one event grows out of those which preceded and enters into those which follow. The human individual is himself a history, a career, and for this reason his biography can be related only as a temporal event. That which comes later explains the earlier quite as truly as the earlier explains the later. Take the individual Abraham Lincoln at one year, at five years, at ten years, at thirty years of age, and imagine everything wiped out, no matter how minutely his life is recorded up to the date set. It is plain beyond the need of words that we then have not his biography but only a fragment of it, while the significance of that fragment is undisclosed. For he did not just exist in a time which eternally surrounded him, but time was the heart of his existence.

Temporal seriality is the very essence, then, of the human individual. It is impossible for a biographer in writing, say the story of the first thirty years of the life of Lincoln, not to bear in mind his later career. Lincoln as an individual *is* a history; any particular event cut off from that history ceases to be a part of his life as an individual. As Lincoln is a particular development in time, so is every other human individual. Individuality is the uniqueness of the history, of the career, not something given once for all at the beginning which then proceeds to unroll as a ball of yarn may be unwound. Lincoln made history. But it is just as true that he made himself as an individual in the history he made.

I have been speaking about human individuality. Now an important part of the problem of time is that what is true of the human individual does not seem to be true of physical individuals. The common saying "as like as two peas" is a virtual denial to one kind of vegetable life of the kind of individuality that marks human beings. It is hard to conceive of the individuality of a given pea in terms of a unique history or career; such individuality as it appears to possess seems to be due in part to spatial separateness and in part to peculiarities that are extremely caused. The same thing holds true of lower forms of animal life. Most persons would resent denial of some sort of unique individuality to their own dogs, but would be slow to attribute it to worms, clams, and bees. Indeed, it seems to be an exclusive prerogative of the romantic novelist to find anything in the way of a unique career in animal lives in general.

When we come to inanimate elements, the prevailing view has been that time and sequential change are entirely foreign to their nature. According to this view they do not have careers; they simply change their relations in space. We have only to think of the classic conception of atoms. The Newtonian atom, for example, moved and was moved, thus changing its position in space, but it was interchangeable in its own being. What it was at the beginning or without any beginning it is always and forever. Owing to the impact of other things it changes its direction and velocity of motion so that it comes closer and further away from other things. But all this was believed to be external to its own substantial being. It had no development, no history, because it had no potentialities. In itself it was like a God, the same yesterday, today, and forever. Time did not enter into its being either to corrode or to develop it. Nevertheless, as an ultimate element it was supposed to have some sort of individuality, to be itself and not something else. Time, in physical science, has been simply a measure of motion in space.

Now, this apparently complete unlikeness in kind between the human and the physical individual is a part of the problem of time. Some philosophers have been content to note the difference and to make it the ground for affirming a sheer dualism between man and other things, a ground for assigning to man a spiritual being in contrast with material things. Others, fewer in numbers, have sought to explain away the seeming disparity, holding that the apparent uniqueness of human individuality is specious, being in fact the effect of the vast number of physical molecules, themselves complex, which make up his being, so that what looks like genuine temporal change or development is really but a function of the number and complexity of changes of constituent fixed elements. Of late, there have been a few daring souls who have held that temporal quality and historical career are a mark of everything, including atomic elements, to which individuality may be attributed.

I shall mention some of the reasons from the side of physical science that have led to this third idea. The first reason is the growing recognition that scientific objects are purely relational and have nothing to do with the intrinsic qualities of individual things and nothing to say about them. The meaning of this statement appears most clearly in the case of scientific laws. It is now a commonplace that a physical law states a correlation of changes or of ways and manners of change. The law of gravitation, for example, states a relation which holds between bodies with respect to distance and mass. It needs no argument to show that distance is a relation. Mass was long regarded as an inherent property of ultimate and individual elements. But even the Newtonian conception was obliged to recognize that mass could be defined only in terms of inertia and that inertia could be defined only in terms, on the one hand, of the resistance it offered to the impact of other bodies, and, on the other hand, of its capacity to exercise impact upon them, impact being measured in terms of motion with respect to acceleration. The idea that mass is an inherent property which caused inertia and momentum was simply a holdover from an old metaphysical idea of force. As far as the findings of science are concerned, independent of the intrusion of metaphysical ideas, mass is inertia-momentum and these are strictly measures and relations. The discovery that mass changes with velocity, a discovery made when minute bodies came under consideration, finally forced surrender of the notion that mass is a fixed and inalienable possession of ultimate elements or individuals, so that time is now considered to be their fourth dimension.

It may be remarked incidentally that the recognition of the relational character of scientific objects completely eliminates an old metaphysical issue. One of the outstanding problems created by the rise of modern science was due to the fact that scientific definitions and descriptions are framed in terms in which qualities play no part. Qualities were wholly superfluous. As long as the idea persisted (an inheritance from Greek metaphysical science) that the business of knowledge is to penetrate into the inner being of objects, the existence of qualities like colors, sounds, etc., was embarrassing. The usual way of dealing with them is to declare that they are merely subjective, existing only in the consciousness of individual knowers. Given the old idea that the purpose of knowledge (represented at its best in science) is to penetrate into the heart of reality and reveal its "true" nature, the conclusion was a logical one. The discovery that the objects of scientific knowledge are purely relational shows that the problem is an artificial one. It was "solved" by the discovery that it needed no solution, since fulfillment of the function and business of science compels disregard of qualities. Using the older language, it was seen that so-called primary qualities are no more inherent properties of ultimate objects than are so-called secondary qualities of odors, sounds, and colors, since the former are also strictly relational; or, as Locke stated in his moments of clear insight, are "retainers" of objects in their connections with other things. The discovery of the nonscientific because of the empirically unverifiable and unnecessary character of absolute space, absolute motion, and absolute time gave the final *coup de grâce* to the traditional idea that solidity, mass, size, etc., are inherent possessions of ultimate individuals.

The revolution in scientific ideas just mentioned is primarily logical. It is due to recognition that the very method of physical science, with its primary standard units of mass, space, and time, is concerned with measurement of relations of change, not with individuals as such. This acknowledgement brought with it a further idea which, in spite of the resistance made to it by adherents of older metaphysical views, is making constant headway. This idea is that laws which purport to be statements of what actually occurs are statistical in character as distinct from so-called dynamic laws that are abstract and mathematical, and disguised definitions. Recognition of the statistical nature of physical laws was first effected in the case of gases when it became evident that generalizations regarding the behavior of swarms of molecules were not descriptions or predictions of the behavior of any individual particle. A single molecule is not and cannot be a gas. It is consequently absurd to suppose that the scientific law is about the elementary constituents of a gas. It is a statement of what happens when a very large number of such constituents interact with one another under certain conditions.

Statistical statements are of the nature of probability formulations. No insurance company makes any prediction as to what will happen to any given person in respect to death, or to any building with respect to destruction by fire. Insurance is conducted upon the basis of observation that out of a large number of persons of a given age such and such a proportionate number will probably live one year more, another proportionate number two years, and so on, while premiums are adjusted on the basis of these probability estimates. The validity of the estimates depends, as in the case of a swarm of molecules, upon the existence of a sufficiently large number of individuals, a knowledge which is a matter of the relative frequency of events of a certain kind to the total number of events which occur. No statement is made about what will take place in the case of an *individual*. The application of scientific formulations of the principle of probability statistically determined is thus a logical corollary of the principle already stated, that the subject matter of scientific findings is relational, not individual. It is for this reason that it is safe to predict the ultimate triumph of the statistical doctrine.

The third scientific consideration is found in Heisenberg's principle of uncertainty or indeterminacy, which may be regarded as a generalization of the ideas already stated. In form, this principle seems to be limited in its application. Classical science was based upon the belief that it is possible to formulate both the position and the velocity at one time of any given particle. It followed that knowledge of the position and velocity of a given number of particles would enable the future behavior of the whole collection to be accurately predicted. The principle of Heisenberg is that given the determination of position, its velocity can be stated only as of a certain order of probability, while if its velocity is determined the correlative factor of position can be stated only as of a certain order of probability. Both cannot be determined at once, from which it follows necessarily that the future of the whole collection cannot possibly be foretold except in terms of some order of probability.

Because of the fundamental place of the conceptions of position and velocity in physical science the principle is not limited in scope but is of the broadest possible significance.

Given the classic conception, Laplace stated its logical outcome when he said "we may conceive the present state of the universe as the effect of its past and the cause of its future. An intellect who at any given instant knew all the forces of animate nature and the mutual positions of the beings who compose it . . . could condense into a single formula the movement both of the greatest body in universe and of its lightest atom. Nothing would be uncertain to such an intellect, for the future, even as the past would be ever present before his eyes." No more sweeping statement of the complete irrelevancy of time to the physical world and of the complete unreality for individuals of time could well be uttered. But the principle of indeterminacy annihilates the premises from which the conclusion follows. The principle is thus a way of acknowledging the pertinency of real time to physical beings. The utmost possible regarding an individual is a statement as to some order of probability about the future. Heisenberg's principle has been seized upon as a basis for wild statements to the effect that the doctrine of arbitrary free will and totally uncaused activity are now scientifically substantiated. Its actual force and significance is generalization of the idea that the individual is a temporal career whose future cannot be *logically* deduced from its past.

As long as scientific knowledge was supposed to be concerned with individuals in their own intrinsic nature, there was no way to bridge the gap between the career of human individuals and that of physical individuals, save by holding that the seeming fundamental place of development and hence of time in the life histories of the former is only seeming or specious. The unescapable conclusion is that as human individuality can be understood only in terms of time as fundamental reality, so for physical individuals time is not simply a measure of predetermined changes in mutual positions, but is something that enters into their being. Laws do not "govern" the activity of individuals. They are a formulation of the frequency-distributions of the behavior of large number of individuals engaged in interactions with one another.

This statement does not mean that physical and human individuality are identical, nor that the things which appear to us to be nonliving have the distinguishing characteristic of organisms. The difference between the inanimate and the animate is not so easily wiped out. But it does show that there is no fixed gap between them. The conclusion which most naturally follows, without indulging in premature speculation, is that the principle of a developing career applies to all things in nature, as well as to human beings—that they are born, undergo qualitative changes, and finally die, giving place to other individuals. The idea of development applied to nature involves differences of forms and qualities as surely as it rules out absolute breaches of continuity. The differences between the amoeba and the human organism are genuinely there even if we accept the idea of organic evolution of species. Indeed, to deny the reality of the differences and their immense significance would be to deny the very idea of development. To wipe out differences because of denial of complete breaks and the need for intervention of some outside power is just as surely a way to deny development as is assertion of gaps which can be bridged only by the intervention of some super-natural force. It is then in terms of development, or if one prefers the more grandiose term, evolution, that I shall further discuss the problem of time.

The issue involved is perhaps the most fundamental one in philosophy at the present time. Are the changes which go on in the world simply external redistributions, rearrangements in space of what previously existed, or are they genuine qualitative changes such as apparently take place in the physiological development of an organism, from the union of ovum and sperm to maturity, and as apparently take place in the personal life career of individuals? When the question is raised, certain misapprehensions must be first guarded against. Development and evolution have historically been eulogistically interpreted. They have been thought of as necessarily proceeding from the lower to the higher, from the relatively worse to the relatively better. But this property was read in from outside moral and theological preoccupations. The real issue is that stated above: Is what happens simply a spatial rearrangement of what existed previously or does it involve something qualitatively new?

From this point of view, cancer is as genuinely a physiological development as is growth in vigor; criminals as well as heroes are a social development; the emergence of totalitarian states is a social evolution out of constitutional states independently of whether we like or approve them.

If we accept the intrinsic connection of time with individuality, they are not mere redistributions of what existed before.

Since it is a *problem* I am presenting, I shall assume that genuine transformations occur, and consider its implications. First and negatively, the idea (which is often identified with the essential meaning of evolution) is excluded that development is a process of unfolding what was previously implicit or latent. Positively it is implied that potentiality is a category of existence, for development cannot occur unless an individual has powers or capacities that are not actualized at a given time. But is also means that these powers are not unfolded from within, but are called out through interaction with other things. While it is necessary to revive the category of potentiality as a characteristic of individuality, it has to be revived in a different form from that of its classic Aristotelian formulation. According to that view, potentialities are connected with a fixed end which the individual endeavors by its own nature or essence to actualize, although its success in actualization depended upon the cooperation of external things and hence might be thwarted by the "accidents" of its surroundings—as not every acorn becomes a tree and few if any acorns become the typical oak.

When the idea that development is due to some indwelling end which tends to control the series of changes passed through is abandoned, potentialities must be thought of in terms of consequences of interactions with other things. Hence potentialities cannot be *known* till *after* the interactions have occurred. There are at a given time unactualized potentialities in an individual because and in as far as there are in existence other things with which it has not yet interacted. Potentialities of milk are known today, for example, that were not known a generation ago, because milk has been brought into interaction with things other than organisms, and hence now has other than furnishing-nutriment consequence. It is now predicted that in the future human beings will be wearing clothes made of glass and that the clothes will be cleaned by throwing them into a hot furnace. Whether this particular prediction is fulfilled or not makes no difference to its value as an illustration. Every new scientific discovery leads to some mode of technology that did not previously exist. As things are brought by new procedures into new contacts and new interactions, new consequences are produced and the powers to produce these new consequences is a recognized potentiality of the thing in question. The idea that potentialities are inherent and fixed by relation to a predetermined end was a product of a highly restricted state of technology. Because of this restriction, the only potentialities recognized were those consequences which were customary in the given state of culture and were accordingly taken to be "natural." When the only possible use of milk was as an article of food, it was "natural" to suppose that it had an inherent tendency to serve that particular end. With the use of milk as a plastic, and with no one able to tell what future consequences may be produced by new techniques which bring it into new interactions, the only reasonable conclusion is that potentialities are not fixed and intrinsic, but are a matter of an indefinite range of interactions in which an individual may engage.

Return for a moment to the human individual. It is impossible to think of the historical career which is the special individuality constituting Abraham Lincoln apart from the particular conditions in which he lived. He did not create, for example, the conditions that formed the issues of States' rights and of slavery, the issues that influenced his development. What his being as an individual would have been without these interacting conditions it is idle to speculate upon. The conditions did not form him from without as wax is supposed to be shaped by external pressure. There is no such thing as interaction that is merely a one-way movement. There were many other persons living under much the same conditions whose careers were very different, because conditions acted upon them and were acted upon by them in different ways. Hence there is no account possible of Lincoln's life that does not portray him interacting day by day with special conditions, with his parents, his wife and children, his neighbors, his economic conditions, his school facilities, the incidents of his profession as a lawyer, and so on. The career which is his unique individuality is the series of interactions in which he was created to be what he was by the ways in which he responded to the occasions with which he was presented. One cannot leave out either conditions as *opportunities* nor yet unique ways of responding to them. An occasion is an opportunity only when it is an evocation of a specific event, while a response is not a necessary effect of a cause but is a way of using an occasion to render it a constituent of an ongoing unique history.

Individuality conceived as a temporal development involves uncertainty, indeterminacy, or contingency. Individuality is the source of whatever is unpredictable in the world. The indeterminate is not change in the sense of violation of law, for laws state probable correlations of change and these probabilities exist no matter what the source of change may be. When a change occurs, *after* it has occurred it belongs to the observable world and is connected with other changes. The nomination of Lincoln for the presidency, his election, his Emancipation Proclamation, his assassination, after they took place can be shown to be related to other events; they can also be shown to have a certain connection with Lincoln's own past. But there was nothing in Lincoln's own life to cause by itself the conjunction of circumstances which brought about any one of these events. As far as he as an individual was concerned, the events were contingent, and as far as the conjunction of circumstances was concerned, his behavior at any given time in response to them was also contingent, or if you please fortuitous.

At critical junctures, his response could not be predicted either from his own past or from the nature of the circumstances, except as a probability. To say this is not arbitrarily to introduce mere chance into the world. It is to say that genuine individuality exists; that individuality is pregnant with new developments; that time is real. If we knew enough about Shakespeare's life we could doubtless show *after Hamlet* was produced how it is connected with other things. We could link it with sources; we could connect its mood with specific experiences of its author, and so on. But no one with the fullest knowledge of Shakespeare's past could have predicted the drama as it stands. If they could have done so, they would have been able to write it. Not even Shakespeare himself could have told in advance just what he was going to say—not if he was an individual, not a nodal point in the spatial redistribution of what already existed.

The mystery of time is thus the mystery of the existence of real individuals. It is a mystery because it is a mystery that anything which exists is just what it is. We are given to forgetting, with our insistence upon causation and upon the necessity of things happening as they do happen, that things exist as just what they qualitatively are. We can account for a change by relating it to other changes, but existences we have to accept for just what they are. Given a butterfly or an earthquake as an event, as a change, we can at least in theory find out and state its connection with other changes. But the individual butterfly or earthquake remains just the unique existence which it is. We forget in explaining its occurrence that it is only the *occurrence* that is explained, not the thing itself. We forget that in explaining the occurrence we are compelled to fall back on other individual things that have just the unique qualities they do have. Go as far back as we please in accounting for present conditions and we still come upon the mystery of things being just what they are.

Their occurrence, their manifestation, may be accounted for in terms of other occurrences, but their own quality of existence is final and opaque. The mystery is that the world is as it is—a mystery that is the source of all joy and all sorrow, of all hope and fear, and the source of development both creative and degenerative. The contingency of all into which time enters is the source of pathos, comedy, and tragedy. Genuine time, if it exists as anything else except the measure of motions in space, is all one with the existence of individuals as individuals, with the creative, with the occurrence of unpredictable novelties. Everything that can be said contrary to this conclusion is but a reminder that an individual may lose his individuality, for individuals become imprisoned in routine and fall to the level of mechanisms. Genuine time then ceases to be an integral element in their being. Our behavior becomes predictable because it is but an external rearrangement of what went before.

In conclusion, I would like to point out two considerations that seem to me to follow, two morals, if you wish to give them that name. I said earlier that the traditional idea of progress and evolution was based upon belief that the fixed structure of the universe is such as automatically brings it about. This optimistic and fatalastic idea is now at a discount. It is easy in the present state of the world to deny all validity whatever to the idea of progress, since so much of the human world seems bent on demonstrating the truth of the old theological doctrine of the fall of man. But the real conclusion is that, while progress is not inevitable, it is up to men as individuals to bring it about. Change is going to occur anyway, and the problem is the control of change in a given direction. The direction, the quality of change, is a matter of individuality. Surrender of individuality by the many to some one who is taken to be a superindividual explains the retrograde movement of society. Dictatorships and totalitarian states, and belief in the inevitability of this or that result coming to pass are, strange as it may sound, ways of denying the reality of time and the creativeness of the individual. Freedom of thought and of expression are not mere rights to be claimed. They have their roots deep in the existence of individuals as developing careers in time. Their denial and abrogation is an application of individuality and a virtual rejection of time as opportunity.

The ground of democratic ideas and practices is faith in the potentialities of individuals, faith in the capacity for positive developments if proper conditions are provided. The weakness of the philosophy originally advanced to justify the democratic movement was that it took individuality to be something given ready-made; that is, in abstraction from time, instead of as a power to develop.

The other conclusion is that art is the complement of science. Science as I have said is concerned wholly with relations, not with individuals. Art, on the other hand, is not only the disclosure of the individuality of the artist but is also a manifestation of individuality as creative of the future, in an unprecedented response to conditions as they were in the past. Some artists in their vision of might be but is not have been conscious rebels. But conscious protest and revolt is not the form which the labor of the artist in creation of the future must necessarily take. Discontent with things as they are is normally the expression of vision of what may be and is not; art, in being the manifestation of individuality, is this prophetic vision. To regiment artists, to make them servants of some particular cause does violence to the very springs of artistic creation. But it does more than that. It betrays the very cause of a better future it would serve, for in its subjection of the individuality of the artist it annihilates the source of that which is genuinely new. Were the regimentation successful, it would cause the future to be but a rearrangement of the past.

The artist in realizing his own individuality reveals potentialities hitherto unrealized. This revelation is the inspiration of other individuals to make the potentialities real, for it is not sheer revolt against things as they are which stirs human endeavor to its depths, but vision of what might be and is not. Subordination of the artists to any special cause no matter how worthy does violence not only to the artist but to the living source of a new and better future. Art is not the possession of the few who are recognized writers, painters, musicians; it is the authentic expression of any and all individuality. Those who have the gift of creative expression in unusually large measure disclose the meaning of the individuality of others to those others. In participating in the work of art, they become artists in their activity. They learn to know and honor individuality in whatever form it appears. The fountains of creative activity are discovered and released. The free individuality which is the source of art is also the final source of creative development in time.

V

Ethical Theory

In the article "Philosophy" that John Dewey wrote for the *Encyclopedia of the Social Sciences,* he proposed a definition of philosophy as a "survey of existence from the standpoint of value." This definition indicates Dewey's belief in an interpretation of philosophy as a discipline that is comprehensive in its scope and seemingly unlimited in its subject matter. For Dewey, however, what distinguishes philosophy from any other comprehensive effort at a general survey of existence, say of the kind undertaken by historians or scientists, is the primacy for philosophy of the moral perspective.

This identification of philosophy with the activity of moral criticism is pervasive in Dewey's writings. As we have seen, it was fundamental to his analysis of the cultural function of philosophy as the agency of cultural coherence and self-consciousness. But it is reflected above all in Dewey's ethical theory. In *Ethics*—an early textbook that Dewey co-authored—he drew a sharp distinction between a pre-philosophical morality of custom and convention and a post-philosophical morality in which customs and conventions have been subjected to a reflective analysis. Dewey argued that philosophy's presence could be noted in the development of a critical attitude toward established custom and conventional values.

The theoretical presupposition of the activity of moral criticism within a society, and indeed of the definition of philosophy as a "survey of existence from the standpoint of value," is a belief in the significance of moral criticism and, hence, in the objective justification of values. For Dewey, then, ethical theory should be able to provide an account of how value judgments function in practice and, further, to demonstrate their objectivity and reliability. The development of such an ethical theory, specifically, an empirical and naturalistic theory of the nature of moral valuation, is a major part of Dewey's philosophy.

It is generally agreed that the tenth chapter of Dewey's *Quest for Certainty,* entitled "The Construction of Good," is the classic source for his naturalistic ethical theory. Here, moral judgments are seen as empirical evaluations that provide decisions in practice about which option among unavoidably competing policies will most adequately satisfy human needs or resolve the problematic situation that generated the moral inquiry in the first place. Crucial to any such evaluation is an analysis of the nature of human needs, and an investigation of the comparative consequences of different methods of satisfying those needs. For Dewey, only scientific methods are competent to determine those needs; and it is his belief that the use of scientific method in moral inquiry will bring about a significant improvement in moral decision making.

Characteristically, Dewey argues for his own objective and naturalistic theses regarding the nature of value judgments by a polemic against two contrary interpretations of how men determine their values. On the one hand, he criticizes any attempt to derive morality from a religious or transcendent source. Moral judgments must be rooted in the desires, wants, or felt needs of human beings within their environment. On the other hand, he argues that it is a distortion of moral experience to believe that all human desires, needs, or preferences are of equal value. Dewey argues that subjectivist accounts of ethical judgment do not allow for the ways in which our moral judgments are continually revised or amended in the light of empirical evidence. The polemical method thus becomes the basis for a demonstration of the naturalistic, empirical, and objective character of moral evaluation.

When Dewey began formulating his views in ethical theory at the turn of the century, he identified the two positions competing with his own thesis as the "transcendental derivation" of ethics and the "subjectivist reduction" of ethics. The former position was adopted primarily by religionists or Kantian absolutists, and the latter was advanced by protagonists of the new anthropological relativity. By the late 1930's, the literature of ethical theories comprised a number of other competing analyses of value judgments. Perhaps the dominant analysis, and certainly the most provocative, was the one identified with logical positivism, which interpreted moral judgments as emotive expressions of the attitudes of the person advancing such judgments. Such expressions were neither true nor false in any empirical or logical sense.

It was against the background of this analysis that Dewey wrote his own formal account of the nature of value judgments in his *Theory of Valuation*, published in 1939, from which the section "Propositions of Appraisal" is taken. In that small work, Dewey sought to defend his own ethical naturalism in the light of current theses. In criticizing the emotivist theory of the logical positivists, Dewey introduced the distinction between an emotive prizing and a judgment of appraisal: While prizings may express emotive attitudes, appraisals require empirical evidence and are open to confirmation or refutation. Hence, as in "The Construction of Good," Dewey argues for a connection between the ways in which scientific method may be employed to determine judgments of fact and judgments of value.

There is an element of irony in the circumstances of the publication of *Theory of Valuation* that should be mentioned. When they were active in European universities in the 1930's, the philosophers of logical positivism had proposed a collaborative encyclopedia of the unified sciences. This encyclopedia would exhibit the philosophical doctrines of logical positivism by showing how the positivists approached such major areas of philosophy as logic, philosophy of history, value theory, and so on. By the late 1930's, many of these philosophers had found refuge in England or America, and the encyclopedia was published in this country. Although the positivist position in ethics had been distinctly different from that of Dewey and other pragmatists, there was then an effort to relate logical positivism to American pragmatism. Both shared a faith in the crucial significance of the acceptance of scientific method for the future of philosophy. Accordingly, John Dewey's *Theory of Valuation* was published as a volume in the *International Encyclopedia of Unified Science*.

11

The Construction of Good

We saw at the outset of our discussion that insecurity generates the quest for certainty. Consequences issue from every experience, and they are the source of our interest in what is present. Absence of arts of regulation diverted the search for security into irrelevant modes of practice, into rite and cult; thought was devoted to discovery of omens rather than of signs of what is to occur. Gradually there was differentiation of two realms, one higher, consisting of the powers which determine human destiny in all important affairs. With this religion was concerned. The other consisted of the prosaic matters in which man relied upon his own skill and his matter-of-fact insight. Philosophy inherited the idea of this division. Meanwhile in Greece many of the arts had attained a state of development which raised them above a merely routine state; there were intimations of measure, order and regularity in materials dealt with which give intimations of underlying rationality. Because of the growth of mathematics, there arose also the ideal of a purely rational knowledge, intrinsically solid and worthy and the means by which the intimations of rationality within changing phenomena could be comprehended within science. For the intellectual class the stay and consolation, the warrant of certainty, provided by religion was henceforth found in intellectual demonstration of the reality of the objects of an ideal realm.

With the expansion of Christianity, ethico-religious traits came to dominate the purely rational ones. The ultimate authoritative

Source: Reprinted by permission of G. P. Putnam's Sons and the Center for Dewey Studies from *The Quest for Certainty* by John Dewey. Copyright 1929 by John Dewey; renewed 1962 by Roberta L. Dewey.

standards for regulation of the dispositions and purposes of the human will were fused with those which satisfied the demands for necessary and universal truth. The authority of ultimate Being was, moreover, represented on earth by the Church; that which in its nature transcended intellect was made known by a revelation of which the Church was the interpreter and guardian. The system endured for centuries. While it endured, it provided an integration of belief and conduct for the western world. Unity of thought and practice extended down to every detail of the management of life; efficacy of its operation did not depend upon thought. It was guaranteed by the most powerful and authoritative of all social institutions.

Its seemingly solid foundation was, however, undermined by the conclusions of modern science. They effected, both in themselves and even more in the new interests and activities they generated, a breach between what man is concerned with here and now and the faith concerning ultimate reality which, in determining his ultimate and eternal destiny, had previously given regulation to his present life. The problem of restoring integration and coöperation between man's beliefs about the world in which he lives and his beliefs about the values and purposes that should direct his conduct is the deepest problem of modern life. It is the problem of any philosophy that is not isolated from that life.

The attention which has been given to the fact that in its experimental procedure science has surrendered the separation between knowing and doing has its source in the fact that there is now provided within a limited, specialized and technical field the possibility and earnest, as far as theory is concerned, of effecting the needed integration in the wider field of collective human experience. Philosophy is called upon to be the theory of the practice, through ideas sufficiently definite to be operative in experimental endeavor, by which the integration may be made secure in actual experience. Its central problem is the relation that exists between the beliefs about the nature of things due to natural science to beliefs about values—using that word to designate whatever is taken to have rightful authority in the direction of conduct. A philosophy which should take up this problem is struck first of all by the fact that beliefs about values are pretty much in the position in which beliefs about nature were before the scientific revolution. There is either a basic distrust of the capacity of experience to develop its own regulative standards, and an appeal to what philosophers call eternal values, in order to ensure regulation of belief and action; or there is acceptance of enjoyments actually experienced irrespective of the method or operation by which they are brought into existence. Complete bifurcation between rationalistic method and an empirical method has its final and most deeply human significance in the ways in which good and bad are thought of and acted for and upon.

As far as technical philosophy reflects this situation, there is division of theories of values into two kinds. On the one hand, goods and evils, in every region of life, as they are concretely experienced, are regarded as characteristic of an inferior order of Being—intrinsically inferior. Just because they are things of human experience, their worth must be estimated by reference to standards and ideals derived from ultimate reality. Their defects and perversion are attributed to the same fact; they are to be corrected and controlled through adoption of methods of conduct derived from loyalty to the requirements of Supreme Being. This philosophic formulation gets actuality and force from the fact that it is a rendering of the beliefs of men in general as far as they have come under the influence of institutional religion. Just as rational conceptions were once superimposed upon observed and temporal phenomena, so eternal values are superimposed upon experienced goods. In one case as in the other, the alternative is supposed to be confusion and lawlessness. Philosophers suppose these eternal values are known by reason; the mass of persons that they are divinely revealed.

Nevertheless, with the expansion of secular interests, temporal values have enormously multiplied; they absorb more and more attention and energy. The sense of transcendent values has become enfeebled; instead of permeating all things in life, it is more and more restricted to special times and acts. The authority of the church to declare and impose divine will and purpose has narrowed. Whatever men say and profess, their tendency in the presence of actual evils is to resort to natural and empirical means to remedy them. But in formal belief, the old doctrine of the inherently disturbed and unworthy character of the goods and standards of ordinary experience persists. This divergence between what men do and what they nominally profess is closely connected with the confusions and conflicts of modern thought.

It is not meant to assert that no attempts have been made to replace the older theory regarding the authority of immutable and transcendent values by conceptions more congruous with the practices of daily life. The contrary is the case. The utilitarian theory, to take one instance, has had great power. The idealistic school is the only one in contemporary philosophies, with the exception of one form of neo-realism, that makes much of the notion of a reality which is all one with ultimate moral and religious values. But this school is also the one most concerned with the conservation of "spiritual" life. Equally significant is the fact that empirical theories retain the notion that thought and judgment are concerned with values that are experienced independently of them. For these theories, emotional satisfactions occupy the same place that sensations hold in traditional empiricism. Values are constituted by liking and enjoyment; to be enjoyed and to be a value are two names for one and the same fact. Since science has extruded values from its objects, these empirical theories do everything possible to emphasize their purely subjective character of value. A psychological theory of desire and liking is supposed to cover the whole ground of the theory of values; in it, immediate feeling is the counterpart of immediate sensation.

I shall not object to this empirical theory as far as it connects the theory of values with concrete experiences of desire and satisfaction. The idea that there is such a connection is the only way known to me by which the pallid remoteness of the rationalistic theory, and the only too glaring presence of the institutional theory of transcendental values can be escaped. The objection is that the theory in question holds down value to objects *antecedently* enjoyed, apart from reference to the method by which they come into existence; it takes enjoyments which are causal because unregulated by intelligent operations to be values in and of themselves. Operational thinking needs to be applied to the judgment of values just as it has now finally been applied in conceptions of physical objects. Experimental empiricism in the field of ideas of good and bad is demanded to meet the conditions of the present situation.

The scientific revolution came about when material of direct and uncontrolled experience was taken as problematic: as supplying material to be transformed by reflective operations into known objects. The contrast between experienced and known objects was found to be a temporal one; namely, one between empirical subject-matters which were had or "given" prior to the acts of experimental variation and redisposition and those which succeeded these acts and issued from them. The notion of an act whether of sense or thought which supplied a valid measure of thought in immediate knowledge was discredited. Consequences of operations became the important thing. The suggestion almost imperatively follows that escape from the defects of transcendental absolutism is not to be had by setting up as values enjoyments that happen anyhow, but in defining value by enjoyments which are the consequences of intelligent action. Without the intervention of thought, enjoyments are not values but problematic goods, becoming values when they re-issue in a changed form from intelligent behavior. The fundamental trouble with the current empirical theory of values is that it merely formulates and justifies the socially prevailing habit of regarding enjoyments as they are actually experienced as values in and of themselves. It completely side-steps the question of regulation of these enjoyments. This issue involves nothing less than the problem of the directed reconstruction of economic, political and religious institutions.

There was seemingly a paradox involved in the notion that if we turned our backs upon the immediately perceived qualities of things, we should be enabled to form valid conceptions of objects, and that these conceptions could be used to bring about a more secure and more significant experience of them. But the method terminated in disclosing the connections or interactions upon which perceived objects, viewed as events, depend. Formal analogy suggests that we regard our direct and original experience of things liked and enjoyed as only *possibilities* of values to be achieved; that enjoyment becomes a value when we discover the relations upon which its presence depends. Such a causal and operational definition gives only a conception of a value, not a value itself. But the utilization of the conception in action results in an object having secure and significant value.

The formal statement may be given concrete content by pointing to the difference between the enjoyed and the enjoyable, the desired and the desirable, the satis*fying* and the satis*factory*. To say that something is enjoyed is to make a statement about a fact, something already in existence; it is not to judge the value of that fact. There is no difference between such a proposition and one which says that something is sweet or sour, red or black. It is just correct or incorrect and that is the end of the matter. But to call an object a value is to assert that it satisfies or fulfills certain conditions. Function and status in meeting conditions is a different matter from bare existence. The fact that something is desired only raises the *question* of its desirability; it does not settle it. Only a child in the degree of his immaturity thinks to settle the question of desirability by reiterated proclamation: "I want it, I want it, I want it." What is objected to in the current empirical theory of values is not connection of them with desire and enjoyment but failure to distinguish between enjoyments of radically different sorts. There are many common expressions in which the difference of the two kinds is clearly recognized. Take for example the difference between the ideas of "satisfying" and "satisfactory." To say that something satisfies is to report something as an isolated finality. To assert that it is satis*factory* is to define it in its connections and interactions. The fact that it pleases or is immediately congenial poses a problem to judgment. How shall the satisfaction be rated. Is it a value or is it not? Is it something to be prized and cherished, *to be* enjoyed? Not stern moralists alone but everyday experience informs us that finding satisfaction in a thing may be a warning, a summons to be on the lookout for consequences. To declare something satis*factory* is to assert that it meets specifiable conditions. It is, in effect, a judgment that the thing "will do." It involves a prediction; it contemplates a future in which the thing will continue to serve; it *will* do. It asserts a consequence the thing will actively institute; it will *do*. That it is satisfying is the content of a proposition of fact; that it is satisfactory is a judgment, an estimate, an appraisal. It denotes an attitude *to be* taken, that of striving to perpetuate and to make secure.

It is worth notice that besides the instances given, there are many other recognitions in ordinary speech of the distinction. The endings "able," "worthy" and "ful" are cases in point. Noted and notable, noteworthy; remarked and remarkable; advised and advisable; wondered at and wonderful; pleasing and beautiful; loved and lovable; blamed and blameable, blameworthy; objected to and objectionable; esteemed and estimable; admired and admirable; shamed and shameful; honored and honorable; approved and approvable, worthy of approbation, etc. The multiplication of words adds nothing to the force of the distinction. But it aids in conveying a sense of the fundamental character of the distinction; of the difference between mere report of an already existent fact and judgment as to the importance and need of bringing a fact into existence; or, if it is already there, of sustaining it in existence. The latter is a genuine practical judgment, and marks the only type of judgment that has to do with the direction of action. Whether or no we reserve the term "value" for the latter (as seems to me proper), is a minor matter; that the distinction be acknowledged as the key to understanding the relation of values to the direction of conduct is the important thing.

This element of direction by an idea of value applies to science as well as anywhere else. For in every scientific undertaking, there is passed a constant succession of estimates; such as "it is worth treating these facts as data or evidence; it is advisable to try this experiment; to make that observation; to entertain such and such a hypothesis; to perform this calculation," etc.

The word "taste" has perhaps got too completely associated with arbitrary liking to express the nature of judgments of value. But if the word be used in the sense of an appreciation at once cultivated and active, one may say that the formation of taste is the chief matter wherever values enter in, whether intellectual, esthetic or moral. Relatively immediate judgments, which we call tact or to which we give the name of intuition, do not precede reflective inquiry, but are the funded products of much thoughtful experience. Expertness of taste is at once the result and the reward of constant exercise of thinking. Instead of there being no disputing about tastes, they are the one thing worth disputing about, if by "dispute" is signified discussion involving reflective inquiry. Taste, if we use the word in its best sense, is the outcome of experience brought cumulatively to bear on the intelligent appreciation of the real worth of likings and enjoyments. There is nothing in which a person so completely reveals himself as in the things which he judges enjoyable and desirable. Such judgments are the sole alternative to the domination of belief by impulse, chance, blind habit and self-interest. The formation of a cultivated and effectively operative good judgment or taste with respect to what is esthetically admirable, intellectually acceptable and morally approvable is the supreme task set to human beings by the incidents of experience.

Propositions about what is or has been liked are of instrumental value in reaching judgments of value, in as far as the conditions and consequences of the thing liked are thought about. In themselves they make no claims; they put forth no demand upon subsequent attitudes and acts; they profess no authority to direct. If one likes a thing he likes it; that *is* a point about which there can be no dispute—although it is not so easy to state just *what* is liked as is frequently assumed. A judgment about what is *to be* desired and enjoyed is, on the other hand, a claim on future action; it possesses *de jure* and not merely *de facto* quality. It is a matter of frequent experience that likings and enjoyments are of all kinds, and that many are such as reflective judgments condemn. By way of self-justification and "rationalization," an enjoyment creates a tendency to assert that the thing enjoyed is a value. This assertion of validity adds authority to the fact. It is a decision that the object has a right to exist and hence a claim upon action to further its existence.

The analogy between the status of the theory of values and the theory of ideas about natural objects before the rise of experimental inquiry may be carried further. The sensationalistic theory of the origin and test of thought evoked, by way of reaction, the transcendental theory of *a priori* ideas. For it failed utterly to account for objective connection, order and regularity in objects observed. Similarly, any doctrine that identifies the mere fact of being liked with the value of the object liked so fails to give direction to conduct when direction is needed that it automatically calls forth the assertion that there are values eternally in Being that are the standards of all judgments and the obligatory ends of all action. Without the introduction of operational thinking, we oscillate between a theory that, in order to save the objectivity of judgments of values, isolates them from experience and nature, and a theory that, in order to save their concrete and human significance, reduces them to mere statements about our own feelings.

Not even the most devoted adherents of the notion that enjoyment and value are equivalent facts would venture to assert that because we have once liked a thing we should go on liking it; they are compelled to introduce the idea that *some* tastes are to be cultivated. Logically, there is no ground for introducing the idea of cultivation; liking is liking, and one is as good as another. If enjoyments *are* values, the judgment of value cannot regulate the form which liking takes; it cannot regulate its own conditions. Desire and purpose, and hence action, are left without guidance, although the question of regulation of their formation is the supreme problem of practical life. Values (to sum up) may be connected inherently with liking, and yet not with *every* liking but only with those that judgment has approved, after examination of the relation upon which the object liked depends. A casual liking is one that happens without knowledge of how it occurs nor to what effect. The difference between it and one which is sought because of a judgment that it is worth having and is to be striven for, makes just the difference between enjoyments which are accidental and enjoyments that have value and hence a claim upon our attitude and conduct.

In any case, the alternative rationalistic theory does not afford the guidance for the sake of which eternal and immutable norms are appealed to. The scientist finds no help in determining the probable truth of some proposed theory by comparing it with a standard of absolute truth and immutable being. He has to rely upon definite operations undertaken under definite conditions—upon method. We can hardly imagine an architect getting aid in the construction of a building from an ideal at large, though we can understand his framing an ideal on the basis of knowledge of actual conditions and needs. Nor does the ideal of perfect beauty in antecedent Being give direction to a painter in producing a particular work of art. In morals, absolute perfection does not seem to be more than a generalized hypostatization of the recognition that there is a good to be sought, an obligation to be met—both being concrete matters. Nor is the defect in this respect merely negative. An examination of history would reveal, I am confident, that these general and remote schemes of value actually obtain a content definite enough and near enough to concrete situations as to afford guidance in action only by consecrating some institution or dogma already having social currency. Concreteness is gained, but it is by protecting from inquiry some accepted standard which perhaps is outworn and in need of criticism.

When theories of values do not afford intellectual assistance in framing ideas and beliefs about values that are adequate to direct action, the gap must be filled by other means. If intelligent method is lacking, prejudice, the pressure of immediate circumstance, self-interest and class-interest, traditional customs, institutions of accidental historic origin, are *not* lacking, and they tend to take the place of intelligence. Thus we are led to our main proposition: *Judgments about values are judgments about the conditions and the results of experienced objects; judgments about that which should regulate the formation of our desires, affections and enjoyments.* For whatever decides their formation will determine the main course of our conduct, personal and social.

If it sounds strange to hear that we should frame our judgments as to what has value by considering the connections in existence of what we like and enjoy, the reply is not far to seek. As long as we do not engage in this inquiry enjoyments (values if we choose to apply that term) are casual; they are given by "nature," not constructed by art. Like natural objects in their qualitative existence, they at most only supply material for elaboration in rational discourse. A *feeling* of good or excellence is as far removed from goodness in fact as a feeling that objects are intellectually thus and so is removed from their being actually so. To recognize that the truth of natural objects can be reached only by the greatest care in selecting and arranging directed operations, and then to suppose that values can be truly determined by the mere fact of liking seems to leave us in an incredible position. All the serious perplexities of life come back to the genuine difficulty of forming a judgment as to the values of the situation; they come back to a conflict of goods. Only dogmatism can suppose that serious moral conflict is between something clearly bad and something known to be good, and that uncertainty lies wholly in the will of the one choosing. Most conflicts of importance are conflicts between things which are or have been satisfying, not between good and evil. And to suppose that we can make a hierarchical table of values at large once for all, a kind of catalogue in which they are arranged in an order of ascending or descending worth, is to indulge in a gloss on our inability to frame intelligent judgments in the concrete. Or else it is to dignify customary choice and prejudice by a title of honor.

The alternative to definition, classification and systematization of satisfactions just as they happen to occur is judgment of them by means of the relations under which they occur. If we know the conditions under which the act of liking, of desire and enjoyment, takes place, we are in a position to know what are the consequences of that act. The difference between the desired and the desirable, admired and the admirable, becomes effective at just this point. Consider the difference between the proposition "That thing has been eaten," and the judgment "That thing is edible." The former statement involves no knowledge of any relation except the one stated; while we are able to judge of the edibility of anything only when we have a knowledge of its interactions with other things sufficient to enable us to foresee its probable effects when it is taken into the organism and produces effects there.

To assume that anything can be known in isolation from its connections with other things is to identify knowing with merely having some object before perception or in feeling, and is thus to lose the key to the traits that distinguish an object as known. It is futile, even silly, to suppose that some quality that is directly present constitutes the whole of the thing presenting the quality. It does not do so when the quality is that of being hot or fluid or heavy, and it does not when the quality is that of giving pleasure, or being enjoyed. Such qualities are, once more, effects, ends in the sense of closing termini of processes involving causal connections. They are something to be investigated, challenges to inquiry and judgment. The more connections and interactions we ascertain, the more we *know* the object in question. Thinking is search for these connections. Heat experienced as a consequence of directed operations has a meaning quite different from the heat that is casually experienced without knowledge of how it came about. The same is true of enjoyments. Enjoyments that issue from conduct directed by insight into relations have a meaning and a validity due to the way in which they are experienced. Such enjoyments are not repented of; they generate no after-taste of bitterness. Even in the midst of direct enjoyment, there is a sense of validity, of authorization, which intensifies the enjoyment. There is solicitude for perpetuation of the *object* having value which is radically different from mere anxiety to perpetuate the *feeling* of enjoyment.

Such statements as we have been making are, therefore, far from implying that there are values apart from things actually enjoyed as good. To find a thing enjoy*able* is, so to say, a *plus* enjoyment. We saw that it was foolish to treat the scientific object as a rival to or substitute for the perceived object, since the former is intermediate between uncertain and settled situations and those experienced under conditions of greater control. In the same way, judgment of the value of an object to be experienced is instrumental to appreciation of it when it is realized. But the notion that every object that happens to satisfy has an equal claim with every other to be a value is like supposing that every object of perception has the same cognitive force as every other. There is no knowledge without perception; but objects perceived are *known* only when they are determined as consequences of connective operations. There is no value except where there is satisfaction, but there have to be certain conditions fulfilled to transform a satisfaction into a value.

The time will come when it will be found passing strange that we of this age should take such pains to control by every means at command the formation of ideas of physical things, even those most remote from human concern, and yet are content with haphazard beliefs about the qualities of objects that regulate our deepest interests; that we are scrupulous as to methods of forming ideas of natural objects, and either dogmatic or else driven by immediate conditions in framing those about values. There is, by implication, if not explicitly, a prevalent notion that values are already well known and that all which is lacking is the will to cultivate them in the order of their worth. In fact the most profound lack is not the will to act upon goods already known but the will to know what they are.

It is not a dream that it is possible to exercise some degree of regulation of the occurrence of enjoyments which are of value. Realization of the possibility is exemplified, for example, in the technologies and arts of industrial life—that is, up to a definite limit. Men desired heat, light, and speed of transit and of communication beyond what nature provides of itself. These things have been attained not by lauding the enjoyment of these things and preaching their desirability, but by study of the conditions of their manifestation. Knowledge of relations having been obtained, ability to produce followed, and enjoyment ensued as a matter of course. It is, however, an old story that enjoyment of these things as goods is no warrant of their bringing only good in their train. As Plato was given to pointing out, the physician may know to heal and the orator to persuade, but the ulterior knowledge of whether it is better for a man to be healed or to be persuaded to the orator's opinion remains unsettled. Here there appears the split between what are traditionally and conventionally called the values of the baser arts and the higher values of the truly personal and humane arts.

With respect to the former, there is no assumption that they can be had and enjoyed without definite operative knowledge. With respect to them it is also clear that the degree in which we value them is measurable by the pains taken to control the conditions of their occurrence. With respect to the latter, it is assumed that no one who is honest can be in doubt what they are; that by revelation, or conscience, or the instruction of others, or immediate feeling, they are clear beyond question. And instead of action in their behalf being taken to be a measure of the extent in which things *are* values to us, it is assumed that the difficulty is to persuade men to act upon what they already know to be good. Knowledge of conditions and consequences is regarded as wholly indifferent to judging what is of serious value, though it is useful in a prudential way in trying to actualize it. In consequence, the existence of values that are by common consent of a secondary and technical sort are under a fair degree of control, while those denominated supreme and imperative are subject to all the winds of impulse, custom and arbitrary authority.

This distinction between higher and lower types of value is itself something to be looked into. Why should there be a sharp division made between some goods as physical and material and others as ideal and "spiritual"? The question touches the whole dualism of the material and the ideal at its root. To denominate anything "matter" or "material" is not in truth to disparage it. It is, if the designation is correctly applied, a way of indicating that the thing in question is a condition or means of the existence of something else. And disparagement of effective means is practically synonymous with disregard of the things that are termed, in eulogistic fashion, ideal and spiritual. For the latter terms if they have any concrete application at all signify something which is a desirable consummation of conditions, a cherished fulfillment of means. The sharp separation between material and ideal good thus deprives the latter of the underpinning of effective support while it opens the way for treating things which should be employed as means as ends in themselves. For since men cannot after all live without some measure of possession of such matters as health and wealth, the latter things will be viewed as values and ends in isolation unless they are treated as integral constituents of the goods that are deemed supreme and final.

The relations that determine the occurrence of what human beings experience, especially when social connections are taken into account, are indefinitely wider and more complex than those that determine the events termed physical; the latter are the outcome of definite selective operations. This is the reason why we know something about remote objects like the stars better than we know significantly characteristic things about our own bodies and minds. We forget the infinite number of things we do not know about the stars, or rather that what we call a star is itself the product of the elimination, enforced and deliberate, of most of the traits that belong to an actual existence. The amount of knowledge we possess about stars would not seem very great or very important if it were carried over to human beings and exhausted our knowledge of them. It is inevitable that genuine knowledge of man and society should lag far behind physical knowledge.

But this difference is not a ground for making a sharp division between the two, nor does it account for the fact that we make so little use of the experimental method of forming our ideas and beliefs about the concerns of man in his characteristic social relations. For this separation religions and philosophies must admit some responsibility. They have erected a distinction between a narrower scope of relations and a wider and fuller one into a difference of kind, naming one kind material, and the other mental and moral. They have charged themselves gratuitously with the office of diffusing belief in the necessity of the division, and with instilling contempt for the material as something inferior in kind in its intrinsic nature and worth. Formal philosophies undergo evaporation of their technical solid contents; in a thinner and more viable form they find their way into the minds of those who know nothing of their original forms. When these diffuse and, so to say, airy emanations re-crystallize in the popular mind they form a hard deposit of opinion that alters slowly and with great difficulty.

What difference would it actually make in the arts of conduct, personal and social, if the experimental theory were adopted not as a mere theory, but as a part of the working equipment of habitual attitudes on the part of everyone? It would be impossible, even were time given, to answer the question in adequate detail, just as men could not foretell in advance the consequences for knowledge of adopting the experimental method. It is the nature of the method that it has to be tried. But there are generic lines of difference which, within the limits of time at disposal, may be sketched.

Change from forming ideas and judgments of value on the basis of conformity to antecedent objects, to constructing enjoyable objects directed by knowledge of consequences, is a change from looking to the past to looking to the future. I do not for a moment suppose that the experiences of the past, personal and social, are of no importance. For without them we should not be able to frame any ideas whatever of the conditions under which objects are enjoyed nor any estimate of the consequences of esteeming and liking them. But past experiences are significant in giving us intellectual instrumentalities of judging just these points. They are tools, not finalities. Reflection upon what we have liked and have enjoyed is a necessity. But it tells us nothing about the *value* of these things until enjoyments are themselves reflectively controlled, or, until, as they are now recalled, we form the best judgment possible about what led us to like this sort of thing and what has issued from the fact that we like it.

We are not, then, to get away from enjoyments experienced in the past and from recall of them, but from the notion that they are the arbiters of things to be further enjoyed. At present, the arbiter is found in the past, although there are many ways of interpreting what in the past is authoritative. Nominally, the most influential conception doubtless is that of a revelation once had or a perfect life once lived. Reliance upon precedent, upon institutions created in the past, especially in law, upon rules of morals that have come to us through unexamined customs, upon uncriticized tradition, are other forms of dependence. It is not for a moment suggested that we can get away from customs and established institutions. A mere break would doubtless result simply in chaos. But there is no danger of such a break. Mankind is too inertly conservative both by constitution and by education to give the idea of this danger actuality. What there is genuine danger of is that the force of new conditions will produce disruption externally and mechanically: this is an ever present danger. The prospect is increased, not mitigated, by the conservatism which insists upon the adequacy of old standards to meet new conditions. What is needed is intelligent examination of the consequences that are actually affected by inherited institutions and customs, in order that there may be intelligent consideration of the ways in which they are to be intentionally modified in behalf of generation of different consequences.

This is the significant meaning of transfer of experimental method from the technical field of physical experience to the wider field of human life. We trust the method in forming our beliefs about things not directly connected with human life. In effect, we distrust it in moral, political and economic affairs. In the fine arts, there are many signs of a change. In the past, such a change has often been an omen and precursor of changes in other human attitudes. But, generally speaking, the idea of actively adopting experimental method in social affairs, in the matters deemed of most enduring and ultimate worth, strikes most persons as a surrender of all standards and regulative authority. But in principle, experimental method does not signify random and aimless action; it implies direction by ideas and knowledge. The question at issue is a practical one. Are there in existence the ideas and the knowledge that permit experimental method to be effectively used in social interests and affairs?

Where will regulation come from if we surrender familiar and traditionally prized values as our directive standards? Very largely from the findings of the natural sciences. For one of the effects of the separation drawn between knowledge and action is to deprive scientific knowledge of its proper service as a guide of conduct—except once more in those technological fields which have been degraded to an inferior rank. Of course, the complexity of the conditions upon which objects of human and liberal value depend is a great obstacle, and it would be too optimistic to say that we have as yet enough knowledge of the scientific type to enable us to regulate our judgments of value very extensively. But we have more knowledge than we try to put to use, and until we try more systematically we shall not know what are the important gaps in our sciences judged from the point of view of their moral and humane use.

For moralists usually draw a sharp line between the field of the natural sciences and the conduct that is regarded as moral. But a moral that frames its judgments of value on the basis of consequences must depend in a most intimate manner upon the conclusions of science. For the knowledge of the relations between changes which enable us to connect things as antecedents and consequences *is* science. The narrow scope which moralists often give to morals, their isolation of some conduct as virtuous and vicious from other large ranges of conduct, thost having to do with health and vigor, business, education, with all the affairs in which desires and affection are implicated, is perpetuated by this habit of exclusion of the subject-matter of natural science from a role in formation of moral standards and ideals. The same attitude operates in the other direction to keep natural science a technical specialty, and it works unconsciously to encourage its use exclusively in regions where it can be turned to personal and class advantage, as in war and trade.

Another great difference to be made by carrying the experimental habit into all matter of practice is that it cuts the roots of what is often called subjectivism, but which is better termed egoism. The subjective attitude is much more widespread than would be inferred from the philosophies which have that label attached. It is as rampant in realistic philosophies as in any others, sometimes even more so, although disguised from those who hold these philosophies under the cover of reverence of and enjoyment of ultimate values. For the implication of placing the standard of thought and knowledge in antecedent existence is that our thought makes no difference in what is significantly real. It then affects only our own attitude toward it.

This constant throwing of emphasis back upon a change made in ourselves instead of one made in the world in which we live seems to me the essence of what is objectionable in "subjectivism." Its taint hangs about even Platonic realism with its insistent evangelical dwelling upon the change made within the mind by contemplation of the realm of essence, and its depreciation of action as transient and all but sordid—a concession to the necessities of organic existence. All the theories which put conversion "of the eye of the soul" in the place of a conversion of natural and social objects that modifies goods actually experienced, is a retreat and escape from existence—and this retraction into self is, once more, the heart of subjective egoisms. The typical example is perhaps the other-worldliness found in religions whose chief concern is with the salvation of the personal soul. But other-worldliness is found as well in estheticism and in all seclusion within ivory towers.

It is not in the least implied that change in personal attitudes, in the disposition of the "subject," is not of great importance. Such change, on the contrary, is involved in any attempt to modify the conditions of the environment. But there is a radical difference between a change in the self that is cultivated and valued as an end, and one that is a means to alteration, through action, of objective conditions. The Aristotelian-medieval conviction that highest bliss is found in contemplative possession of ultimate Being presents an ideal attractive to some types of mind; it sets forth a refined sort of enjoyment. It is a doctrine congenial to minds that despair of the effort involved in creation of a better world of daily experience. It is, apart from theological attachments, a doctrine sure to recur when social conditions are so troubled as to make actual endeavor seem hopeless. But the subjectivism so externally marked in modern thought as compared with ancient is either a development of the old doctrine under new conditions or is of merely technical import. The medieval version of the doctrine at least had the active support of a great social institution by means of which man could be brought into the state of mind that prepared him for ultimate enjoyment of eternal Being. It had a certain solidity and depth which is lacking in modern theories that would attain the result by merely emotional or speculative procedures, or by any means not demanding a change in objective existence so as to render objects of value more empirically secure.

The nature in detail of the revolution that would be wrought by carrying into the region of values the principle now embodied in scientific practice cannot be told; to attempt it would violate the fundamental idea that we know only after we have acted and in consequences of the outcome of action. But it would surely effect a transfer of attention and energy from the subjective to the objective. Men would think of themselves as agents not as ends; ends would be found in experienced enjoyment of the fruits of a transforming activity. In as far as the subjectivity of modern thought represents a discovery of the part played by personal responses, organic and acquired, in the causal production of the qualities and values of objects, it marks the possibility of a decisive gain. It puts us in possession of some of the conditions that control the occurrence of experienced objects, and thereby it supplies us with an instrument of regulation. There is something querulous in the sweeping denial that things as experienced, as perceived and enjoyed, in any way depend upon interaction with human selves. The error of doctrines that have exploited the part played by personal and subjective reactions in determining what is perceived and enjoyed lies either in exaggerating this factor of constitution into the sole condition—as happens in subjective idealism—or else in treating it as a finality instead of, as with all knowledge, an instrument in direction of further action.

A third significant change that would issue from carrying over experimental method from physics to man concerns the import of standards, principles, rules. With the transfer, these, and all tenets and creeds about good and goods, would be recognized to be hypotheses. Instead of being rigidly fixed, they would be treated as intellectual instruments to be tested and confirmed—and altered—through consequences effected by acting upon them. They would lose all pretence of finality—the ulterior source of dogmatism. It is both astonishing and depressing that so much of the energy of mankind has gone into fighting for (with weapons of the flesh as well as of the spirit) the truth of creeds, religious, moral and political, as distinct from what has gone into effort to try creeds by putting them to the test of acting upon them. The change would do away with the intolerance and fanaticism that attend the notion that beliefs and judgments are capable of inherent truth and authority; inherent in the sense of being independent of what they lead to when used as directive principles. The transformation does not imply merely that men are responsible for acting upon what they profess to believe; that is an old doctrine. It goes much further. Any belief as such is tentative, hypothetical; it is not just to be acted upon, but is to be *framed* with reference to its office as a guide to action. Consequently, it should be the last thing in the world to be picked up casually and then clung to rigidly. When it is apprehended as a tool and only a tool, an instrumentality of direction, the same scrupulous attention will go to its formation as now goes into the making of instruments of precision in technical fields. Men, instead of being proud of accepting and asserting beliefs and "principles" on the ground of loyalty, will be as ashamed of that procedure as they would now be to confess their assent to a scientific theory out of reverence for Newton or Helmholz or whomever, without regard to evidence.

If one stops to consider the matter, is there not something strange in the fact that men should consider loyalty to "laws," principles, standards, ideals to be an inherent virtue, accounted unto them for righteousness? It is as if they were making up for some secret sense of weakness by rigidity and intensity of insistent attachment. A moral law, like a law in physics, is not something to swear by and stick to at all hazards; it is a formula of the way to respond when specified conditions present themselves. Its soundness and pertinence are tested by what happens when it is acted upon. Its claim or authority rests finally upon the imperativeness of the situation that has to be dealt with, not upon its own intrinsic nature—as any tool achieves dignity in the measure of needs served by it. The idea that adherence to standards external to experienced objects is the only alternative to confusion and lawlessness was once held in science. But knowledge became steadily progressive when it was abandoned, and clews and tests found within concrete acts and objects were employed. The test of consequences is more exacting than that afforded by fixed general rules. In addition, it secures constant development, for when new acts are tried new results are experienced, while the lauded immutability of eternal ideals and norms is in itself a denial of the possibility of development and improvement.

The various modifications that would result from adoption in social and humane subjects of the experimental way of thinking are perhaps summed up in saying that it would place *method and means* upon the level of importance that has, in the past, been imputed exclusively to ends. Means have been regarded as menial, and the useful as the servile. Means have been treated as poor relations to be endured, but not inherently welcome. The very meaning of the word "ideals" is significant of the divorce which has obtained between means and ends. "Ideals" are thought to be remote and inaccessible of attainment; they are too high and fine to be sullied by realization. They serve vaguely to arouse "aspiration," but they do not evoke and direct strivings for embodiment in actual existence. They hover in an indefinite way over the actual scene; they are expiring ghosts of a once significant kingdom of divine reality whose rule penetrated to every detail of life.

It is impossible to form a just estimate of the paralysis of effort that has been produced by indifference to means. Logically, it is truistic that lack of consideration for means signifies that so-called ends are not taken seriously. It is as if one professed devotion to painting pictures conjoined with contempt for canvas, brush and paints; or love of music on condition that no instruments, whether the voice or something external, be used to make sounds. The good workman in the arts is known by his respect for his tools and by his interest in perfecting his technique. The glorification in the arts of ends at the expense of means would be taken to be a sign of complete insincerity or even insanity. Ends separated from means are either sentimental indulgences or if they happen to exist are merely accidental. The ineffectiveness in action of "ideals" is due precisely to the supposition that means and ends are not on exactly the same level with respect to the attention and care they demand.

It is, however, much easier to point out the formal contradiction implied in ideals that are professed without equal regard for the instruments and techniques of their realization, than it is to appreciate the concrete ways in which belief in their separation has found its way into life and borne corrupt and poisonous fruits. The separation marks the form in which the traditional divorce of theory and practice has expressed itself in actual life. It accounts for the relative impotency of arts concerned with enduring human welfare. Sentimental attachment and subjective eulogy take the place of action. For there is no art without tools and instrumental agencies. But it also explains the fact that in actual behavior, energies devoted to matters nominally thought to be inferior, material and sordid, engross attention and interest. After a polite and pious deference has been paid to "ideals," men feel free to devote themselves to matters which are more immediate and pressing.

It is usual to condemn the amount of attention paid by people in general to material ease, comfort, wealth, and success gained by competition, on the ground that they give to mere means the attention that ought to be given to ends, or that they have taken for ends things which in reality are only means. Criticisms of the place which economic interest and action occupy in present life are full of complaints that men allow lower aims to usurp the place that belongs to higher and ideal values. The final source of the trouble is, however, that moral and spiritual "leaders" have propagated the notion that ideal ends may be cultivated in isolation from "material" means, as if means and material were not synonymous. While they condemn men for giving to means the thought and energy that ought to go to ends, the condemnation should go to them. For they have not taught their followers to think of material and economic activities as *really* means. They have been unwilling to frame their conception of the values that should be regulative of human conduct on the basis of the actual conditions and operations by which alone values can be actualized.

Practical needs are imminent; with the mass of mankind they are imperative. Moreover, speaking generally, men are formed to act rather than to theorize. Since the ideal ends are so remotely and accidentally connected with immediate and urgent conditions that need attention, after lip service is given to them, men naturally devote themselves to the latter. If a bird in the hand is worth two in a neighboring bush, an actuality in hand is worth, for the direction of conduct, many ideals that are so remote as to be invisible and inaccessible. Men hoist the banner of the ideal, and then march in the direction that concrete conditions suggest and reward.

Deliberate insincerity and hypocrisy are rare. But the notion that action and sentiment are inherently unified in the constitution of human nature has nothing to justify it. Integration is something to be achieved. Division of attitudes and responses, compartmentalizing of interests, is easily acquired. It goes deep just because the acquisition is unconscious, a matter of habitual adaptation to conditions. Theory separated from concrete doing and making is empty and futile; practice then becomes an immediate seizure of opportunities and enjoyments which conditions afford without the direction which theory—knowledge and ideas—has power to supply. The problem of the relation of theory and practice is not a problem of theory alone; it is that, but it is also the most practical problem of life. For it is the question of how intelligence may inform action, and how action may bear the fruit of increased insight into meaning: a clear view of the values that are worth while and of the means by which they are to be made secure in experienced objects. Construction of ideals in general and their sentimental glorification are easy; the responsibilities both of studious thought and of action are shirked. Persons having the advantage of positions of leisure and who find pleasure in abstract theorizing—a most delightful indulgence to those to whom it appeals—have a large measure of liability for a cultivated diffusion of ideals and aims that are separated from the conditions which are the means of actualization. Then other persons who find themselves in positions of social power and authority readily claim to be the bearers and defenders of ideal ends in church and state. They then use the prestige and authority their representative capacity as guardians of the highest ends confers on them to cover actions taken in behalf of the harshest and narrowest of material ends.

The present state of industrial life seems to give a fair index of the existing separation of means and ends. Isolation of economics from ideal ends, whether of morals or of organized social life, was proclaimed by Aristotle. Certain things, he said, are conditions of a worthy life, personal and social, but are not constituents of it. The economic life of man, concerned with satisfaction of wants, is of this nature. Men have wants and they must be satisfied. But they are only prerequisites of a good life, not intrinsic elements in it. Most philosophers have not been so frank nor perhaps so logical. But upon the whole, economics has been treated as on a lower level than either morals or politics. Yet the life which men, women and children actually lead, the opportunities open to them, the values they are capable of enjoying, their education, their share in all the things of art and science are mainly determined by economic conditions. Hence we can hardly expect a moral system which ignores economic conditions to be other than remote and empty.

Industrial life is correspondingly brutalized by failure to equate it as the means by which social and cultural values are realized. That the economic life, thus exiled from the pale of higher values, takes revenge by declaring that it is the only social reality, and by means of the doctrine of materialistic determination of institutions and conduct in all fields, denies to deliberate morals and politics any share of causal regulation, is not surprising.

When economists were told that their subject-matter was merely material, they naturally thought they could be "scientific" only by excluding all reference to distinctively human values. Material wants, efforts to satisfy them, even the scientifically regulated technologies highly developed in industrial activity, are then taken to form a complete and closed field. If any reference to social ends and values is introduced it is by way of an external addition, mainly hortatory. That economic life largely determines the conditions under which mankind has access to concrete values may be recognized or it may not be. In either case, the notion that it is the means to be utilized in order to secure significant values as the common and shared possession of mankind is alien and inoperative. To many persons, the idea that the ends professed by morals are impotent save as they are connected with the working machinery of economic life seems like deflowering the purity of moral values and obligations.

The social and moral effects of the separation of theory and practice have been merely hinted at. They are so manifold and so pervasive that an adequate consideration of them would involve nothing less than a survey of the whole field of morals, economics and politics. It cannot be justly stated that these effects are in fact direct consequences of the quest for certainty by thought and knowledge isolated from action. For, as we have seen, this quest was itself a reflex product of actual conditions. But it may be truly asserted that this quest, undertaken in religion and philosophy, has had results which have reinforced the conditions which originally brought it about. Moreover, search for safety and consolation amid the perils of life by means other than intelligent action, by feeling and thought alone, began when actual means of control were lacking, when arts were undeveloped. It had then a relative historic justification that is now lacking. The primary problem for thinking which lays claim to be philosophic in its breadth and depth is to assist in bringing about a reconstruction of all beliefs rooted in a basic separation of knowledge and action; to develop a system of operative ideas congruous with present knowledge and with present facilities of control over natural events and energies.

We have noted more than once how modern philosophy has been absorbed in the problem of affecting an adjustment between the conclusions of natural science and the beliefs and values that have authority in the direction of life. The genuine and poignant issue does not reside where philosophers for the most part have placed it. It does not consist in accommodation to each other of two realms, one physical and the other ideal and spiritual, nor in the reconciliation of the "categories" of theoretical and practical reason. It is found in that isolation of executive means and ideal interests which has grown up under the influence of the separation of theory and practice. For this, by nature, involves the separation of the material and the spiritual. Its solution, therefore, can be found only in action wherein the phenomena of material and economic life are equated with the purposes that command the loyalties of affection and purpose, and in which ends and ideals are framed in terms of the possibilities of actually experienced situations. But while the solution cannot be found in "thought" alone, it can be furthered by thinking which is operative—which frames and defines ideas in terms of what may be done, and which uses the conclusions of science as instrumentalities. William James was well within the bounds of moderation when he said that looking forward instead of backward, looking to what the world and life might become instead of to what they have been, is an alteration in the "seat of authority."

It was incidentally remarked earlier in our discussion that the serious defect in the current empirical philosophy of values, the one which identifies them with things actually enjoyed irrespective of the conditions upon which they depend, is that it formulates and in so far consecrates the conditions of our present social experience. Throughout these chapters, primary attention has perforce been given to the methods and statements of philosophic theories. But these statements are technical and specialized in formulation only. In origin, content and import they are reflections of some condition or some phase of concrete human experience. Just as the theory of the separation of theory and practice has a practical origin and a momentous practical consequence, so the empirical theory that values are identical with whatever men actually enjoy, no matter how or what, formulates an aspect, and an undesirable one, of the present social situation.

For while our discussion has given more attention to the other type of philosophical doctrine, that which holds that regulative and authoritative standards are found in transcendent eternal values, it has not passed in silence over the fact that actually the greater part of the activities of the greater number of human beings is spent in effort to seize upon and hold onto such enjoyments as the actual scene permits. Their energies and their enjoyments are controlled in fact, but they are controlled by external conditions rather than by intelligent judgment and endeavor. If philosophies have any influence over the thoughts and acts of men, it is a serious matter that the most widely held empirical theory should in effect justify this state of things by identifying values with the objects of any interest as such. As long as the only theories of value placed us for intellectual assent alternate between sending us to a realm of eternal and fixed values and sending us to enjoyments such as actually obtain, the formulation, even as only a theory, of an experimental empiricism which finds values to be identical with goods that are the fruit of intelligently directed activity has its measure of practical significance.

12

Propositions of Appraisal

Any survey of the experiences in which ends-in-view are formed, and in which earlier impulsive tendencies are shaped through deliberation into a *chosen* desire, reveals that the object finally valued as an end to be reached is determined in its concrete makeup by appraisal of existing conditions as means. However, the habit of completely separating the conceptions of ends from that of means is so ingrained because of a long philosophical tradition that further discussion is required.

1. The common assumption that there is a sharp separation between things, on the one hand, as useful or helpful, and, on the other hand, as *intrinsically* good, and hence that there exists a separation between propositions as to what is expedient, prudent, or advisable and what is inherently desirable, does not, in any case, state a *self-evident* truth. The fact that such words as "prudent," "sensible," and "expedient," in the long run, or after survey of all conditions, merge so readily into the word "wise" suggests (though, of course, it does not prove) that ends framed in separation from consideration of things as means are foolish to the point of irrationality.

2. Common sense regards some desires and interests as shortsighted, "blind," and others, in contrast, as enlightened, farsighted. It does not for a moment lump all desires and interests together as having the same status with respect to end-values. Discrimination between their respective shortsightedness and farsightedness is made precisely on the ground of whether the object of a given desire is

Source: From *Theory of Valuation* (*International Encyclopedia of Unified Science*, II, 4, 1939). By permission of the University of Chicago Press.

viewed as, in turn, itself a conditioning means of further consequences. Instead of taking a laudatory view of "immediate" desires and valuations, common sense treats refusal to mediate as the very essence of short-view judgment. For treating the end as *merely* immediate and exclusively final is equivalent to refusal to consider what will happen after and because a particular end is reached.

3.   The words "inherent," "intrinsic," and "immediate" are used ambiguously, so that a fallacious conclusion is reached. Any quality or property that actually belongs to any object or event is properly said to be immediate, inherent, or intrinsic. The fallacy consists in interpreting what is designated by these terms as out of relation to anything else and hence as absolute. For example, *means* are by definition relational, mediated, and mediating, since they are intermediate between an existing situation and a situation that is to be brought into existence by their use. But the relational character of the *things* that are employed as means does not prevent the things from having their own immediate qualities. In case the things in question are prized and cared for, then, according to the theory that connects the property of value with prizing, they necessarily have an immediate quality of value. The notion that, when means and instruments are valued, the value-qualities which result are only instrumental is hardly more than a bad pun. There is nothing in the nature of prizing or desiring to prevent their being directed to things which are means, and there is nothing in the nature of means to militate against their being desired and prized. In empirical fact, the measure of the value a person attaches to a given end is not what he *says* about its preciousness but the care he devotes to obtaining and using the *means* without which it cannot be attained. No case of notable achievement can be cited in any field (save as a matter of sheer accident) in which the persons who brought about the end did not give loving care to the instruments and agencies of its production. The dependence of ends attained upon means employed is such that the statement just made reduces in fact to a tautology. Lack of desire and interest are proved by neglect of, and indifference to, required means. As soon as an attitude of desire and interest has been developed, then, because without full-hearted attention an end which is professedly prized will not be attained, the desire and interest in question automatically attach themselves to whatever other things are seen to be required means of attaining the end.

The considerations that apply to "immediate" apply also to "intrinsic" and "inherent." A quality, including that of value, is inherent if it actually belongs to something, and the question of whether or not it belongs is one of *fact* and not a question that can be decided by dialectical manipulation of the concept of inherency. If one has an ardent desire to obtain certain things as means, then the quality of value belongs to, or inheres in, those things. For the time being, producing or obtaining those means *is* the end-in-view. The notion that only that which is out of relation to everything else can justly be called *inherent* is not only itself absurd but is contradicted by the very theory that connects the value of objects as ends with desire and interest, for this view expressly makes the value of the end-object relational, so that, if the inherent is identified with the nonrelational, there are, according to this view, no inherent values at all. On the other hand, if it is the fact that the quality exists in this case because that to which it belongs is conditioned by a relation, then the relational character of means cannot be brought forward as evidence that their value is not inherent. The same considerations apply to the terms "intrinsic" and "extrinsic" as applied to value-qualities. Strictly speaking, the phrase "extrinsic value" involves a contradiction in terms. Relational properties do not lose their intrinsic quality of being just what they are because their coming into being is *caused* by something "extrinsic." The theory that such is the case would terminate logically in the view that there are no intrinsic qualities whatever, since it can be shown that such intrinsic qualities as *red, sweet, hard*, etc., are causally conditioned as to their occurrence. The trouble, once more, is that a dialectic of concepts has taken the place of examination of actual empirical facts. The extreme instance of the view that to be intrinsic is to be out of any relation is found in those writers who hold that, since values *are* intrinsic, they cannot depend upon *any* relation whatever, and certainly not upon a relation to human beings. Hence this school attacks those who connect value-properties with desire and interest on exactly the same ground that the latter equate the distinction between the values of means and ends with the distinction between instrumental and intrinsic values. The views of this extreme nonnaturalistic school may, accordingly, be regarded as a definite exposure of what happens when an analysis of the abstract concept of "intrinsicalness" is substituted for analysis of empirical occurrences.

The more overtly and emphatically the valuation of objects as ends is connected with desire and interest, the more evident it should be that, since desire and interest are ineffectual save as they co-operatively interact with environing conditions, valuation of desire and interest, as means correlated with other means, is the sole condition for valid appraisal of objects as ends. If the lesson were learned that the object of scientific knowledge is *in any case* an ascertained correlation of changes, it would be seen, beyond the possibility of denial, that anything taken *as end* is in its own content or constituents a correlation of the energies, personal and extra-personal, which operate as means. An end as an *actual* consequence, as an existing outcome, is, like any other occurrence which is scientifically analyzed, nothing but the interaction of the conditions that bring it to pass. Hence it follows necessarily that the *idea* of the object of desire and interest, the *end-in-view* as distinct from the end or outcome actually effected, is warranted in the precise degree in which it is formed in terms of these operative conditions.

4.   The chief weakness of current theories of valuation which relate the latter to desire and interest is due to failure to make an empirical analysis of concrete desires and interests as they actually exist. When such an analysis is made, certain relevant considerations at once present themselves.

(i)   Desires are subject to frustration and interests are subject to defeat. The likelihood of the occurrence of failure in attaining desired ends is in direct ratio to failure to form desire and interest (and the objects they involve) on the basis of conditions that operate either as obstacles (negatively valued) or as positive resources. The difference between reasonable and unreasonable desires and interests is precisely the difference between those which arise casually and are not reconstituted through consideration of the conditions that will actually decide the outcome and those which are formed on the basis of existing liabilities and potential resources. That desires as they first present themselves are the product of a mechanism consisting of native organic tendencies and acquired habits is an undeniable fact. All growth in maturity consists in *not* immediately giving way to such tendencies but in remaking them in their first manifestation through consideration of the consequences they will occasion *if* they are acted upon—an operation which is equivalent to judging or evaluating them as means operating in connection with extra-personal conditions as also means. Theories of valuation which relate it to desire and interest cannot both eat their cake and have it. They cannot continually oscillate between a view of desire and interest that identifies the latter with impulses just as they happen to occur (as products of organic mechanisms) and a view of desire as a modification of a raw impulse through foresight of its outcome; the latter alone being desire, the whole difference between impulse and desire is made by the presence in desire of an end-in-view, of objects *as* foreseen consequences. The foresight will be dependable in the degree in which it is constituted by examination of the conditions that will in fact decide the outcome. If it seems that this point is being hammered in too insistently, it is because the issue at stake is nothing other and nothing less than the possibility of distinctive valuation-propositions. For it cannot be denied that propositions having evidential warrant and experimental test are possible in the case of evaluation of things as means. Hence it follows that, if these propositions enter into the formation of the interests and desires which are valuations of ends, the latter are thereby constituted the subject matter of authentic empirical affirmations and denials.

(ii)   We commonly speak of "learning from experience" and the "maturity" of an individual or a group. What do we mean by such expressions? At the very least, we mean that in the history of individual persons and of the human race there takes place a change from original, comparatively unreflective, impulses and hard-and-fast habits to desires and interests that incorporate the results of critical inquiry. When this process is examined, it is seen to take place chiefly on the basis of careful observation of differences found between desired and proposed ends (ends-*in-view*) and attained ends or actual consequences. Agreement between what is wanted and anticipated and what is actually obtained confirms the selection of conditions which operate as a means to the desired end; discrepancies, which are experienced as frustrations and defeats, lead to an inquiry to discover the causes of failure. This inquiry consists of more and more thorough examination of the conditions under which impulses and habits are formed and in which they operate. The result is formation of desires and interests which are what they are through the union of the affective-motor conditions of action with the intellectual or ideational. The latter is there in any case if there is an end-in-view of any sort, no matter how casually formed, while it is adequate in just the degree in which the end is constituted in terms of the conditions of its actualization. For, wherever there is an *end-in-view* of any sort whatever, there is affective-*ideational*-motor activity; or, in terms of the dual meaning of valuation, there is union of prizing and appraising. Observation of results obtained, of *actual* consequences in their agreement with and difference from ends anticipated or held in view, thus provides the conditions by which desires and interests (and hence valuations) are matured and tested. Nothing more contrary to common sense can be imagined than the notion that we are incapable of changing our desires and interests by means of learning what the consequences of acting upon them are, or, as it is sometimes put, of *indulging* them. It should not be necessary to point in evidence to the spoiled child and the adult who cannot "face reality." Yet, as far as valuation and the theory of values are concerned, any theory which isolates valuation of ends from appraisal of means equates the spoiled child and the irresponsible adult to the mature and sane person.

(iii)   Every person in the degree in which he is capable of learning from experience draws a distinction between what is desired and what is desirable whenever he engages in formation and choice of competing desires and interests. There is nothing far-fetched or "moralistic" in this statement. The contrast referred to is simply that between the object of a desire as it first presents itself (because of the existing mechanism of impulses and habits) and the object of desire which emerges as a revision of the first-appearing impulse, after the latter is critically judged in reference to the conditions which will decide the actual result. The "desirable," or the object which *should* be desired (valued), does not descend out of the a priori blue nor descend as an imperative from a moral Mount Sinai. It presents itself because past experience has shown that hasty action upon uncriticized desire leads to defeat and possibly to catastrophe. The "desirable" as distinct from the "desired" does not then designate something at large or a priori. It points to the difference between the operation and consequences of unexamined impulses and those of desires and interests that are the product of investigation of conditions and consequences. Social conditions and pressures are part of the conditions that affect the execution of desires. Hence they have to be taken into account in framing ends in terms of available means. But the distinction between the "is" in the sense of the object of a casually emerging desire and the "should be" of a desire framed in relation to actual conditions is a distinction which in any case is bound to offer itself as human beings grow in maturity and part with the childish disposition to "indulge" every impulse as it arises.

Desires and interests are, as we have seen, themselves causal conditions of results. As such they are potential means and have to be appraised as such. This statement is but a restatement of points already made. But it is worth making because it forcibly indicates how far away some of the theoretical views of valuation are from practical common-sense attitudes and beliefs. There is an indefinite number of proverbial sayings which in effect set forth the necessity of not treating desires and interests as final in their first appearance but of treating them as means—that is, of appraising them and forming objects or ends-in-view on the ground of what consequences they will tend to produce in practice. "Look before you leap"; "Act in haste, repent at leisure"; "A stitch in time saves nine"; "When angry count ten"; "Do not put your hand to the plow until the cost has been counted"—are but a few of the many maxims. They are summed up in the old saying, *"Respice finem"*—a saying which marks the difference between simply *having* an end-in-view for which *any* desire suffices, and *looking,* examining, to make sure that the consequences that will actually result are such as will be actually prized and valued when they occur. Only the exigencies of a preconceived theory (in all probability one seriously infected by the conclusions of an uncritically accepted "subjectivistic" psychology) will ignore the concrete differences that are made in the content of "likings" and "prizings," and of desires and interests, by evaluating them in their respective causal capacities when they are taken as means.

VI

Social and Political Philosophy

The ultimate test of a philosophy, for Dewey, is the way in which it fulfills its social function. Dewey believed that those philosophical scenarios in which a completely isolated human being resolves the ultimate questions about the nature of things or of self, of God or of the right, are conceptually incoherent. Philosophy is an activity born out of the conflict of opinions and disagreements about methods of inquiry in a specific culture. Its function is the clarification of the nature of that conflict and the resolution of the disagreements about intellectual method. Abstracted from social context, there could be no philosophical discussion.

These general considerations concerning the social basis of all philosophical thought led Dewey to a sustained analysis of the role of philosophy in the contemporary social context. Thus documents taken from that analysis illuminate the recurrent themes in Dewey's reflection on the social and political problems of our time.

Social philosophy, he believed, could carry out two related tasks in the reconstruction of social institutions so as to respond more adequately to the genuine needs of all the members of the society. In his small book *Reconstruction in Philosophy* (1920), he sketched these two tasks. The first is the development of a conceptual interpretation of the relationship between the "individual" and the "social" that would undo the damage caused by those views that interpret society either in terms of "atomic individuals" or of an "organic whole."

The second task is the clarification of the methodological shift required in order to transfer the attention of political philosophers to the study of how particular forms of social organization would lead to particular expressions of individuality. Dewey argued that the problem of achieving a more democratic society may be insoluble in terms of the relationship between an entity described as "the individual" and the entity of "society" as such. It becomes open to creative solution if we shift to an investigation of the social conditions that enhance the development of certain kinds of individuality.

Dewey's criticism of the concept of the "atomic individual" was part of his continuous criticism of the inadequacy of nineteenth-century formulations of liberalism in terms of economic and political individualism. The concept of liberty that such an individualism delineated was a negative one, in which freedom is interpreted not in terms of the possibilities of self-realization but solely in terms of the ability of presumably completed individuals to resist incursions from government or society. Dewey developed this theme historically on several occasions, both in a small volume entitled *Liberalism and Social Action* and in a number of papers. Here, it is developed in the selection "The Future of Liberalism," which was written for *The Journal of Philosophy* in 1935.

The growth of individual personality was, for Dewey, the goal of a democratic society. Yet political democracy as an institutional mechanism for electing national leaders between competing political parties seemed remote from any such goal or ideal. Free personalities, he argued, would be the product of societies in which capacities were developed by participation in the decision-making processes of the society. The American political agenda was then to see if the Great Society, that is, the large industrialized society, may become the Great Community, the society of participating individuals. The method for realizing this possibility is the development of democracy in the secondary and voluntary associations of the Great Society: the schools, trade unions, and local government. In this context, Dewey develops his concept of democracy as the idea of the individual participating in the shared experiences of the community. In *The Public and Its Problems* (1927), from which the section "Search for the Great Community" is taken, Dewey aimed at a realistic assessment of some of the risks and some of the possibilities for the emergence of a democratic society under modern social and industrial conditions.

13

Reconstruction as Affecting Social Philosophy

How can philosophic change seriously affect social philosophy? As far as fundamentals are concerned, every view and combination appears to have been formulated already. Society is composed of individuals: this obvious and basic fact no philosophy, whatever its pretensions to novelty, can question or alter. Hence these three alternatives: Society must exist for the sake of individuals; or individuals must have their ends and ways of living set for them by society; or else society and individuals are correlative, organic, to one another, society requiring the service and subordination of individuals and at the same time existing to serve them. Beyond these three views, none seems to be logically conceivable. Moreover, while each of the three types includes many subspecies and variations within itself, yet the changes seem to have been so thoroughly rung that at most only minor variations are now possible.

Especially would it seem true that the "organic" conception meets all the objections to the extreme individualistic and extreme socialistic theories, avoiding the errors alike of Plato and Bentham. Just because society is composed of individuals, it would seem that individuals and the associative relations that hold them together must be of coequal importance. Without strong and competent individuals, the bonds and ties that form society have nothing to lay hold on. Apart from associations with one another, individuals are

SOURCE: From *Reconstruction in Philosophy*, 1920. Reprinted with the permission of The Center for Dewey Studies, Southern Illinois University at Carbondale.

isolated from one another and fade and wither; or are opposed to one another and their conflicts injure individual development. Law, state, church, family, friendship, industrial association, these and other institutions and arrangements are necessary in order that individuals may grow and find their specific capacities and functions. Without their aid and support human life is, as Hobbes said, brutish, solitary, nasty.

We plunge into the heart of the matter by asserting that these various theories suffer from a common defect. They are all committed to the logic of general notions under which specific situations are to be brought. What we want light upon is this or that group of individuals, this or that concrete human being, this or that special institution or social arrangement. For such a logic of inquiry, the traditionally accepted logic substitutes discussion of the meaning of concepts and their dialectical relationship to one another. The discussion goes on in terms of *the* state, *the* individual; the nature of institutions as such, society in general.

We need guidelines in dealing with particular perplexities in domestic life, and are met by dissertations on the Family or by assertions of the sacredness of individual Personality. We want to know about the worth of the institution of private property as it operates under given conditions of definite time and place. We meet with the reply of Proudhon that property generally is theft, or with that of Hegel that the realization of will is the end of all institutions, and that private ownership as the expression of mastery of personality over physical nature is a necessary element in such realization. Both answers may have a certain suggestiveness in connection with specific situations. But the conceptions are not proffered for what they may be worth in connection with special historic phenomena. They are general answers supposed to have a universal meaning that covers and dominates all particulars. Hence they do not assist inquiry. They close it. They are not instrumentalities to be employed and tested in clarifying concrete social difficulties. They are ready-made principles to be imposed upon particulars in order to determine their nature. They tell us about *the* state when we want to know about *some* state. But the implication is that what is said about *the* state applies to any state that we happen to wish to know about.

In transferring the issue from concrete situations to definitions and conceptual deductions, the effect, especially of the organic theory, is to supply the apparatus for intellectual justification of the established order. Those most interested in practical social progress and the emancipation of groups from oppression have turned a cold shoulder to the organic theory. The effect, if not the intention, of

German idealism as applied in social philosophy was to provide a bulwark for the maintenance of the political *status quo* against the tide of radical ideas coming from revolutionary France. Although Hegel asserted in explicit form that the end of states and institutions is to further the realization of the freedom of all, his effect was to consecrate the Prussian State and to enshrine bureaucratic absolutism. Was this apologetic tendency accidental, or did it spring from something in the logic of the notions that were employed?

Surely the latter. If we talk about *the* state and *the* individual, rather than about this or that political organization and this or that group of needy and suffering human beings, the tendency is to throw the glamor and prestige, the meaning and value attached to the general notion, over the concrete situation and thereby to cover up the defects of the latter and disguise the need of serious reforms. The meanings which are found in the general notions are injected into the particulars that come under them. Quite properly so if we once grant the logic of rigid universals under which the concrete cases have to be subsumed in order to be understood and explained.

Again, the tendency of the organic point of view is to minimize the significance of specific conflicts. Since the individual and the state or social institution are but two sides of the same reality, since they are already reconciled in principle and conception, the conflict in any particular case can be but apparent. Since in theory the individual and the state are reciprocally necessary and helpful to one another, why pay much attention to the fact that in *this* state a whole group of individuals are suffering from oppressive conditions? In "reality" their interests cannot be in conflict with those of the state to which they belong; the opposition is only superficial and casual. Capital and labor cannot "really" conflict because each is an organic necessity to the other, and both to the organized community as a whole. There cannot "really" be any sex-problem because men and women are indispensable both to one another and to the state. In his day, Aristotle could easily employ the logic of general concepts superior to individuals to show that the institution of slavery was in the interests both of the state and of the slave class. Even if the intention is not to justify the existing order the effect is to divert attention from special situations. Rationalistic logic formerly made men careless in observation of the concrete in physical philosophy. It now operates to depress and retard observation in specific social phenomena. The social philosopher, dwelling in the region of his concepts, "solves" problems by showing the relationship of ideas, instead of helping men solve problems in the concrete by supplying them hypotheses to be used and tested in projects of reform.

Meanwhile, of course, the concrete troubles and evils remain.

They are not magically waived out of existence because in theory society is organic. The region of concrete difficulties, where the assistance of intelligent method for tentative plans for experimentation is urgently needed, is precisely where intelligence fails to operate. In this region of the specific and concrete, men are thrown back upon the crudest empiricism, upon short-sighted opportunism and the matching of brute forces. In theory, the particulars are all neatly disposed of; they come under their appropriate heading and category; they are labelled and go into an orderly pigeon-hole in a systematic filing cabinet labelled political science or sociology. But in empirical fact they remain as perplexing, confused and unorganized as they were before. So they are dealt with not by even an endeavor at scientific method but by blind rule of thumb, citation of precedents, considerations of immediate advantage, smoothing things over, use of coercive force and the clash of personal ambitions. The world still survives; it has therefore got on somehow—so much cannot be denied. The method of trial and error and competition of selfishnesses has somehow wrought out many improvements. But social theory nevertheless exists as an idle luxury rather than as a guiding method of inquiry and planning. In the question of methods concerned with reconstruction of special situations, rather than in any refinements in the general concepts of institution, individuality, state, freedom, law, order, progress, etc., lies the true impact of philosophical reconstruction.

Consider the conception of the individual self. The individualistic school of England and France in the eighteenth and nineteenth centuries was empirical in intent. It based its individualism, philosophically speaking, upon the belief that individuals are alone real, that classes and organizations are secondary and derived. They are artificial, while individuals are natural. In what way then can individualism be said to come under the animadversions that have been passed? To say the defect was that this school overlooked those connections with other persons which are a part of the constitution of every individual is true as far as it goes; but unfortunately it rarely goes beyond the point of just that wholesale justification of institutions which has been criticized.

The real difficulty is that the individual is regarded as something *given,* something already there. Consequently, he can only be something to be catered to, something whose pleasures are to be magnified and possessions multiplied. When the individual is taken as something given already, anything that can be done to him or for him can only be by way of external impressions and belongings: sensations of pleasure and pain, comforts, securities. Now it is true that social arrangements, laws, institutions are made for man, rather than that man is made for them; that they are means and agencies of human welfare and progress. But they are not means for obtaining something for individuals, not even happiness. They are means of *creating* individuals. Only in the physical sense of physical bodies that to the senses are separate is individuality an original datum. Individuality in a social and moral sense is something to be wrought out. It means initiative, inventiveness, varied resourcefulness, assumption of responsibility in choice of belief and conduct. These are not gifts, but achievements. As achievements, they are not absolute but relative to the use that is to be made of them. And this use varies with the environment.

The import of this conception comes out in considering the fortunes of the idea of self-interest. All members of the empirical school emphasized this idea. It was the sole motive of mankind. Virtue was to be attained by making benevolent action profitable to the individual; social arrangements were to be reformed so that egoism and altruistic consideration of others would be identified. Moralists of the opposite school were not backward in pointing out the evils of any theory that reduced both morals and political science to means of calculating self-interest. Consequently they threw the whole idea of interest overboard as obnoxious to morals. The effect of this reaction was to strengthen the cause of authority and political obscurantism. When the play of interest is eliminated, what remains? What concrete moving forces can be found? Those who identified the self with something ready-made and its interest with acquisition of pleasure and profit took the most effective means possible to reinstate the logic of abstract conceptions of law, justice, sovereignty, freedom, etc.—all of those vague general ideas that for all their seeming rigidity can be manipulated by any clever politician to cover up his designs and to make the worse seem the better cause. Interests are specific and dynamic; they are the natural terms of any concrete social thinking. But they are damned beyond recovery when they are identified with the things of a petty selfishness. They can be employed as vital terms only when the self is seen to be in process, and interest to be a name for whatever is concerned in furthering its movement.

The same logic applies to the old dispute of whether reform should start with the individual or with institutions. When the self is regarded as something complete within itself, then it is readily argued that only internal moralistic changes are of importance in general reform. Institutional changes are said to be merely external. They may add conveniences and comforts to life, but they cannot effect moral improvements. The result is to throw the burden for social improvement upon free-will in its most impossible form. Moreover, social and economic passivity are encouraged. Individuals are led to concentrate in moral introspection upon their own vices and virtues, and to neglect the character of the environment. Morals withdraw from active concern with detailed economic and political conditions. Let us perfect ourselves within, and in due season changes in society will come of themselves is the teaching. And while saints are engaged in introspection, burly sinners run the world. But when self-hood is perceived to be an active process it is also seen that social modifications are the only means of the creation of changed personalities. Institutions are viewed in their educative effect—with reference to the types of individuals they foster. The interest in individual moral improvement and the social interest in objective reform of economic and political conditions are identified. And inquiry into the meaning of social arrangements gets definite point and direction. We are led to ask what the specific stimulating, fostering and nurturing power of each specific social arrangement may be. The old-time separation between politics and morals is abolished at its root.

Consequently we cannot be satisfied with the general statement that society and the state is organic to the individual. The question is one of specific causations. Just what response does *this* social arrangement, political or economic, evoke, and what effect does it have upon the disposition of those who engage in it? Does it release capacity? If so, how widely? Among a few, with a corresponding depression in others, or in an extensive and equitable way? Is this capacity which is set free also directed in some coherent way, so that it becomes a power, or its manifestation spasmodic and capricious? Since responses are of an indefinite diversity of kind, these inquiries have to be detailed and specific. Are men's senses rendered more delicately sensitive and appreciative, or are they blunted and dulled by this and that form of social organization? Are their minds trained so that the hands are more deft and cunning? Is curiosity awakened or blunted? What is its quality: is it merely esthetic, dwelling on the forms and surfaces of things or is it also an intellectual searching into their meaning? Such questions as these (as well as the more obvious ones about the qualities conventionally labelled moral), become the starting-points of inquiries about every institution of the community when it is recognized that individuality is not originally given but is created under the influences of associated life. Like utilitarianism, the theory subjects every form of organization to continued scrutiny and criticism. But instead of leading us to ask what it does in the way of causing pains and pleasures to individuals already in existence, it inquires what is done to release specific capacities and co-ordinate them into working powers. What sort of individuals are created?

The waste of mental energy due to conducting discussion of social affairs in terms of conceptual generalities is astonishing. How far would the biologist and the physician progress if when the subject of respiration is under consideration, discussion confined itself to bandying back and forth the concepts of organ and organism—If for example one school thought respiration could be known and understood by insisting upon the fact that it occurs in an individual body and therefore is an "individual" phenomenon, while an opposite school insisted that it is simply one function in organic interaction with others and can be known or understood therefore only by reference to other functions taken in an equally general or wholesale way? Each proposition is equally true and equally futile. What is needed is specific inquiries into a multitude of specific structures and interactions. Not only does the solemn reiteration of categories of individual and organic or social whole not further these definite and detailed inquiries, but it checks them. It detains thought within pompous and sonorous generalities wherein controversy is as inevitable as it is incapable of solution. It is true enough that if cells were not in vital interaction with one another, they could neither conflict nor co-operate. But the fact of the existence of an "organic" social group, instead of answering any questions merely marks the fact that questions exist: Just what conflicts and what co-operations occur, and what are their specific causes and consequences? But because of the persistence within social philosophy of the order of ideas that has been expelled from natural philosophy, even sociologists take conflict or co-operation as general categories upon which to base their science, and condescend to empirical facts only for illustrations. As a rule, their chief "problem" is a purely dialectical one, covered up by a thick quilt of empirical anthropological and historical citations: How do individuals unite to form society? How are individuals socially controlled? And the problem is justly called dialectical because it springs from antecedent conceptions of "individual" and "social."

Just as "individual" is not one thing, but is a blanket term for the immense variety of specific reactions, habits, dispositions and powers of human nature that are evoked, and confirmed under the influences of associated life, so with the term "social." Society is one word, but infinitely many things. It covers all the ways in which by associating together men share their experiences, and build up common interests and aims; street gangs, schools for burglary, clans, social cliques, trades unions, joint stock corporations, villages and international alliances. The new method takes effect in substituting inquiry into these specific, changing and relative facts (relative to problems and purposes, not metaphysically relative) for solemn manipulation of general notions.

Strangely enough, the current conception of the state is a case in point. For one direct influence of the classic order of fixed species arranged in hierarchical order is the attempt of German political philosophy in the nineteenth century to enumerate a definite number of institutions, each having its own essential and immutable meaning; to arrange them in an order of "evolution" which corresponds with the dignity and rank of the respective meanings. The National State was placed at the top as the consummation and culmination, and also the basis of all other institutions.

Hegel is a striking example of this industry, but he is far from the only one. Many who have bitterly quarrelled with him, have only differed as to the details of the "evolution" or as to the particular meaning to be attributed as essential *Begriff* to some one of the enumerated institutions. The quarrel has been bitter only because the underlying premises were the same. Particularly have many schools of thought, varying even more widely in respect to method and conclusion, agreed upon the final consummating position of the state. They may not go as far as Hegel in making the sole meaning of history to be the evolution of National Territorial States, each of which embodies more than the prior form of the essential meaning or conception of *the* State and consequently displaces it, until we arrive at that triumph of historical evolution, the Prussian State. But they do not question the unique and supreme position of the State in the social hierarchy. Indeed that conception has hardened into unquestionable dogma under the title of sovereignty.

There can be no doubt of the tremendously important role played by the modern territorial national state. The formation of these states has been the centre of modern political history. France, Great Britain, Spain were the first peoples to attain nationalistic organization, but in the nineteenth century their example was followed by Japan, Germany and Italy, to say nothing of a large number of smaller states, Greece, Servia, Bulgaria, etc. As everybody knows, one of the most important phases of the recent world war was the struggle to complete the nationalistic movement, resulting in the erection of Bohemia, Poland, etc., into independent states, and the accession of Armenia, Palestine, etc., to the rank of candidates.

The struggle for the supremacy of the State over other forms of organization was directed against the power of minor districts, provinces, principalities, against the dispersion of power among feudal lords as well as, in some countries, against the pretensions of an ecclesiastic potentate. The "State" represents the conspicuous culmination of the great movement of social integration and consolidation taking place in the last few centuries, tremendously accelerated by the concentrating and combining forces of steam and electricity. Naturally, inevitably, the students of political science have been preoccupied with this great historic phenomenon, and their intellectual activities have been directed to its systematic formulation. Because the contemporary progressive movement was to establish the unified state against the inertia of minor social units and against the ambitions of rivals for power, political theory developed the dogma of the sovereignty of the national state, internally and externally.

As the work of integration and consolidation reaches its climax, the question arises, however, whether the national state, once it is firmly established and no longer struggling against strong foes, is not just an instrumentality for promoting and protecting other and more voluntary forms of association, rather than a supreme end in itself. Two actual phenomena may be pointed to in support of an affirmative answer. Along with the development of the larger, more inclusive and more unified organization of the state has gone the emancipation of individuals from restrictions and servitudes previously imposed by custom and class status. But the individuals freed from external coercive bonds have not remained isolated. Social molecules have at once recombined in new associations and organizations. Compulsory associations have been replaced by voluntary ones; rigid organizations by those more amenable to human choice and purposes—more directly changeable at will. What upon one side looks like a movement toward individualism, turns out to be really a movement toward multiplying all kinds and varieties of associations: Political parties, industrial corporations, scientific and artistic organizations, trade unions, churches, schools, clubs and societies without number, for the cultivation of every conceivable interest that men have in common. As they develop in number and importance, the state tends to become more and more a regulator and adjuster among them; defining the limits of their actions, preventing and settling conflicts.

Its "supremacy" approximates that of the conductor of an orchestra, who makes no music himself but who harmonizes the activities of those who in producing it are doing the thing intrinsically worth while. The state remains highly important—but its importance consists more and more in its power to foster and co-ordinate the activities of voluntary groupings. Only nominally is it in any modern community the end for the sake of which all the other societies and organizations exist. Groupings for promoting the diversity of goods that men share have become the real social units. They occupy the place which traditional theory has claimed either for mere isolated individuals or for the supreme and single political organization. Pluralism is well ordained in present political practice and demands a modification of hierarchical practice and monistic theory. Every combination of human forces that adds its own contribution of value to life has for that reason its own unique and ultimate worth. It cannot be degraded into a means to glorify the State. One reason for the increased demoralization of war is that it forces the State into an abnormally supreme position.

The other concrete fact is the opposition between the claim of independent sovereignty in behalf of the territorial national state and the growth of international and what have well been called trans-national interests. The weal and woe of any modern state is bound up with that of others. Weakness, disorder, false principles on the part of any state are not confined within its boundaries. They spread and infect other states. The same is true of economic, artistic and scientific advances. Moreover the voluntary associations just spoken of do not coincide with political boundaries. Associations of mathematicians, chemists, astronomers; business corporations, labor organizations, churches are trans-national because the interests they represent are worldwide. In such ways as these, internationalism is not an aspiration but a fact, not a sentimental ideal but a force. Yet these interests are cut across and thrown out of gear by the traditional doctrine of exclusive national sovereignty. It is the vogue of this doctrine, or dogma, that represents the strongest barrier to the effective formation of an international mind which alone agrees with the moving forces of present-day labor, commerce, science, art and religion.

Society, as was said, is many associations, not a single organization. Society means association; coming together in joint intercourse and action for the better realization of any form of experience which is augmented and confirmed by being shared. Hence there are as many associations as there are goods which are enhanced by being mutually communicated and participated in. And these are literally indefinite in number. Indeed, capacity to endure publicity and communication is the test by which it is decided whether a pretended good is genuine or spurious. Moralists have always insisted upon the fact that good is universal, objective, not just private, particular. But too often, like Plato, they have been content with a metaphysical universality or, like Kant, with a logical universality. Communication, sharing, joint participation are the only actual ways of universalizing the moral law and end. We insist upon the unique character of every intrinsic good. But the counterpart of this proposition is that the situation in which a good is consciously realized is not one of transient sensations or private appetites but one of sharing and communication—public, social. Even the hermit communes with gods or spirits; even misery loves company; and the most extreme selfishness includes a band of followers or some partner to share in the attained good. Universalization means socialization, the extension of the area and range of those who share in a good.

The increasing acknowledgment that goods exist and endure only through being communicated and that association is the means of conjoint sharing lies back of the modern sense of humanity and democracy. It is the saving salt in altruism and philanthropy, which without this factor degenerate into moral condescension and moral interference, taking the form of trying to regulate the affairs of others under the guise of doing them good or of conferring upon them some right as if it were a gift of charity. It follows that organization is never an end in itself. It is a means of promoting *association,* of multiplying effective points of contact between persons, directing their intercourse into the modes of greatest fruitfulness.

The tendency to treat organization as an end in itself is responsible for all the exaggerated theories in which individuals are subordinated to some institution to which is given the noble name of society. Society is the *process* of associating in such ways that experiences, ideas, emotions, values are transmitted and made common. To this active process, both the individual and the institutionally organized may truly be said to be subordinate. The individual is subordinate because except in and through communication of experience from and to others, he remains dumb, merely sentient, a brute animal. Only in association with fellows does he become a conscious centre of experience. Organization, which is what traditional theory has generally meant by the term Society or State, is also subordinate because it becomes static, rigid, institutionalized whenever it is not employed to facilitate and enrich the contacts of human beings with one another.

The long-time controversy between rights and duties, law and freedom is another version of the strife between the Individual and Society as fixed concepts. Freedom for an individual means growth, ready change when modification is required.

It signifies an active process, that of release of capacity from whatever hems it in. But since society can develop only as new resources are put at its disposal, it is absurd to suppose that freedom has positive significance for individuality but negative meaning for social interests. Society is strong, forceful, stable against accident only when all its members can function to the limit of their capacity. Such functioning cannot be achieved without allowing a leeway of experimentation beyond the limits of established and sanctioned custom. A certain amount of overt confusion and irregularity is likely to accompany the granting of the margin of liberty without which capacity cannot find itself. But socially as well as scientifically the great thing is not to avoid mistakes but to have them take place under conditions such that they can be utilized to increase intelligence in the future.

If British liberal social philosophy tended, true to the spirit of its atomistic empiricism, to make freedom and the exercise of rights ends in themselves, the remedy is not to be found in recourse to a philosophy of fixed obligations and authoritative law such as characterized German political thinking. The latter, as events have demonstrated, is dangerous because of its implicit menace to the free self-determination of other social groups. But it is also weak internally when put to the final test. In its hostility to the free experimentation and power of choice of the individual in determining social affairs, it limits the capacity of many or most individuals to share effectively in social operations, and thereby deprives society of the full contribution of all its members. The best guarantee of collective efficiency and power is liberation and use of the diversity of individual capacities in initiative, planning, foresight, vigor and endurance. Personality must be educated, and personality cannot be educated by confining its operations to technical and specialized things, or to the less important relationships of life. Full education comes only when there is a responsible share on the part of each person, in proportion to capacity, in shaping the aims and policies of the social groups to which he belongs. This fact fixes the significance of democracy. It cannot be conceived as a sectarian or racial thing nor as a consecration of some form of government which has already attained constitutional sanction. It is but a name for the fact that human nature is developed only when its elements take part in directing things which are common, things for the sake of which men and women form groups—families, industrial companies, governments, churches, scientific associations and so on. The principle holds as much of one form of association, say in industry and commerce, as it does in government. The identification of democracy with political democracy which is responsible for most of its failures is, however, based upon the traditional ideas which make the individual and the state ready-made entities in themselves.

14

The Future of Liberalism

Liberalism as a conscious and aggressive movement arose in Great Britain as two different streams flowed into one.

One of these streams was the humanitarian and philanthropic zeal that became so active late in the eighteenth century and that in various forms is still a mighty current. It was expressed in the feeling that man is his brother's keeper and that the world is full of suffering and evil that are caused by failure to recognize this fact. In consequence of the failure, political and social institutions are horribly and tragically harsh and cruel in their effect upon the mass of men, women and children.

This humanitarian movement itself represents the conflux of many separate streams. There was, for example, the tremendous influence exerted by Rousseau, the real author of the doctrine of the forgotten man and the forgotten masses. His influence was quite as great in literature as in politics. It helped create the novel of the common man in England in the eighteenth century, a literary influence that found such vivid expression in the nineteenth century in the novels of Dickens.

Independent of Rousseau, but reinforced by his influence, there was a reaction against the importance attached by most eighteenth-century thought to "reason." Reason, it was felt if not argued, is a prerogative of a select few. The mass of men are influenced by feeling and instinct, and the hope of the world lies in giving free

SOURCE: From the *Journal of Philosophy*, vol. XXXII, no. 9 (April 1935), pp. 225–230. Reprinted by permission of the *Journal of Philosophy*.

play to the instinct of sympathy, rather than to logic and reason.

This new attitude found expression in the deification of the "man of sentiment" so characteristic of one period of English thought. The interest in the "noble savage" is another expression of the same attitude. Aside from the fact that he was supposed, in a wholly illusory way, to be independent and free from the constraints of convention and custom, he was idealized as the creature of instinct and emotion.

Another influence that finally joined in to form the humanitarian current was the religious. In England it was stimulated by the Wesleyan movement, with its peculiar appeal to the "lower" and neglected classes. But it affected the established church as well. Ardent, aggressive missionary zeal for saving the souls of men, especially those of the humble and poor, ran over into efforts to improve their condition by abolishing harsh and cruel inequalities.

The movement, instigated by religion, was active in attack upon slavery, upon the abuses of prison life, upon brutal and mechanical methods of administering charity, and, through the factory laws, upon the inhuman conditions of labor of women and children in mines and factories. In every one of these movements evangelical zeal was the motive force.

The other great stream that entered into the formation of liberalism sprang from the stimulus to manufacturing and trade that came from the application of steam to industry. The great intellectual leader of this movement was Adam Smith. His theories found practical reinforcement in the endeavor of manufacturers and traders to get free from the immense number of laws and customs that restricted the freedom of movement of laborers, that subjected the market price to prices legally fixed and that hampered freedom of exchange especially with foreign markets.

This mass of restrictions that tended to strangle at birth the new infant industry held over from agrarian feudalism and was kept in force by the influence of landed interests. Because the restrictive and oppressive conditions were embodied in law and because law was the voice of government in control of human action, government was taken to be the great enemy of liberty; interference with human industry engaged in satisfaction of human needs was taken to be the chief cause why progress was retarded and why a reign of harmony of interests and peace did not exist.

Freedom of production would, it was held, lead to the maximum stimulation of human effort and automatically direct abilities into the channels in which, in bringing most reward to the individual, they would also be most serviceable to society. Freedom of exchange would create an interdependence that would automatically create harmony of interests. The negative side of the doctrine, its opposition to governmental action in production and trade, came to full flower in the principle of *laissez-faire*: hands off on the part of government and the maximum of free activity on the part of producer and trader in the advancement of his own interests.

This historical summary is more than historical. It is indispensable to any understanding of liberalism as a social and political movement. For, while the two streams came together, they never coalesced.

Although the humanitarian movement expressed itself most actively in personal and voluntary effort, it was far from averse to employing governmental agencies to achieve its reforms. Most of them, in fact, like abolition of the slave trade, prison reform, removal of abuses attending the labor of women and children, could not be effected without some intervention on the part of government.

The whole movement toward what is known as social legislation, with its slogan of social justice, derives from this source and involves more and more appeal to governmental action. Hence there was from the beginning an inner split in liberalism. Any attempt to define liberalism in terms of one or the other of its two strains will be vehemently denied by those attached to the other strain.

Historically, the split was embodied in the person of one of the chief representatives of nineteenth-century liberalism, Jeremy Bentham. Whether he was aware of it or not, his leading principle, that of the greatest happiness of the greatest number, was derived from the philanthropic and humanitarian movement. But when it came to the realization of this goal, he ranked himself, with some exceptions, such as public health and public education, with *laissez-faire* liberalism.

He was strong for political action to reform abuses of judicial procedure, of lawmaking and methods of electing lawmakers, but he regarded the abuses to be corrected as the product of the failure of government in the past to confine itself to its proper sphere. When the abuses of governmental action by government were once removed, he believed that the free play of individual initiative and effort would furnish the sure road to progress and to producing the greatest happiness of the greatest number.

As I have indicated, the inner breach in liberalism has never been healed. On the Continent, so-called liberal parties have been almost universally the political representatives of big industry, banking and commerce. In Great Britain, true to the spirit of tradition and compromise so strong in English affairs, liberalism has been a mixture of the two strains, leaning now in one direction and now in another.

In the United States liberalism has been identified largely with the idea of the use of governmental agencies to remedy evils from which the less-fortunate classes suffer. It was "forward-looking" in the Progressive movement; it lies, nominally at least, behind Square Deals and New Deals. It has favored employer-liability acts, laws regulating hours and conditions of labor, anti-sweatshop legislation, supplementation of private charity by public relief and public works, generous appropriations for public schools, graded higher taxation of larger incomes and of inheritances; in general, when there has been a conflict between labor and employers it has sided with labor.

Its philosophy has rarely been clear cut. But so far as it has had a philosophy it has been that government should regularly intervene to help equalize conditions between the wealthy and the poor, between the overprivileged and the underprivileged. For this reason liberals of the other, or *laissez-faire*, schools have always attacked it as pink socialism, as disguised radicalism; while at the present time the favorite charge is that it is instigated, of all places in the world, from Moscow.

As a matter of fact, up to this time in this country political liberalism has never attempted to change the fundamental conditions of the economic system or to do more than ameliorate the estate in which the mass of human beings live. For this reason liberalism at present is under more violent attack from radicals than from conservatives. In the mouth of radicals liberalism is a term of hissing and reproach.

In spite of the extreme clash, both schools of liberalism profess devotion to the same ultimate ideal and goal. The slogan of both schools is the utmost possible liberty of the individual. The difference between them concerns the province in which liberty and individuality are most important and the means by which they are to be realized.

One has only to read any outgiving of the adherents of *laissez-faire* liberalism to see that it is the liberty of the entrepreneur in business undertakings which they prize and which they come close to identifying with the heart of all liberty.

To the spokesmen of the Liberty League and to ex-President Hoover in his doctrine of rugged individualism, any governmental action that interferes with this particular kind of liberty is an attack upon liberty itself. The ruggedness, independence, initiative and vigor of individuals upon which they set chief store is that of the individuals who have come to the top in the existing economic system of finance capitalism. They are exposed to the charge of identifying the meaning of liberty and of rugged individualism with the maintenance of the system under which they have prospered.

The charge is given force by the fact that they have for the most part supported the system of protective tariffs, against which original simon-pure *laissez-faire* liberals directed some of their most violent attacks. The author of the phrase "rugged individualism" used the government to come to the aid of industry when it was in straits by means of the Reconstruction Finance Corporation, and, as far as I know, the opponents of governmental intervention made no protest at this flagrant case of governmental interference with the free course of private industry.

The most vocal spokesmen for this special form of liberty have never attacked land monopoly and, if they think at all about Henry George, they think of him as one of the subversive and dangerous radicals. They have themselves built up financial and industrial systems so concentrated as to be semi-monopolies or monopolies proper.

Liberals of the other school are those who point to things like those just mentioned and who assert that the system of industry for private profit without regard to social consequences has had in fact a most unfavorable effect upon the real liberty of the mass of individuals.

Their conception of what I called the province of liberty and individuality is broader and more generous than is that of those who come forward as the self-appointed champions of liberty. They think that liberty is something that affects every aspect and phase of human life—liberty of thought, of expression, of cultural opportunity—and that it is not to be had, even in the economic sphere, without a degree of security that is denied to millions by the present economic system.

They point out that industry, banking and commerce have reached a point where there is no such thing as merely private initiative and enterprise. For the consequences of private business enterprise affect so many persons and in such deep and enduring ways that all business is affected with a public interest. Since the consequences of business are social, society must itself look after, by means of increased organized control, the industrial and financial causes of these consequences.

There is, accordingly, no doubt in my own mind that *laissez-faire* liberalism is played out, largely because of the fruits of its own policies. Any system that cannot provide elementary security for millions has no claim to the title of being organized in behalf of liberty and the development of individuals. Any person and any movement whose interest in these ends is genuine and not a cover for personal advantage and power must put primary emphasis in thought and action upon the means of their attainment.

At present those means lie in the direction of increased social control and increased collectivism of effort. Humane liberalism in order to save itself must cease to deal with symptoms and go to the causes of which inequalities and oppressions are but the symptoms. In order to endure under present conditions, liberalism must become radical in the sense that, instead of using social power to ameliorate the evil consequences of the existing system, it shall use social power to change the system.

Radicalism in the minds of many, however, both among its professed adherents and its bitter enemies, is identified with a particular method of changing the system. To them, it means the change of the present system by violent overthrow. Radicalism of this sort is opposed to liberalism, and liberalism is opposed to it. For liberalism both by its history and by its own nature is committed to democratic methods of effecting social change.

The idea of forcing men to be free is an old idea, but by nature it is opposed to freedom. Freedom is not something that can be handed to men as a gift from outside, whether by old-fashioned dynastic benevolent despotisms or by new-fashioned dictatorships, whether of the proletarian or of the fascist order. It is something which can be had only as individuals participate in winning it, and this fact, rather than some particular political mechanism, is the essence of democratic liberalism.

The denial of the democratic method of achieving social control is in part the product of sheer impatience and romantic longing for a short-cut which if it were taken would defeat its own end. It is in part the fruit of the Russian revolution, oblivious of the fact that Russia never had any democratic tradition in its whole history and was accustomed to dictatorial rule in a way that is foreign to the spirit of every Western country. In part, it is the product of the capture of the machinery of democratic legislation and administration by the dominant economic power, known for short as plutocracy or "the interests."

Discontent with democracy as it operates under conditions of exploitation by special interests has justification. But the notion that the remedy is violence and a civil war between classes is a counsel of despair.

If the method of violence and civil war be adopted, the end will be either fascism, open and undisguised, or the common ruin of both parties to the struggle. The democratic method of social change is slow; it labors under many and serious handicaps imposed by the undemocratic character of what passes for democracy. But it is the method of liberalism, with its belief that liberty is the means as well as the goal and that only through the development of individuals in their voluntary cooperation with one another can the development of individuality be made secure and enduring.

II

The emphasis of earlier liberalism upon individuality and liberty defines the focal points of discussion of the philosophy of liberalism today. This earlier liberalism was itself an outgrowth, in the late eighteenth and nineteenth centuries, of the earlier revolt against oligarchical government, one which came to its culmination in the "glorious revolution" of 1688. The latter was fundamentally a demand for freedom of the taxpayer from government arbitrary action in connection with a demand for confessional freedom in religion by the Protestant churches. In the liberalism, expressly so called, demand for liberty and individual freedom of action came primarily from the rising industrial and trading class and was directed against restrictions placed by government, in legislation, common law and judicial action, and other institutions having connection with the political state, upon freedom of economic enterprise. In both cases, governmental action and the desired freedom were placed in antithesis to each other. This way of conceiving liberty has persisted; it was strengthened in this country by the revolt of the colonies and by pioneer conditions.

Nineteenth-century philosophic liberalism added, more or less because of its dominant economic interest, the conception of natural laws to that of natural rights of the Whig movement. There are natural laws, it held, in social matters as well as in physical, and these natural laws are economic in character. Political laws, on the other hand, are man-made and in that sense artificial. Governmental intervention in industry and exchange was thus regarded as a violation not only of inherent individual liberty but also of natural laws—of which supply and demand is a sample. The proper sphere of governmental action was simply to prevent and to secure redress for infringement by one, in the exercise of his liberty, of like and equal liberty of action on the part of others.

Nevertheless, the demand for freedom in initiation and conduct of business enterprise did not exhaust the content of earlier liberalism. In the minds of its chief promulgators there was included an equally strenuous demand for the liberty of mind, freedom of thought and its expression in speech, writing, print and assemblage. The earlier interest in confessional freedom was generalized, and thereby deepened as well as broadened. This demand was a product of the rational enlightenment of the eighteenth century and of the growing importance of science. The great tide of reaction that set in after the defeat of Napoleon, the demand for order and discipline, gave the agitation for freedom of thought and its expression plenty of cause and plenty of opportunity.

The earlier liberal philosophy rendered valiant service. It finally succeeded in sweeping away, especially in its home, Great Britain, an innumerable number of abuses and restrictions. The history of social reforms in the nineteenth century is almost one with the history of liberal social thought. It is not then from ingratitude that I shall emphasize its defects, for recognition of them is essential to an intelligent statement of the elements of liberal philosophy for the present and any nearby future. The fundamental defect was its lack of perception of historic relativity. This lack is expressed in the conception of the individual as something given, complete in itself, and of liberty as a ready-made possession of the individual, only needing the removal of external restrictions in order to manifest itself. The individual of earlier liberalism was a Newtonian atom having only external time and space relations to other individuals, save in that each social atom was equipped with inherent freedom. These ideas might not have been especially harmful if they had been merely a rallying cry for practical movements. But they formed part of a philosophy and of a philosophy in which these particular ideas of individuality and freedom were asserted to be absolute and eternal truths; good for all times and all places.

This absolutism, this ignoring and denial of temporal relativity is one great reason why the earlier liberalism degenerated so easily into pseudo-liberalism. For the sake of saving time, I shall identify what I mean by this spurious liberalism, the kind of social ideas represented by the "Liberty League" and ex-President Hoover. I call it a pseudo-liberalism because it ossified and narrowed generous ideas and aspirations. Even when words remain the same, they mean something very different when they are uttered by a minority struggling against repressive measures and when expressed by a group that has attained power and then uses ideas that were once weapons of emancipation as instruments for keeping the power and wealth they have obtained. Ideas that at one time are means of producing social change assume another guise when they are used as means of preventing further social change. This fact is itself an illustration of historic relativity, and an evidence of the evil that lay in the assertion by earlier liberalism of the immutable and eternal character of their ideas. Because of this latter fact, the *laissez-faire* doctrine was held by the degenerate school of liberals to express the very order of nature itself. The outcome was the degradation of the idea of individuality until in the minds of many who are themselves struggling for a wider and fuller development of individuality, individualism has become a term of hissing and reproach, while many can see no remedy for the evils that have come from the use of socially unrestrained liberty in business enterprise, save change produced by violence. The historic tendency to conceive the whole question of liberty as a matter in which individual and government are opposed parties has borne bitter fruit. Born of despotic government, it has continued to influence thinking and action after government had become popular and *in theory* the servant of the people.

I pass now to what the philosophy of liberalism would be were its inheritance of absolutism eliminated. In the first place such liberalism knows that an individual is nothing fixed, given ready-made. It is something achieved, and achieved not in isolation, but with the aid and support of conditions, cultural and physical, including in "cultural" economic, legal and political institutions as well as science and art. Liberalism knows that social conditions may restrict, distort and almost prevent the development of individuality. It therefore takes an active interest in the working of social institutions that have a bearing, positive or negative, upon the growth of individuals who shall be rugged in fact and not merely in abstract theory. It is as much interested in the positive construction of favorable institutions, legal, political and economic, as it is in the work of removing abuses and overt oppressions.

In the second place, liberalism is committed to the idea of historic relativity. It knows that the content of the individual and freedom change with time; that this is as true of social change as it is of individual development from infancy to maturity. The positive counterpart of opposition to doctrinal absolutism is experimentalism. The connection between historic relativity and experimental method is intrinsic. Time signifies change. The significance of individuality with respect to social policies alter with change of the conditions in which individuals live. The earlier liberalism in being absolute was also unhistoric. Underlying it there was a philosophy of history which assumed that history, like time in the Newtonian scheme, means only modification of external relations; that it is quantitative, not qualitative and internal. The same thing is true of any theory that assumes, like the one usually attributed to Marx, that temporal changes in society are inevitable—that is to say, are governed by a law that is not itself historical. The fact is that the historicism and the evolutionism of nineteenth-century doctrine were only half-way doctrines. They assumed that historical and developmental processes were subject to some law or formula outside temporal processes.

The commitment of liberalism to experimental procedure carries with it the idea of continuous reconstruction of the ideas of individuality and of liberty in intimate connection with changes in social relations. It is enough to refer to the changes in productivity and distribution since the time when the earlier liberalism was formulated, and the effect of these transformations, due to science and technology, upon the terms on which men associate together. An experimental method is the recognition of this temporal change in ideas and policies so that the latter shall coordinate with the facts instead of being opposed to them. Any other view maintains a rigid conceptualism and implies that facts should conform to concepts that are framed independently of temporal or historical change.

The two things essential, then, to thorough-going social liberalism are, first, realistic study of existing conditions in their movement, and, secondly, leading ideas, in the form of policies for dealing with these conditions in the interest of development of increased individuality and liberty. The first requirement is so obviously implied that I shall not elaborate it. The second point needs some amplification. Experimental method is not just messing around nor doing a little of this and a little of that in the hope that things will improve. Just as in the physical sciences, it implies a coherent body of ideas, a theory, that gives direction to effort. What is implied, in contrast to every form of absolutism, is that the ideas and theory be taken as methods of action tested and continuously revised by the consequences they produce in actual social conditions. Since they are operational in nature, they modify conditions, while the first requirement, that of basing them upon realistic study of actual conditions, brings about their continuous reconstruction.

It follows, finally, that there is no opposition in principle between liberalism as social philosophy and radicalism in action, if by radicalism is signified the adoption of policies that bring about drastic instead of piecemeal social changes. It is all a question of what kind of procedures the intelligent study of changing conditions discloses. These changes have been so tremendous in the last century, yes, in the last forty years, that it looks to me as if radical methods were now necessary. But all that the argument here requires is recognition of the fact that there is nothing in the nature of liberalism that makes it a milk-water doctrine, committed to compromise and minor "reforms." It is worth noting that the earlier liberals were regarded in their days as subversive radicals.

What has been said should make it clear that the question of method in formation and execution of policies is the central thing in liberalism. The method indicated is that of maximum reliance upon intelligence. This fact determines its opposition to those forms of radicalism that place chief dependence upon violent overthrow of existing institutions as the method of effecting desired social change. A genuine liberal will emphasize as crucial the complete correlation between the means used and the consequences that follow. The same principle which makes him aware that the means employed by pseudo-liberalism only perpetuate and multiply the evils of existing conditions makes him aware also that dependence upon sheer massed force as the means of social change decides the kind of consequences that actually result. Doctrines, whether proceeding from Mussolini or from Marx, which assume that because certain ends are desirable therefore those ends and nothing else will result from the use of force to attain them is but another example of the limitations put upon intelligence by any absolute theory. In the degree in which mere force is resorted to, actual consequences are themselves so compromised that the ends originally in view have in fact to be worked out afterwards by the method of experimental intelligence.

In saying this, I do not wish to be understood as meaning that radicals of the type mentioned have any monopoly of the use of force. The contrary is the case. The reactionaries are in possession of force, in not only the army and police, but in the press and the schools. The only reason they do not advocate the use of force is the fact that they are already in possession of it, so their policy is to cover up its existence with idealistic phrases—of which their present use of individual initiative and liberty is a striking example.

These facts illustrate the essential evil of reliance upon sheer force. Action and reaction are equal and in opposite directions, and force as such is physical. Dependence upon force sooner or later calls out force on the other side. The whole problem of the relation of intelligence to force is much too large to go into here. I can only say that when the forces in possession are so blind and stubborn as to throw all their weight against the use of liberty of inquiry and of communication, of organization to effect social change, they not only encourage the use of force in those who want social change, but they give the latter the most justification they ever have. The emphasis of liberalism upon the method of intelligence does not commit it to unqualified pacificism, but to the unremitting use of every method of intelligence that conditions permit, and to search for all that are possible.

In conclusion, I wish to emphasize one point implied in the early part of the paper. The question of the practical signficance of liberty is much wider than that of the relation of government to the individual, to say nothing of the monstrosity of the doctrine that assumes that under all conditions governmental action and individual liberty are found in separate and independent spheres. Government is one factor and an important one. But it comes into the picture only in relation to other matters. At present, these other matters are economic and cultural. With respect to the first point, it is absurd to conceive liberty as that of the business entrepreneur and ignore the immense regimentation to which workers are subjected, intellectual as well as manual workers. As to the second point, the full freedom of the human spirit and of individuality can be achieved only as there is effective opportunity to share in the cultural resources of civilization. No economic state of affairs is merely economic. It has a profound effect upon the presence or absence of cultural freedom. Any liberalism that does not make full cultural freedom supreme and that does not see the relation between it and genuine industrial freedom as a way of life is degenerate and delusive liberalism.

15

Search for the Great Community

Regarded as an idea, democracy is not an alternative to other principles of associated life. It is the idea of community life itself. It is an ideal in the only intelligible sense of an ideal: namely, the tendency and movement of some thing which exists carried to its final limit, viewed as completed, perfected. Since things do not attain such fulfillment but are in actuality distracted and interfered with, democracy in this sense is not a fact and never will be. But neither in this sense is there or has there ever been anything which is a community in its full measure, a community unalloyed by alien elements. The idea or ideal of a community presents, however, actual phases of associated life as they are freed from restrictive and disturbing elements, and are contemplated as having attained their limit of development. Wherever there is conjoint activity whose consequences are appreciated as good by all singular persons who take part in it, and where the realization of the good is such as to effect an energetic desire and effort to sustain it in being just because it is a good shared by all, there is in so far a community. The clear consciousness of a communal life, in all its implications, constitutes the idea of democracy.

Only when we start from a community as a fact, grasp the fact in thought so as to clarify and enhance its constituent elements, can we reach an idea of democracy which is not utopian. The conceptions and shibboleths which are traditionally associated with the idea of democracy take on a veridical and directive meaning only when they

SOURCE: From *The Public and Its Problems*, 1927. Reprinted with the permission of The Center for Dewey Studies, Southern Illinois University at Carbondale.

are construed as marks and traits of an association which realizes the defining characteristics of a community. Fraternity, liberty and equality isolated from communal life are hopeless abstractions. Their separate assertion leads to mushy sentimentalism or else to extravagant and fanatical violence which in the end defeats its own aims. Equality then becomes a creed of mechanical identity which is false to facts and impossible of realization. Effort to attain it is divisive of the vital bonds which hold men together; as far as it puts forth issue, the outcome is a mediocrity in which good is common only in the sense of being average and vulgar. Liberty is then thought of as independence of social ties, and ends in dissolution and anarchy. It is more difficult to sever the idea of brotherhood from that of a community, and hence it is either practically ignored in the movements which identify democracy with Individualism, or else it is a sentimentally appended tag. In its just connection with communal experience, fraternity is another name for the consciously appreciated goods which accrue from an association in which all share, and which give direction to the conduct of each. Liberty is that secure release and fulfillment of personal potentialities which take place only in rich and manifold association with others: the power to be an individualized self making a distinctive contribution and enjoying in its own way the fruits of association. Equality denotes the unhampered share which each individual member of the community has in the consequences of associated action. It is equitable because it is measured only by need and capacity to utilize, not by extraneous factors which deprive one in order that another may take and have. A baby in the family is equal with others, not because of some antecedent and structural quality which is the same as that of others, but in so far as his needs for care and development are attended to without being sacrificed to the superior strength, possessions and matured abilities of others. Equality does not signify that kind of mathematical or physical equivalence in virtue of which any one element may be substituted for another. It denotes effective regard for whatever is distinctive and unique in each, irrespective of physical and psychological inequalities. It is not a natural possession but is a fruit of the community when its actions is directed by its character as a community.

Associated or joint activity is a condition of the creation of a community. But association itself is physical and organic, while communal life is moral, that is emotionally, intellectually, consciously sustained. Human beings combine in behavior as directly and unconsciously as do atoms, stellar masses and cells; as directly and unknowingly as they divide and repel. They do so in virtue of their own structure, as man and woman unite, the baby seeks the breast and the breast is there to supply its need. They do so from external circumstances, pressure from without, as atoms combine or separate in presence of an electric charge, or as sheep huddle together from the cold. Associated activity needs no explanation; things are made that way. But no amount of aggregated collective action of itself constitutes a community. For beings who observe and think, and whose ideas are absorbed by impulses and become sentiments and interests, "we" is as inevitable as "I." But "we" and "our" exist only when the consequences of combined action are perceived and become an object of desire and effort, just as "I" and "mine" appear on the scene only when a distinctive share in mutual action is consciously asserted or claimed. Human associations may be ever so organic in origin and firm in operation, but they develop into societies in a human sense only as their consequences, being known, are esteemed and sought for. Even if "society" were as much an organism as some writers have held, it would not on that account be society. Interactions, transactions, occur *de facto* and the results of interdependence follow. But participation in activities and sharing in results are additive concerns. They demand *communication* as a prerequisite.

Combined activity happens among human beings; but when nothing else happens it passes as inevitably into some other mode of interconnected activity as does the interplay of iron and the oxygen of water. What takes place is wholly describable in terms of energy, or, as we say in the case of human interactions, of force. Only when there exist *signs* or *symbols* of activities and of their outcome can the flux be viewed as from without, be arrested for consideration and esteem, and be regulated. Lightning strikes and rives a tree or rock, and the resulting fragments take up and continue the process of interaction, and so on and on. But when phases of the process are represented by signs, a new medium is interposed. As symbols are related to one another, the important relations of a course of events are recorded and are preserved as meanings. Recollection and foresight are possible; the new medium facilitates calculation, planning, and a new kind of action which intervenes in what happens to direct its course in the interest of what is foreseen and desired.

Symbols in turn depend upon and promote communications. The results of conjoint experience are considered and transmitted. Events cannot be passed from one to another, but meanings may be shared by means of signs. Wants and impulses are then attached to common meanings. They are thereby transformed into desires and purposes, which, since they implicate a common or mutually understood meaning, present new ties, converting a conjoint activity into a community of interest and endeavor. Thus there is generated what, metaphorically, may be termed a general will and social consciousness: desire and choice on the part of individuals in behalf of activities that, by means of symbols, are communicable and shared by all concerned. A community thus presents an order of energies transmuted into one of meanings which are appreciated and mutually referred by each to every other on the part of those engaged in combined action. "Force" is not eliminated but is transformed in use and direction by ideas and sentiments made possible by means of symbols.

The work of conversion of the physical and organic phase of associated behavior into a community of action saturated and regulated by mutual interest in shared meanings, consequences which are translated into ideas and desired objects by means of symbols, does not occur all at once nor completely. At any given time, it sets a problem rather than marks a settled achievement. We are born organic beings associated with others, but we are not born members of a community. The young have to be brought within the traditions, outlook and interests which characterize a community by means of education: by unremitting instruction and by learning in connection with the phenomena of overt association. Everything which is distinctively human is learned, not native, even though it could not be learned without native structures which mark man off from other animals. To learn in a human way and to human effect is not just to acquire added skill through refinement of original capacities.

To learn to be human is to develop through the give-and-take of communication an effective sense of being an individually distinctive member of a community; one who understands and appreciates its beliefs, desires and methods, and who contributes to a further conversion of organic powers into human resources and values. But this translation is never finished. The old Adam, the unregenerate element in human nature, persists. It shows itself wherever the method obtains of attaining results by use of force instead of by the method of communication and enlightenment. It manifests itself more subtly, pervasively and effectually when knowledge and the instrumentalities of skill which are the product of communal life are employed in the service of wants and impulses which have not themselves been modified by reference to a shared interest. To the doctrine of "natural" economy which held that commercial exchange would bring about such an interdependence that harmony would automatically result, Rousseau gave an adequate answer in advance. He pointed out that interdependence provides just the situation which makes it possible and worth while for the stronger and abler to exploit others for their own ends, to keep others in a state of subjection where they can be utilized as animated tools. The remedy he suggested, a return to a condition of independence based on isolation, was hardly seriously meant. But its desperateness is evidence of the urgency of the problem. Its negative character was equivalent to surrender of any hope of solution. By contrast it indicates the nature of the only possible solution: the perfecting of the means and ways of communication of meanings so that genuinely shared interest in the consequences of interdependent activities may inform desire and effort and thereby direct action. . . .

The strongest point to be made in behalf of even such rudimentary political forms as democracy has already attained, popular voting, majority rule and so on, is that to some extent they involve a consultation and discussion which uncover social needs and troubles. This fact is the great asset on the side of the political ledger. De Tocqueville wrote it down almost a century ago in his survey of the prospects of democracy in the United States. Accusing a democracy of a tendency to prefer mediocrity in its elected rulers, and admitting its exposure to gusts of passion and its openness to folly, he pointed out in effect that popular government is educative as other modes of political regulations are not. It forces a recognition that there are common interests, even though the recognition of *what* they are is confused; and the need it enforces of discussion and publicity brings about some clarification of what they are. The man who wears the shoe knows best that it pinches and where it pinches, even if the expert shoemaker is the best judge of how the trouble is to be remedied. Popular government has at least created public spirit even if its success in informing that spirit has not been great.

A class of experts is inevitably so removed from common interests as to become a class with private interests and private knowledge, which in social matters is not knowledge at all. The ballot is, as often said, a substitute for bullets. But what is more significant is that counting of heads compels prior recourse to methods of discussion, consultation and persuasion, while the essence of appeal to force is to cut short resort to such methods. Majority rule, just as majority rule, is as foolish as its critics charge it with being. But it never is *merely* majority rule. As a practical politician, Samuel J. Tilden, said a long time ago: "The means by which a majority comes to be a majority is the more important thing": antecedent debates, modification of views to meet the opinions of minorities, the relative satisfaction given the latter by the fact that it has had a chance and that next time it may be successful in becoming a majority. Think of the meaning of the "problem of minorities" in certain European states, and compare it with the status of minorities in countries having popular government. It is true that all valuable as well as new ideas begin with minorities, perhaps a minority of one. The important consideration is that opportunity be given that idea to spread and to become the possession of the multitude. No government by experts in which the masses do not have the chance to inform the experts as to their needs can be anything but an oligarchy managed in the interests of the few. And the enlightenment must proceed in ways which force the administrative specialists to take account of the needs. The world has suffered more from leaders and authorities than from the masses.

The essential need, in other words, is the improvement of the methods and conditions of debate, discussion and persuasion. That is *the* problem of the public. We have asserted that this improvement depends essentially upon freeing and perfecting the processes of inquiry and of dissemination of their conclusions. Inquiry, indeed, is a work which devolves upon experts. But their expertness is not shown in framing and executing policies, but in discovering and making known the facts upon which the former depend. They are technical experts in the sense that scientific investigators and artists manifest *expertise*. It is not necessary that the many should have the knowledge and skill to carry on the needed investigations; what is required is that they have the ability to judge of the bearing of the knowledge supplied by others upon common concerns.

It is easy to exaggerate the amount of intelligence and ability demanded to render such judgments fitted for their purpose. In the first place, we are likely to form our estimate on the basis of present conditions. But indubitably one great trouble at present is that the data for good judgment are lacking; and no innate faculty of mind can make up for the absence of facts. Until secrecy, prejudice, bias, misrepresentation, and propaganda as well as sheer ignorance are replaced by inquiry and publicity, we have no way of telling how apt for judgment of social policies the existing intelligence of the masses may be. It would certainly go much further than at present. In the second place, *effective* intelligence is not an original, innate endowment. No matter what are the differences in native intelligence (allowing for the moment that intelligence can be native), the actuality of mind is dependent upon the education which social conditions effect. Just as the specialized mind and knowledge of the past is embodied in implements, utensils, devices and technologies which those of a grade of intelligence which could not produce them can now intelligently use, so it will be when currents of public knowledge blow through social affairs.

The level of action fixed by *embodied* intelligence is always the important thing. In savage culture a superior man will be superior to his fellows, but his knowledge and judgment will lag in many matters far behind that of an inferiorly endowed person in an advanced civilization. Capacities are limited by the objects and tools at hand. They are still more dependent upon the prevailing habits of attention and interest which are set by tradition and institutional customs. Meanings run in the channels formed by instrumentalities of which, in the end, language, the vehicle of thought as well as of communication, is the most important. A mechanic can discourse of ohms and amperes as Sir Isaac Newton could not in his day. Many a man who has tinkered with radios can judge of things which Faraday did not dream of. It is aside from the point to say that if Newton and Faraday were now here, the amateur and mechanic would be infants beside them. The retort only brings out the point: the difference made by different objects to think of and by different meanings in circulation. A more intelligent state of social affairs, one more informed with knowledge, more directed by intelligence, would not improve original endowments one whit, but it would raise the level upon which the intelligence of all operates. The height of this level is much more important for judgment of public concerns than are differences in intelligence quotients. As Santayana has said: "Could a better system prevail in our lives a better order would establish itself in our thinking. It has not been for want of keen senses, or personal genius, or a constant order in the outer world, that mankind has fallen back repeatedly into barbarism and superstition. It has been for want of good character, good example, and good government." The notion that intelligence is a personal endowment or personal attainment is the great conceit of the intellectual class, as that of the commercial class is that wealth is something which they personally have wrought and possess.

A point which concerns us in conclusion passes beyond the field of intellectual method, and trenches upon the question of practical re-formation of social conditions. In its deepest and richest sense a community must always remain a matter of face-to-face intercourse. This is why the family and neighborhood, with all their deficiencies, have always been the chief agencies of nurture, the means by which dispositions are stably formed and ideas acquired which laid hold on the roots of character. The Great Community, in the sense of free and full intercommunication, is conceivable. But it can never possess all the qualities which mark a local community. It will do its final work in ordering the relations and enriching the experience of local associations. The invasion and partial destruction of the life of the latter by outside uncontrolled agencies is the immediate source of the instability, disintegration and restlessness which characterize the present epoch. Evils which are uncritically and indiscriminately laid at the door of industrialism and democracy might, with greater intelligence, be referred to the dislocation and unsettlement of local communities. Vital and thorough attachments are bred only in the intimacy of an intercourse which is of necessity restricted in range.

Is it possible for local communities to be stable without being static, progressive without being merely mobile? Can the vast, innumerable and intricate currents of the trans-local associations be so banked and conducted that they will pour the generous and abundant meanings of which they are potential bearers into the smaller intimate unions of human beings living in immediate contact with one another? Is it possible to restore the reality of the lesser communal organizations and to penetrate and saturate their members with a sense of local community life? There is at present, at least in theory, a movement away from the principle of territorial organization to that of "functional," that is to say, occupational organization. It is true enough that older forms of territorial association do not satisfy present needs. It is true that ties formed by sharing in common work, whether in what is called industry or what are called professions, have now a force which formerly they did not possess. But these ties can be counted upon for an enduring and stable organization, which at the same time is flexible and moving, only as they grow out of immediate intercourse and attachment. The theory, as far as it relies upon associations which are remote and indirect, would if carried into effect soon be confronted by all the troubles and evils of the present situation in a transposed form. There is no substitute for the vitality and depth of close and direct intercourse and attachment.

VII

Philosophy of Education

The philosophy of John Dewey affected American society most directly and most broadly in the field of education. Dewey's educational theories, as interpreted by leading figures in the teachers colleges and schools of education throughout the country, had an important part in the change and reformation of American education over several decades. There was also a great receptivity to his educational philosophy in a number of foreign countries that adapted his views to their schools and even to the planning of whole educational systems.

The movement for educational reform associated with Dewey came to be identified with the movement for "progressive education," and developed into the subject of intense controversy. Dewey's writings were certainly cited by advocates of reform in education, though the legitimacy of derivation of certain educational practices or institutions from those writings itself became a question at issue.

The two selections in this section both show Dewey's special interest in the relationship between education and democracy. Dewey argues that the educational methods of a democratic society must necessarily differ from those that have prevailed in nondemocratic societies. The reasons for this difference are not related simply to the change in educational techniques or curricula that would follow once education of a small minority of the population—customary in a nondemocratic society—was replaced by an effort at universal education. They are also related to the fact that, independent of this kind of change, a society that is based on the value of democracy would, Dewey argues, require that the democratic spirit and process be exhibited in the classroom and the school system. Further, a democratic society must also be one that is committed to free inquiry, and hence to a willingness to experiment in its educational methods.

Dewey formulated his attitude toward educational reform and democratic education on the basis of his experience in education in the latter part of the nineteenth century and the first decades of the twentieth century. The first statement presented here is from *Democracy and Education,* written in 1916. There is a melancholy wisdom that asserts that no theory of social criticism or social reform no matter how trenchant its views against the prevailing orthodoxy, can survive the experience of acceptance, adoption, and implementation. Dewey's educational theories suffered that fate in the three decades after 1916. At the same time, he himself believed that American society had failed to narrow the gap, as he had hoped it would, between the reliability of its knowledge in technology or the physical sciences as compared with the social and psychological sciences. Against this background, it is instructive to see how Dewey reflected on the relationship between the democratic faith and education in a late essay written in 1944.

16

The Democratic Conception in Education

For the most part, save incidentally, we have hitherto been concerned with education as it may exist in any social group. We have now to make explicit the differences in the spirit, material, and method of education as it operates in different types of community life. To say that education is a social function, securing direction and development in the immature through their participation in the life of the group to which they belong, is to say in effect that education will vary with the quality of life which prevails in a group. Particularly is it true that a society which not only changes but which has the ideal of such change as will improve it, will have different standards and methods of education from one which aims simply at the perpetuation of its own customs. To make the general ideas set forth applicable to our own educational practice, it is, therefore, necessary to come to closer quarters with the nature of present social life.

1. *The Implications of Human Association*

Society is one word, but many things. Men associate together in all kinds of ways and for all kinds of purposes. One man is concerned in a multitude of diverse groups, in which his associates may be quite different. It often seems as if they had nothing in common except that they are modes of associated life. Within every larger

SOURCE: From *Democracy and Education*, 1916. Reprinted by permission of Macmillan Publishing Co., Inc. A footnote, containing a cross-reference, has been omitted.

social organization there are numerous minor groups: not only political subdivisions, but industrial, scientific, religious, associations. There are political parties with differing aims, social sets, cliques, gangs, corporations, partnerships, groups bound closely together by ties of blood, and so in endless variety. In many modern states, and in some ancient, there is great diversity of populations, of varying languages, religions, moral codes, and traditions. From this standpoint, many a minor political unit, one of our large cities, for example, is a congeries of loosely associated societies, rather than an inclusive and permeating community of action and thought.

The terms society, community, are thus ambiguous. They have both a eulogistic or normative sense, and a descriptive sense; a meaning *de jure* and a meaning *de facto*. In social philosophy, the former connotation is almost always uppermost. Society is conceived as one by its very nature. The qualities which accompany this unity, praiseworthy community of purpose and welfare, loyalty to public ends, mutuality of sympathy, are emphasized. But when we look at the facts which the term *denotes* instead of confining our attention to its intrinsic *connotation,* we find not unity, but a plurality of societies, good and bad. Men banded together in a criminal conspiracy, business aggregations that prey upon the public while serving it, political machines held together by the interest of plunder are included. If it is said that such organizations are not societies because they do not meet the ideal requirements of the notion of society, the answer, in part, is that the conception of society is then made so "ideal" as to be of no use, having no reference to facts; and in part, that each of these organizations, no matter how opposed to the interests of other groups, has something of the praiseworthy qualities of "Society" which hold it together. There is honor among thieves, and a band of robbers has a common interest as respects its members. Gangs are marked by fraternal feeling, and narrow cliques by intense loyalty to their own codes. Family life may be marked by exclusiveness, suspicion, and jealousy as to those without, and yet be a model of amity and mutual aid within. Any education given by a group tends to socialize its members, but the quality and value of the socialization depends upon the habits and aims of the group.

Hence, once more, the need of a measure for the worth of any given mode of social life. In seeking this measure, we have to avoid two extremes. We cannot set up, out of our heads, something we regard as an ideal society. We must base our conception upon societies which actually exist, in order to have any assurance that our ideal is a practicable one. But, as we have just seen, the ideal cannot simply repeat the traits which are actually found. The problem is to extract the desirable traits of forms of community life which actually exist, and employ them to criticize undesirable features and suggest improvement. Now in any social group whatever, even in a gang of thieves, we find some interest held in common, and we find a certain amount of interaction and cooperative intercourse with other groups. From these two traits we derive our standard. How numerous and varied are the interests which are consciously shared? How full and free is the interplay with other forms of association? If we apply these considerations to, say, a criminal band, we find that the ties which consciously hold the members together are few in number, reducible almost to a common interest in plunder; and that they are of such a nature as to isolate the group from other groups with respect to give and take of the values of life. Hence, the education such a society gives is partial and distorted. If we take, on the other hand, the kind of family life which illustrates the standard, we find that there are material, intellectual, aesthetic interests in which all participate and that the progress of one member has worth for the experience of other members—it is readily communicable—and that the family is not an isolated whole, but enters intimately into relationships with business groups with schools, with all the agencies of culture, as well as with other similar groups, and that it plays a due part in the political organization and in return receives support from it. In short, there are many interests consciously communicated and shared; and there are varied and free points of contact with other modes of association.

I. Let us apply the first element in this criterion to a despotically governed state. It is not true there is no common interest in such an organization between governed and governors. The authorities in command must make some appeal to the native activities of the subjects, must call some of their powers into play. Talleyrand said that a government could do everything with bayonets except sit on them. This cynical declaration is at least a recognition that the bond of union is not merely one of coercive force. It may be said, however, that the activities appealed to are themselves unworthy and degrading—that such a government calls into functioning activity simply capacity for fear. In a way, this statement is true. But it overlooks the fact that fear need not be an undesirable factor in experience. Caution, circumspection, prudence, desire to foresee future events so as to avert what is harmful, these desirable traits are as much a product of calling the impulse of fear into play as is cowardice and abject submission. The real difficulty is that the appeal to fear is *isolated*. In evoking dread and hope of specific tangible reward—say comfort and ease—many other capacities are left untouched. Or rather, they are affected, but in such a way as to pervert them. Instead of operating on their own account they are reduced to mere servants of attaining pleasure and avoiding pain.

This is equivalent to saying that there is no extensive number of common interests; there is no free play back and forth among the members of the social group. Stimulation and response are exceedingly one sided. In order to have a large number of values in common, all the members of the group must have an equable opportunity to receive and to take from others. There must be a large variety of shared undertakings and experiences. Otherwise, the influences which educate some into masters educate others into slaves. And the experience of each party loses in meaning, when the free interchange of varying modes of life-experience is arrested. A separation into a privileged and a subject-class prevents social endosmosis. The evils thereby affecting the superior class are less material and less perceptible, but equally real. Their culture tends to be sterile, to be turned back to feed on itself; their art becomes a showy display and artificial; their wealth luxurious; their knowledge overspecialized; their manners fastidious rather than humane.

Lack of the free and equitable intercourse which springs from a variety of shared interests makes intellectual stimulation unbalanced. Diversity of stimulation means novelty, and novelty means challenge to thought. The more activity is restricted to a few definite lines—as it is when there are rigid class lines preventing adequate interplay of experiences—the more action tends to become routine on the part of the class at a disadvantage, and capricious, aimless, and explosive on the part of the class having the materially fortunate position. Plato defined a slave as one who accepts from another the purposes which control his conduct. This condition obtains even where there is no slavery in the legal sense. It is found wherever men are engaged in activity which is socially serviceable, but whose service they do not understand and have no personal interest in. Much is said about scientific management of work. It is a narrow view which restricts the science which secures efficiency of operation to movements of the muscles. The chief opportunity for science is the discovery of the relations of a man to his work—including his relations to others who take part—which will enlist his intelligent interest in what he is doing. Efficiency in production often demands division of labor. But it is reduced to a mechanical routine unless workers see the technical, intellectual, and social relationships involved in what they do, and engage in their work because of the motivation furnished by such perceptions. The tendency to reduce such things as efficiency of activity and scientific management to purely technical externals is evidence of the one-sided stimulation of thought given to those in control of industry—those who supply its aims. Because of their lack of all-round and well-balanced social interest, there is not sufficient stimulus for attention to the human factors and relationships in industry. Intelligence is narrowed to the factors concerned with technical production and marketing of goods. No doubt, a very acute and intense intelligence in these narrow lines can be developed, but the failure to take into account the significant social factors means none the less an absence of mind, and a corresponding distortion of emotional life.

II. This illustration (whose point is to be extended to all associations lacking reciprocity of interest) brings us to our second point. The isolation and exclusiveness of a gang or clique brings its anti-social spirit into relief. But this same spirit is found wherever one group has interests "of its own" which shut it out from full interaction with other groups, so that its prevailing purpose is the protection of what it has got, instead of reorganization and progress through wider relationships. It marks nations in their isolation from one another; families which seclude their domestic concerns as if they had no connection with a larger life; schools when separated from the interest of home and community; the divisions of rich and poor; learned and unlearned. The essential point is that isolation makes for rigidity and formal institutionalizing of life, for static and selfish ideals within the group. That savage tribes regard aliens and enemies as synonymous is not accidental. It springs from the fact that they have identified their experience with rigid adherence to their past customs. On such a basis it is wholly logical to fear intercourse with others, for such contact might dissolve custom. It would certainly occasion reconstruction. It is a commonplace that an alert and expanding mental life depends upon an enlarging range of contact with the physical environment. But the principle applies even more significantly to the field where we are apt to ignore it—the sphere of social contacts.

Every expansive era in the history of mankind has coincided with the operation of factors which have tended to eliminate distance between peoples and classes previously hemmed off from one another. Even the alleged benefits of war, so far as more than alleged, spring from the fact that conflict of peoples at least enforces intercourse between them and thus accidentally enables them to learn from one another, and thereby to expand their horizons. Travel, economic and commercial tendencies have at present gone far to break down external barriers; to bring peoples and classes into closer and more perceptible connection with one another. It remains for the most part to secure the intellectual and emotional significance of this physical annihilation of space.

2. *The Democratic Ideal*

The two elements in our criterion both point to democracy. The first signifies not only more numerous and more varied points of shared common interest, but greater reliance upon the recognition of mutual interests as a factor in social control. The second means not only freer interaction between social groups (once isolated so far as intention could keep up a separation) but change in social habit—its continuous readjustment through meeting the new situations produced by varied intercourse. And these two traits are precisely what characterize the democratically constituted society.

Upon the educational side, we note first that the realization of a form of social life in which interests are mutually interpenetrating, and where progress, or readjustment, is an important consideration, makes a democratic community more interested than other communities have cause to be in deliberate and systematic education. The devotion of democracy to education is a familiar fact. The superficial explanation is that a government resting upon popular suffrage cannot be successful unless those who elect and who obey their governors are educated. Since a democratic society repudiates the principle of external authority, it must find a substitute in voluntary disposition and interest; these can be created only by education. But there is a deeper explanation. A democracy is more than a form of government; it is primarily a mode of associated living, of conjoint communicated experience. The extension in space of the number of individuals who participate in an interest so that each has to refer his own action to that of others, and to consider the action of others to give point and direction to his own, is equivalent to the breaking down of those barriers of class, race, and national territory which kept men from perceiving the full import of their activity. These more numerous and more varied points of contact denote a greater diversity of stimuli to which an individual has to respond; they consequently put a premium on variation in his action. They secure a liberation of powers which remain suppressed as long as the incitations to action are partial, as they must be in a group which in its exclusiveness shuts out many interests.

The widening of the area of shared concerns, and the liberation of a greater diversity of personal capacities which characterize a democracy are not of course the product of deliberation and conscious effort. On the contrary, they were caused by the development of modes of manufacture and commerce, travel, migration, and intercommunication which flowed from the command of science over natural energy. But after greater individualization on one hand, and a broader community of interest on the other have come into existence, it is a matter of deliberate effort to sustain and extend them. Obviously a society to which stratification into separate classes would be fatal must see to it that intellectual opportunities are accessible to all on equable and easy terms. A society marked off into classes need be specially attentive only to the education of its ruling elements. A society which is mobile, which is full of channels for the distribution of a change occurring anywhere, must see to it that its members are educated to personal initiative and adaptability. Otherwise, they will be overwhelmed by the changes in which they are caught and whose significance or connections they do not perceive. The result will be a confusion in which a few will appropriate to themselves the results of the blind and externally directed activities of others.

17

The Democratic Faith and Education

Not even the most far-seeing of men could have predicted, no longer ago than fifty years, the course events have taken. The expectations that were entertained by men of generous outlooks are in fact chiefly notable in that the actual course of events has moved, and with violence, in the opposite direction. The ardent and hopeful social idealist of the last century or so has been proved so wrong that a reaction to the opposite extreme has taken place. A recent writer has even proposed a confraternity of pessimists who should live together in some sort of social oasis. It is a fairly easy matter to list the articles of that old faith which, from the standpoint of today, have been tragically frustrated.

The first article on the list had to do with the prospects of the abolition of war. It was held that the revolution which was taking place in commerce and communication would break down the barriers which had kept the peoples of the earth alien and hostile and would create a state of interdependence which in time would insure lasting peace. Only an extreme pessimist ventured to suggest that interdependence might multiply points of friction and conflict.

Another item of that creed was the belief that a general development of enlightenment and rationality was bound to follow the increase in knowledge and the diffusion which would result from the revolution in science that was taking place. Since it had long been held that rationality and freedom were intimately allied, it was held that the movement toward democratic institutions and

SOURCE: Copyright by the Antioch Review, Inc., 1944. First published in *The Antioch Review,* Vol. 4, No. 2. Reprinted by permission of the editors.

popular government which had produced in succession the British, American, and French Revolutions was bound to spread until freedom and equality were the foundations of political government in every country of the globe.

A time of general ignorance and popular unenlightenment and a time of despotic and oppressive governmental rule were taken to be practically synonymous. Hence the third article of faith. There was a general belief among social philosophers that governmental activities were necessarily more or less oppressive; that governmental action tended to be an artificial interference with the operation of natural laws. Consequently the spread of enlightenment and democratic institutions would produce a gradual but assured withering away of the powers of the political state. Freedom was supposed to be so deeply rooted in the very nature of men that, given the spread of rational enlightenment, it would take care of itself with only a minimum of political action confined to insuring external police order.

The other article of faith to be mentioned was the general belief that the vast, the almost incalculable, increase in productivity resulting from the industrial revolution was bound to raise the general standard of living to a point where extreme poverty would be practically eliminated. It was believed that the opportunity to lead a decent, self-respecting, because self-sufficient, economic life would be assured to everyone who was physically and morally normal.

The course of events culminating in the present situation suffices to show without any elaborate argument how grievously these generous expectations have been disappointed. Instead of universal peace, there occurred two wars worldwide in extent and destructive beyond anything known in all history. Instead of uniform and steady growth of democratic freedom and equality, we have seen the rise of powerful totalitarian states with thoroughgoing suppression of liberty of belief and expression, outdoing the most despotic states of previous history. We have an actual growth in importance and range of governmental action in legislation and administration as necessary means of rendering freedom on the part of the many an assured actual fact. Instead of promotion of economic security and movement toward the elimination of poverty, we now have a great increase in the extent and the intensity of industrial crises with great increase of inability of workers to find employment. Social instability has reached a point that may portend revolution if it goes on unchecked.

Externally it looks as if the pessimists had the best of the case. But before we reach a conclusion on that point, we have to inquire concerning the solidity of the premise upon which the idealistic optimists rested their case. This principle was that the more desirable goals in view were to be accomplished by a complex of forces to which in their entirety the name "Nature" was given. In practical effect, acceptance of this principle was equivalent to adoption of a policy of drift as far as human intelligence and effort were concerned. No conclusion is warranted until we have inquired how far failure and frustration are consequences of putting out trust in a policy of drift; a policy of letting "George" in the shape of Nature and Natural Law do the work which only human intelligence and effort could possibly accomplish. No conclusion can be reached until we have considered an alternative: What is likely to happen if we recognize that the responsibility for creating a state of peace internationally, and of freedom and economic security internally, has to be carried by deliberate cooperative human effort? Technically speaking the policy known as *laissez-faire* is one of limited application. But its limited and technical significance is one instance of a manifestation of widespread trust in the ability of impersonal forces, popularly called Nature, to do a work that has to be done by human insight, foresight, and purposeful planning.

Not all the men of the earlier period were of the idealistic type. The idealistic philosophy was a positive factor in permitting those who prided themselves upon being realistic to turn events so as to produce consequences dictated by their own private and class advantage. The failure of cooperative and collective intelligence and effort to intervene was an invitation to immediate short-term intervention by those who had an eye to their own profit. The consequences were wholesale destruction and waste of natural resources, increase of social instability, and mortgaging of the future to a transitory and brief present of so-called prosperity. If "idealists" were misguided in what they failed to do, "realists" were wrong in what they did. If the former erred in supposing that the drift (called by them progress or evolution) was inevitably toward the better, the latter were more actively harmful because their insistence upon trusting to natural laws was definitely in the interest of personal and class profit.

The omitted premise in the case of both groups is the fact that neither science nor technology is an impersonal cosmic force. They operate only in the medium of human desire, foresight, aim, and effort. Science and technology are transactions in which man and nature work together and in which the human factor is that directly open to modification and direction. That man takes part along with physical conditions in invention and use of the devices, implements, and machinery of industry and commerce, no one would think of denying.

But in practice, if not in so many words, it has been denied that man has any responsibility for the consequences that result from what he invents and employs. This denial is implicit in our widespread refusal to engage in large-scale collective planning. Not a day passes, even in the present crisis, when the whole idea of such planning is not ridiculed as an emanation from the brain of starry-eyed professors or of others equally inept in practical affairs. And all of this in the face of the fact that there is not a successful industrial organization that does not owe its success to persistent planning within a limited field—with an eye to profit—to say nothing of the terribly high price we have paid in the way of insecurity and war for putting our trust in drift.

Refusal to accept responsibility for looking ahead and for planning in matters national and international is based upon refusal to employ in social affairs, in the field of human relations, the methods of observation, interpretation, and test that are matters of course in dealing with physical things, and to which we owe the conquest of physical nature. The net result is a state of imbalance, of profoundly disturbed equilibrium between our physical knowledge and our social-moral knowledge. This lack of harmony is a powerful factor in producing the present crisis with all its tragic features. For physical knowledge and physical technology have far outstripped social or humane knowledge and human engineering. Our failure to use in matters of direct human concern the scientific methods which have revolutionized physical knowledge has permitted the latter to dominate the social scene.

The change in the physical aspect of the world has gone on so rapidly that there is probably no ground for surprise in the fact that our psychological and moral knowledge has not kept pace. But there is cause for astonishment in the fact that, after the catastrophe of war, insecurity, and the threat to democratic institutions have shown the need for moral and intellectual attitudes and habits which will correspond with the changed state of the world, there should be a definite campaign to make the scientific attitude the scapegoat for present evils, while a return to the beliefs and practices of a prescientific and pretechnological age is urged as the road to our salvation.

The organized attack made from time to time against science and against technology as inherently materialistic and as usurping the place properly held by abstract moral precepts—abstract because divorcing ends from the means by which they must be realized—

defines the issue we now have to face. Shall we go backwards or shall we go ahead to discover and put into practice the means by which science and technology shall be made fundamental in the promotion of human welfare? The failure to use scientific methods in creating understanding of human relationships and interests and in planning measures and policies that correspond in human affairs to the technologies in physical use is easily explained in historical terms. The new science began with things at the furthest remove from human affairs, namely with the stars of the heavens. From astronomy the new methods went on to win their victories in physics and chemistry. Still later science was applied in physiological and biological subject-matter. At every state, the advance met determined resistance from the representatives of established institutions who felt their prestige was bound up with maintenance of old beliefs and found their class control of others being threatened. In consequence, many workers in science found that the easiest way in which to procure an opportunity to carry on their inquiries was to adopt an attitude of extreme specialization. The effect was equivalent to the position that their methods and conclusions were not and could not be "dangerous," since they had no point of contact with man's serious moral concerns. This position in turn served to perpetuate and confirm the older separation of man as man from the rest of nature and to intensify the split between the "material" and the moral and "ideal."

Thus it has come about that when scientific inquiry began to move from its virtually complete victories in astronomy and physics and its partial victory in the field of living things over into the field of human affairs and concerns, the interests and institutions which offered resistance to its earlier advance gathered themselves together for a final attack upon that aspect of science which in truth constitutes its supreme and culminating significance. On the principle that offense is the best defense, respect for science and loyalty to its outlook are attacked as the chief source of all our present social ills. One may read, for example, in current literature such a condescending concession as marks the following passage: "Of course, the scientific attitude, though often leading to such a catastrophe, is not to be condemned, "the immediate context showing that the particular "catastrophe" in mind consists of "errors leading to war . . . derived from an incorrect theory of truth." Since these errors are produced by belief in the applicability of scientific method to human as well as physical facts, the remedy, according to this writer, is to abandon "the erroneous application of the methods and results of natural science to the problems of human life."

In three respects the passage is typical of such organized campaigns in active operation. There is first the assertion that such catastrophes as that of the recent war are the result of devotion to scientific method and conclusions. The denunciation of "natural" science as applied to human affairs carries, in the second place, the implication that man is outside of and above nature, and the consequent necessity of returning to the medieval prescientific doctrine of a supernatural foundation and outlook in all social and moral subjects. Then thirdly there is the assumption, directly contrary to fact, that the scientific method has at the present time been seriously and systematically applied to the problems of human life.

I dignify the passage quoted by this reference to it because it serves quite as well as a multitude of other passages from reactionaries to convey a sense of the present issues. It is true that the *results* of natural science have had a large share, for evil as well as for good, in bringing the world to its present pass. But it is equally true that "natural" science has been identified with *physical* science in a sense in which the physical is set over against the human. It is true that the interests and institutions which are now attacking science are just the forces which in behalf of a supernatural center of gravity are those that strive to maintain this tragic split in human affairs. Now the issue, as is becoming clearer every day, is whether we shall go backward or whether we shall go forward toward recognition in theory and practice of the indissoluble unity of the humanistic and the naturalistic.

What has all this to do with education? The answer to this question may be gathered from the fact that those who are engaged in assault upon science center their attacks upon the increased attention given by our schools to science and to its application in vocational training. In a world which is largely what it is today because of science and technology they propose that education should turn its back upon even the degree of recognition science and technology have received. They propose we turn our face to the medievalism in which so-called "liberal" arts were identified with literary arts: a course natural to adopt in an age innocent of knowledge of nature, an age in which the literary arts were the readiest means of rising above barbarism through acquaintance with the achievements of Greek-Roman culture. Their proposal is so remote from the facts of the present world, it involves such a bland ignoring of actualities, that there is a temptation to dismiss it as idle vaporing. But it would be a tragic mistake to take the reactionary assaults so lightly. For they are an expression of just the forces that keep science penned up in a compartment labelled "materialistic and anti-human." They strengthen all the habits and institutions which render that which is morally "ideal" impotent in action and which leave the "material" to operate without humane direction.

Let me return for the moment to my initial statement that the basic error of social idealists was the assumption that something called "natural law" could be trusted, with only incidental cooperation by human beings, to bring about the desired ends. The lesson to be learned is that human attitudes and efforts are the strategic center for promotion of the generous aims of peace among nations; promotion of economic security; the use of political means in order to advance freedom and equality; and the worldwide cause of democratic institutions. Anyone who starts from this premise is bound to see that it carries with it the basic importance of education in creating the habits and the outlook that are able and eager to secure the ends of peace, democracy, and economic stability.

When this is seen, it will also be seen how little has actually been done in our schools to render science and technology active agencies in creating the attitudes and dispositions and in securing the kinds of knowledge that are capable of coping with the problems of men and women today. Externally a great modification has taken place in subjects taught and in methods of teaching them. But when the changes are critically examined it is found that they consist largely in emergency concessions and accommodation to the urgent conditions and issues of the contemporary world. The standards and the controlling methods in education are still mainly those of a pre-scientific and pretechnological age.

This statement will seem to many persons to be exaggerated. But consider the purposes which as a rule still govern instruction in just those subjects that are taken to be decisively "modern," namely science and vocational preparation. Science is taught upon the whole as a body of ready-made information and technical skills. It is not taught as furnishing in its method the pattern for all effective intelligent conduct. It is taught upon the whole not with respect to the way in which it actually enters into human life, and hence as a supremely humanistic subject, but as if it had to do with a world which is "external" to human concerns. It is not presented in connection with the ways in which it actually enters into every aspect and phase of present human life. And it is hardly necessary to add that still less is it taught in connection with what scientific knowledge of human affairs might do in overcoming sheer drift. Scientific method and conclusions will not have gained a fundamentally important place in education until they are seen and treated as supreme agencies in giving direction to collective and cooperative human behavior.

The same sort of thing is to be said about the kind of use now made in education of practical and vocational subjects so called. The reactionary critics are busy urging that the latter subjects be taught to the masses—who are said to be incapable of rising to the plane of the "intellectual" but who do the useful work which somebody has to do, and who may be taught by vocational education to do it more effectively. This view is of course an open and avowed attempt to return to that dualistic separation of ideas and action, of the "intellectual" and the "practical," of the liberal and servile arts, that marked the feudal age. And this reactionary move in perpetuation of the split from which the world is suffering is offered as a cure, a panacea, not as the social and moral quackery it actually is. As is the case with science, the thing supremely needful is to go forward. And the forward movement in the case of technology as in the case of science is to do away with the chasm which ancient and medieval educational practice and theory set up between the liberal and the vocational, not to treat the void, the hole, constituted by this chasm, as if it were a foundation for the creation of free society.

There is nothing whatever inherent in the occupations that are socially necessary and useful to divide them into those which are "learned" professions and those which are menial, servile, and illiberal. As far as such a separation exists in fact it is an inheritance from the earlier class structure of human relations. It is a denial of democracy. At the very time when an important, perhaps *the* important, problem in education is to fill education having an occupational direction with a genuinely liberal content, we have, believe it or not, a movement, such as is sponsored for example by President Hutchins, to cut vocational training off from any contact with what is liberating by relegating it to special schools devoted to inculcation of technical skills. Inspiring vocational education with a liberal spirit and filling it with a liberal content is not a utopian dream. It is a demonstrated possibility in schools here and there in which subjects usually labelled "practically useful" are taught charged with scientific understanding and with a sense of the social-moral applications they potentially possess.

If little is said in the foregoing remarks specifically upon the topic of democratic faith, it is because their bearing upon a democratic outlook largely appears upon their very face. Conditions in this country when the democratic philosophy of life and democratic institutions were taking shape were such as to encourage a belief that the latter were so natural to man, so appropriate to his very being, that if they were once established they would tend to maintain themselves. I cannot rehearse here the list of events that have given this naive faith a shock. They are contained in every deliberate attack upon democracy and in every expression of cynicism about its past failures and pessimism about its future—attacks and expressions which have to be taken seriously if they are looked at as signs of trying to establish democracy as an end in separation from the concrete means upon which the end depends.

Democracy is not an easy road to take and follow. On the contrary, it is, as far as its realization is concerned in the complex conditions of the contemporary world, a supremely difficult one. Upon the whole we are entitled to take courage from the fact that it has worked as well as it has done. But to this courage we must add, if our courage is to be intelligent rather than blind, the fact that successful maintenance of democracy demands the utmost in use of the best available methods to procure a social knowledge that is reasonably commensurate with our physical knowledge, and the invention and use of forms of social engineering reasonably commensurate with our technological abilities in physical affairs.

This then is the task indicated. It is, if we employ large terms, to humanize science. This task in the concrete cannot be accomplished save as the fruit of science, which is named technology, is also humanized. And the task can be executed in the concrete only as it is broken up into vital applications of intelligence in a multitude of fields to a vast diversity of problems so that science and technology may be rendered servants of the democratic hope and faith. The cause is capable of inspiring loyalty in thought and deed. But there has to be joined to aspiration and effort the formation of free, wide-ranging, trained attitudes of observation and understanding such as incorporate within themselves, as a matter so habitual as to be unconscious, the vital principles of scientific method. In this achievement science, education, and the democratic cause meet as one. May we be equal to the occasion. For it is our human problem. If a solution is found it will be through the medium of human desire, human understanding, and human endeavor.

VIII

Philosophy of Religion

The philosophical agenda of our times, in Dewey's view, is the reconciliation of the inherited traditions of our culture with the progressive revelations of scientific method. Such a reconciliation often requires a radical revision or reconstruction of the tradition. The reconciliation of religious tradition with scientific method is obviously an extremely difficult undertaking. Many products of the religious tradition express a sensibility that is remote from scientific methodology. So many efforts at the rationalization of religious views or artificial reconciliations have taken place that any such reconciliation suggests a compromise with intellectual honesty.

Yet since the rise of modern science, from Spinoza through Matthew Arnold and John Stuart Mill, there have been continuous efforts to reinterpret religious belief in a manner compatible with scientific method and scientific knowledge. These efforts usually required a redefinition of the nature of religious belief, or of God, or of religious knowledge. In redefining fundamental aspects of religion, however, the philosophers concerned believed that they had preserved continuity with certain vital features of the religious tradition.

Dewey's philosophy of religion follows in this path of what has been termed "religious naturalism" or "religious liberalism." Dewey's sense of the philosophical agenda drew him to a concern with the reconciliation between our inherited views on social, political, and moral questions and the methods of science, rather than to the problems science poses for religious belief. Essentially, his contribution in this area was one small volume, *A Common Faith* (1934).

A Common Faith is a coherent and thoughtful formulation of religious naturalism. Religious belief, it claims, can be consistent with the adoption of scientific method as the only reliable way to knowledge if it is prepared to abandon any assertion of supernatural or transcendental entities or experience. After such surrender, there remain all those aspects of religious belief and religious experience that involve the imaginative construction of an unification of ideal ends, called God. Further, the celebration or commemoration of the possibility of those ends being realized in the world of our experience has not been abandoned.

Many naturalists and pragmatists found in Dewey's willingness to sanction the use of the term "God" an evasion of the implications of his consistent naturalistic point of view in metaphysics or theory of knowledge. It is the associations of the term "God" not only with the supernatural, but also with the conception that there is a guarantee for the outcome of natural and historical process that suggest that a naturalistic use of the term is equivocal. For many philosophical naturalists the introduction of a naturalist conception of God violated the canons of semantic parsimony.

Many religionists and theologians argue that conceptions of a naturalistic or limited divinity ignore the centrality of the transcendent and the irrational for the theory and practice of religion. They believe, accordingly, that works that reconcile religious tradition with scientific method do not do justice to the richness of that tradition in its own settings.

Dewey had set for himself a limited goal in *A Common Faith*. Within the context of the effort to develop a contemporary religious liberalism or religious naturalism, he sought to formulate a statement of that religious option. The second chapter of *A Common Faith* posits the feasibility and appeal of a naturalistic interpretation of religious belief.

18

Faith and Its Object

All religions, as I pointed out in the preceding chapter, involve specific intellectual beliefs, and they attach—some greater, some less—importance to assent to these doctrines as true, true in the intellectual sense. They have literatures held especially sacred, containing historical material with which the validity of the religions is connected. They have developed a doctrinal apparatus it is incumbent upon "believers" (with varying degrees of strictness in different religions) to accept. They also insist that there is some special and isolated channel of access to the truths they hold.

No one will deny, I suppose, that the present crisis in religion is intimately bound up with these claims. The skepticism and agnosticism that are rife and that from the standpoint of the religionist are fatal to the religious spirit are directly bound up with the intellectual contents, historical, cosmological, ethical, and theological, asserted to be indispensable in everything religious. There is no need for me here to go with any minuteness into the causes that have generated doubt and disbelief, uncertainty and rejection, as to these contents. It is enough to point out that all the beliefs and ideas in question, whether having to do with historical and literary matters, or with astronomy, geology and biology, or with the creation and structure of the world and man, are connected with the supernatural, and that this connection is the factor that has brought doubts upon them; the factor that from the standpoint of historic and institutional religions in sapping the religious life itself.

The obvious and simple facts of the case are that some views

Source: From *A Common Faith*, 1934. Reprinted by permission of Yale University Press.

about the origin and constitution of the world and man, some views about the course of human history and personages and incidents in that history, have become so interwoven with religion as to be identified with it. On the other hand, the growth of knowledge and of its methods and tests has been such as to make acceptance of these beliefs increasingly onerous and even impossible for large numbers of cultivated men and women. With such persons, the result is that the more these ideas are used as the basis and justification of a religion, the more dubious that religion becomes.

Protestant denominations have largely abandoned the idea that particular ecclesiastic sources can authoritatively determine cosmic, historic and theological beliefs. The more liberal among them have at least mitigated the older belief that individual hardness and corruption of heart are the causes of intellectual rejection of the intellectual apparatus of the Christian religion. But these denominations have also, with exceptions numerically insignificant, retained a certain indispensable minimum of intellectual content. They ascribe peculiar religious force to certain literary documents and certain historic personages. Even when they have greatly reduced the bulk of intellectual content to be accepted, they have insisted at least upon theism and the immortality of the individual.

It is no part of my intention to rehearse in any detail the weighty facts that collectively go by the name of the conflict of science and religion—a conflict that is not done away with by calling it a conflict of science with theology, as long as even a minimum of intellectual assent is prescribed as essential. The impact of astronomy not merely upon the older cosmogony of religion but upon elements of creeds dealing with historic events—witness the idea of ascent into heaven—is familiar. Geological discoveries have displaced creation myths which once bulked large. Biology has revolutionized conceptions of soul and mind which once occupied a central place in religious beliefs and ideas, and this science has made a profound impression upon ideas of sin, redemption, and immortality. Anthropology, history and literary criticism have furnished a radically different version of the historic events and personages upon which Christian religions have built. Psychology is already opening to us natural explanations of phenomena so extraordinary that once their supernatural origin was, so to say, the natural explanation.

The significant bearing for my purpose of all this is that new methods of inquiry and reflection have become for the educated man today the final arbiter of all questions of fact, existence, and intellectual assent. Nothing less than a revolution in the "seat of intellectual authority" has taken place. This revolution, rather than

any particular aspect of its impact upon this and that religious belief, is the central thing. In this revolution, every defeat is a stimulus to renewed inquiry; every victory won is the open door to more
discoveries, and every discovery is a new seed planted in the soil of
intelligence, from which grow fresh plants with new fruits. The
mind of man is being habituated to a new method and ideal: There
is but one sure road of access to truth—the road of patient, cooperative inquiry operating by means of observation, experiment,
record and controlled reflection.

The scope of the change is well illustrated by the fact that whenever a particular outpost is surrendered it is usually met by the
remark from a liberal theologian that the particular doctrine or
supposed historic or literary tenet surrendered was never, after all,
an intrinsic part of religious belief, and that without it the true
nature of religion stands out more clearly than before. Equally significant is the growing gulf between fundamentalists and liberals in
the churches. What is not realized—although perhaps it is more
definitely seen by fundamentalists than by liberals—is that the issue
does not concern this and that piecemeal *item* of belief, but centers
in the question of the method by which any and every item of intellectual belief is to be arrived at and justified.

The positive lesson is that religious qualities and values if they
are real at all are not bound up with any single item of intellectual
assent, not even that of the existence of the God of theism; and that,
under existing conditions, the religious function in experience can
be emancipated only through surrender of the whole notion of
special truths that are religious by their own nature, together with
the idea of peculiar avenues of access to such truths. For were we
to admit that there is but one method for ascertaining fact and
truth—that conveyed by the word "scientific" in its most general
and generous sense—no discovery in any branch of knowledge and
inquiry could then disturb the faith that is religious. I should describe this faith as the unification of the self through allegiance to
inclusive ideal ends, which imagination presents to us and to which
the human will responds as worthy of controlling our desires and
choices.

It is probably impossible to imagine the amount of intellectual
energy that has been diverted from normal processes of arriving at
intellectual conclusions because it has gone into rationalization of
the doctrines entertained by historic religions. The set that has
thus been given the general mind is much more harmful, to my
mind, than are the consequences of any one particular item of belief, serious as have been those flowing from acceptance of some of

them. The modern liberal version of the intellectual content of Christianity seems to the modern mind to be more rational than some of the earlier doctrines that have been reacted against. Such is not the case in fact. The theological philosophers of the Middle Ages had no greater difficulty in giving rational form to all the doctrines of the Roman church than has the liberal theologian of today in formulating and justifying intellectually the doctrines he entertains. This statement is as applicable to the doctrine of continuing miracles, penance, indulgences, saints and angels, etc., as to the trinity, incarnation, atonement and the sacraments. The fundamental question, I repeat, is not of this and that article of intellectual belief but of intellectual habit, method and criterion.

One method of swerving aside the impact of changed knowledge and method upon the intellectual content of religion is the method of division of territory and jurisdiction into two parts. Formerly these were called the realm of nature and the realm of grace. They are now often known as those of revelation and natural knowledge. Modern religious liberalism has no definite names for them, save, perhaps, the division, referred to in the last chapter, between scientific and religious experience. The implication is that in one territory the supremacy of scientific knowledge must be acknowledged, while there is another region, not very precisely defined, of intimate personal experience wherein other methods and criteria hold sway.

This method of justifying the peculiar and legitimate claim of certain elements of belief is always open to the objection that a positive conclusion is drawn from a negative fact. Existing ignorance or backwardness is employed to assert the existence of a division in the nature of the subject-matter dealt with. Yet the gap may only reflect, at most, a limitation now existing but in the future to be done away with. The argument that because some province or aspect of experience has not yet been "invaded" by scientific methods it is not subject to them, is as old as it is dangerous. Time and time again, in some particular reserved field, it has been invalidated. Psychology is still in its infancy. He is bold to the point of rashness who asserts that intimate personal experience will never come within the ken of natural knowledge.

It is more to the present point, however, to consider the region that is claimed by religionists as a special reserve. It is mystical experience. The difference, however, between mystic experience and the theory about it that is offered to us must be noted. The experience is a fact to be inquired into. The theory, like any theory, is an interpretation of the fact. The idea that by its very nature the experience is a veridical realization of the direct presence of God does not rest so much upon examination of the facts as it does upon importing into their interpretation a conception that is formed outside them. In its dependence upon a prior conception of the supernatural, which is the thing to be proved, it begs the question.

History exhibits many types of mystic experience, and each of these types is contemporaneously explained by the concepts that prevail in the culture and the circle in which the phenomena occur. There are mystic crises that arise, as among some North American Indian tribes, induced by fasting. They are accompanied by trances and semi-hysteria. Their purpose is to gain some special power, such perhaps as locating a person who is lost or finding objects that have been secreted. There is the mysticism of Hindoo practice now enjoying some vogue in Western countries. There is the mystic ecstasy of Neoplatonism with its complete abrogation of the self and absorption into an impersonal whole of Being. There is the mysticism of intense aesthetic experience independent of any theological or metaphysical interpretation. There is the heretical mysticism of William Blake. There is the mysticism of sudden unreasoning fear in which the very foundations seem shaken beneath one—to mention but a few of the types that may be found.

What common element is there between, say, the Neoplatonic conception of a super-divine Being wholly apart from human needs and conditions and the medieval theory of an immediate union that is fostered through attention to the sacraments or through concentration upon the heart of Jesus? The contemporary emphasis of some Protestant theologians upon the sense of inner personal communion with God, found in religious experience, is almost as far away from medieval Christianity as it is from Neoplatonism or Yoga. Interpretations of the experience have not grown from the experience itself with the aid of such scientific resources as may be available. They have been imported by borrowing without criticism from ideas that are current in the surrounding culture.

The mystic states of the shaman and of some North American Indians are frankly techniques for gaining a special power—*the* power as it is conceived by some revivalist sects. There is no especial intellectual objectification accompanying the experience. The knowledge that is said to be gained is not that of Being but of particular secrets and occult modes of operation. The aim is not to gain knowledge of superior divine power, but to get advice, cures for the sick, prestige, etc. The conception that mystic experience is a normal mode of religious experience by which we may acquire knowledge of God and divine things is a nineteenth-century interpretation that has gained vogue in direct ratio to the decline of older methods of religious apologetics.

There is no reason for denying the existence of experiences that are called mystical. On the contrary, there is every reason to suppose that, in some degree of intensity, they occur so frequently that they may be regarded as normal manifestations that take place at certain rhythmic points in the movement of experience. The assumption that denial of a particular interpretation of their objective content proves that those who make the denial do not have the experience in question, so that if they had it they would be equally persuaded of its objective source in the presence of God, has no foundation in fact. As with every empirical phenomenon, the occurrence of the state called mystical is simply an occasion for inquiry into its mode of causation. There is no more reason for converting the experience itself into an immediate knowledge of its cause than in the case of an experience of lightning or any other natural occurrence.

My purpose, then, in this brief reference to mysticism is not to throw doubt upon the existence of particular experiences called mystical. Nor is it to propound any theory to account for them. I have referred to the matter merely as an illustration of the general tendency to mark off two distinct realms in one of which science has jurisdiction, while in the other, special modes of immediate knowledge of religious objects have authority. This dualism as it operates in contemporary interpretation of mystic experience in order to validate certain beliefs is but a reinstatement of the old dualism between the natural and the supernatural, in terms better adapted to the cultural conditions of the present time. Since it is the conception of the supernatural that science calls in question, the circular nature of this type of reasoning is obvious.

Apologists for a religion often point to the shift that goes on in scientific ideas and materials as evidence of the unreliability of science as a mode of knowledge. They often seem peculiarly elated by the great, almost revolutionary, change in fundamental physical conceptions that has taken place in science during the present generation. Even if the alleged unreliability were as great as they assume (or even greater), the question would remain: Have we any other recourse for knowledge? But in fact they miss the point. Science is not constituted by any particular body of subject-matter. It is constituted by a method, a method of changing beliefs by means of tested inquiry as well as of arriving at them. It is its glory, not its condemnation, that its subject-matter develops as the method is improved. There is no special subject-matter of belief that is sacrosanct. The identification of science with a particular set of beliefs and ideas is itself a hold-over of ancient and still current dogmatic habits of thought which are opposed to science in its actuality and which science is undermining.

For scientific method is adverse not only to dogma but to doctrine as well, provided we take "doctrine" in its usual meaning—a body of definite beliefs that need only to be taught and learned as true. This negative attitude of science to doctrine does not indicate indifference to truth. It signifies supreme loyalty to the method by which truth is attained. The scientific-religious conflict ultimately is a conflict between allegiance to this method and allegiance to even an irreducible minimum of belief so fixed in advance that it can never be modified.

The method of intelligence is open and public. The doctrinal method is limited and private. This limitation persists even when knowledge of the truth that is religious is said to be arrived at by a special mode of experience, that termed "religious." For the latter is assumed to be a very special kind of experience. To be sure it is asserted to be open to all who obey certain conditions. Yet the mystic experience yields, as we have seen, various results in the way of belief to different persons, depending upon the surrounding culture of those who undergo it. As a method, it lacks the public character belonging to the method of intelligence. Moreover, when the experience in question does not yield consciousness of the presence of God, in the sense that is alleged to exist, the retort is always at hand that it is not a genuine religious experience. For by definition, only that experience *is* religious which arrives at this particular result. The argument is circular. The traditional position is that some hardness or corruption of heart prevents one from having the experience. Liberal religionists are now more humane. But their logic does not differ.

It is sometimes held that beliefs about religious matters are symbolic, like rites and ceremonies. This view may be an advance upon that which holds to their literal objective validity. But as usually put forward it suffers from an ambiguity. Of what are the beliefs symbols? Are they symbols of things experienced in other modes than those set apart as religious, so that the things symbolized have an independent standing? Or are they symbols in the sense of standing for some transcendental reality—transcendental because not being the subject-matter of experience generally? Even the fundamentalist admits a certain quality and degree of symbolism in the latter sense in objects of religious belief. For he holds that the objects of these beliefs are so far beyond finite human capacity that our beliefs must be couched in more or less metaphorical terms. The conception that faith is the best available substitute for knowledge in our present estate still attaches to the notion of the symbolic character of the materials of faith; unless by ascribing to them a symbolic nature we mean that these materials stand for something that is verifiable in general and public experience.

Were we to adopt the latter point of view, it would be evident not only that the intellectual articles of a creed must be understood to be symbolic of moral and other ideal values, but that the facts taken to be historic and used as concrete evidence of the intellectual articles are themselves symbolic. These articles of a creed present events and persons that have been made over by the idealizing imagination in the interest, at their best, of moral ideals. Historic personages in their divine attributes are materializations of the ends that enlist devotion and inspire endeavor. They are symbolic of the reality of ends moving us in many forms of experience. The ideal values that are thus symbolized also mark human experience in science and art and the various modes of human association: they mark almost everything in life that rises from the level of manipulation of conditions as they exist. It is admitted that the objects of religion are ideal in contrast with our present state. What would be lost if it were also admitted that they have authoritative claim upon conduct just because they are ideal? The assumption that these objects of religion exist already in some realm of Being seems to add nothing to their force, while it weakens their claim over us as ideals, in so far as it bases that claim upon matters that are intellectually dubious. The question narrows itself to this: Are the ideals that move us genuinely ideal or are they ideal only in contrast with our present estate?

The import of the question extends far. It determines the meaning given to the word "God." On one score, the word can mean only a particular Being. On the other score, it denotes the unity of all ideal ends arousing us to desire and actions. Does the unification have a claim upon our attitude and conduct because it is already, apart from us, in realized existence, or because of its own inherent meaning and value? Suppose for the moment that the word "God" means the ideal ends that at a given time and place one acknowledges as having authority over his volition and emotion, the values to which one is supremely devoted, as far as these ends, through imagination, take on unity. If we make this supposition, the issue will stand out clearly on contrast with the doctrine of religions that "God" designates some kind of Being having prior and therefore non-ideal existence.

The word "non-ideal" is to be taken literally in regard to some religions that have historically existed, to all of them as far as they are neglectful of moral qualities in their divine beings. It does not apply in the same *literal* way to Judaism and Christianity. For they have asserted that the Supreme Being has moral and spiritual attributes. But it applies to them none the less in that these moral and spiritual characters are thought of as properties of a particular existence and are thought to be of religious value for us because of this embodiment in such an existence. Here, as far as I can see, is the ultimate issue as to the difference between *a* religion and the religious as a function of experience.

The idea that "God" represents a unification of ideal values that is essentially imaginative in origin when the imagination supervenes in conduct is attended with verbal difficulties owing to our frequent use of the word "imagination" to denote fantasy and doubtful reality. But the reality of ideal ends as ideals is vouched for by their undeniable power in action. An ideal is not an illusion because imagination is the organ through which it is apprehended. For *all* possibilities reach us through the imagination. In a definite sense the only meaning that can be assigned the term "imagination" is that things unrealized in fact come home to us and have power to stir us. The unification effected through imagination is not fanciful, for it is the reflex of the unification of practical and emotional attitudes. The unity signifies not a single Being, but the unity of loyalty and effort evoked by the fact that many ends are one in the power of their ideal, or imaginative, quality to stir and hold us.

We may well ask whether the power and significance in life of the traditional conceptions of God are not due to the ideal qualities referred to by them, the hypostatization of them into an existence being due to a conflux of tendencies in human nature that converts the object of desire into an antecedent reality, in beliefs that have prevailed in the cultures of the past. For in the older cultures the idea of the supernatural was "natural," in the sense in which "natural" signifies something customary and familiar. It seems more credible that religious persons have been supported and consoled by the reality with which ideal values appeal to them than that they have been upborne by sheer matter-of-fact existence. That, when once men are inured to the idea of the union of the ideal and the physical, the two should be so bound together in emotion that it is difficult to institute a separation, agrees with all we know of human psychology.

The benefits that will accrue, however, from making the separation are evident. The dislocation frees the religious values of experience once for all from matters that are continually becoming more dubious. With that release there comes emancipation from the necessity of resort to apologetics. The reality of ideal ends and values in their authority over us is an undoubted fact. The validity of justice, affection, and that intellectual correspondence of our ideas with realities that we call truth, is so assured in its hold upon humanity that it is unnecessary for the religious attitude to encumber itself with the apparatus of dogma and doctrine. Any other conception of the religious attitude, when it is adequately analyzed, means that those who hold it care more for force than for ideal values—since all that an Existence can add is force to establish, to punish, and to reward. There are, indeed, some persons who frankly say that their own faith does not require any guarantee that moral values are backed up by physical force, but who hold that the masses are so backward that ideal values will not affect their conduct unless in the popular belief these values have the sanction of a power that can enforce them and can execute justice upon those who fail to comply.

There are some persons, deserving of more respect, who say: "We agree that the beginning must be made with the primacy of the ideal. But why stop at this point? Why not search with the utmost eagerness and vigor for all the evidence we can find, such as is supplied by history, by presence of design in nature, which may lead on to the belief that the ideal is already extant in a Personality having objective existence?"

One answer to the question is that we are involved by this search in all the problems of the existence of evil that have haunted theology in the past and that the most ingenious apologetics have not faced, much less met. If these apologists had not identified the existence of ideal goods with that of a Person supposed to originate and support them—a Being, moreover, to whom omnipotent power is attributed—the problem of the occurrence of evil would be gratuitous. The significance of ideal ends and meaning is, indeed, closely connected with the fact that there are in life all sorts of things that are evil to us because we would have them otherwise. Were existing conditions wholly good, the notion of possibilities to be realized would never emerge.

But the more basic answer is that while if the search is conducted upon a strictly empirical basis there is no reason why it should not take place, as a matter of fact it is always undertaken in the interest of the supernatural. Thus it diverts attention and energy from ideal values and from the exploration of actual conditions by means of which they may be promoted. History is testimony to this fact. Men have never fully used the powers they possess to advance the good in life, because they have waited upon some power external to themselves and to nature to do the work they are responsible for doing. Dependence upon an external power is the counterpart of surrender of human endeavor. Nor is emphasis on exercising our own powers for good an egoistical or a sentimentally optimistic recourse. It is not the first, for it does not isolate man, either individually or collectively, from nature. It is not the second, because it makes no assumption beyond that of the need and responsibility for human endeavor, and beyond the conviction that, if human desire and endeavor were enlisted in behalf of natural ends, conditions would be bettered. It involves no expectation of a millennium of good.

Belief in the supernatural as a necessary power for apprehension of the ideal and for practical attachment to it has for its counterpart a pessimistic belief in the corruption and impotency of natural means. That is axiomatic in Christian dogma. But this apparent pessimism has a way of suddenly changing into an exaggerated optimism. For according to the terms of the doctrine, if the faith in the supernatural is of the required order, regeneration at once takes place. Goodness, in all essentials, is thereby established; if not, there is proof that the established relation to the supernatural has been vitiated. This romantic optimism is one cause for the excessive attention to individual salvation characteristic of traditional Christianity. Belief in a sudden and complete transmutation through conversion and in the objective efficacy of prayer, is too easy a way out of difficulties. It leaves matters in general just about as they were before; that is, sufficiently bad so that there is additional support for the idea that only supernatural aid can better them. The position of natural intelligence is that there exists a *mixture* of good and evil, and that reconstruction in the direction of the good which is indicated by ideal ends must take place, if at all, through continued cooperative effort. There is at least enough impulse toward justice, kindliness, and order so that if it were mobilized for action, not expecting abrupt and complete transformation to occur, the disorder, cruelty, and oppression that exist would be reduced.

The discussion has arrived at a point where a more fundamental objection to the position I am taking needs consideration. The misunderstanding upon which this objection rests should be pointed out. The view I have advanced is sometimes treated as if the identification of the divine with ideal ends left the ideal wholly without roots in existence and without support from existence. The objection implies that my view commits one to such a separation of the ideal and the existent that the ideal has no chance to find lodgment even as a seed that might grow and bear fruit. On the contrary, what I have been criticizing is the *identification* of the ideal with a particular Being, especially when that identification makes necessary the conclusion that this Being is outside of nature, and what I have tried to show is that the ideal itself has its roots in natural conditions; it emerges when the imagination idealizes existence by laying hold of the possibilities offered to thought and action. There are values, goods, actually realized upon a natural basis—the goods of human association, of art and knowledge. The idealizing imagination seizes upon the most precious things found in the climacteric moments of experience and projects them. We need no external criterion and guarantee for their goodness. They are had, they exist as good, and out of them we frame our ideal ends.

Moreover, the ends that result from our projection of experienced goods into objects of thought, desire and effort exist, only they exist *as* ends. Ends, purposes, exercise determining power in human conduct. The aims of philanthropists, of Florence Nightingale, of Howard, of Wilberforce, of Peabody, have not been idle dreams. They have modified institutions. Aims, ideals, do not exist simply in "mind"; they exist in character, in personality and action. One might call the roll of artists, intellectual inquirers, parents, friends, citizens who are neighbors to show that purposes exist in an *operative* way. What I have been objecting to, I repeat, is not the idea that ideals are linked with existence and that they themselves exist, through human embodiment, as forces, but the idea that their authority and value depend upon some prior complete embodiment—as if the efforts of human beings in behalf of justice, or knowledge or beauty, depended for their effectiveness and validity upon assurance that there already existed in some supernal region a place where criminals are humanely treated, where there is no serfdom or slavery, where all facts and truths are already discovered and possessed, and all beauty is eternally displayed in actualized form.

The aims and ideals that move us are generated through imagination. But they are not made out of imaginary stuff. They are made of the hard stuff of the world of physical and social experience. The locomotive did not exist before Stevenson, nor the telegraph before the time of Morse. But the conditions for their existence were there in physical material and energies and in human capacity. Imagination seized hold upon the idea of a rearrangement of existing things that would evolve new objects. The same thing is true of a painter, a musician, a poet, a philanthropist, a moral prophet. The new vision does not arise out of nothing, but emerges through seeing, in terms of possibilities, that is, of imagination, old things in new relations serving a new end which the new end aids in creating.

Moreover the process of creation is experimental and continuous. The artist, scientific man, or good citizen depends upon what others have done before him and are doing around him. The sense of new values that become ends to be realized arises first in dim and uncertain form. As the values are dwelt upon and carried forward in action they grow in definiteness and coherence. Interaction between aim and existent conditions improves and tests the ideal; and conditions are at the same time modified. Ideals change as they are applied in existent conditions. The process endures and advances with the life of humanity. What one person and one group accomplish becomes the standing ground and starting point of those who succeed them. When the vital factors in this natural process are generally acknowledged in emotion, thought and action, the process will be both accelerated and purified through elimination of that irrelevant element that culminates in the idea of the supernatural. When the vital factors attain the religious force that has been drafted into supernatural religions, the resulting reinforcement will be incalculable.

These considerations may be applied to the idea of God, or, to avoid misleading conceptions, to the idea of the divine. This idea is, as I have said, one of ideal possibilities unified through imaginative realization and projection. But this idea of God, or of the divine, is also connected with all the natural forces and conditions—including man and human association—that promote the growth of the ideal and that further its realization. We are in the presence neither of ideals completely embodied in existence nor yet of ideals that are mere rootless ideals, fantasies, utopias. For there are forces in nature and society that generate and support the ideals. They are further unified by the action that gives them coherence and solidity. It is this *active* relation between ideal and actual to which I would give the name "God." I would not insist that the name *must* be given. There are those who hold that the associations of the term with the supernatural are so numerous and close that any use of the word "God" is sure to give rise to misconception and be taken as a concession to traditional ideas.

They may be correct in this view. But the facts to which I have referred are there, and they need to be brought out with all possible clearness and force. There exist concretely and experimentally goods—the values of art in all its forms, of knowledge, of effort and of rest after striving, of education and fellowship, of friendship and love, of growth in mind and body. These goods are there and yet they are relatively embryonic. Many persons are shut out from generous participation in them; there are forces at work that threaten and sap existent goods as well as prevent their expansion. A clear and intense conception of a union of ideal ends with actual conditions is capable of arousing steady emotion. It may be fed by every experience, no matter what its material.

In a distracted age, the need for such an idea is urgent. It can unify interests and energies now dispersed; it can direct action and generate the heat of emotion and the light of intelligence. Whether one gives the name "God" to this union, operative in thought and action, is a matter for individual decision. But the *function* of such a working union of the ideal and actual seems to me to be identical with the force that has in fact been attached to the conception of God in all the religions that have a spiritual content; and a clear idea of that function seems to me urgently needed at the present time.

The sense of this union may, with some persons, be furthered by mystical experiences, using the term "mystical" in its broadest sense. That result depends largely upon temperament. But there is a marked difference between the union associated with mysticism and the union which I had in mind. There is nothing mystical about the latter; it is natural and moral. Nor is there anything mystical about the perception or consciousness of such union. Imagination of ideal ends pertinent to actual conditions represents the fruition of a disciplined mind. There is, indeed, even danger that resort to mystical experiences will be an escape, and that its result will be the passive feeling that the union of actual and ideal is already accomplished. But in fact this union is active and practical; it is a *uniting*, not something given.

One reason why personally I think it fitting to use the word "God" to denote that uniting of the ideal and actual which has been spoken of lies in the fact that aggressive atheism seems to me to have something in common with traditional supernaturalism. I do not mean merely that the former is mainly so negative that it fails to give positive direction to thought, though that fact is pertinent. What I have in mind especially is the exclusive preoccupation of both militant atheism and supernaturalism with man in isolation. For in spite of supernaturalism's reference to something beyond nature, it conceives of this earth as the moral center of the universe and of man as the apex of the whole scheme of things. It regards the drama of sin and redemption enacted within the isolated and lonely soul of man as the one thing of ultimate importance. Apart from man, nature is held either accursed or negligible. Militant atheism is also affected by lack of natural piety. The ties binding man to nature that poets have always celebrated are passed over lightly. The attitude taken is often that of man living in an indifferent and hostile world and issuing blasts of defiance. A religious attitude, however, needs the sense of a connection of man, in the way of both dependence and support, with the enveloping world that the imagination feels is a universe. Use of the words "God" or "divine" to convey the union of actual with ideal may protect man from a sense of isolation and from consequent despair or defiance.

In any case, whatever the name, the meaning is selective. For it involves no miscellaneous worship of everything in general. It selects those factors in existence that generate and support our idea of good as an end to be striven for. It excludes a multitude of forces that at any given time are irrelevant to this function. Nature produces whatever gives reinforcement and direction but also what occasions discord and confusion. The "divine" is thus a term of human choice and aspiration. A humanistic religion, if it excludes our relation to nature, is pale and thin, as it is presumptuous, when it takes humanity as an object of worship. Matthew Arnold's conception of a "power not ourselves" is too narrow in its reference to operative and sustaining conditions. While it is selective, it is too narrow in its basis of selection—righteousness. The conception thus needs to be widened in two ways. The powers that generate and support the good as experienced and as ideal, work *within* as well as without. There seems to be a reminiscence of an external Jehovah in Arnold's statement. And the powers work to enforce other values and ideals than righteousness. Arnold's sense of an opposition between Hellenism and Hebraism resulted in exclusion of beauty, truth, and friendship from the list of the consequences toward which powers work within and without.

In the relation between nature and human ends and endeavors, recent science has broken down the older dualism. It has been engaged in this task for three centuries. But as long as the conceptions of science were strictly mechanical (mechanical in the sense of assuming separate things acting upon one another purely externally by push and pull), religious apologists had a standing ground in pointing out the differences between man and physical nature. The differences could be used for arguing that something supernatural had intervened in the case of man. The recent acclaim, however, by apologists for religion of the surrender by science of the classic type of mechanicalism* seems ill-advised from their own point of view. For the change in the modern scientific view of nature simply brings man and nature nearer together. We are no longer compelled to choose between explaining away what is distinctive in man through reducing him to another form of a mechanical model and the doctrine that something literally supernatural marks him off from nature. The less mechanical—in its older sense— physical nature is found to be, the closer is man to nature.

In his fascinating book, *The Dawn of Conscience,* James Henry Breasted refers to Haeckel as saying that the question he would most wish to have answered is this: Is the universe friendly to man? The question is an ambiguous one. Friendly to man in what respect? With respect to ease and comfort, to material success, to egoistic ambitions? Or to his aspiration to inquire and discover, to invent and create, to build a more secure order for human existence? In whatever form the question be put, the answer cannot in all honesty be an unqualified and absolute one. Mr. Breasted's answer, as a historian, is that nature has been friendly to the emergence and development of conscience and character. Those who will have all or nothing cannot be satisfied with this answer. Emergence and growth are not enough for them. They want something more than growth accompanied by toil and pain. They want final achievement. Others who are less absolutist may be content to think that, morally speaking, growth is a higher value and ideal than is sheer attainment. They will remember also that growth has not been confined to conscience and character; that it extends also to discovery, learning and knowledge, to creation in the arts, to furtherance of ties that hold men together in mutual aid and affection. These persons at least will be satisfied with an intellectual view of the religious function that is based on continuing choice directed toward ideal ends.

For, I would remind readers in conclusion, it is the intellectual side of the religious attitude that I have been considering. I have suggested that the religious element in life has been hampered by conceptions of the supernatural that were imbedded in those cultures wherein man had little control over outer nature and little in the way of sure method of inquiry and test. The crisis today as to the intellectual content of religious belief has been caused by the change in the intellectual climate due to the increase of our

---

* I use this term because science has not abandoned its beliefs in working mechanisms in giving up the idea that they are of the nature of a strictly mechanical contact of discrete things.

knowledge and our means of understanding. I have tried to show that this change is not fatal to the religious values in our common experience, however adverse its impact may be upon historic religions. Rather, provided that the methods and results of intelligence at work are frankly adopted, the change is liberating.

It clarifies our ideals, rendering them less subject to illusion and fantasy. It relieves us of the incubus of thinking of them as fixed, as without power of growth. It discloses that they develop in coherence and pertinency with increase of natural intelligence. The change gives aspiration for natural knowledge a definitely religious character, since growth in understanding of nature is seen to be organically related to the formation of ideal ends. The same change enables man to select those elements in natural conditions that may be organized to support and extend the sway of ideals. All purpose is selective, and all intelligent action includes deliberate choice. In the degree in which we cease to depend upon belief in the supernatural, selection is enlightened and choice can be made in behalf of ideals whose inherent relations to conditions and consequences are understood. Were the naturalistic foundations and bearings of religion grasped, the religious element in life would emerge from the throes of the crisis in religion. Religion would then be found to have its natural place in every aspect of human experience that is concerned with estimate of possibilities, with emotional stir by possibilities as yet unrealized, and with all action in behalf of their realization. All that is significant in human experience falls within this frame.

IX

Philosophy of Art

In 1931, John Dewey was invited to give the William James Lectures at Harvard University. His theme was the philosophy of art, which developed into the book *Art as Experience* (1934).

Since its publication, *Art as Experience* has commanded serious attention from philosophical students of aesthetics as well as from art educators and art critics, particularly in the United States. One explanation of this interest is the way in which the book combines a comprehensive theory of the nature of art with illuminating or provocative interpretations of particular works of art.

Dewey's philosophy of art is a characteristically naturalistic one, taking as its point of departure the creation or appreciation of a work of art as the activity of a human organism interacting with its environment. The challenge becomes the clarification of the experience that constitutes the making or enjoying of a work of art.

Dewey systematically considers various aspects of that experience that have been central to various modern aesthetic theories of intuition, representation, form, or expression. As in other works of his philosophical criticism, Dewey's methodology stresses the bifurcation of integral experience that is required by philosophical views that isolate and hypostasize some aspect of experience. He formulates his philosophical goal as clarification of the total character of the experience that constitutes artistic activity.

In a sense, Dewey's philosophy of art involves him in a polemical criticism of various dualisms: the separation of artistic form from subject matter, or of the expression of an artist's internal emotional state from the objective structuring of the medium, or of the intuitive vision of the artist from the technical concern with adequacy of structure and representation, or of art as consummatory experience from art as a means of communication.

Each of the three selections from *Art as Experience* presented here shows Dewey's effort to overcome duality. In the first, "The Live Creature and 'Etherial Things,'" Dewey analyses the distinction between the fine arts and the applied or technological arts. He stresses the connection between these two kinds of activity. And in so doing, he formulates once again a characteristic theme of American naturalism: the importance of recognizing and understanding the relationship between the material origins or conditions of an event and its ideal fulfillment or realization.

In the second selection, from the chapter "The Act of Expression," Dewey seeks to reconcile the claims of expressionism in accounting for the function and intensity of a work of art with the awareness of the environment and medium in which emotional expression becomes significant as a work of art.

The third selection is a brief comment on the relationship between art and knowledge from the chapter entitled "The Challenge to Philosophy."

19

The Live Creature and "Etherial Things"*

Why is the attempt to connect the higher and ideal things of experience with basic vital roots so often regarded as betrayal of their nature and denial of their value? Why is there repulsion when the high achievements of fine art are brought into connection with common life, the life that we share with all living creatures? Why is life thought of as an affair of low appetite, or at its best a thing of gross sensation, and ready to sink from its best to the level of lust and harsh cruelty? A complete answer to the question would involve the writing of a history of morals that would set forth the conditions that have brought about contempt for the body, fear of the senses, and the opposition of flesh to spirit.

One aspect of this history is so relevant to our problem that it must receive at least passing notice. The institutional life of mankind is marked by disorganization. This disorder is often disguised by the fact that it takes the form of static division into classes, and this static separation is accepted as the very essence of order as long as it is so fixed and so accepted as not to generate open conflict. Life is compartmentalized and the institutionalized compartments are

SOURCE: Reprinted by permission of G. P. Putnam's Sons and The Center for Dewey Studies from *Art as Experience* by John Dewey. Copyright 1934 by John Dewey; renewed 1962 by Roberta L. Dewey.

* "The Sun, the Moon, the Earth and its contents, are material to form greater things, that is, etherial things—greater things than the Creator himself made." —JOHN KEATS.

classified as high and as low; their values as profane and spiritual,
as material and ideal. Interests are related to one another externally
and mechanically, through a system of checks and balances. Since
religion, morals, politics, business has each its own compartment,
within which it is fitting each should remain, art, too, must have
its peculiar and private realm. Compartmentalization of occupations
and interests brings about separation of that mode of activity commonly called "practice" from insight, of imagination from executive doing, of significant purpose from work, of emotion from
thought and doing. Each of these has, too, its own place in which
it must abide. Those who write the anatomy of experience then
suppose that these divisions inhere in the very constitution of
human nature.

Of much of our experience as it is actually lived under present
economic and legal institutional conditions, it is only too true that
the separations hold. Only occasionally in the lives of many are the
senses fraught with the sentiment that comes from deep realization
of intrinsic meanings. We undergo sensations as mechanical stimuli
or as irritated stimulations, without having a sense of the reality
that is in them and behind them: in much of our experience our
different senses do not unite to tell a common and enlarged story.
We see without feeling; we hear, but only a second-hand report,
second hand because not reenforced by vision. We touch, but the
contact remains tangential because it does not fuse with qualities of
senses that go below the surface. We use the senses to arouse passion
but not to fulfill the interest of insight, not because that interest is
not potentially present in the exercise of sense but because we
yield to conditions of living that force sense to remain an excitation
on the surface. Prestige goes to those who use their minds without
participation of the body and who act vicariously through control
of the bodies and labor of others.

Under such conditions, sense and flesh get a bad name. The
moralist, however, has a truer sense of the intimate connections of
sense with the rest of our being than has the professional psychologist and philosopher, although his sense of these connections takes
a direction that reverses the potential facts of our living in relation
to the environment. Psychologist and philosopher have in recent
times been so obsessed with the problem of knowledge that they
have treated "sensations" as mere elements of knowledge. The
moralist knows that sense is allied with emotion, impulse and
appetition. So he denounces the lust of the eye as part of the surrender of spirit to flesh. He identifies the sensuous with the sensual
and the sensual with the lewd. His moral theory is askew, but at
least he is aware that the eye is not an imperfect telescope designed

for intellectual reception of material to bring about knowledge of distant objects.

"Sense" covers a wide range of contents: the sensory, the sensational, the sensitive, the sensible, and the sentimental, along with the sensuous. It includes almost everything from bare physical and emotional shock to sense itself—that is, the meaning of things present in immediate experience. Each term refers to some real phase and aspect of the life of an organic creature as life occurs through sense organs. But sense, as meaning so directly embodied in experience as to be its own illuminated meaning, is the only signification that expresses the function of sense organs when they are carried to full realization. The senses are the organs through which the live creature participates directly in the on-goings of the world about him. In this participation the varied wonder and splendor of this world are made actual for him in the qualities he experiences. This material cannot be opposed to action, for motor apparatus and "will" itself are the means by which this participation is carried on and directed. It cannot be opposed to "intellect," for mind is the means by which participation is rendered fruitful through sense; by which meanings and values are extracted, retained, and put to further service in the intercourse of the live creature with his surroundings.

Experience is the result, the sign, and the reward of that interaction of organism and environment which, when it is carried to the full, is a transformation of interaction into participation and communication. Since sense-organs with their connected motor apparatus are the means of this participation, any and every derogation of them, whether practical or theoretical, is at once effect and cause of a narrowed and dulled life-experience. Oppositions of mind and body, soul and matter, spirit and flesh all have their origin, fundamentally, in fear of what life may bring forth. They are marks of contraction and withdrawal. Full recognition, therefore, of the continuity of the organs, needs and basic impulses of the human creature with his animal forbears, implies no necessary reduction of man to the level of the brutes. On the contrary, it makes possible the drawing of a ground-plan of human experience upon which is erected the superstructure of man's marvelous and distinguishing experience. What is distinctive in man makes it possible for him to sink below the level of the beasts. It also makes it possible for him to carry to new and unprecedented heights that unity of sense and impulse, of brain and eye and ear, that is exemplified in animal life, saturating it with the conscious meanings derived from communication and deliberate expression.

Man excels in complexity and minuteness of differentiations.

This very fact constitutes the necessity for many more comprehensive and exact relationships among the constituents of his being.
Important as are the distinctions and relations thus made possible,
the story does not end here. There are more opportunities for
resistance and tension, more drafts upon experimentation and invention, and therefore more novelty in action, greater range and
depth of insight and increase of poignancy in feeling. As an organism increases in complexity, the rhythms of struggle and consummation in its relation to its environment are varied and prolonged, and
they come to include within themselves an endless variety of sub-
rhythms. The designs of living are widened an enriched. Fulfillment
is more massive and more subtly shaded.

Space thus becomes something more than a void in which to roam
about, dotted here and there with dangerous things and things that
satisfy the appetite. It becomes a comprehensive and enclosed scene
within which are ordered the multiplicity of doings and undergoings in which man engages. Time ceases to be either the endless
and uniform flow of the succession of instantaneous points which
some philosophers have asserted it to be. It, too, is the organized
and organizing medium of the rhythmic ebb and flow of expectant
impulse, forward and retracted movement, resistance and suspense,
with fulfillment and consummation. It is an ordering of growth
and maturations—as James said, we learn to skate in summer after
having commenced in winter. Time as organization in change is
growth, and growth signifies that a varied series of change enters
upon intervals of pause and rest; of completions that become the
initial points of new processes of development. Like the soil, mind
is fertilized while it lies fallow, until a new burst of bloom ensues.

When a flash of lightning illumines a dark landscape, there is a
momentary recognition of objects. But the recognition is not itself
a mere point in time. It is the focal culmination of long, slow
processes of maturation. It is the manifestation of the continuity
of an ordered temporal experience in a sudden discrete instant of
climax. It is as meaningless in isolation as would be the drama of
Hamlet were it confined to a single line or word with no context.
But the phrase "the rest is silence" is infinitely pregnant as the conclusion of a drama enacted through development in time; so may
be the momentary perception of a natural scene. Form, as it is
present in the fine arts, is the art of making clear what is involved
in the organization of space and time prefigured in every course of a
developing life-experience.

Moments and places, despite physical limitation and narrow
localization, are charged with accumulations of long-gathering en-

ergy. A return to a scene of childhood that was left long years before floods the spot with a release of pent-up memories and hopes. To meet in a strange country one who is a casual acquaintance at home may arouse a satisfaction so acute as to bring a thrill. Mere recognitions occur only when we are occupied with something else than the object or person recognized. It marks either an interruption or else an intent to use what is recognized as a means for something else. To see, to perceive, is more than to recognize. It does not identify something present in terms of a past disconnected from it. The past is carried into the present so as to expand and deepen the content of the latter. There is illustrated the translation of bare continuity of external time into the vital order and organization of experience. Identification nods and passes on. Or it defines a passing moment in isolation, it marks a dead spot in experience that is merely filled in. The extent to which the process of living in any day or hour is reduced to labeling situations, events, and objects as "so-and-so" in mere succession marks the cessation of a life that is a conscious experience. Continuities realized in an individual, discrete form are the essence of the latter.

Art is thus prefigured in the very processes of living. A bird builds its nest and a beaver its dam when internal organic pressures cooperate with external materials so that the former are fulfilled and the latter are transformed in a satisfying culmination. We may hesitate to apply the word "art," since we doubt the presence of directive intent. But all deliberation, all conscious intent, grows out of things once performed organically through the interplay of natural energies. Were it not so, art would be built on quaking sands, nay, on unstable air. The distinguishing contribution of man is consciousness of the relations found in nature. Through consciousness, he converts the relations of cause and effect that are found in nature into relations of means and consequence. Rather, consciousness itself is the inception of such a transformation. What was mere shock becomes an invitation; resistance becomes something to be used in changing existing arrangements of matter; smooth facilities become agencies for executing an idea. In these operations, an organic stimulation becomes the bearer of meanings, and motor responses are changed into instruments of expression and communication; no longer are they mere means of locomotion and direct reaction. Meanwhile, the organic substratum remains as the quickening and deep foundation. Apart from relations of cause and effect in nature, conception and invention could not be. Apart from the relation of processes of rhythmic conflict and fulfillment in animal life, experience would be without design and pattern. Apart from organs inherited from animal ancestry, idea and purpose would be without a mechanism of realization. The primeval arts of nature and animal life are so much the material, and, in gross outline, so much the model for the intentional achievements of man, that the theologically minded have imputed conscious intent to the structure of nature—as man, sharing many activities with the ape, is wont to think of the latter as imitating his own performances.

The existence of art is the concrete proof of what has just been stated abstractly. It is proof that man uses the materials and energies of nature with intent to expand his own life, and that he does so in accord with the structure of his organism—brain, sense-organs, and muscular system. Art is the living and concrete proof that man is capable of restoring consciously, and thus on the plane of meaning, the union of sense, need, impulse and action characteristic of the live creature. The intervention of consciousness adds regulation, power of selection, and redisposition. Thus it varies the arts in ways without end. But its intervention also leads in time to the *idea* of art as a conscious idea—the greatest intellectual achievement in the history of humanity.

The variety and perfection of the arts in Greece led thinkers to frame a generalized conception of art and to project the ideal of an art of organization of human activities as such—the art of politics and morals as conceived by Socrates and Plato. The ideas of design, plan, order, pattern, purpose emerged in distinction from and relation to the materials employed in their realization. The conception of man as the being that uses art became at once the ground of the distinction of man from the rest of nature and of the bond that ties him to nature. When the conception of art as the distinguishing trait of man was made explicit, there was assurance that, short of complete relapse of humanity below even savagery, the possibility of invention of new arts would remain, along with use of old arts, as the guiding ideal of mankind. Although recognition of the fact still halts, because of traditions established before the power of art was adequately recognized, science itself is but a central art auxiliary to the generation and utilization of other arts.*

It is customary, and from some points of view necessary, to make

* I have developed this point in *Experience and Nature*, in Chapter Nine, on Experience, Nature and Art. As far as the present point is concerned, the conclusion is contained in the statement that "art, the mode of activity that is charged with meanings capable of immediately enjoyed possession, is the complete culmination of nature, and that science is properly a handmaiden that conducts natural events to this happy issue."

a distinction between fine art and useful or technological art. But the point of view from which it is necessary is one that is extrinsic to the work of art itself. The customary distinction is based simply on acceptance of certain existing social conditions. I suppose the fetiches of the negro sculptor were taken to be useful in the highest degree to his tribal group, more so even than spears and clothing. But now they are fine art, serving in the twentieth century to inspire renovations in arts that had grown conventional. But they are fine art only because the anonymous artist lived and experienced so fully during the process of production. An angler may eat his catch without thereby losing the esthetic satisfaction he experienced in casting and playing. It is this degree of completeness of living in the experience of making and of perceiving that makes the difference between what is fine or esthetic in art and what is not. Whether the thing made is put to use, as are bowls, rugs, garments, weapons, is, *intrinsically* speaking, a matter of indifference. That many, perhaps most, of the articles and utensils made at present for use are not genuinely esthetic happens, unfortunately, to be true. But it is true for reasons that are foreign to the relation of the "beautiful" and "useful" as such. Wherever conditions are such as to prevent the act of production from being an experience in which the whole creature is alive and in which he possesses his living through enjoyment, the product will lack something of being esthetic. No matter how useful it is for special and limited ends, it will not be useful in the ultimate degree—that of contributing directly and liberally to an expanding and enriched life. The story of the severance and final sharp opposition of the useful and the fine is the history of that industrial development through which so much of production has become a form of postponed living and so much of consumption a superimposed enjoyment of the fruits of the labor of others.

Usually there is a hostile reaction to a conception of art that connects it with the activities of a live creature in its environment. The hostility to association of fine art with normal processes of living is a pathetic, even a tragic, commentary on life as it is ordinarily lived. Only because that life is usually so stunted, aborted, slack, or heavy laden is the idea entertained that there is some inherent antagonism between the process of normal living and creation and enjoyment of works of esthetic art. After all, even though "spiritual" and "material" are separated and set in opposition to one another, there must be conditions through which the ideal is capable of embodiment and realization—and this is all, fundamentally, that "matter" signifies. The very currency which the opposition has acquired testifies, therefore, to a widespread operation of forces that convert what might be means of executing liberal ideas into oppressive burdens and that cause ideals to be loose aspirations in an uncertain and ungrounded atmosphere.

While art itself is the best proof of the existence of a realized and therefore realizable, union of material and ideal, there are general arguments that support the thesis in hand. Wherever continuity is possible, the burden of proof rests upon those who assert opposition and dualism. Nature is the mother and the habitat of man, even if sometimes a stepmother and an unfriendly home. The fact that civilization endures and culture continues—and sometimes advances—is evidence that human hopes and purposes find a basis and support in nature. As the developing growth of an individual embryo to maturity is the result of interaction of organism with surroundings, so culture is the product not of efforts of men put forth in a void or just upon themselves, but of prolonged and cumulative interaction with environment. The depth of the responses stirred by works of art shows *their* continuity with the operations of this enduring experience. The works and the responses they evoke are continuous with the very processes of living as these are carried to unexpected happy fulfillment.

As to absorption of the esthetic in nature, I cite a case duplicated in some measure in thousands of persons, but notable because expressed by an artist of the first order, W. H. Hudson. "I feel when I am out of sight of living, growing grass, and out of the sound of birds' voices and all rural sounds, that I am not properly alive." He goes on to say, ". . . when I hear people say that they have not found the world and life so agreeable and interesting as to be in love with it, or that they look with equanimity to its end, I am apt to think that they have never been properly alive, nor seen with clear vision the world they think so meanly of or anything in it— not even a blade of grass." The mystic aspect of acute esthetic surrender, that renders it so akin as an experience to what religionists term ecstatic communion, is recalled by Hudson from his boyhood life. He is speaking of the effect the sight of acacia trees had upon him. "The loose feathery foliage on moonlight nights had a peculiar hoary aspect that made this tree seem more intensely alive than others, more conscious of me and of my presence. . . . Similar to a feeling a person would have if visited by a supernatural being if he was perfectly convinced that it was there in his presence, albeit silent and unseen, intently regarding him and divining every thought in his mind." Emerson is often regarded as an austere thinker. But it was Emerson as an adult who said, quite in the spirit of the passage quoted from Hudson: "Crossing a bare common, in snow puddles, at twilight, under a clouded sky, without having in my thought any occurrence of special good fortune, I have enjoyed a perfect exhilaration. I am glad to the brink of fear."

I do not see any way of accounting for the multiplicity of experiences of this kind (something of the same quality being found in every spontaneous and uncoerced esthetic response), except on the basis that there are stirred into activity resonances of dispositions acquired in primitive relationships of the living being to its surroundings, and irrecoverable in distinct or intellectual consciousness. Experiences of the sort mentioned take us to a further consideration that testifies to natural continuity. There is no limit to the capacity of immediate sensuous experience to absorb into itself meanings and values that in and of themselves—that is in the abstract—would be designated "ideal" and "spiritual." The animistic strain of religious experience, embodied in Hudson's memory of his childhood days, is an instance on one level of experience. And the poetical, in whatever medium, is always a close kin of the animistic. And if we turn to an art that in many ways is at the other pole, architecture, we learn how ideas, wrought out at first perhaps in highly technical thought like that of mathematics, are capable of direct incorporation in sensuous form. The sensible surface of things is never merely a surface. One can discriminate rock from flimsy tissue-paper by the surface alone, so completely have the resistances of touch and the solidities due to stresses of the entire muscular system been embodied in vision. The process does not stop with incarnation of other sensory qualities that give depth of meaning to surface. Nothing that a man has ever reached by the highest flight of thought or penetrated by any probing insight is inherently such that it may not become the heart and core of sense. . . .

20

The Act of Expression

Every experience, of slight or tremendous import, begins with an impulsion, rather *as* an impulsion. I say "impulsion" rather than "impulse." An impulse is specialized and particular; it is, even when instinctive, simply a part of the mechanism involved in a more complete adaptation with the environment. "Impulsion" designates a movement outward and forward of the whole organism to which special impulses are auxiliary. It is the craving of the living creature for food as distinct from the reactions of tongue and lips that are involved in swallowing; the turning toward light of the body as a whole, like the heliotropism of plants, as distinct from the following of a particular light by the eyes.

Because it is the movement of the organism in its entirety, impulsion is the initial stage of any complete experience. Observation of children discovers many specialized reactions. But they are not, therefore, inceptive of complete experiences. They enter into the latter only as they are woven as strands into an activity that calls the whole self into play. Overlooking these generalized activities and paying attention only to the differentiations, the divisions of labor, which render them more efficient are pretty much the source and cause of all further errors in the interpretation of experience.

Impulsions are the beginnings of complete experience because they proceed from need; from a hunger and demand that belongs to the organism as a whole and that can be supplied only by instituting definite relations (active relations, interactions) with the

SOURCE: Reprinted by permission of G. P. Putnam's Sons and The Center for Dewey Studies from *Art as Experience* by John Dewey. Copyright 1934 by John Dewey; renewed 1962 by Roberta L. Dewey.

environment. The epidermis is only in the most superficial way an indication of where an organism ends and its environment begins. There are things inside the body that are foreign to it, and there are things outside of it that belong to it *de jure,* if not *de facto;* that must, that is, be taken possession of if life is to continue. On the lower scale, air and food materials are such things; on the higher, tools, whether the pen of the writer or the anvil of the blacksmith, utensils and furnishings, property, friends and institutions—all the supports and sustenances without which a civilized life cannot be. The need that is manifest in the urgent impulses that demand completion through what the environment—and it alone—can supply, is a dynamic acknowledgment of this dependence of the self for wholeness upon its surroundings.

It is the fate of a living creature, however, that it cannot secure what belongs to it without an adventure in a world that as a whole it does not own and to which it has no native title. Whenever the organic impulse exceeds the limit of the body, it finds itself in a strange world and commits in some measure the fortune of the self to external circumstance. It cannot pick just what it wants and automatically leave the indifferent and adverse out of account. If, and as far as, the organism continues to develop, it is helped on as a favoring wind helps the runner. But the impulsion also meets many things on its outbound course that deflect and oppose it. In the process of converting these obstacles and neutral conditions into favoring agencies, the live creature becomes aware of the intent implicit in its impulsion. The self, whether it succeed or fail, does not merely restore itself to its former state. Blind surge has been changed into a purpose; instinctive tendencies are transformed into contrived undertakings. The attitudes of the self are informed with meaning.

An environment that was always and everywhere congenial to the straightaway execution of our impulsions would set a term to growth as surely as one always hostile would irritate and destroy. Impulsion forever boosted on its forward way would run its course thoughtless, and dead to emotion. For it would not have to give an account of itself in terms of the things it encounters, and hence they would not become significant objects. The only way it can become aware of its nature and its goal is by obstacles surmounted and means employed; means which are only means from the very beginning are too much one with an impulsion, on a way smoothed and oiled in advance, to permit of consciousness of them. Nor without resistance from surroundings would the self become aware of itself; it would have neither feeling nor interest, neither fear nor hope, neither disappointment nor elation. Mere opposition that completely thwarts, creates irritation and rage. But resistance that calls out thought generates curiosity and solicitous care, and, when it is overcome and utilized, eventuates in elation.

That which merely discourages a child and one who lacks a matured background of relevant experiences is an incitement to intelligence to plan and convert emotion into interest, on the part of those who have previously had experiences of situations sufficiently akin to be draw upon. Impulsion from need starts an experience that does not know where it is going; resistance and check bring about the conversion of direct forward action into re-flection; what is turned back upon is the relation of hindering conditions to what the self possesses as working capital in virtue of prior experiences. As the energies thus involved re-enforce the original impulsion, this operates more circumspectly with insight into end and method. Such is the outline of every experience that is clothed with meaning.

That tension calls out energy and that total lack of opposition does not favor normal development are familiar facts. In a general way, we all recognize that a balance between furthering and retarding conditions is the desirable state of affairs—provided that the adverse conditions bear intrinsic relation to what they obstruct instead of being arbitrary and extraneous. Yet what is evoked is not just quantitative, or just more energy, but is qualitative, a transformation of energy into thoughtful action, through assimilation of meanings from the background of past experiences. The junction of the new and old is not a mere composition of forces, but is a re-creation in which the present impulsion gets form and solidity while the old, the "stored," material is literally revived, given new life and soul through having to meet a new situation.

It is this double change which converts an activity into an act of expression. Things in the environment that would otherwise be mere smooth channels or else blind obstructions become means, media. At the same time, things retained from past experience that would grow stale from routine or inert from lack of use, become coefficients in new adventures and put on a raiment of fresh meaning. Here are all the elements needed to define expression. The definition will gain force if the traits mentioned are made explicit by contrast with alternative situations. Not all outgoing activity is of the nature of expression. At one extreme, there are storms of passion that break through barriers and that sweep away whatever intervenes between a person and something he would destroy.

There is activity, but not, from the standpoint of the one acting, expression. An onlooker may say "What a magnificent expression of rage!" But the enraged being is only raging, quite a different matter from *expressing* rage. Or, again, some spectator may say "How that man is expressing his own dominant character in what he is doing or saying." But the last thing the man in question is thinking of is to express his character; he is only giving way to a fit of passion. Again the cry or smile of an infant may be expressive to mother or nurse and yet not be an act of expression of the baby. To the onlooker it is an expression because it tells something about the state of the child. But the child is only engaged in doing something directly, no more expressive from his standpoint than is breathing or sneezing—activities that are also expressive to the observer of the infant's condition.

Generalization of such instances will protect us from the error—which has unfortunately invaded esthetic theory—of supposing that the mere giving way to an impulsion, native or habitual, constitutes expression. Such an act is expressive not in itself but only in reflective interpretation on the part of some observer—as the nurse may interpret a sneeze as the sign of an impending cold. As far as the act itself is concerned, it is, if purely impulsive, just a boiling over. While there is no expression unless there is urge from within outwards, the welling up must be clarified and ordered by taking into itself the values of prior experiences before it can be an act of expression. And these values are not called into play save through objects of the environment that offer resistance to the direct discharge of emotion and impulse. Emotional discharge is a necessary but not a sufficient condition of expression.

There is no expression without excitement, without turmoil. Yet an inner agitation that is discharged at once in a laugh or cry, passes away with its utterance. To discharge is to get rid of, to dismiss; to express is to stay by, to carry forward in development, to work out to completion. A gush of tears may bring relief, a spasm of destruction may give outlet to inward rage. But where there is no administration of objective conditions, no shaping of materials in the interest of embodying the excitement, there is no expression. What is sometimes called an act of self-expression might better be termed one of self-exposure; it discloses character—or lack of character—to others. In itself, it is only a spewing forth.

The transition from an act that is expressive from the standpoint of an outside observer to one intrinsically expressive is readily illustrated by a simple case. At first a baby weeps, just as it turns its head to follow light; there is an inner urge but nothing to express. As the infant matures, he learns that particular acts effect different consequences, that, for example, he gets attention if he cries, and that smiling induces another definite response from those about him. He thus begins to be aware of the *meaning* of what he does. As he grasps the meaning of an act at first performed from sheer internal pressure, he becomes capable of acts of true expression. The transformation of sounds, babblings, lalling, and so forth, into language is a perfect illustration of the way in which acts of expression are brought into existence and also of the difference between them and mere acts of discharge.

There is suggested, if not exactly exemplified, in such cases the connection of expression with art. The child who has learned the effect his once spontaneous act has upon those around him performs "on purpose" an act that was blind. He begins to manage and order his activities in reference to their consequences. The consequences undergone because of doing are incorporated as the meaning of subsequent doings because the relation between doing and undergoing is perceived. The child may now cry for a purpose, because he wants attention or relief. He may begin to bestow his smiles as inducements or as favors. There is now art in incipiency. An activity that was "natural"—spontaneous and unintended—is transformed because it is undertaken as a means to a consciously entertained consequence. Such transformation marks every deed of art. The result of the transformation may be artful rather than esthetic. The fawning smile and conventional smirk of greeting are artifices. But the genuinely gracious act of welcome contains also a change of an attitude that was once a blind and "natural" manifestation of impulse into an act of art, something performed in view of its place or relation in the processes of intimate human intercourse.

The difference between the artificial, the artful, and the artistic lies on the surface. In the former there is a split between what is overtly done and what is intended. The appearance is one of cordiality; the intent is that of gaining favor. Wherever this split between what is done and its purpose exists, there is insincerity, a trick, a simulation of an act that intrinsically has another effect. When the natural and the cultivated blend in one, acts of social intercourse are works of art. The animating impulse of genial friendship and the deed performed completely coincide without intrusion of ulterior purpose. Awkwardness may prevent adequacy of expression. But the skillful counterfeit, however skilled, goes *through* the form of expression; it does not have the form of friendship and abide in it. The substance of friendship is untouched.

An act of discharge or mere exhibition lacks a medium. Instinctive crying and smiling no more require a medium than do sneezing and winking. They occur through some channel, but the means of outlet are not used as immanent means of an end. The act that *expresses* welcome uses the smile, the outreached hand, the lighting up of the face as media, not consciously but because they have become organic means of communicating delight upon meeting a valued friend. Acts that were primitively spontaneous are converted into means that make human intercourse more rich and gracious—just as a painter converts pigment into means of expressing an imaginative experience. Dance and sport are activities in which acts once performed spontaneously in separation are assembled and converted from raw, crude material into works of expressive art. Only where material is employed as media is there expression and art. Savage taboos that look to the outsider like mere prohibitions and inhibitions externally imposed may be to those who experience them media of expressing social status, dignity, and honor. Everything depends upon the way in which material is used when it operates as medium.

The connection between a medium and the act of expression is intrinsic. An act of expression always employs natural material, though it may be natural in the sense of habitual as well as in that of primitive or native. It becomes a medium when it is employed in view of its place and role, in its relations, an inclusive situation —as tones become music when ordered in a melody. The same tones might be uttered in connection with an attitude of joy, surprise, or sadness, and be natural outlets of particular feelings. They are *expressive* of one of these emotions when other tones are the medium in which one of them occurs.

Etymologically, an act of expression is a squeezing out, a pressing forth. Juice is expressed when grapes are crushed in the wine press; to use a more prosaic comparison, lard and oil are rendered when certain fats are subjected to heat and pressure. Nothing is pressed forth except from original raw or natural material. But it is equally true that the mere issuing forth or discharge of raw material is not expression. Through interaction with something external to it, the wine press, or the treading foot of man, juice results. Skin and seeds are separated and retained; only when the apparatus is defective are they discharged. Even in the most mechanical modes of expression there is interaction and a consequent transformation of the primitive material which stands as raw material for a product of art in relation to what is actually pressed out. It takes the wine press as well as grapes to ex-press juice, and it takes environing and resisting objects as well as internal emotion and impulsion to constitute an *expression* of emotion.

Speaking of the production of poetry, Samuel Alexander remarked that "the artist's work proceeds not from a finished imaginative experience to which the work of art corresponds, but from passionate excitement about the subject matter. . . . The poet's poem is wrung from him by the subject which excites him." The passage is a text upon which we may hang four comments. One of these comments may pass for the present as a reenforcement of a point made in previous chapters. The real work of art is the building up of an integral experience out of the interaction of organic and environmental conditions and energies. Nearer to our present theme is the second point: The thing expressed is wrung from the producer by the pressure exercised by objective things upon the natural impulses and tendencies—so far is expression from being the direct and immaculate issue of the latter. The third point follows. The act of expression that constitutes a work of art is a construction in time, not an instantaneous emission. And this statement signifies a great deal more than that it takes time for the painter to transfer his imaginative conception to canvas and for the sculptor to complete his chipping of marble. It means that the expression of the self in and through a medium, constituting the work of art, is *itself* a prolonged interaction of something issuing from the self with objective conditions, a process in which both of them acquire a form and order they did not at first possess. Even the Almighty took seven days to create the heaven and the earth, and, if the record were complete, we should also learn that it was only at the end of that period that he was aware of just what He set out to do with the raw material of chaos that confronted Him. Only an emasculated subjective metaphysics has transformed the eloquent myth of Genesis into the conception of a Creator creating without any unformed matter to work upon.

The final comment is that when excitement about subject matter goes deep, it stirs up a store of attitudes and meanings derived from prior experience. As they are aroused into activity they become conscious thoughts and emotions, emotionalized images. To be set on fire by a thought or scene is to be inspired. What is kindled must either burn itself out, turning to ashes, or must press itself out in material that changes the latter from crude metal into a refined product. Many a person is unhappy, tortured within, because he has at command no art of expressive action. What under happier conditions might be used to convert objective material into material of an intense and clear experience, seethes within in unruly turmoil which finally dies down after, perhaps, a painful inner disruption.

Materials undergoing combustion because of intimate contacts and mutually exercised resistances constitute inspiration. On the side of the self, elements that issue from prior experience are stirred into action in fresh desires, impulsions and images. These proceed from the subconscious, not cold or in shapes that are identified with particulars of the past, not in chunks and lumps, but fused in the fire of internal commotion. They do not seem to come from the self, because they issue from a self not consciously known. Hence, by a just myth, the inspiration is attributed to a god, or to the muse. The inspiration, however, is initial. In itself, at the outset, it is still inchoate. Inflamed inner material must find objective fuel upon which to feed. Through the interaction of the fuel with material already afire the refined and formed product comes into existence. The act of expression is not something which supervenes upon an inspiration already complete. It is the carrying forward to completion of an inspiration by means of the objective material of perception and imagery.*

An impulsion cannot lead to expression save when it is thrown into commotion, turmoil. Unless there is com-pression nothing is ex-pressed. The turmoil marks the place where inner impulse and contact with environment, in fact or in idea, meet and create a ferment. The war dance and the harvest dance of the savage do not issue from within except there be an impending hostile raid or crops are to be gathered. To generate the indispensable excitement there must be something at stake, something momentous and uncertain—like the outcome of a battle or the prospects of a harvest. A sure thing does not arouse us emotionally. Hence it is not mere excitement that is expressed but excitement-about-something; hence, also, it is that even mere excitement, short of complete panic, will utilize channels of action that have been worn by prior activities that dealt with objects. Thus, like the movements of an actor who goes through his part automatically, it stimulates ex-

---

* In his interesting "The Theory of Poetry," Mr. Lascelles Abercrombie wavers between two views of inspiration. One of them takes what seems to me the correct interpretation. In the poem, an inspiration "completely and exquisitely defines itself." At other times, he says the inspiration *is* the poem; "something self-contained and self-sufficient, a complete and entire whole." He says that "each inspiration is something which did not and could not originally exist as words." Doubtless such is the case; not even a trigonometric function exists merely as words. But if it is already self-sufficient and self-contained, why does it seek and find words as a medium of expression?

pression. Even an undefined uneasiness seeks outlet in song or pantomime, striving to become articulate.

Erroneous views of the nature of the act of expression almost all have their source in the notion that an emotion is complete in itself within, only when uttered having impact upon external material. But, in fact, an emotion is *to* or *from* or *about* something objective, whether in fact or in idea. An emotion is implicated in a situation, the issue of which is in suspense and in which the self that is moved in the emotion is vitally concerned. Situations are depressing, threatening, intolerable, triumphant. Joy in the victory won by a group with which a person is identified is not something internally complete, nor is sorrow upon the death of a friend anything that can be understood save as an interpenetration of self with objective conditions.

This latter fact is especially important in connection with the individualization of works of art. The notion that expression is a direct emission of an emotion complete in itself entails logically that individualization is specious and external. For, according to it, fear is fear, elation is elation, love is love, each being generic, and internally differentiated only by differences of intensity. Were this idea correct, works of art would necessarily fall within certain types. This view has infected criticism but not so as to assist understanding of concrete works of art. Save nominally, there is no such thing as *the* emotion of fear, hate, love. The unique, unduplicated character of experienced events and situations impregnates the emotion that is evoked. Were it the function of speech to reproduce that to which it refers, we could never speak of fear, but only of fear-of-this-particular-oncoming-automobile, with all its specifications of time and place, or fear-under-specified-circumstances-of-drawing-a-wrong-conclusion from just-such-and-such data. A lifetime would be too short to reproduce in words a single emotion. In reality, however, poet and novelist have an immense advantage over even an expert psychologist in dealing with an emotion. For the former build up a concrete situation and permit *it* to evoke emotional response. Instead of a description of an emotion in intellectual and symbolic terms, the artist "does the deed that breeds" the emotion.

That art is selective is a fact universally recognized. It is so because of the role of emotion in the act of expression. Any predominant mood automatically excludes all that is uncongenial with it. An emotion is more effective than any deliberate challenging sentinel could be. It reaches out tentacles for that which is cognate, for things which feed it and carry it to completion. Only when emotion dies or is broken to dispersed fragments, can material to which it is alien enter consciousness. The selective operation of materials so powerfully exercised by a developing emotion in a series of continued acts extracts matter from a multitude of objects, numerically and spatially separated, and condenses what is abstracted in an object that is an epitome of the values belonging to them all. This function creates the "universality" of a work of art.

If one examines into the reason why certain works of art offend us, one is likely to find that the cause is that there is no personally felt emotion guiding the selecting and assembling of the materials presented. We derive the impression that the artist, say the author of a novel, is trying to regulate by conscious intent the nature of the emotion aroused. We are irritated by a feeling that he is manipulating materials to secure an effect decided upon in advance. The facets of the work, the variety so indispensable to it, are held together by some external force. The movement of the parts and the conclusion disclose no logical necessity. The author, not the subject matter, is the arbiter.

In reading a novel, even one written by an expert craftsman, one may get a feeling early in the story that hero or heroine is doomed, doomed not by anything inherent in situations and character but by the intent of the author who makes the character a puppet to set forth his own cherished idea. The painful feeling that results is resented not because it is painful but because it is foisted upon us by something that we feel comes from outside the movement of the subject matter. A work may be much more tragic and yet leave us with an emotion of fulfillment instead of irritation. We are reconciled to the conclusion because we feel it is inherent in the movement of the subject matter portrayed. The incident is tragic but the world in which such fateful things happen is not an arbitrary and imposed world. The emotion of the author and that aroused in us are occasioned by scenes in that world and they blend with subject matter. It is for similar reasons that we are repelled by the intrusion of a moral design in literature while we esthetically accept any amount of moral content if it is held together by a sincere emotion that controls the material. A white flame of pity or indignation may find material that feeds it and it may fuse everything assembled into a vital whole.

Just because emotion is essential to that act of expression which produces a work of art, it is easy for inaccurate analysis to misconceive its mode of operation and conclude that the work of art has emotion for its signficant content. One may cry out with joy or even weep upon seeing a friend from whom one has been long separated. The outcome is not an expressive object—save to the on-looker. But if the emotion leads one to gather material that is affiliated to the mood which is aroused, a poem may result. In the direct outburst, an objective situation is the stimulus, the cause, of the emotion. In the poem, objective material becomes the content and matter of the emotion, not just its evocative occasion.

In the development of an expressive act, the emotion operates like a magnet drawing to itself appropriate material: appropriate because it has an experienced emotional affinity for the state of mind already moving. Selection and organization of material are at once a function and a test of the quality of the emotion experienced. In seeing a drama, beholding a picture, or reading a novel, we may feel that the parts do not hang together. Either the maker had no experience that was emotionally toned, or, although having at the outset a felt emotion, it was not sustained, and a succession of unrelated emotions dictated the work. In the latter case, attention wavered and shifted, and an assemblage of incongruous parts ensued. The sensitive observer or reader is aware of junctions and seams, of holes arbitrarily filled in. Yes, emotion must operate. But it works to effect continuity of movement, singleness of effect amid variety. It is selective of material and directive of its order and arrangement. But it is not *what* is expressed. Without emotion, there may be craftsmanship, but not art; it may be present and be intense, but if it is directly manifested the result is also not art.

There are other works that are overloaded with emotion. On the theory that manifestation of an emotion is its expression, there could be no overloading; the more intense the emotion, the more effective the "expression." In fact, a person overwhelmed by an emotion is thereby incapacitated for expressing it. There is at least that element of truth in Wordsworth's formula of "emotion recollected in tranquility." There is, when one is mastered by an emotion, too much undergoing (in the language by which having an experience has been described) and too little active response to permit a balanced relationship to be struck. There is too much "nature" to allow of the development of art. Many of the paintings of Van Gogh, for example, have an intensity that arouses an answering chord. But with the intensity, there is an explosiveness due to absence of assertion of control. In extreme cases of emotion, it works to disorder instead of ordering material. Insufficient emotion shows itself in a coldly "correct" product. Excessive emotion obstructs the necessary elaboration and definition of parts.

The determination of the *mot juste,* of the right incident in the right place, of exquisiteness of proportion, of the precise tone, hue, and shade that helps unify the whole while it defines a part, is accomplished by emotion. Not every emotion, however, can do this work, but only one informed by material that is grasped and gathered. Emotion is informed and carried forward when it is spent indirectly in search for material and in giving it order, not when it is directly expended.

21

The Challenge to Philosophy

The sense of increase of understanding, of a deepened intelligibility on the part of objects of nature and man, resulting from esthetic experience has led philosophic theorists to treat art as a mode of knowledge, and has induced artists, especially poets, to regard art as a mode of revelation of the inner nature of things that cannot be had in any other way. It has led to treating art as a mode of knowledge superior not only to that of ordinary life but to that of science itself. The notion that art is a form of knowledge (though not one superior to the scientific mode) is implicit in Aristotle's statement that poetry is more philosophical than history. The assertion has been expressly made by many philosophers. A reading of these philosophers in connection with one another suggests, however, that they either have not had an esthetic experience or have allowed preconceptions to determine their interpretation of it. For the alleged knowledge can hardly be at the same time that of fixed species, as with Aristotle; of Platonic Ideas, as with Schopenhauer; of the rational structure of the universe, as with Hegel; of states of mind, as with Croce; and of sensations with associated images, as with the sensational school; to mention a few of the outstanding philosophic instances. The varieties of incompatible conceptions put forth prove that the philosophers in question were anxious to carry a dialectical development of conceptions framed without regard to art into esthetic experience more than they were willing to allow this experience to speak for itself.

SOURCE: Reprinted by permission of G. P. Putnam's Sons and The Center for Dewey Studies from *Art as Experience* by John Dewey. Copyright 1934 by John Dewey; renewed 1962 by Roberta L. Dewey.

Nevertheless, the sense of disclosure and of heightened intelligibility of the world remains to be accounted for. That knowledge enters deeply and intimately into the production of a work is proved by the works themselves. Theoretically, it follows of necessity from the part played by mind, by the meanings funded from prior experiences that are actively incorporated in esthetic production and perception. There are artists who have been definitely influenced in their work by the science of their time—as Lucretius, Dante, Milton, Shelley, and, although not to advantage of their paintings, Leonardo and Dürer in the larger compositions of the latter. But there is a great difference between the transformation of knowledge that is effected in imaginative and emotional vision, and in expression through union with sense-material and knowledge. Wordsworth declared that "poetry is the breath and finer spirit of all knowledge; it is the impassioned expression which is in the countenance of all science." Shelley said: "Poetry . . . is at once the center and circumference of all knowledge; it is that which comprehends all science and to which all science must be referred."

But these men were poets and are speaking imaginatively. "Breath and finer spirit" of knowledge are far from being knowledge in any literal sense, and Wordsworth goes on to say that poetry "carries sensation into the objects of science." And Shelley also says, "poetry awakens and enlarges the mind by rendering it the receptacle of a thousand unapprehended combinations of thought." I cannot find in such remarks as these any intention to assert that esthetic experience is to be *defined* as a mode of knowledge. What is intimated to my mind is that in both production and enjoyed perception of works of art, knowledge is transformed; it becomes something more than knowledge because it is merged with non-intellectual elements to form an experience worth while as an experience. I have from time to time set forth a conception of knowledge as being "instrumental." Strange meanings have been imputed by critics to this conception. Its actual content is simple: Knowledge is instrumental to the enrichment of immediate experience through the control over action that it exercises. I would not emulate the philosophers I have criticized and force this interpretation into the ideas set forth by Wordsworth and Shelley. But an idea similar to that I have just stated seems to me to be the most natural translation of their intent.

Tangled scenes of life are made more intelligible in esthetic experience: not, however, as reflection and science render things more intelligible by reduction to conceptual form, but by presenting their meanings as the matter of a clarified, coherent, and intensified or "impassioned" experience . . .

Philosophy like art moves in the medium of imaginative mind, and, since art is the most direct and complete manifestation there is of experience *as* experience, it provides a unique control for the imaginative ventures of philosophy.

In art as an experience, actuality and possibility or ideality, the new and the old, objective material and personal response, the individual and the universal, surface and depth, sense and meaning, are integrated in an experience in which they are all transfigured from the significance that belongs to them when isolated in reflection. "Nature," said Goethe, "has neither kernel nor shell." Only in esthetic experience is this statement completely true. Of art as experience it is also true that nature has neither subjective nor objective being; is neither individual nor universal, sensuous nor rational. The significance of art as experience is, therefore, incomparable for the adventure of philosophic thought.

067